Free Speech Theory

Studies in Law and Politics

David A. Schultz
General Editor

Vol. 5

―――――――――

The Studies in Law and Politics series
is part of the Peter Lang Politics and Economics list.
Every volume is peer reviewed and meets the highest
quality standards for content and production.

―――――――――

PETER LANG
New York • Bern • Berlin
Brussels • Vienna • Oxford • Warsaw

Free Speech Theory

Understanding the Controversies

Edited by
Helen J. Knowles and
Brandon T. Metroka

PETER LANG
New York • Bern • Berlin
Brussels • Vienna • Oxford • Warsaw

Library of Congress Cataloging-in-Publication Data
Names: Knowles, Helen J., editor. | Metroka, Brandon T., editor.
Title: Free speech theory: understanding the controversies / edited by
Helen J. Knowles and Brandon T. Metroka.
Description: New York: Peter Lang, 2020.
Series: Studies in law and politics; vol. 5 | ISSN 1083-3366
Includes bibliographical references and index.
Identifiers: LCCN 2019033901 | ISBN 978-1-4331-5595-6 (hardback: alk. paper)
ISBN 978-1-4331-5596-3 (ebook pdf) | ISBN 978-1-4331-5597-0 (epub)
ISBN 978-1-4331-5598-7 (mobi)
Subjects: LCSH: Freedom of speech.
Classification: LCC JC591.F7745 | DDC 323.44/301—dc23
LC record available at https://lccn.loc.gov/2019033901
DOI 10.3726/b13431

Bibliographic information published by **Die Deutsche Nationalbibliothek**.
Die Deutsche Nationalbibliothek lists this publication in the "Deutsche
Nationalbibliografie"; detailed bibliographic data are available
on the Internet at http://dnb.d-nb.de/.

The paper in this book meets the guidelines for permanence and durability
of the Committee on Production Guidelines for Book Longevity
of the Council of Library Resources.

© 2020 Peter Lang Publishing, Inc., New York
29 Broadway, 18th floor, New York, NY 10006
www.peterlang.com

All rights reserved.
Reprint or reproduction, even partially, in all forms such as microfilm,
xerography, microfiche, microcard, and offset strictly prohibited.

Printed in the United States of America

For John, who always encourages
people to stand up for their views

In memory of Jenny,
taken from us far too soon; fly high my angel

For Brad. To borrow from John Steinbeck, he knows why (or should).

"Practical freedom of speech, graduate-level freedom of speech, is not a black-and-white issue, not just a matter of misquoting Voltaire; it is a subtly calibrated scale. It involves questions about social context, and discretion."
—Archie Bland

Table of Contents

Acknowledgments   xi

Introduction: Why Free Speech Theory Matters   1
    HELEN J. KNOWLES AND BRANDON T. METROKA

1. *No Neutrality: Hobbesian Constitutionalism in the Internet Age*   33
    JAMES C. FOSTER

2. *Freedoms of Speech in the Multiversity*   67
    MARK A. GRABER

3. *Free Speech, Free Press, and Fake News: What If the Marketplace of Ideas Isn't About Identifying Truth?*   95
    KEITH J. BYBEE AND LAURA E. JENKINS

4. *Free Speech and Confederate Symbols*   119
    LOGAN STROTHER AND NATHAN T. CARRINGTON

5. *Speech and National Past Times: The NFL, the Flag, and Professional Athletes*   139
    AARON LORENZ

6. *The Slants and Blurred Lines: The Conflict Between Free Speech and Intellectual Property Law*   157
    JASON ZENOR

7. *Free Speech Debates in Australia: Contemporary Controversies*   183
    KATHARINE GELBER

8. Parliamentary and Judicial Treatments of Free Speech Interests
in the UK   205
    IAN CRAM

Conclusion: It's Still Complicated   227
    HELEN J. KNOWLES AND BRANDON T. METROKA

Contributors   239

Index   243

Acknowledgments

"Variety's the very spice of life, That gives it all its flavour."[1] Without our dedicated contributors, this volume would not exist. Just like the proverb suggests, they have given this book life by providing us with an eclectic and engaging variety of perspectives on using theories of expressive freedom to understand contemporary free speech controversies. There is no one (right or wrong) way to approach the subject, and the chapters that follow reflect that belief. They do not obey a specific pattern or appropriate one single method of organization, and they do not apply the same theories in the same manner. This, we believe, is one of the strengths of this book. The diversity of the chapters embraces and reflects the truth of Archie Bland's words, the words of the epigraph with which we open this book: "Practical freedom of speech, graduate-level freedom of speech, is not a black-and-white issue, not just a matter of misquoting Voltaire; it is a subtly calibrated scale. It involves questions about social context, and discretion."[2] Our contributors ask many questions, and provide some theory-grounded answers, all of which take social context and discretion very seriously. We are exceptionally grateful for their hard work.

The gratitude of the editors and contributors alike extends to Nick Stubba and Linda Tettamant for the work they undertook for us. Nick is a very talented SUNY Oswego alumnus ('19) who did the detailed, laborious, and absolutely essential work (all while completing his undergraduate studies) of checking the accuracy of all of the quotations included in the book. Linda performed the Herculean task of casting her careful copyediting eye over the entire manuscript. Whatever errors remain are, of course, the sole responsibility of the editors and contributors alike.

We also extend our very sincere thanks to the Institute for Humane Studies for awarding us a Hayek Fund for Scholars Grant that enabled us to hire Nick and Linda. In particular, we are grateful to Tommy Creegan at the IHS, and Julie Marte and Michele Frazier at SUNY Oswego, for helping us with the paperwork related to the administration of this grant.

Although Helen daily finds herself herding four cats (and one horse), she considers that task infinitely easier than editing a book. Therefore, she is exceptionally grateful that Brandon agreed to sign on to this project. He truly picked up the slack when she could not (especially after emergency surgery left her without the normal use of her dominant hand for an extended period of time). Thank you, Brandon, for being a wonderful co-editor. I have enjoyed this journey!

Of course, it would be remiss of Helen not to mention, very quickly, that she is also very grateful to the aforementioned menagerie—Doc (neigh), Clementine, Smokey, Faith, and Toffee (meow, meow, meow, meow)—for their love and support (special credit goes to Toffee who repeatedly donned the editor-in-chief cap when he thought Brandon and Helen were going astray). Last, but by no means least, Helen owes everything to John, who is never short of something to say about free speech, and is never short of love to give to Helen. She dedicates this book to John, and to the memory of Jenny, the stepdaughter, who on July 5, 2019, was taken from this world far, far, far too soon.

Brandon extends his appreciation and gratitude to his family for their love, laughs, and encouragement: Cynthia & Sean; Robert & Sue (and Dalton); Ryan & Christen; Blaise & Brittany; Riana (and Brydon!); Kathy & Gary; Donna & Charlie; and many others. He is also appreciative of the support of numerous individuals who influenced and supported work contributing to this volume's completion, including incredible colleagues Lydia Andrade and Scott Dittloff at the University of the Incarnate Word; Robert & Lisa Matson, Jim Alexander, and Ray Wrabley at the University of Pittsburgh at Johnstown; Tom Keck and Keith Bybee at Syracuse University; Craig Warkentin and Helen Knowles at SUNY Oswego; the talented staff at each of these institutions (including Candy Brooks, Jacquie Meyer, Sally Greenfield, Kelly Coleman, and Bethany Walawender at Syracuse; Lisa Teters and Patti Tifft at Oswego; and Lorraine Ewers, Rosalinda Villarreal, Kathy Allwein, and Matt Gonzalez at Incarnate Word) and Peter Lang Publishing; those offering critiques and feedback at regional conferences on earlier work on this subject; the contributors to this volume; and the many students he continues to teach and learn from. Most importantly, completion of this project would not have been possible without the friendship, love, and support of Adam E. Brnardic (and Katie!); Zachary R. Cacicia (and Kayla!); Ron J. Gathagan (and Linh!); Brandon M. Miller; Brad S. Penrose (and Tiff!); and Jason A. Piccone.

HJK, Clinton, NY
BTM, San Antonio, TX

Note

1. William Cowper, *The Task and Other Poems* (1899), last accessed July 13, 2019, https://www.gutenberg.org/files/3698/3698-h/3698-h.htm
2. Archie Bland, "Freedom of Speech: Is It My Right to Offend You?" *Independent*, February 2, 2014, https://www.independent.co.uk/news/uk/politics/freedom-of-speech-is-it-my-right-to-offend-you-9101650.html

Introduction: Why Free Speech Theory Matters

HELEN J. KNOWLES AND BRANDON T. METROKA

As David Gilmour's iconic Pink Floyd song, "Lost For Words," suggests, it is neither healthy nor productive to try and respond to the words and ideas with which one disagrees by developing a "tunnel vision" of "spite."[1] If we simply attempt to shut (or, perhaps, shout) down our opponents by labeling them as "wrong" or "fake," we ultimately create an impoverished, unproductive, and undemocratic dialogue. This is because when we allow ourselves to become cocooned within a world of free speech defined by nothing more than speech on our terms, we rarely (if at all) stop to think (because we do not have to) about *why* we value our particular viewpoints or *why* we are free to hold and express them. Consequently, we believe we are at liberty to ignore the effects of our speech on those around us.

If we do stop to consider those effects, we will not be able to fully comprehend their origins and meanings unless we acknowledge the value of the competing perspectives. Indeed, invoking "free speech" as an authority for a preferred political position is a form of question begging, because it assumes that a rhetorical appeal to a value alone (here, free speech) somehow decides a particular issue. The contributors to this volume provide analyses of particular "free speech" conflicts with the specific goal of critically assessing *why* and *how* "free speech" *might* resolve a particular conflict. Their chapters are united by the belief that the incantation of "free speech" is a starting point rather than the end game of any argument, and that normative inquiries—establishing "rules or ideal standards" for deciding *what ought to be*—need to be part of the expressive freedom conversation.

Within the realm of free speech, all of the chapters address the following inquiry: "How can we answer the question of how things ought to be?"

Jonathan Wolff provides an answer to this question that speaks to the goal of this volume:

> The uncomfortable fact is that there ... [are] no easy answer[s]. But, despite this, very many philosophers have attempted to solve these normative political problems, and they have not been short of things to say ... philosophers reason about politics in just the way they do about other philosophical issues. They draw distinctions, they examine whether propositions are self-contradictory, or whether two or more propositions are logically consistent ... In short, they present arguments.[2]

The contributors to this volume pick up where too many citizens and pundits have left off—they present arguments that examine modern political controversies through different normative lenses, magnifying the assumptions that underlie shouts of "free speech!" They share a belief that in order to appreciate why free speech is relevant when deciding political controversies, one must first examine why free speech is valuable.

We view this problem on two different levels. First, such considerations get lost in the shuffle when one rejects the value of "disapprov[ing] of what you say, but ... defend[ing] to the death your right to say it."[3] In the United States in the 21st century, there are disturbing signs that many in society are indeed willing to distance themselves from a commitment to tolerate diverse views. They seem ready to reject the profound statement made by Justice William J. Brennan, Jr. in his opinion for the U.S. Supreme Court in *Texas v. Johnson* (1989). Striking down a state law prohibiting flag desecration, Brennan wrote: "We can imagine no more appropriate response to burning a flag than waving one's own, no better way to counter a flag burner's message than by saluting the flag that burns..."[4] This message of tolerance appears to have fallen on deaf ears, across the political spectrum. It is our collective belief that the true value of expressive freedom—which means more than just having the freedom to shout loudly at (or over) one's perceived opponents—can best be understood by using prominent philosophical approaches to unpack contemporary free speech controversies (controversies which all too frequently involve inadequate doses of tolerance).

An example of a controversy which has developed in recent years, and which would benefit from being put under this free speech theory microscope, is the propensity of many (predominantly liberal) administrators on college campuses to (strongly) encourage their faculty to use "trigger warnings" to alert students to the presence, in course material, of controversial subject matter that might offend and/or psychologically injure students. Rather than defend the concept of a classroom as a vibrant debate forum, it is suggested to educators that they either eradicate (aka censor) certain "non-conforming" viewpoints, or discuss them with caution and/ or disdain. In his welcoming letter to incoming students, John Ellison, dean of students at the University of Chicago, denounced this practice as a threat to "our commitment to freedom of inquiry and expression."[5] Other conservatives and self-described "classical liberals" have expressed this concern less kindly, indicting American universities for subverting a value long thought to be a "lodestar" of democracy. Terms like "regressive left" and "authoritarian" have been wielded as scythes against various constituent parts of this nebulous evil that seeks to destroy the lifeblood of a democratic body politic.[6] Take, for example, the words of Dennis Prager, a conservative commentator and talk show host, who lambasts the idea of campus "safe spaces":

> The worst offenders in protecting free speech are professors, and deans, and presidents of colleges. It's a moral cesspool, our university. And unless we are prepared to say that over and over, because just like big lies get believed, so do big truths. This is a big truth: the university in America is a wasteland—it is a moral and intellectual wasteland. It is the center of American hatred, of Western civilization hatred.[7]

Critics like Prager see political correctness run amuck; they believe that academics and others are either systematically or unwittingly (it is tough to tell which, at times) allowing good intentions to guide society down a primrose path to totalitarian hell.

Blind spots abound in this free expression debate. While vociferously denouncing the perceived elevation of "liberal" ideas in the university, many members of the "conservative" vanguard were noticeably silent over such matters as the suspension and subsequent resignation of Drexel University Associate Professor George Ciccariello-Maher, who first came under fire in 2016 for a "tweet" (that he described as satirical) which said: "All I want for Christmas is white genocide."[8] A 2018 article in the *Chronicle of Higher Education* provides a number of examples of conservative efforts to silence or deter liberal speakers on college campuses, suggesting the double-standard accusation levied against the political left could apply in equal force to the political right.[9] Similarly, there has been a remarkable lack of outrage from self-appointed free expression guardians in light of some local efforts to have books featuring LGBTQ characters removed from libraries, and in the aftermath of a Florida law that, until struck down by the Eleventh Circuit Court of Appeals, prevented doctors from discussing guns with patients in the course of standard inquiries about risks to safety and health.[10] This sort of tunnel vision gets us nowhere. If we stop to ask *why* people engage in such expressions (and use theories to structure that inquiry), rather than uncritically embracing or rejecting their positions, our understanding of the dialogue will be that much richer.

We do caution, however, that as much as we believe such theoretical inquiries are needed, we do not believe that the sky is falling. The United States is no stranger to private and public challenges to expressive freedom. From the Sedition Acts of 1798 to the anti-communist sentiment of World War I, from the southern gag orders on discussions of slavery in legislatures to the tarring and feathering of Jehovah's Witnesses during World War II (and beyond), the graveyard of American history is littered with tombstones that say "here lie the bones of yet another (primarily unsuccessful) challenge to free speech."[11]

However, one cannot ignore the fact that much of this divisive rhetoric—which is frequently defended in the name of "Free Speech!"—either emerged in its current form, or intensified in volume (spatially and audibly) during Donald J. Trump's presidential campaign in 2016, a trend that showed no signs of abating (quite the opposite, in fact) once Trump became the 45th President of the United States. Eschewing press conferences in favor of 140-character Twitter missives,[12] and engaging in actions that suggest an insatiable desire for widespread public dissemination (although not necessarily approval) of his actions, Trump has taken the "rhetorical presidency" to a whole new level.[13] This level has, most prominently, featured a constant clarion call condemnation of "fake news." Admittedly, Trump is not the first politician (American or otherwise) to rail against news reports by decrying their accuracy. However, his accusations of "fake news" play an unprecedented role in his presidential rhetoric. Polls conducted at the end of Trump's first year in office showed a disturbing increase in the percentage of Americans distrustful of the media.[14] And those accusations are issued in a hyper-partisan manner.[15] Therefore, in many ways Trump's exhibitions of expressive intolerance are no different from those of the aforementioned college campus administrators and trigger-warnings-implementing educators. After all, one rarely finds the President seeking to suppress (via Twitter or other media mechanisms) conservative news outlets. Conveniently, the "fake" news comes from the President's opponents, such as "the failing @nytimes" (the President habitually refers to the *New York Times* this way in his tweets). As Lara Trump observed, when "Real News Update" was created by her father-in-law's 2020 presidential reelection campaign, it was intended to be an online news program which would "bring you"—"you [who] are tired of all the fake news out there…nothing but the facts." What would these "facts" be? They would be "about all the accomplishments the president had this week," accomplishments which had not received the coverage they were entitled to "because there's so much fake news out there."[16]

Although one can point to these incidents as examples of societal intolerance, we must remember that they are also examples of free speech in action. For example, when the former San Francisco 49ers quarterback Colin Kaepernick took a knee during the playing of the national anthem to protest the state of race relations in America, he was just as much exercising his expressive freedom as was Vice President Mike Pence when he decided to walk out of an NFL game in condemnation of the players who had chosen to follow Kaepernick's lead.[17] And when Heather Heyer gathered with counter-protesters in Charlottesville, Virginia, on that fateful day in August, 2017, she was in one sense exercising the very same freedom as the "Unite the Right" white nationalists to whom she stood vehemently opposed.

It is just as important to remember, though, that words can have powerful consequences that are oftentimes non-expressive. Words sometimes speak louder than actions, and words sometimes beget actions that ultimately drown out those words. Kaepernick's efforts to draw attention to racial inequality have made him a prominent national spokesman on the subject, but at what cost? In response to his expressive actions the American Civil Liberties Union (ACLU) awarded him its 2017 Eason Monroe Courageous Advocate Award and in 2018 Nike made him the face of its "Just Do It" campaign.[18] However, he has not played in the NFL since 2016, and his unemployment is widely perceived to be the result of the controversy surrounding his anthem protest. Tragically, for Heather Heyer the price that she paid for exercising her expressive freedom was far greater; when an individual drove his car, at high speed, into a crowd of the counterprotesters, he killed Heather and wounded dozens more.[19] Thus, the situation is complicated by the fact that there is no clear line between what constitutes speech and what constitutes conduct.[20] If we stand on the street corner and wave United States flags as the Labor Day parade goes by, is that speech or conduct? The answer is probably a higgledy-piggledy mess of "speech," "conduct," and "it depends."

How do we make sense of all of these controversies? This brings us to our second argument. The irony is that while "Free Speech!" is increasingly in the news, and bandied about as something of value, that value remains under-theorized and, perhaps as an unintended consequence, is under threat; it is in danger of existing exclusively as a political slogan without substance. At best, it has become a rhetorical flourish in the spirit of political arguments, but at its worst it is a disingenuous mask for advancing extreme agendas and delegitimizing entire vocations, political factions, and positions about which reasonable people can (and do) disagree. If we agree that free speech is worth protecting, the next logical step is to examine its value to society. Some proponents may view expression as intrinsically valuable; this *non-consequentialist* conception of free expression tends to view speech as an end in and of itself rather than a particular avenue for achieving other social values. On the other hand, proponents may argue that free expression is valuable for its effects. The role of free expression in realizing other social values is also known as a *consequentialist* defense.[21] All of the contributors to this volume share the goal of more carefully examining how and when free expression is valuable to civic society, and they also explore what we believe is a less discussed issue: how and when free expression is complementary to or in conflict with other social values. Whether one agrees with the idea of free speech being valuable for its consequences and effects or not, anyone who believes speech has social value should take responsibility in explaining how that value can or should be balanced against competing values, or integrated so as to achieve a wider range of social commitments. This is not merely the province of courts, which make difficult decisions on this front on a case-by-case basis.

Two circumstances—a failure to engage with foundational assumptions about the value of free expression, and uncritical, partisan sloganeering drawing on the exalted status of free expression in the pantheon of fundamental rights—have contributed to an impoverished civic discourse that obscures more than it illuminates. We instinctively know that driving a car into a crowd of protesters because one disagrees with their views is not something that can legitimately be welcomed under the umbrella of "free speech." Similarly, although the hijackers of American Airlines flights 11 and 77, and United Airlines flights 175 and 93 probably operated under some belief that their actions were expressions of their opposition to American values, there is nothing controversial about saying that these "expressions" were not protected "free speech." The *harm* associated with the terrorists flying those planes into buildings on September 11, 2001, is categorically different from, and far greater than that which is associated with, for example, glimpsing someone walking through a courthouse wearing a jacket emblazoned with the words "Fuck the Draft."[22] Consequently, there is a far greater, and far more legitimate governmental interest in preventing the "expressive" actions of the terrorists than there is in clamping down on profane sartorial choices. And the law recognizes these differing governmental interests.[23] However, for every easy case there are hundreds of far harder ones. Is the creation of a wedding cake by a Christian baker a form of individual, artistic expression? Must that value supersede all others, such as an equality commitment that businesses serving the public avoid discriminating against same-sex couples? Look no farther than oral arguments in *Masterpiece Cakeshop, Ltd. v. Colorado Civil Rights Commission* for examples of U.S. Supreme Court justices struggling with this exercise in line-drawing.[24]

Introduction: Why Free Speech Theory Matters

The goal of this volume is to try and make sense of contemporary free speech controversies by engaging in critical analysis of them using theories of expressive freedom. One could simply say that the expressive actions and words of Colin Kaepernick, Heather Heyer, President Trump, and Professor George Ciccariello-Maher were examples of a "preferred" freedom being exercised. However, in terms of understanding their actions and words, that empirical statement does not get us very far, and certainly does not help us to understand *why* their actions and words should (or, perhaps, should not) be tolerated. Rather, if we use expressive freedom theories to engage in the normative inquiry that asks *why*, we are able to reach a far greater level of understanding of these contributions to the current societal dialogue. Indeed, if we do not, the dialogue ultimately looks more like a monologue.

Taking Free Speech Theory Seriously

Of course, at first blush many readers might seek to situate the idea of engaging in discussions using specific free speech theories and the works of philosophers somewhere along a continuum that runs from daunting, through frightening, to damn nigh impossible. The authors of the chapters in this volume are united in a belief that free speech theories do not have to be scary. We all encourage you, the reader, to "open your door" to theories, and not to view them as "enemies."[25] After all, whether you (the reader) know it or not, you have almost certainly already encountered many of the theoretical concepts that the contributors will discuss. Does a "marketplace of ideas" sound familiar? Or perhaps the "harm principle"?

Indeed, college students—who have sometimes been characterized as "snowflakes" seeking "safe spaces" from expression—appear to have found the proverbial treasure without a map, and may be in the vanguard in this "open door" effort. A recent *New York Times* article reported the results of a national survey of over 3,000 undergraduates who were directly asked about attitudes toward open and free debate and what is often framed as a competing, mutually exclusive concern for inclusivity and tolerance. The results of the survey are striking, and indicate students are actively wrestling with the normative questions we seek to expand upon in this volume. Among other findings, the survey found that "[c]ollege students believe about equally in free expression and pluralism, with nearly 90 percent saying that free expression protections are very or extremely important to democracy and more than 80 percent saying the same of promoting an inclusive and diverse society." And while majorities across survey subgroups (except for men and Republicans) tended to rank the importance of the latter over the former in the abstract, the survey also found that "the vast majority of students say they would rather have a learning environment that is open and permits offensive speech to one that is positive but limits it." This sentiment holds across all demographic and partisan subgroups of those surveyed. The survey and *New York Times* report also noted that majorities of students surveyed are willing to support restrictions on "hate speech" while also allowing for "free speech zones" to exist on campuses, and that students—contra some conventional accounts—do worry about the erosion of First Amendment protections.[26] Looking beyond this survey, the advocacy of David Hogg, Emma González, Cameron Kasky, Kyle Kashuv, and other survivors of the February 14, 2018, mass shooting at Marjory Stoneman Douglas High School in Parkland, Florida, suggests that the next generation of undergraduates is not at all shy about exercising First Amendment rights (just ask Fox News personality Laura Ingraham).[27] Taken together, these empirical findings strongly suggest to us that the "snowflake" claim is more slogan than substance, and that undergraduates are engaged in something more than recreational outrage.

In sum, there is good reason to believe that the spirit of philosophical inquiry is alive and well on college campuses, and is ripe for continued flourishing. We collectively view this volume as the next step in this robust philosophical debate. The chapters in this volume examine contemporary controversies concerning freedom of expression through a critical, theoretical lens. Each author walks the reader through the positions taken by commentators, ideologues, and partisans in recent controversies featuring cries of "Free Speech!" via assessments of competing justifications for freedom of expression. We use the reasons why polities value freedom of expression in the first place to engage in critical assessments and analytical explanations of contemporary controversies both in America and abroad. By the end of each chapter—and, for those brave souls, by the end of this volume—the reader will have a newfound appreciation of the underlying assumptions about human nature and the goals freedom of expression are meant to achieve.

Although this volume is a broad exercise in normative reasoning, we hope it is obvious that we do not seek to give primacy to any one theoretical justification for freedom of expression. It does not make an unqualified claim that free speech "absolutism"—freedom of expression must always trump all other fundamental commitments in any and all possible contexts—is the normative baseline against which all other positions are to be judged. Indeed, far too many of the current debates assume, without carefully examining, the value of freedom of expression, and assume there is only one value served by freedom of expression—a negative liberty on behalf of the individual—without sufficient attention to competing justifications that may be in substantial tension with one another. Freedom of expression is one important value among many, and its antecedent assumptions deserve more critical scrutiny and discussion than they currently receive in the modern political culture.

This survey of the theoretical landscape should not be interpreted as privileging some writers and thinkers over others. Far more has been written about normative philosophies of freedom of expression than we could ever hope to fit in a single introductory chapter (or perhaps single book). As such, the illustrative examples that follow were chosen because they represent "ideal types." They are canonical—any survey of the free speech theoretical landscape would be noticeably barren without them. For readers interested in additional readings touching upon the theories surveyed, citations are provided in the endnotes to this chapter. Ultimately, while the contributors to this volume may or may not adopt these particular normative lenses, each chapter points to our general thesis: If "free speech" is to be more than a rhetorical flourish in political debate, substantive rather than blind authority, we must first attempt to answer the question of *why* free speech is valuable.

Beyond the First Amendment and the Supreme Court

Before perusing that theoretical landscape, however, it behooves us to say a few words about the explanatory paths not taken in this book. This is because speech theories are by no means the only way to understand expressive freedom controversies. When attempting to sort through such controversies, in the United States one might be inclined to consult the pages of the U.S. Reports for the First Amendment decisions and opinions of the U.S. Supreme Court, and accompanying commentary. There is no shortage of material to choose from. Many forests have fallen in the service of producing texts that describe and attempt to explain the evolution of freedom of expression doctrine generated by that Court.[28] However, there are a number of problems associated with following the First Amendment path to the imposing bronze doors of the Court's building on First Street NE in Washington, D.C.

1. Fourteen Pesky Words

First, the language of the First Amendment might seem clear, but for the entirety of its existence the meaning of that language has been hotly debated as competing interpretations have abounded. As one of our contributors, Professor Jim Foster, eloquently expressed elsewhere:

> First Amendment speech and press guarantees did not spring fully grown—Athena-like—from the collective brow of the Founding generation. On the

contrary, despite the foremost placement and categorical language of those fourteen little words—'Congress shall make no law ... abridging the freedom of speech, or of the press'—the Founders, along with their political allies and their political enemies, often opted to punish instead of protect oppositional speech.[29]

The only thing that there has been real agreement upon has been the number of words in the Amendment.

2. Fourteen, Sometimes Inapplicable, Words

The second reason why neither the First Amendment nor the Supreme Court alone can be relied upon to help us make sense of an expressive freedom conflict in the United States is that not all such conflicts are constitutional ones. People all too often forget that the First Amendment limits the actions of the government; it does not limit private actors.[30] So, when Jerry Jones, the owner of the Dallas Cowboys, threatened to punish his players for actions which, in his opinion, are "disrespecting the flag," the First Amendment could not have stood in his way.[31] Similarly, when Google terminated the employment of James Damore after he published a document sharply critical of the company's diversity hiring practices, the "fourteen little words" offered him no protection.[32] They were not applicable, because those words only serve to limit the actions of governments in the United States.

3. The Slow-Moving Wheels of Justice

Third, the decisions of the U.S. Supreme Court simply do not help us to understand the current free speech controversies mentioned above, and dissected in the chapters that follow. In 2015, one of us opened the Conclusion to *Judging Free Speech*, a volume of essays tracing the evolution of the U.S. Supreme Court's expressive freedom jurisprudence, with the following hypothetical:

> Imagine that you are a politics professor (whose area of study focuses on law and courts) working at a private, small liberal arts college. You receive an unsolicited email from a member of Congress; using offensive language, that politician bitterly criticizes your work, implying that you are contributing to the 'vast gay conspiracy' by failing to expose the US Supreme Court's gay rights decisions for what they are, namely 'moral abominations that are rapidly sending the country to hell in a hand basket.' Viewing the email as a rather pathetic piece of ideological screed, you post the text of it on your personal, private Facebook page (which is only viewable by your friends—twenty-five in total). You also mention that the politician's words are proof that he is an 'intolerant, homophobic nut-job who would benefit from doing what he did last weekend—namely, to f*** his mother in a portable toilet.'

Introduction: Why Free Speech Theory Matters   11

> Thinking that this is the end of your bizarre day, you drive home, only to find two items in your mailbox. Knowing that you are an animal lover, an organization has sent you an unsolicited package containing a DVD bearing the label "God's creatures" and featuring pictures of beautiful animals on the cover (computer hackers told the organization that you regularly purchase cat litter at the local pet store). You and your cat are distraught when you play the DVD and discover it contains multiple "animal crush" scenes—of scantily clad women wearing stilettos, taking sexual pleasure from stomping on kittens strapped to the floor (you subsequently realize that the women are locally elected officials). Frustrated, in the middle of the night you climb into your car, drive to the local town hall, walk up to the steps of the building, douse two flags—Old Glory and the local town flag—in lighter fuel and set fire to them. As you leave the scene, you notice that an elderly gentleman, who was sitting on a nearby bench and playing a guitar, has now begun to collect up the ashes of the flags while gently weeping.[33]

As the chapters in *Judging Free Speech* illustrated, in 2015 the answer to the question "To what extent can governments in the United States regulate and/or restrict these forms of expression?" was "not much."[34] This is because at the time the Court was more protective of free speech (or at least of the types of claims it chose to review) than it had ever been.[35] And, not much has changed. In the intervening years the free speech decisions issued by the justices have generally continued to embrace a belief that expressive freedom should be robustly and rigorously protected.[36] Societal views are far more complex, and the contemporary controversies discussed in the chapters of this book suggest (unlike the Court's jurisprudence) that it is by no means a sure thing that the future of expressive freedom will be progressive rather than regressive.

4. The Court of Public Opinion

Fourth, discussions about free speech conflicts are not confined to courtrooms or lawyers' offices. Although courts have a fascinating history of giving meaning to the First Amendment, the debates that implicate free expression often occur in the court of public opinion and rely on philosophical or moral justifications that are never fully articulated. The chapters in this volume all enable us to better understand contemporary free speech controversies because they are examined using precisely those otherwise unarticulated justifications.

The court of public opinion, by contrast, operates very differently, and plays by an entirely separate set of rules (or, sometimes, by no rules at all). Just ask the Canadian feminist author Margaret Atwood. When she dared to criticize the ways in which the #MeToo movement condemned those accused of sexual harassment, she found out, firsthand, how the court of public opinion can even all too easily reject something as fundamental to the Anglo-American system of law as due process (which is, ironically, a principle designed to protect individual liberty from authoritarian encroachment).[37] And the problems associated with the court of public opinion are often intensified by the fact that increasingly it renders its decisions via individual-centric technologies such as Facebook, Instagram, and Twitter. The irony of the new media is that extended discussions of the theories of expressive freedom are often absent from such debates even though convenient and frequently (mis)used slogans such as "clear and present danger" and "shouting fire in a crowded theater" have their own very well-used Twitter hash tags.[38]

5. Global Citizenship

Finally, we wish to remind readers that the U.S. free speech tradition does not stand alone in the world. Whatever one's political convictions, Americans are indisputably members of a global economy and society. Unfortunately, available data continue to suggest that Americans have an incredibly limited sense of world affairs, from current events to simply locating other nations on a map.[39] Other comparable, western democracies, through their own forms of judicial review, have established free speech traditions as well. Yet, the lines drawn and the values served tend to vary from court to court, and polity to polity.

At first blush, one might assume that the United Kingdom and Australia (the two western liberal democracies beyond the shores of the United States that are featured in this volume) provide their citizens with wide-ranging speech protections comparable to those enjoyed by Americans. After all, their legal systems share much in common with that of the United States. Indeed, the data contained in indices such as the Cato Institute's "Human Freedom Index" and the Freedom House "Freedom in the World Report" support the expectation that there are more similarities than differences.[40] The truth is more complex.

Just consider what the average undergraduate taking an American politics course in the United States is likely to know about the laws and politics of the United Kingdom. Perhaps he or she knows that the UK does not have a written constitution. That is a good start. However, whether they are aware of, have stopped to consider, or have been engaged in classroom contemplation about the implications of the UK's constitutional tradition is less likely. Surely, they might think, the United Kingdom, home to the Royal Family (which appears to have considerable public support in the US);[41] iconic tourist attractions such as Big Ben, red telephone boxes, and those guards with big fuzzy hats; the producers of quality television programs such as Game of Thrones and Dr. Who; and generally a population of people with very cool accents, is nothing less than a bastion of democratic constitutionalism, with protections of rights and liberties such as those enjoyed by the Americans with whom the British have historically enjoyed a "special relationship."[42] Those undergraduates will probably be shocked to find out that there is no system of checks and balances akin to that in the United States—for example, the "chief executive" (aka the Prime Minister) is actually a member of the legislative branch (aka Parliament). And there are very few formal ways in which to check the lawmaking power of that branch. Indeed, growing up in Great Britain, one of us vividly remembers the way in which the Parliament, under the leadership of Prime Minister Margaret Thatcher in 1988, responded to increasing episodes of Northern Ireland violence (generally referred to as "the Troubles") by legally requiring United Kingdom broadcasters to censor the voices of members of numerous Irish republican groups—most prominently, members of Sinn Fein.[43] That governmental censorship was perfectly legal in the UK. Although the ban was lifted in 1994, it serves as a vivid reminder of the very different censorial powers held by the British Parliament and the U.S. Congress.

Surveying the Theoretical Landscape

In the remainder of this introduction, we lay the theoretical groundwork for the chapters that follow by providing an abbreviated overview of three important theoretical justifications for, and conceptions of freedom of expression.

1. The Marketplace of Ideas

"You can't handle the truth!" One of the most famous movie quotations in history,[44] this forceful proclamation came from the mouth of Colonel Nathan R. Jessup (played by Jack Nicholson) in his epic courtroom confrontation with Lieutenant Daniel Kaffee (played by Tom Cruise) in the 1992 film *A Few Good Men*. A quarter of a century later, many of the individuals referenced in the examples outlined in the previous pages of this Introduction— especially those who decry "fake news"—seem unable to handle anything that they have not deemed to be the truth. And they certainly seem unlikely to engage in truth-related discussions that take free speech theories seriously as useful analytical tools.

To those individuals who want "truth" on their own terms, much solace might be found in the following sentences:

> Persecution for the expression of opinions seems to me perfectly logical. If you have no doubt of your premises or your power, and want a certain result with all your heart, you naturally express your wishes in law, and sweep away all opposition. To allow opposition by speech seems to indicate that you think the speech impotent, as when a man says that he has squared the circle, or that you do not care wholeheartedly for the result, or that you doubt either your power or your premises.[45]

However, initial looks can be deceiving. This passage comes from one of the most famous opinions about freedom of speech ever written by a member of the U.S. Supreme Court—the dissenting opinion penned by Justice Oliver Wendell Holmes, Jr. in *Abrams v. United States* (1919), an otherwise unexceptional case in a line of decisions unsympathetic to the rights of unpopular World War I dissenters. It is only one passage, however; the entirety of Holmes's opinion gives very little aid and comfort to those seeking to suppress what they deem to be incorrect (i.e., opposing) views. The sentences reprinted above were quickly followed by these immortal words:

> *But* when men have realized that time has upset many fighting faiths, they may come to believe even more than they believe the very foundations of their own conduct that the ultimate good desired is better reached by free trade in ideas—*that the best test of truth is the power of the thought to get itself accepted in the competition of the market, and that truth is the only ground upon which their wishes safely can be carried out.* That, at any rate, is the theory of our Constitution. It is an experiment, as all life is an experiment. Every year, if not every day, we have to wager our salvation upon some prophecy based upon imperfect knowledge. While that experiment is part of our system, I think that we should be eternally vigilant against attempts to check the expression of opinions that we loathe and believe to be fraught with death, unless they so imminently threaten immediate interference with the lawful and pressing purposes of the law that an immediate check is required to save the country.[46]

As we can see, Holmes did not use the precise words "marketplace of ideas." Nevertheless, it is from this dissent that we get the *concept* underpinning that famous aphorism. This market metaphor is one of the most well-known conceptual means of achieving the end of "the truth." Holmes was hardly the first to come up with the idea, yet his concept remains powerful, in large part because it provides us with a convenient visual image of this particular rationale for expressive freedom. A "marketplace of ideas" conjures up an image of a vibrant and bustling bazaar filled with people trading in competing thoughts and ideas. As Holmes suggests, if "the best test of truth is the power of the thought to get itself accepted in the competition of the market," then the marketplace will naturally sort out truths from falsities.[47]

Of course, that is a big "if." The marketplace analogy is far from perfect, because a great many things can prevent the truth (or anything remotely resembling it) from prevailing.[48] After all, sometimes markets fail. However, in Holmes's defense, all he was saying is that this was the "theory of our [U.S.] Constitution"—the theory of the principal document which, in the United States, stands in the way of governmental censorship of expressive freedom—and that "[i]t is an experiment, as all life is an experiment. Every year, if not every day, we have to wager our salvation upon some prophecy based upon imperfect knowledge." As the chapters that follow seek to demonstrate, the inevitable imperfections in our knowledge can be offset by analysis that engages in thoughtful and incisive examinations that draw upon canonical theoretical justifications for free speech, justifications such as the Holmesian marketplace analogy.

Perhaps the most egregious way in which the government can suppress views is through imposing a prior restraint on the press. Rather than *punishing* someone for the views that they publish, prior restraint involves *preventing* those views from seeing the light of day in the first place. In the United States, protecting publishers from prior restraint is considered to be "the chief purpose" of the Free Press Clause of the First Amendment—which is "a virtually insurmountable barrier between government and the print media so far as government tampering, in advance of publication, with news and editorial content is concerned."[49]

Writing in 1644, British author John Milton sharply condemned Parliament's recently enacted press licensing requirements and the discretionary power they gave to officials to impose prior restraints. In *Areopagitica*, he offered an argument that, like Holmes's dissent in *Abrams*, is a powerful statement of the marketplace of ideas theory. In his appeal to the better angels of Parliament, Milton identified a theoretical reason against press licensing—preservation of "truth":

> And though all the windes of doctrin were let loose to play upon the earth, so Truth be in the field, we do injuriously, by licencing and prohibiting to misdoubt her strength. Let her and Falshood grapple; who ever knew Truth put to the wors, in a free and open encounter. Her confuting is the best and surest suppressing ... When a man hath bin labouring the hardest labour in the deep mines of knowledge, hath furnisht out his findings in all their equipage, drawn forth his reasons as it were a battell raung'd, scatter'd and defeated all objections in his way, calls out his adversary into the plain, offers him the advantage of wind and sun, if he please; only that he may try the matter by dint of argument, for his opponents then to sculk, to lay ambushments, to keep a narrow bridge of licencing where the challenger should passe, though it be valour anough in souldiership, is but weaknes and cowardice in the wars of Truth. For who knows not

that Truth is strong next to the Almighty; she needs no policies, nor stratagems, nor licencings to make her victorious, those are the shifts and the defences that error uses against her power...[50]

"Truth" also entered into the discussion of prior restraint that appeared in William Blackstone's *Commentaries on the Laws of England*, a 1760s treatise on the common law that greatly influenced the United States legal system during the years of the early American Republic. When discussing the importance of preventing prior restraints, Blackstone said:

> The liberty of the press is indeed essential to the nature of a free state; but this consists in laying no previous restraints upon publications, and not in freedom from censure for criminal matter when published. Every freeman has an undoubted right to lay what sentiments he pleases before the public; to forbid this, is to destroy the freedom of the press...[51]

Blackstone went on to emphasize, however, that if a person "publishes what is improper, mischievous or illegal, he must take the consequence of his own temerity."[52] In other words, he did not believe that one could hide behind a "this is the truth!" defense if one spoke with bad intentions.

A far broader discussion of the "truth" rationale for protecting freedom of expression—a discussion that has more sympathy for the views expressed by Milton than for those of Blackstone—came in the mid-nineteenth century with the publication of John Stuart Mill's *On Liberty* (1859):

> If all mankind minus one were of one opinion, and only one person were of the contrary opinion, mankind would be no more justified in silencing that one person, than he, if he had the power, would be justified in silencing mankind—But the peculiar evil of silencing the expression of an opinion is, that it is robbing the human race; posterity as well as the existing generation; those who dissent from the opinion, still more than those who hold it. If the opinion is right, they are deprived of the opportunity of exchanging error for truth: if wrong, they lose, what is almost as great a benefit, the clearer perception and livelier impression of truth, produced by its collision with error.[53]

Mill's truth defense is generally framed as a conflict between individuals holding unpopular, minority opinions, and a governing authority, through law and with the backing of majority opinion, seeking to quell the expression of those opinions. However, Mill also alludes to the way in which majority opinion, outside of its entrenchment in law, can be dangerous to the unearthing of truth:

> Like other tyrannies, the tyranny of the majority was at first, and is still vulgarly, held in dread, chiefly as operating through the acts of the public authorities. But reflecting persons perceived that when society is itself the tyrant—society

> collectively over the separate individuals who compose it—its means of tyrannizing are not restricted to the acts which it may do by the hands of its political functionaries. Society can and does execute its own mandates: and if it issues wrong mandates instead of right, or any mandates at all in things with which it ought not to meddle, it practices a social tyranny more formidable than many kinds of political oppression, since, though not usually upheld by such extreme penalties, it leaves fewer means of escape, penetrating much more deeply into the details of life, and enslaving the soul itself. Protection, therefore, against the tyranny of the magistrate is not enough: there needs protection also against the tyranny of the prevailing opinion and feeling; against the tendency of society to impose, by other means than civil penalties, its own ideas and practices as rules of conduct on those who dissent from them…[54]

The tenets of Mill's tract are no less relevant today than they were in the 1850s, and these tenets shed much-needed light on modern free expression controversies. In the United States, Blackstone's views were immensely influential; however, his belief that speech (even the "truth") could be suppressed because of the "bad tendencies" associated with it has long since fallen by the wayside, replaced (since the middle of the twentieth century) by a far more libertarian view of expressive freedom, a far more Millian and Holmesian view.[55]

2. Democratic Self-Governance

What has become known as an argument from democracy—and later, the self-government rationale—gained legal traction in Justice Louis D. Brandeis's concurring opinion in *Whitney v. California* (1927). Brandeis's rationale subtly differed from Justice Holmes's in emphasizing a value distinct from truth:

> Those who won our independence believed that the final end of the State was to make men free to develop their faculties, and that, in its government, the deliberative forces should prevail over the arbitrary. They valued liberty both as an end, and as a means. They believed liberty to be the secret of happiness, and courage to be the secret of liberty. They believed that freedom to think as you will and to speak as you think are means indispensable to the discovery and spread of political truth; that, without free speech and assembly, discussion would be futile; that, with them, discussion affords ordinarily adequate protection against the dissemination of noxious doctrine; that the greatest menace to freedom is an inert people; that public discussion is a political duty, and that this should be a fundamental principle of the American government. They recognized the risks to which all human institutions are subject. But they knew that order cannot be secured merely through fear of punishment for its infraction; that it is hazardous to discourage thought, hope and imagination; that fear breeds repression; that repression breeds hate; that hate menaces stable government; that the path of safety lies in the opportunity to discuss freely supposed grievances and proposed

remedies, and that the fitting remedy for evil counsels is good ones. Believing in the power of reason as applied through public discussion, they eschewed silence coerced by law—the argument of force in its worst form. Recognizing the occasional tyrannies of governing majorities, they amended the Constitution so that free speech and assembly should be guaranteed.[56]

This is widely regarded as one of the greatest U.S. Supreme Court opinions (within and beyond the realm of the First Amendment) ever written.[57] Its justification for free expression did not eschew the Mill-centered logic of Holmes's dissent in *Abrams*; however, it did suggest that expressive freedom was the means for achieving a different end—the goal of deliberative, civic discourse that is a necessary condition for democratic self-government. Whereas individual liberty (Mill) and truth (Holmes) were both ends in their own right, Brandeis's concurrence suggested that these are means to the realization of a robust democracy.

In 1948, the American philosopher Alexander Meiklejohn published a forceful defense of the democratic self-governance rationale for protecting free speech.[58] *Free Speech and Its Relation to Self-Government*, his seminal work on the subject, recognized that no member of the American polity could justifiably be prevented from speaking on *public matters* because of an authority's judgment on truth and content. Meiklejohn made the case that free expression is *almost exclusively tied to the project of self-governance*. Beginning with a recitation of the First Amendment's speech clause, Meiklejohn extoled the virtues of human capacity for thought and development while also noting that the subject of free expression is not immune from government action:

> First, let it be noted that, by those words, Congress is not debarred from all action upon freedom of speech. Legislation which abridges that freedom is forbidden, but not legislation to enlarge and enrich it. The freedom of mind which befits the members of a self-governing society is not a given and fixed part of human nature. It can be increased and established by learning, by teaching, by the unhindered flow of accurate information, by giving men health and vigor and security, by bringing them together in activities of communication and mutual understanding...[59]

For Meiklejohn, democratic self-governance was the end, and individual development was but the means. Self-governance was only possible if certain kinds of speech were restrained. To Meiklejohn, the Constitution was fundamentally about self-governing, not prevailing in the marketplace of ideas. "We Americans," he wrote, "when thinking in that vein, have taken the 'competition of the market' principle to mean that as separate thinkers, we have no obligation to test our thinking, to make sure that it is worthy of a citizen who is one of the 'rulers of the nation.' "[60] Limiting the marketplace did not amount to "abridging" speech, because it was the only way to realize the *freedom* of speech given the baseline of democracy:

> In the town meeting the people of a community assemble to discuss and to act upon matters of public interest—roads, schools, poorhouses, health, external defense, and the like. Every man is free to come. They meet as political equals. Each has a right and a duty to think his own thoughts, to express them, and to listen to the arguments of others. The basic principle is that the freedom of speech shall be unabridged. And yet the meeting cannot even be opened unless, by common consent, speech is abridged. A chairman or moderator is, or has been, chosen. He 'calls the meeting to order.' And the hush which follows that call is a clear indication that restrictions upon speech have been set up ... The meeting has been assembled, not primarily to talk, but primarily by means of talking to get business done. And the talking must be regulated and abridged as the doing of the business under actual conditions may require. If a speaker wanders from the point at issue, if he is abusive or in other ways threatens to defeat the purpose of the meeting, he may be and should be declared 'out of order.' He must then stop speaking, at least in that way. And if he persists in breaking the rules, he may be 'denied the floor' or, in the last resort, 'thrown out' of the meeting. The town meeting, as it seeks for freedom of public discussion of public problems, would be wholly ineffectual unless speech were thus abridged. It is not a Hyde Park. It is a parliament or congress. It is a group of free and equal men, cooperating in a common enterprise, and using for that enterprise responsible and regulated discussion. It is not a dialectical free-for-all. It is self-government.[61]

Meiklejohn's justification for expression is at once intensely protective and the least protective. It views freedom of speech as a means of realizing the most virtuous public good. However, it is explicitly less concerned with private speech. In 1948, Meiklejohn saw the First Amendment as extending protection:

> only to speech which bears, directly or indirectly, upon issues with which voters have to deal—only, therefore, to the consideration of matters of public interest. Private speech, or private interest in speech, on the other hand, has no claim whatever to the protection of the First Amendment. If men are engaged, as we so commonly are, in argument, or inquiry, or advocacy, or incitement which is directed toward our private interests, private privileges, private possessions, we are, of course, entitled to 'due process' protection of those activities. *But the First Amendment has no concern over such protection.*[62]

Some of his later publications suggested that, over time, Meiklejohn's understanding of the types of speech that would contribute to democratic self-governance expanded.[63] Nevertheless, his distinction between private and public speech remains a potent one, especially as one seeks—as some of the contributors to this volume do—to make sense of free speech controversies in the 21st century, when social media platforms have come to replace Meiklejohn's physical town hall parable.

3. Individual Autonomy

The third, and perhaps the most under-theorized of the principal justifications for free expression is individual autonomy—sometimes described as individual self-fulfillment. Scholars identify this justification with a natural right to individual freedom and dignity. As Stephen Heyman observes: "The core meaning of freedom is self-determination: a free person is the author of his or her own thoughts and actions."[64] On this account, expressive freedom may produce valuable consequences—such as finding the "truth" or promoting democratic self-governance; however, its principal value instead derives from the fact that free speech is the very essence of free individuals. As C.E. Baker explains, "A person's autonomy might reasonably be conceived as her capacity to pursue successfully the life she endorses—self-authored at least in the sense that, no matter how her image of a meaningful life originates, she now can endorse that life for reasons that she accepts."[65]

Protecting an individual's "capacity to pursue successfully the life" they "endorse" means, of course, protecting forms of expression that many people in society would view as not only morally reprehensible but also *harmful* to society in physical and psychological ways. The U.S. Supreme Court addressed this conflict in *Ashcroft v. Free Speech Coalition* (2002), in which, by a vote of 7–2, it struck down the Child Pornography Prevention Act of 1996 (CPPA), a law extending the federal ban on child pornography to "any visual depiction including any photograph, film, video, picture, or computer or computer-generated image or picture" that "is, or appears to be, of a minor engaging in sexually explicit conduct" (virtual child pornography).[66] The Court distinguished between pornography created using real children—which could be banned because of the associated sexual abuse of children and the creation of a "permanent record" that would negatively affect the child beyond the material's initial creation—and virtual child pornography with which these consequences were not clearly associated. The Court viewed the CPPA as a congressional attempt to regulate a harm that resulted from the "content of the images."[67] And the First Amendment does not permit the suppression of speech simply because a crime might result from the expression. Writing for his colleagues, in his majority opinion Justice Anthony M. Kennedy expressed their collective disgust at the material in question. However, for the reasons outlined above, the justices concluded that the material had to be constitutionally protected:

> The mere tendency of speech to encourage unlawful acts is not a sufficient reason for banning it. The government 'cannot constitutionally premise legislation on the desirability of controlling a person's private thoughts'... First Amendment freedoms are most in danger when the government seeks to control thought or

to justify its laws for that impermissible end. *The right to think is the beginning of freedom, and speech must be protected from the government because speech is the beginning of thought.*[68]

The ability to express one's self is a necessary condition for maximizing autonomy, but it is a justification that is admittedly difficult to cabin, and it is a justification that requires us to tolerate that which we might find the most difficult to tolerate. Indeed, if one concludes that individuals have the right to control their own expressions, regardless of the truth, and regardless of any potentially harmful or malicious intentions—if, in other words, they have the right to control their own expressions without regard to consequences—then "free expression" has the potential to be reduced to the meaningless "all expressions are free." As discussed above, instinctually the acts of terrorism witnessed on September 11, 2001, are no doubt "expressive" acts of conduct; yet society does not understand them as such. Similarly, let us suppose that on the way to work, a person decides to exceed the speed limit. Once pulled over by law enforcement, the person argues that she cannot be ticketed because the act of speeding was, in fact, an expression of disagreement with the posted speed limit laws. To fulfill her autonomy, one might argue, the expressive act was the fullest realization of the self. Where, then, might one draw the line?[69]

This is one of the crucial questions explored by the contributors to this volume as they apply theories of expressive freedom—including those outlined above—to contemporary issues wherein line-drawing is far from easy, and inherently controversial.

Critical Responses. As noted from the outset, we urge readers to recognize that "Free Speech!" is not the only value cherished by members of the polity, in the U.S. and abroad. Scholars from feminist and critical race theory traditions have long argued that the elevation of free expression has come at the cost of other values, including broad commitments to egalitarianism. They view the expressive freedom line-drawing enterprise in a very different context. Although their critical arguments may not feature as prominently in the chapters that follow as, for example, those of Mill and Meiklejohn, their contributions to free speech theory are nevertheless extremely important to consider.

By making the argument that one condones rape when one condones expressive freedom protection for pornography, Catharine MacKinnon forces us to reconsider the relationship between words and actions/conduct. As she contends in *Only Words*:

> What pornography does, it does in the real world, not only in the mind ... In pornography, women are gang raped so they can be filmed. They are not gang raped by the idea of a gang rape. It is for pornography, and not by the ideas in it,

that women are hurt and penetrated, tied and gagged, undressed and genitally spread and sprayed with lacquer and water so sex pictures can be made. Only for pornography are women killed to make a sex movie, and it is not the idea of sex killing that kills them. It is unnecessary to do any of these things to express, as ideas, the ideas pornography expresses. It is essential to do them to make pornography...

Pornography contains ideas, like any other social practice. But the way it works is not as a thought or through its ideas as such, at least not in the way thoughts and ideas are protected as speech. Its place in abuse requires understanding it more in active than in passive terms, as constructing and performative rather than as merely referential or connotative. The message of these materials, and there is one, as there is to all conscious activity, is 'get her,' pointing at all women, to the perpetrators' benefit often billion dollars a year and counting. This message is addressed directly to the penis, delivered through an erection, and taken out on women in the real world ... How many women's bodies have to stack up here even to register against male profit and pleasure presented as First Amendment principle?[70]

Recall that in *Free Speech Coalition*, Justice Kennedy wrote the opinion striking down a law banning virtual child pornography, saying that "[t]he right to think is the beginning of freedom, and speech must be protected from the government because speech is the beginning of thought."[71] The logic of opposition to pornography, for MacKinnon, can be extended to even computer-generated pornographic images because those images might have a tendency to produce violent behavior (especially against women), and whet the appetites of sexual predators. So, one might legitimately ask, "How many women's bodies have to stack up here" before we dare to restrict even a "right" accurately described as "the beginning of freedom"?

Courts in the United States have generally not accepted MacKinnon's views.[72] Libertarian views akin to those expressed in Justice Kennedy's opinion have generally triumphed (both within courts of law and the broader court of public opinion) at the expense of MacKinnon-esque feminist positions. However, if the #MeToo movement has proven anything thus far, it is that simply because "something has always been that way" is not an automatically adequate justification for defending views and/or conduct.

It is for the very same reason that the writings of scholars operating in the discipline known as "critical race theory" need to be given a voice in conversations about free speech theory. Those scholars have drawn attention to the ways in which the exalted status of free expression serves to marginalize the experiences of those on the receiving end of speech. Mari Matsuda, for example, engaged in "legal storytelling" to highlight the ways in which free expression not only helps preserve racial hierarchies, but also negatively affects members of dominant racial and social classes:

Introduction: Why Free Speech Theory Matters 23

> The negative effects of hate messages are real and immediate for the victims. Victims of vicious hate propaganda have experienced physiological symptoms and emotional distress ranging from fear in the gut, rapid pulse rate and difficulty in breathing, nightmares, post-traumatic stress disorder, hypertension, psychosis, and suicide ...
>
> Victims are restricted in their personal freedom. In order to avoid receiving hate messages, victims have had to quit jobs, forgo education, leave their homes, avoid certain public places, curtail their own exercise of speech rights, and otherwise modify their behavior and demeanor. The recipient of hate messages struggles with inner turmoil ...
>
> Dominant-group members who rightfully, and often angrily, object to hate propaganda share a guilty secret: their relief that they are not themselves the target of the racist attack ... at some level, no matter how much both victims and well-meaning dominant-group members resist it, racial inferiority is planted in our minds as an idea that may hold some truth. The idea is improbable and abhorrent, but it is there before us, because it is presented repeatedly. 'Those people' are lazy, dirty, sexualized, money-grubbing, dishonest, inscrutable, we are told. We reject the idea, but the next time we sit next to one of 'those people' the dirt message, the sex message, is triggered. We stifle it, reject it as wrong, but it is there, interfering with our perception and interaction with the person next to us. For the victim, similarly, the angry rejection of the message of inferiority is coupled with absorption of the message. When a dominant-group member responds favorably, there is a moment of relief—the victims of hate messages do not always believe in their insides that they deserve decent treatment. This obsequious moment is degrading and dispiriting when the self-aware victim acknowledges it.[73]

To fully appreciate the implications of free expression controversies in society, informed citizens must take seriously these accounts of countervailing values and consider how and when the elevation of free speech may aggravate, rather than cure, social ills. It would be blinking at reality to ignore how racial and sexual overtones weave through the debates we wish to critically examine in this volume. Omission of these critical voices from the conversation fails to do justice to the scope of the subject matter that is "free speech theory."

...

One fails to do justice to the scope of that subject matter any time one succumbs to the temptation to cry "Free Speech!" in an uncritical and/or purely partisan manner. It is because so many commentators—within and beyond the United States—*do not* resist that temptation that we have put this book together. In the chapters that follow, our contributors unpack contemporary free speech controversies, united by a belief that it is important to "answer the question of how things ought to be." As Professor Wolff observes, although "[t]he uncomfortable fact is that there is no easy answer" to that question, this should not stop us from addressing this inquiry. Our contributors do just that, by "draw[ing] distinctions ... examin[ing] whether propositions are self-contradictory," and asking "whether two or more propositions are logically consistent."[74] Simply put, "they present arguments," arguments that are critically analytically in nature, and which apply canonical free speech theories in pursuit of the goal of better understanding why we value the ability to freely express ourselves.[75] You could simply keep on arguing, "engulfed in a fever of spite."[76] We believe, however, that your time would be better spent if you stopped to consider *why* any particular argument matters (instead of simply observing that the arguments exist). Therefore, in the pages that follow what you will not find yourself engulfed in is a "fever of spite," but rather you will be surrounded by an intense application of free speech theory.

Notes

1. "Lost For Words," Pink Floyd, *The Division Bell*, 1994 (2011 remastered version (explicit)), track 10, Sony Legacy, 2016, compact disc.
2. Jonathan Wolff, *An Introduction to Political Philosophy* (New York: Oxford University Press, 2006), 3.
3. Although frequently attributed to Voltaire, these words actually come from a book about Voltaire. See S. G. Tallentyre, *The Friends of Voltaire* (London: Smith, Elder, & Co., 1906), 199.
4. 491 U.S. 397, 420 (1989).
5. Leonor Vivanco and Dawn Rhodes, "U. Of C. Tells Incoming Freshmen It Does Not Support 'Trigger Warnings' or 'Safe Spaces,'" *Chicago Tribune*, August 25, 2016. For the text of the letter, see https://news.uchicago.edu/sites/default/files/attachments/Dear_Class_of_2020_Students.pdf
6. See, for example, popular YouTube commentator Dave Rubin's various segments criticizing the "regressive left," as well as controversial (and popular) University of Toronto Professor Jordan B. Peterson, who suggested that legal requirements to address transgender individuals by their preferred pronoun (rather than one based on biological sex at birth) amount to thought control. "The Left is No Longer Liberal," *The Rubin Report*, January 25, 2017, accessed November 13, 2018, https://www.youtube.com/watch?v=Tq86Beh3T70; "Jordan Peterson and Dave Rubin: Gender Pronouns and the Free Speech War," *The Rubin Report*, November 18, 2016, accessed November 13, 2018, https://www.youtube.com/watch?v=5n8zn-R10qM.
7. Quoted in Red Alert Politics, "Top 5 Quotes from Dennis Prager on Campus Free Speech," *Washington Examiner*, December 5, 2017, accessed November 13, 2018, https://www.washingtonexaminer.com/top-5-quotes-from-dennis-prager-on-campus-free-speech.
8. Scott Jaschik, "Controversial Professor Placed on Leave," *Inside Higher Ed*, October 11, 2017, accessed November 13, 2018, https://www.insidehighered.com/news/2017/10/11/drexel-places-controversial-professor-leave; Marwa Eltagouri, "Professor Who Tweeted, 'All I Want for Christmas Is White Genocide,' Resigns After Year of Threats," *Washington Post*, December 29, 2017.

9. Aaron R. Hanlon, "Political Correctness Has Run Amok—on the Right," *Chronicle of Higher Education*, January 7, 2018, accessed November 13, 2018, https://www.chronicle.com/article/Political-Correctness-Has-Run/242143.
10. Macey Morales, "New Report Chronicles Library Community's Front Line Battles Against Fake News, Censorship, Bigotry," American Library Association, April 10, 2017, accessed November 13, 2018, http://www.ala.org/news/press-releases/2017/04/new-report-chronicles-library-community-s-front-line-battles-against-fake; Rebecca Hersher, "Court Strikes Down Florida Law Barring Doctors From Discussing Guns With Patients," *NPR*, February 17, 2017, accessed November 13, 2018, https://www.npr.org/sections/thetwo-way/2017/02/17/515764335/court-strikes-down-florida-law-barring-doctors-from-discussing-guns-with-patient.
11. Useful works on this history include Michael Kent Curtis, *Free Speech, 'The People's Darling Privilege': Struggles for Freedom of Expression in American History* (Durham, NC: Duke University Press, 2000); Geoffrey R. Stone, *Perilous Times: Free Speech in Wartime, From the Sedition Act of 1798 to the War on Terrorism* (New York: W.W. Norton, 2004); Rodney A. Smolla, *Free Speech in an Open Society* (New York: Vintage, 1992); David M. Rabban, *Free Speech in Its Forgotten Years* (New York: Cambridge University Press, 1997); Mark A. Graber, *Transforming Free Speech: The Ambiguous Legacy of Civil Libertarianism* (Berkeley: University of California Press, 1991); Richard W. Garnett and Andrew Koppelman, eds., *First Amendment Stories* (New York: Foundation Press, 2011); Anthony Lewis, *Make No Law: The Sullivan Case and the First Amendment* (New York: Random House, 1991).
12. Between November 7, 2016, when he was elected, and November 7, 2017, Trump tweeted 2,461 times. Jessica Estepa, "Trump Has Tweeted 2,461 Times Since the Election. Here's a Breakdown of His Twitter Use," *USA Today*, November 7, 2017. By contrast, during his first year in office he held only one press conference, a number that pales in comparison to those of his predecessors. Gerhard Peters, "Presidential News Conferences," *The American Presidency Project*, accessed November 13, 2018, http://www.presidency.ucsb.edu/data/newsconferences.php.
13. Carlyn Reichel, "Shadow Government: Trump Has Reshaped Presidential Rhetoric into an Unrecognizable Grotesque," *FP*, July 7, 2017, accessed November 13, 2018, http://foreignpolicy.com/2017/07/07/trump-has-reshaped-presidential-rhetoric-into-an-unrecognizable-grotesque/. The classic work on this aspect of the presidency is Jeffrey Tulis, *The Rhetorical Presidency* (Princeton, NJ: Princeton University Press, 1987).
14. Beatrice Dupuy, "Nearly Half of Republicans Think Negative Stories Are 'Fake News' While Trust in Media Hits All-Time Low, Poll Shows," *Newsweek*, January 16, 2018, accessed November 13, 2018, http://www.newsweek.com/republicans-fake-news-trust-media-low-poll-783116.
15. Apparently, they are also believed in a hyper-partisan manner: "Half of Americans feel that media outlets allow readers to cut through bias, a drop from 66 percent in previous polling. Only 27 percent of Americans say they are 'very confident' in spotting factual news. When they share news, 68 percent say they are doing it with people who hold the same views as them." Ibid.
16. Sophia Tesfaye, "Trump's Daughter-in-Law Pushes His Propaganda: Lara Trump Launches 'Real News' Show to Praise the President," *Salon*, August 2, 2017, accessed November 13, 2018, https://www.salon.com/2017/08/02/

trumps-daughter-in-law-pushes-his-propaganda-lara-trump-launches-real-news-show-to-praise-the-president/. In this respect, there was nothing surprising about the winners of the "2017 Fake News Awards" unveiled on the Republican Party's website on January 17, 2018. "The Highly-Anticipated 2017 Fake News Awards," January 17, 2018, accessed November 13, 2018, https://gop.com/the-highly-anticipated-2017-fake-news-awards/.

17. Cindy Boren, "Trump Says He Directed Pence to Walk Out of Game If 49ers Protested During National Anthem," *Washington Post*, October 8, 2017.

18. "'Human Rights Cannot Be Compromised': Colin Kaepernick Honored by ACLU, Time Magazine," *Washington Post*, December 4, 2017; Kevin Draper and Ken Belson, "Colin Kaepernick's Nike Campaign Keeps N.F.L. Anthem Kneeling in Spotlight," *New York Times*, September 4, 2018.

19. Sheryl Gay Stolberg and Brian M. Rosenthal, "Man Charged After White Nationalist Rally in Charlottesville Ends in Deadly Violence," *New York Times*, August 12, 2017.

20. This is one of the primary reasons why Justice Hugo L. Black is best described as a "*qualified* absolutist," his absolutist statement about the First Amendment's free speech clause (that "no law" means "no law") notwithstanding. He repeatedly drew a sharp distinction between speech and conduct, concluding that the Amendment only protected the former. See Michael Paris and Kevin J. McMahon, "Absolutism and Democracy: Hugo L. Black's Free Speech Jurisprudence," in *Judging Free Speech: First Amendment Jurisprudence of US Supreme Court Justices*, ed. Helen J. Knowles and Steven B. Lichtman (New York: Palgrave Macmillan, 2015).

21. For an extended discussion of free speech principles, including the terms "consequentialist" and "non-consequentialist," see Kent Greenawalt, "Free Speech Justifications," *Columbia Law Review* 89, no. 1 (1989).

22. Paul Robert Cohen's decision to wear exactly this kind of jacket inside the Los Angeles Municipal Court on April 20, 1968 is what led to the landmark U.S. Supreme Court decision in *Cohen v. California*, 403 U.S. 15 (1971). Overturning Cohen's disturbing the peace conviction, the Court held that a State could not "excise, as 'offensive conduct,' one particular scurrilous epithet from the public discourse, either upon the theory of the court below that its use is inherently likely to cause violent reaction or upon a more general assertion that the States, acting as guardians of public morality, may properly remove this offensive word from the public vocabulary." 403 U.S. at 22–23.

23. In particular, see the test outlined by the U.S. Supreme Court in *United States v. O'Brien*, 391 U.S. 367 (1968) (upholding the conviction of David Paul O'Brien for violating a law that made it a crime to burn one's draft card (as O'Brien did on the steps of the South Boston Courthouse on March 31, 1966), a law which the Court concluded was not related to the suppression of expression). The test the Court established for such occasions consists of four components: "This Court has held that when 'speech' and 'nonspeech' elements are combined in the same course of conduct, a sufficiently important governmental interest in regulating the nonspeech element can justify incidental limitations on First Amendment freedoms. To characterize the quality of the governmental interest which must appear, the Court has employed a variety of descriptive terms: compelling; substantial; subordinating; paramount; cogent; strong. Whatever imprecision inheres in these terms, we think it clear that *a government regulation is sufficiently justified if it is within the constitutional power of the Government; if it furthers an important or substantial governmental interest; if the*

governmental interest is unrelated to the suppression of free expression; and if the incidental restriction on alleged First Amendment freedoms is no greater than is essential to the furtherance of that interest." 391 U.S. at 376–77 (italics added).
24. "Oyez: *Masterpiece Cakeshop, Ltd. v. Colorado Civil Rights Commission*, 584 U.S. (2018), U.S. Supreme Court Oral Argument," accessed November 13, 2018 https://www.oyez.org/cases/2017/16-111.
25. This is a reference to another verse of "Lost for Words." Of course, we will not convert everyone; not every reader will walk away from this book committed to the belief that free speech theories matter. Although, we hope that they do not respond in accordance with the next line of that song. If they do so, however, we will defend their free speech freedom to do so.
26. Niraj Chokshi, "What College Students Really Think About Free Speech," *New York Times*, April 4, 2018. We are very grateful to Craig Warkentin for bringing this article to our attention.
27. Allyson Chiu, "'Bullies on the Left': Laura Ingraham Returns With Promise to Fight 'Stalinist' Forces," *Washington Post*, April 10, 2018.
28. Including the volume one of us co-edited. See Knowles and Lichtman, eds., *Judging Free Speech*.
29. James C. Foster, "Justice Civility: William J. Brennan Jr.'s Free Speech Jurisprudence," in ibid., 123.
30. Equally importantly, one might say, the First Amendment gives nothing to the citizenry. With one hand it taketh away from the government (the power to abridge citizens' speech and press freedoms), but with the other it does not giveth to the populace. As one commentator has observed: "Were the First Amendment, for example, to be structured in the same kind of *purposive fashion* as the Second Amendment, the Free Speech Clause might read as follows: 'A well-educated polity being necessary for the preservation of democracy, the right of the people to speak and assemble freely shall not be infringed.'" Steven B. Lichtman, "Aspirational Negation: Our Backwards Constitution" (paper presented at the Annual Meeting of the New England Political Science Association, Portsmouth, NH, April 27, 2012), 4.
31. Mark Maske and Des Bieler, "Jerry Jones Says Cowboys Players 'Disrespecting the Flag' Won't Play," *Washington Post*, October 8, 2017.
32. Under some circumstances, federal labor laws might offer some protection for workplace speech. On the Google controversy, the First Amendment, and these labor laws, see Jena McGregor, "The Google Memo is a Reminder That We Generally Don't Have Free Speech at Work," *Washington Post*, August 8, 2017; Jim Edwards, "James Damore, the Google Employee Fired for His Controversial Manifesto, Is (Almost Certainly) Not a Victim of a Free-Speech Violation," *Business Insider*, August 8, 2017, accessed November 13, 2018, http://www.businessinsider.com/james-damore-google-anti-diversity-manifesto-free-speech-2017-8.
33. Helen J. Knowles and Steven B. Lichtman, "Conclusion: It's Complicated," in *Judging Free Speech*, 239–40.
34. Ibid., 240.
35. The extent to which the Roberts Court has a distinctly "pro-speech" track record has been a subject of debate for some time now. Erwin Chemerinsky, Dean of Berkeley Law School, points out that the pro-speech reputation gained traction even as the Court limited the free speech rights of students (*Morse v. Frederick*, 551 U.S. 393

(2007)); government employees (*Garcetti v. Ceballos*, 547 U.S. 410 (2006)); and prisoners (*Beard v. Banks*, 548 U.S. 521 (2006)). Erwin Chemerinsky, "The Roberts Court and Freedom of Speech," *Federal Communications Law Journal* 63, no. 3 (2011). More recently, Laurence Tribe and Joshua Matz characterized the tension between reputation and reality as such: "Partly because of rulings like [*Entertainment Merchants Association v.*] *Brown* and *Snyder* [*v. Phelps*], the Roberts Court enjoys a strong 'pro-speech' reputation. Appearances deceive. A closer look reveals that the Court is deeply torn over its vision of free speech. In many ways, the Court is not as libertarian as it sometimes seems." Laurence Tribe and Joshua Matz, *Uncertain Justice: The Roberts Court and the Constitution* (New York: Henry Holt, 2014), 152–53.
36. Indeed, if one examines the voting alignments of the justices from the 2006 through 2014 terms of the Court, the pattern is also consistent with a partisan or ideological explanation, as the majority of "pro-speech" decisions are consistent with broader conservative or Republican commitments. Brandon Metroka, "The Roberts Court Constitution of Freedom of Speech: Preferences, Principles, and the Study of Supreme Court Decision-Making" (Ph.D. diss., Syracuse University, 2017), chapters 3 and 4.
37. Ashifa Kassam, "Margaret Atwood Faces Feminist Backlash on Social Media over #Metoo," *The Guardian*, January 15, 2018.
38. Unlike "falsely shouting fire in a crowded theater," which is the real line used by Justice Oliver Wendell Holmes, Jr. in *Schenck v. United States*, 249 U.S. 47, 52 (1919) ("The most stringent protection of free speech would not protect a man in falsely shouting fire in a theatre and causing a panic").
39. Sanford J. Ungar, "American Ignorance." *Inside HigherEd*, March 23, 2015, accessed November 13, 2018, https://www.insidehighered.com/views/2015/03/23/essay-problems-american-ignorance-world.
40. Ian Vasquez and Tanja Porcnik, *The Human Freedom Index 2016: A Global Measurement of Personal, Civil, and Economic Freedom* (Washington, DC: CATO Institute, 2016); Freedom House, "Freedom in the World 2018: Democracy in Crisis," accessed November 13, 2018, https://freedomhouse.org/report/freedom-world/freedom-world-2018.
41. Liam Stack, "Do Americans Love the British Royal Family? Quite," *New York Times*, December 4, 2017.
42. On this relationship, see John Dumbrell, *A Special Relationship: Anglo-American Relations from the Cold War to Iraq*, 2nd ed. (Basingstoke, England: Palgrave, 2006).
43. Robert J. Savage, *The BBC's 'Irish Troubles': Television, Conflict and Northern Ireland* (Manchester, England: Manchester University Press, 2017).
44. In 2005, the American Film Institute listed it at number 29 on its list of the top 100 greatest movie quotations of all time. American Film Institute, "AFI's 100 Greatest Movie Quotes of All Time," accessed November 13, 2018, http://www.afi.com/100years/quotes.aspx.
45. *Abrams v. United States*, 250 U.S. 616, 630 (Holmes, J., joined by Brandeis, J., dissenting).
46. Ibid. (italics added).
47. On the way in which this aspect of Holmes's intellectual, jurisprudential development occurred, see Thomas Healy, *The Great Dissent: How Oliver Wendell Holmes Changed His Mind—And Changed the History of Free Speech in America*

(New York: Metropolitan Books, 2013). Compare Edwin Cannan, ed. *Adam Smith, the Wealth of Nations (1776)* (New York: Modern Library, 1994).
48. One might argue that this is precisely what has happened in the United States because of the take-over of the electoral process by "big money"—a take-over facilitated, in large part, by a series of U.S. Supreme Court decisions removing regulatory limits on campaign finance. For discussions of this, see, for example, Timothy Kuhner, *Capitalism v. Democracy: Money in Politics and the Free Market Constitution* (Stanford, CA: Stanford University Press, 2014); Robert C. Post, ed., *Citizens Divided: Campaign Finance Reform and the Constitution* (Cambridge, MA: Harvard University Press, 2014); Yasmin Dawood, "Campaign Finance and American Democracy," *Annual Review of Political Science* 18, no. 1 (2015). For a more general critique of the entire "marketplace of ideas" and "truth" justifications, see Stanley Ingber, "The Marketplace of Ideas: A Legitimizing Myth," *Duke Law Journal* 1984, no. 1 (1984).
49. *Near v. Minnesota*, 283 U.S. 697, 713 (1931); *Miami Herald Publishing Co. v. Tornillo*, 418 U.S. 241, 259 (1974) (White, J., concurring).
50. William Poole, ed. *John Milton, Areopagitica and Other Writings* (New York: Penguin Classics, 2016), 137 (original spelling preserved).
51. William Blackstone, *Commentaries on the Laws of England: A Facsimile of the First Edition of 1765–1769* (Chicago: University of Chicago Press, 1979), 4: 150–53.
52. Ibid.
53. John Stuart Mill, "On Liberty," in *John Stuart Mill, On Liberty: Annotated Text, Sources, and Background Criticism*, ed. David Spitz (New York: W.W. Norton, 1975), 21.
54. Ibid., 8.
55. For a useful overview of the development of this free speech tradition in the United States, see Frederick P. Lewis, "Oliver Wendell Holmes Jr. and the 'Marketplace of Ideas': Experience Proves to Be the 'Life of the Law,'" in *Judging Free Speech*, 28–30. Also see Leonard W. Levy, *Legacy of Suppression: Freedom of Speech and Press in Early American History* (Cambridge, MA: Harvard University Press, 1960).
56. 274 U.S. 357, 375–76 (Brandeis, J., concurring).
57. For a superb discussion of the *Whitney* case, see Philippa Strum, *Speaking Freely: Whitney v. California and American Speech Law* (Lawrence: University Press of Kansas, 2015). On the significance of Brandeis's concurrence, see, for example, Vincent Blasi, "The First Amendment and the Ideal of Civil Courage: The Brandeis Opinion in *Whitney v. California*," *William and Mary Law Review* 29, no. 4 (1988).
58. Meiklejohn was born in England but moved to the United States with his family when he was eight. "Dr. Alexander Meiklejohn Dead," *New York Times*, December 17, 1964.
59. Alexander Meiklejohn, *Free Speech and Its Relation to Self-Government* (New York: Harper, 1948), 16–17.
60. Ibid., 86.
61. Ibid., 22–23.
62. Ibid., 94 (italics added).
63. See, for example, Alexander Meiklejohn, "The First Amendment Is an Absolute," *Supreme Court Review* 1961 (1961); Alexander Meiklejohn, "The Balancing of Self-Preservation Against Political Freedom," *California Law Review* 49, no. 1 (1961). Indeed, such was the extent to which Meiklejohn eventually became associated with

free speech absolutism, that his memorial service was the only time that Justice Black interrupted a conference of the justices at the Court to go to an outside function. George Anastaplo, "*In Re* Justice Hugo La Fayette Black (1866–1971): My More or Less 'Personal' Experience of Him," *Loyola University Chicago Law Journal* 44 (2013): 1275.
64. Steven J. Heyman, *Free Speech & Human Dignity* (New Haven, CT: Yale University Press, 2008), 38.
65. C. Edwin Baker, "Autonomy and Free Speech," *Constitutional Commentary* 27 (2011): 253.
66. 535 U.S. 234, 241 (2002).
67. Ibid., at 242.
68. Ibid., at 253 (italics added).
69. We are grateful to Keith Bybee for this example.
70. Catharine Mackinnon, *Only Words* (Cambridge, MA: Harvard University Press, 1993), 15, 21–22.
71. 535 U.S. at 253.
72. Most famously, see *American Booksellers Ass'n, Inc. v. Hudnut*, 771 F.2d 323 (7th Cir. 1985). In this case the Seventh Circuit Court of Appeals struck down the Indianapolis Antipornography Civil Rights Ordinance, which was one of a number of ordinances, co-authored by MacKinnon and Andrea Dworkin, which banned pornography on the basis that it was a form of sexual discrimination that threatened the health, safety, and welfare of women.
73. Mari J. Matsuda, "Public Response to Racist Speech: Considering the Victim's Story," *Michigan Law Review* 87, no. 8 (1989): 2336–40.
74. Wolff, *An Introduction to Political Philosophy*, 3.
75. Ibid.
76. "Lost for Words."

References

Anastaplo, George. "In Re Justice Hugo La Fayette Black (1866–1971): My More or Less 'Personal' Experience of Him." *Loyola University Chicago Law Journal* 44 (2013): 1271–322.

Baker, C. Edwin. "Autonomy and Free Speech." *Constitutional Commentary* 27 (2011): 251–82.

Blackstone, William. *Commentaries on the Laws of England: A Facsimile of the First Edition of 1765—1769*. Chicago: University of Chicago Press, 1979.

Blasi, Vincent. "The First Amendment and the Ideal of Civil Courage: The Brandeis Opinion in *Whitney v. California*." *William and Mary Law Review* 29, no. 4 (1988): 653–97.

Cannan, Edwin, ed. *Adam Smith, the Wealth of Nations (1776)*. New York: Modern Library, 1994.

Chemerinsky, Erwin. "The Roberts Court and Freedom of Speech." *Federal Communications Law Journal* 63, no. 3 (2011): 579–89.

Curtis, Michael Kent. *Free Speech, 'The People's Darling Privilege': Struggles For Freedom of Expression in American History*. Durham, NC: Duke University Press, 2000.

Dawood, Yasmin. "Campaign Finance and American Democracy." *Annual Review of Political Science* 18, no. 1 (2015): 329–48.

Dumbrell, John. *A Special Relationship: Anglo-American Relations From the Cold War to Iraq*, 2nd ed. Basingstoke, England: Palgrave, 2006.

Foster, James C. "Justice Civility: William J. Brennan Jr.'s Free Speech Jurisprudence." In Knowles and Lichtman, *Judging Free Speech*, 123–46.

Garnett, Richard W., and Andrew Koppelman, eds. *First Amendment Stories*. New York: Foundation Press, 2011.

Graber, Mark A. *Transforming Free Speech: The Ambiguous Legacy of Civil Libertarianism*. Berkeley: University of California Press, 1991.

Greenawalt, Kent. "Free Speech Justifications." *Columbia Law Review* 89, no. 1 (1989): 119–55.

Healy, Thomas. *The Great Dissent: How Oliver Wendell Holmes Changed His Mind—And Changed the History of Free Speech in America*. New York: Metropolitan Books, 2013.

Heyman, Steven J. *Free Speech & Human Dignity*. New Haven, CT: Yale University Press, 2008.

Ingber, Stanley. "The Marketplace of Ideas: A Legitimizing Myth." *Duke Law Journal* 1984, no. 1 (1984).

Knowles, Helen J., and Steven B. Lichtman, eds. *Judging Free Speech: First Amendment Jurisprudence of US Supreme Court Justices*. New York: Palgrave Macmillan, 2015.

Knowles, Helen J., and Steven B. Lichtman. "Conclusion: It's Complicated." In Knowles and Lichtman, *Judging Free Speech*, 239–54.

Kuhner, Timothy. *Capitalism v. Democracy: Money in Politics and the Free Market Constitution*. Stanford, CA: Stanford University Press, 2014.

Levy, Leonard W. *Legacy of Suppression: Freedom of Speech and Press in Early American History*. Cambridge, MA: Harvard University Press, 1960.

Lewis, Anthony. *Make No Law: The Sullivan Case and the First Amendment*. New York: Random House, 1991.

Lewis, Frederick P. "Oliver Wendell Holmes Jr. and the 'Marketplace of Ideas': Experience Proves to Be the 'Life of the Law.'" In Knowles and Lichtman, *Judging Free Speech*, 27–48.

Lichtman, Steven B. "Aspirational Negation: Our Backwards Constitution." Paper presented at the Annual Meeting of the New England Political Science Association, Portsmouth, NH, April 2012.

MacKinnon, Catharine. *Only Words*. Cambridge, MA: Harvard University Press, 1993.

Matsuda, Mari J. "Public Response to Racist Speech: Considering the Victim's Story." *Michigan Law Review* 87, no. 8 (1989): 2320–81.

Meiklejohn, Alexander. "The Balancing of Self-Preservation Against Political Freedom." *California Law Review* 49, no. 1 (1961): 4–14.

———. "The First Amendment Is an Absolute." *Supreme Court Review* 1961 (1961): 245–66.

———. *Free Speech and Its Relation to Self-Government.* New York: Harper, 1948.

Metroka, Brandon. "The Roberts Court Constitution of Freedom of Speech: Preferences, Principles, and the Study of Supreme Court Decision-Making." Ph.D. diss., Syracuse University, 2017.

Mill, John Stuart. "On Liberty." In *John Stuart Mill, on Liberty: Annotated Text, Sources, and Background Criticism,* edited by David Spitz, 1–106. New York: W.W. Norton, 1975.

Paris, Michael, and Kevin J. McMahon. "Absolutism and Democracy: Hugo L. Black's Free Speech Jurisprudence." In Knowles and Lichtman, *Judging Free Speech,* 75–97.

Pink Floyd. "Lost For Words." The Division Bell. Sony Legacy B019VQSBQI, 2016, compact disc. 2011 remastered version (explicit). Originally released in 1994.

Poole, William, ed. *John Milton, Areopagitica and Other Writings.* New York: Penguin Classics, 2016.

Post, Robert C., ed. *Citizens Divided: Campaign Finance Reform and the Constitution.* Cambridge, MA: Harvard University Press, 2014.

Rabban, David M. *Free Speech in Its Forgotten Years.* New York: Cambridge University Press, 1997.

Savage, Robert J. *The BBC's 'Irish Troubles': Television, Conflict and Northern Ireland.* Manchester, England: Manchester University Press, 2017.

Smolla, Rodney A. *Free Speech in an Open Society.* New York: Vintage, 1992.

Stone, Geoffrey R. *Perilous Times: Free Speech in Wartime, From the Sedition Act of 1798 to the War on Terrorism.* New York: W.W. Norton, 2004.

Strum, Philippa. *Speaking Freely:* Whitney v. California *and American Speech Law.* Lawrence: University Press of Kansas, 2015.

Tallentyre, S. G. *The Friends of Voltaire.* London: Smith, Elder, & Co., 1906.

Tribe, Laurence, and Joshua Matz. *Uncertain Justice: The Roberts Court and the Constitution.* New York: Henry Holt, 2014.

Tulis, Jeffrey. *The Rhetorical Presidency.* Princeton, NJ: Princeton University Press, 1987.

Vasquez, Ian, and Tanja Porcnik. *The Human Freedom Index 2016: A Global Measurement of Personal, Civil, and Economic Freedom.* Washington, DC: CATO Institute, 2016.

Wolff, Jonathan. *An Introduction to Political Philosophy.* New York: Oxford University Press, 2006.

1. No Neutrality: Hobbesian Constitutionalism in the Internet Age

JAMES C. FOSTER

> The dogmas of the quiet past, are inadequate to the stormy present. The occasion is piled high with difficulty, and we must rise—with the occasion. As our case is new, so we must think anew, and act anew. We must disenthrall ourselves, and then we shall save our country.
> ~ Abraham Lincoln to Congress, December 1, 1862

First Amendment theories do not exist in a vacuum. First Amendment conceptualizations reflect the social circumstances within which they are embedded. As the editors of this book emphasize in their Introduction, if free speech is not to be an arid abstraction it must be situated within a particular time and place. This insight is the primary point of departure for the contributors to this volume. Contextualizing various understandings of free speech underpins the several chapters of this book, an approach that also informs this chapter. In the present case, neo-Hobbesian tribalism colors free speech.

Our Republic is in crisis—along with its core principle, freedom of speech. Fueling this calamity is a pervasive tribalism, which is a potent combination of fear and hate, anger and distrust, combined with a zero-sum/in-group-out-group mentality. Our crisis is the 21st century version of Thomas Hobbes' State of Nature. Hobbes returned to England in 1651, after taking refuge in France during the English Civil War (1642–1651). In his dedication to the English edition of *De Cive: Philosophical Rudiments Concerning Government and Society*, he set out that "… Man to Man is an arrant Wolfe [homo homini lupus est] … [M]en must defend themselves by taking to them for a Sanctuary the two daughters of War, Deceipt [sic] and Violence."[1] In Hobbesian terms, contemporary Internet speech often consists of dog-whistles—code words for racist and other discriminatory ideas—and other more explicit feral behaviors, in pursuit of wolf-like outcomes.

Over three and a half centuries after Hobbes described his State of Nature, retiring U.S. Senator Bob Corker (R-TN) echoed Hobbes in March 2018, observing that: "[t]he president is, as you know—you've seen his numbers among the Republican base—very strong. It's more than strong, it's tribal in nature[.] ... [W]hat matters most ... is what GOP voters think of lawmakers' tribal loyalty to Trump..."[2] Here are two takes, then, on the fundamental source of our constitutional crisis, 367 years apart: Hobbes' *bellum omnium contra omnes* (the war of all against all); and "Corker's ... suggest[ion] that GOP voters equate being 'with Trump' in a 'tribal' sense..."[3] Be it 17th-century Roundhead Parliamentarians versus Cavalier Royalists, or 21st century Internet data mining and viral memes and trolls and weaponized bots and doxing, Hobbes trenchantly described tribalism's atavistic return of humans to a State of Nature: "No arts; no letters; no society; and which is worst of all, continual fear, and danger of violent death: and the life of man, solitary, poor, nasty, brutish and short."[4]

Whether imaginary or actual—Hobbes' thought experiment or contemporary Americans' tribal culture war skirmishes—our contemporary State of Nature threatens the end of civil discourse and, most direly, the death of civil society itself. In our Internet Age, there is no "net neutrality." On the contrary, online combat prevails throughout the *anti*social media characteristic of our Internet apocalypse. Flaming is foreclosing community. And what of free speech? Is weaponized speech legally protected speech? Do criteria exist that would enable distinguishing between legitimate and illegitimate speech? We require a First Amendment theory adequate to our contemporary State of Nature. Circumstances are rendering the First Amendment free speech and free press clause obsolete. Can those 14 little words (and the values they serve) be made current?

Four Vignettes

This chapter opens with an excerpt from Abraham Lincoln's eloquent 1862 address to Congress. Lincoln's words accomplish two purposes. First, they capture the urgency of living through "the stormy present." His words sound a clarion call of warning. Second, Lincoln's words serve as a road map to this chapter. Our inquiry begins with four vignettes (examples) designed to illustrate aspects of the vitriolic and capricious online worlds within which many Americans engage in speech acts. Examining the culture of tribalism underlying these worlds follows that inquiry. In Lincoln's terms, together these two sections detail several ways in which our times are "piled high with difficulty." Spite and untruths abound in this world, defining interactions.

No Neutrality

Tribalism prevails.[5] Finally—and ultimately—the last section suggests a way "we shall save our country." Doing so entails rejecting "[t]he dogmas of the quiet past," "disenthrall[ing] ourselves," and most crucially, "think[ing] anew, and act[ing] anew."

The initial two conflicts examined below pit male tribesmen against interlopers—read women. The arenas—gender battlefields, if you will—are online gaming and Silicone Valley boardrooms. Gender gaming wars are vicious. In Silicon Valley clubby slights are the *modus operandi*.

Item: Gamergate

"Gamergate" describes a campaign of online assaults which began in August 2014. These attacks involved harassment, initially targeting a specific woman, then eventually women video gamers in general. Game developer Zoe Quinn initially was at the center of this vicious maelstrom. Drawing on her personal experience, being diagnosed at 14 with clinical depression, Quinn had designed and released a game she called "Depression Quest." Her game was not in the predominate chase 'em, shoot 'em-up, destroy 'em genre. On the contrary, Quinn's game was about living while being afflicted with depression. Her game could be played for free, with voluntary proceeds going to the National Suicide Prevention Lifeline.

The term "GamerGate" was coined by actor Adam Baldwin as his Twitter hashtag #GamerGate. What apparently started as something of a vendetta, involving a few aggrieved people who were part of a love triangle, escalated into a freewheeling virtual firefight involving charges, counter-charges, and counter-counter-charges. What had originated as petty, mean-spirited flaming blew up into full scale doxing, hacking, tit-for-tat character assassination, and misogynist intimidation complete with rape and death threats. One consequential attack occurred after Quinn's estranged boyfriend, Eron Gjoni, posted ("Zoe Post") her home address on line. Threats of bodily harm to her and family members drove Quinn out of her house. One October 2014 estimate posited 10,000 #GamerGate postings: pro and con. Eventually, in September 2015, the FBI opened, then closed an investigation into cyber harassment.

Caitlin Dewey, *Washington Post* reporter, offers this incisive analysis of Gamergate and its continuing social significance:

> If you're not personally a gamer, it can be tempting to dismiss… [Gamergate] as subcultural drama. But … that couldn't be further from the truth: The issues that Gamergate struggles over are also issues of great conflict, and importance, to American culture as a whole. In fact, in many respects, Gamergate is just a proxy

war for a greater cultural battle over space and visibility and inclusion, a battle over who belongs to the mainstream—and as such, it's a battle for our cultural soul. Just writ really small.[6]

Dewey's account sounds several themes useful for understanding Net tribalism. First, she discerns that Gamergate is symptomatic of fundamental contemporary cultural cleavages in the United States. It would be a mistake, she contends, to dismiss Gamergate by consigning it to the realm of, say, adolescent bullying. To be sure, Gamergate entails bullying. At base, though, Gamergate marks a pathology: a manifestation of tribal social deformation. Second, Dewey recognizes the in-group/out-group dynamic fueling Gamergate. Gamergate is no frivolous playground contest à la Capture the Flag. It is ruinously serious, employing Internet speech to ferret out and destroy people deemed "others." Third, Dewey apprehends the contesting identities, the naming and gaming fights characterizing Gamergate. What makes Gamergate "the perfect representation of our times"[7] is that it is about the zero-sum struggle to define and to police "who is and is not allowed to have a voice in mainstream culture."[8]

Item: Bro-culture in the Valley

Tribalism need not be vicious to be insidious. Tribalism can be characterized more by fraternal bonding than the law of the jungle; more "Animal House" than *Lord of the Flies*. The core of bro-culture tribal expression is twofold: alienation—a pervasive sense of finding women strange (in German, *Entfremdung*, the condition of being a stranger), plus a strict sexual binary mindset generating bifurcated, hierarchical relationships. These either/or dichotomous relations actually can take on the appearance of innocuous fun and games. For instance, journalist Emily Chang, author of what she terms "Brotopia," discusses sex parties in Silicon Valley where "men play, women pay."[9]

> [The guys] don't necessarily see themselves as predatory. When they look in the mirror, they see individuals setting a new paradigm of behavior by pushing the boundaries of social mores and values. 'What's making [sex parties] possible is the same progressiveness and open-mindedness that allows us to be creative and disruptive about ideas,' [one ambitious, world-traveling entrepreneur] told me. ... It's worth asking, however, if these sexual adventurers are so progressive, why do these parties seem to lean so heavily toward male-heterosexual fantasies? Women are often expected to be involved in threesomes that include other women; male gay and bisexual behavior is conspicuously absent. 'Oddly, it's completely unthinkable that guys would be bisexual or curious,' says one [venture capitalist] who attends and is married (I'll call him Married V.C.). 'It's

a total double standard.' In other words, at these parties men don't make out with other men. And, outside of the new types of drugs, these stories might have come out of the Playboy Mansion circa 1972.[10]

This double standard, shaping Silicon Valley men at play, is evident in the ways they speak and write about women at work. The resulting speech acts might be termed Hugh Hefner's sensibility filtered through the clubby, clannish values of super star, PayPal founder, Peter Thiel, and an aggrieved Google employee, James Damore. The former's "PayPal Mafia" reveals the underpinnings informing the latter's infamous 2017 Damore Memo.

Peter Thiel is "still seen by many as the philosopher-king of Silicon Valley."[11] He is the Genius—capital G—who founded PayPal and then went on to invest in Facebook, Tesla, and alternative energy. (Thiel's sterling reputation among Silicon Valley elites has been somewhat tarnished by his bankrolling of several lawsuits that eventually bankrupted the gossipy blog *Gawker*.) Thiel's startup success at PayPal had as much to do with his tribal approach to organization building as his entrepreneurial acumen. Specifically, hiring the best people—"meritocracy"—meant, in practice, "hiring only people like us."[12] " 'Let's get people like us' became ingrained as company culture."[13] "When it came to the idea of hiring your friends or 'people like us' ... [the PayPal Mafia] didn't just perpetuate it; they turned it into a fine art."[14] *Zero to One: Notes on Startups, or How to Build the Future* is Thiel's *magnum opus*. It is a worldwide best seller, an industry-leader's Bible, considered required reading for aspiring entrepreneurs. The words "woman" or "women" do not appear in its 195 pages. On the contrary, as Emily Chang observes: "[I]n *Zero to One*, [Thiel] embraces the term 'PayPal Mafia,' a moniker that is deeply fraught with connotations of misogyny, male dominance, and the brutal exclusion of anyone outside the group."[15]

Google engineer James Damore traced the exclusion of women throughout Silicon Valley to biological determinism. For Damore, the paucity of women was not the result of sex discrimination. It was a consequence of their sex. In July 2017 he circulated an internal memo titled "Google's Ideological Echo Chamber: How bias clouds our thinking about diversity and inclusion." Damore wrote: "I'm simply stating that the distribution of preferences and abilities of men and women differ in part due to biological causes and that these differences may explain why we don't see equal representation of women in tech and leadership."[16] Why, then, don't we see equal representation of women in tech and leadership? Because women are stereotyped as a functionally different species, ill-suited to succeeding in the Brotopia. Female biology excludes women from the Brotopia tribe.

Item: Parkland Students Virtually Pilloried

Students at Marjory Stoneman Douglas (MSD) High School in Parkland, Florida were traumatized twice.[17] First, they survived the February 14, 2018 murderous assault[18] that killed 14 of their fellow students and three MSD staff members. Then, when many MSD students organized to advocate for stricter gun laws, creating Never Again MSD, they were vilified and demonized online. *Washington Post* staffer, Cleve R. Wootson, Jr., described the situation:

> As they've stepped out of the hallways of Marjory Stoneman Douglas High School and into the national spotlight, the Parkland, Fla., teenagers have become Twitter influencers, TV news show mainstays and the stoic-faced subjects of a *Time* magazine cover. But they've also increasingly become targets[.][19]

All manner of Internet critics castigated the advocacy efforts of MSD students as all manner of conspiracy. Prominent voices and powerful groups dismissed the students' efforts as inappropriate, ineffectual, self-serving, or all three. Much of the reaction played out in familiar terms, pitting the actual tribe of Second Amendment supporters against an imagined tribe of adolescent "gun-grabbers."

The scurrilous ways in which Emma González and David Hogg, two "organic intellectuals"[20] of the MSD student movement, are attacked illustrates further the tribal Hobbesian world of no neutrality: give no quarter to those deemed beyond the pale. As *GQ* reporter, Mari Uyehara, put it: "The Sliming of David Hogg and Emma Gonzáles."[21] For example, Gonzáles is called a "skinhead lesbian."[22] This tweeted epithet demonstrates the tone of the attacks leveled against this eloquent spokesperson for the student-led Never Again MSD movement. "Brown bald lesbian girl"[23] is another. A photoshopped hoax pictures Gonzáles tearing up a copy of the U.S. Constitution. Hogg is called a "bald-faced liar,"[24] and, according to Justice Clarence Thomas' wife Virginia, a "special kind of stupid."[25] Conservative talk show host Alex Jones referred to Hogg and his fellow MSD activists as Nazis.[26] "[Ex] Sinclair broadcaster, Jamie Allman, went so far as to say he'd use a hot poker to sexually assault [Hogg]."[27] And what fuels this inflammatory vitriol? Tribalism, and the resulting breakdown in civil discourse.

"When you see people fighting in a debate, most people don't really care about the content of the message," explained Dan Kahan, a Yale law professor and head of the Cultural Cognition Project. "They're using the identity of the fighters to figure out whose side they should be on." Most people determine their opinions,' Kahan continued:

Based not on cold analysis of the facts but on their 'affinity group.' If people like you are for guns, then you are for guns. More important, if people that you consider weird, different or bad ... have a pronounced opinion, that inclines you to take the opposite view.[28]

Professor Kahan explains the nexus between personal identity and opinion formation. People typically embrace the ideas held by their primary social group, rejecting world views espoused by people deemed different. Such embrace or rejection is not so much a matter of rationality than of emotional attachment; knee-jerk acceptance, not reasoned analysis. Usually agreement follows affiliation. One way to understand what is playing out in the MSD tragedy is that a tribe of gun-rights-supporting conservatives is waging war on surprisingly engaged student-activists, threatening these students: return to class, sit down and shut up—or else. Opposing those who identify with gun-owners on the Right are students who identify with young people who fear the possibility of being vulnerable children slaughtered at school.

Item: Fraudulent Online Comments Fundamentally Flaw FCC Review Process

The Federal Communications Commission's (FCC) own 2017 net neutrality public notice and comment process evidences further how *no neutrality* exists in our Hobbesian world. "Net neutrality" requires equal Internet access. Without getting too far into the weeds,

> net neutrality is a network design paradigm that argues for broadband network providers to be completely detached from what information is sent over their networks. In essence, it argues that no bit of information should be prioritized over another. This principle implies that an information network such as the internet is most efficient and useful to the public when it is less focused on a particular audience and instead attentive to multiple users.[29]

This description, tying utility to multiplicity and implicitly contending for government regulations prohibiting providers from prioritizing, is vociferously contested. The underlying crux of the controversy is a familiar American debate over whether government regulatory policy, or markets, should shape Internet access: the regulatory tribe versus the free-market tribe.

As Columbia Law Professor Tim Wu, the person who coined the term "network neutrality" in 2003, muses: "A neutral network might be designed without legal prodding—as in the original internet. In an ideal world, either competition or enlightened self-interest might drive carriers to design neutral networks."[30] Needless to say (and mixing metaphors), the Wild, Wild West/neo-Hobbesian Internet is hardly an ideal world. *Au contraire.*

The current tussle traces back to 2004 during the George W. Bush administration. Then FCC Chair, Michael Powell, articulated what he believed were four fundamental Internet freedoms: "The freedom to access any Web content of their choice, so long as it was legal; the freedom to use any online application; the freedom to use their home broadband connections on any device; and the freedom to get subscription information from their own providers." Powell added: "Our belief at the time was that the Internet needed to retain a light regulatory environment to get broadband moving."[31] Such a so-called "light-touch regulatory environment"[32] was modified significantly during the Obama administration. In 2015, FCC Chair Tom Wheeler reclassified Internet sources as "telecom providers" instead of "information services." The change affected the regulatory environment, because telecom providers are subject to a greater range of FCC oversight, and FCC-imposed obligations. The change kindled a raging debate between consumer protection advocates and industry groups. Thus the stage was set for the arrival of the Trump Administration, and a new FCC Chair, Ajit Pai.

Under Pai's leadership, on December 14, 2017, the FCC voted 3–2 to scrap the Obama FCC net neutrality rule. For our purposes, this outcome is less salient than the bizarre rule-making process that produced it. A single headline out of many sketches the story:

NET NEUTRALITY: MILLIONS OF FCC COMMENTS WERE FAKED, INCLUDING MINE.[33]

Just how bifurcated was the FCC net neutrality comment process? *Washington Post* staffer Brian Fung reported that:

> The sharp divides on net neutrality show that what began as a bipartisan issue has hardened into two distinct sides. 'Tribal partisanship is dominating our public policy debates,' said Marc Martin, a communications lawyer at the firm Perkins Coie. 'It wasn't always this way. First adopted and enforced during the Bush administration, net neutrality began as a noncontroversial policy to protect consumers' use of online platforms.'[34]

Once again, online tribalism reared its ugly head—in spectacular and consequential fashion. The public comments process, created by the 1946 Administrative Procedures Act, is a key aspect of regulatory rule-making. The FCC does not merely count comments, giving the nod to the most posts. Evidence-based comments reflecting personal or professional experience, related to the proposed rule, are influential. If this process is corrupted, the entire undertaking is called into question. Tribalism tainted the record.

The Pew Research Center downloaded all FCC comments from the official comment period from April to August 2017, and found that only six percent of online comments used unique text. At the other extreme, they found the top five comments each repeated over 800,000 times. Such prolific posting can only happen with the help of software: on over 100 separate occasions, more than 25,000 copies of the same message posted instantaneously. Overall, 57 percent of comments contained addresses that either repeated between comments or came from disposable accounts.[35]

The Pew data analysis, cited in a Brookings Institution publication, demonstrates the extent to which the FCC comment process had been weaponized. Ultimately, debate over the FCC scrapping net neutrality became less about the rule change itself than a proxy war pitting supporters of the Trump administration against its opponents. This proxy combat had its share of irony. It likewise illustrated how tribalism is more about identity than self-interest in any narrow sense. For instance, allied with Trump, Breitbart News advocated overturning net neutrality, a policy designed to level the playing field between small outlets like Breitbart and media giants like the Cable News Network (CNN).[36]

Three Concepts

These four vignettes illustrate just how endemic and pervasive Internet tribalism has become during our stormy present. In line with the major concern of this book, Hobbesian tribalism is the context within which debates about the First Amendment take place.[37] Internet tribalism is an organic subset of American constitutional tribalism. How we might theorize free speech in our Hobbesian world is the key subject to which we eventually direct our attention. However, first, in order to analyze free speech theory within the context of Internet tribalism, it is initially necessary to distinguish between three essential and related concepts. Clarifying, and distinguishing between these three ideas is the first step toward inventing new ways to think about free speech. The three concepts are:

    the Constitution (capital C)—textual;

    the ¢onstitution (lower-case c)—cultural;

    constitutionalism (foundational conversations)—politics

Now, clarifying and distinguishing among these three concepts might seem elementary. After all, every American knows what the Constitution is. Or do we? Loose talk about "The Constitution this..." and "The Constitution that..."

risks obscuring understanding and frustrating communication.[38] Worse, loose talk facilitates weaponizing constitutional language. Constitutional ambiguity, compounded by tribal animosities, arms-competing factions. It is precisely because of pervasive constitutional confusion that conceptual clarity is in order. Far from being elementary, conceptual clarification is elemental.

To elucidate these distinctions, it is useful to focus specifically on the "Second Amendment"[39] as an example. Consider guns and the Constitution. Or better: consider the several widely divergent things one can mean by referring to "guns" and "the Constitution."

The <u>C</u>onstitution (capital C) refers, in part, to the parchment document which resides in the National Archives in Washington, D.C. The <u>C</u>onstitution also refers to the judicial gloss added to that document whenever judges interpret its wording. Ironically, although lawyers are given to presenting the Constitution as black-letter law (i.e., law free from doubt or dispute), the Constitution always has been thoroughly contestable. With reference to the Second Amendment, the Constitution lay dormant for 84 years, silent between 1791 and 1875. The pertinent words existed on paper: "A well regulated Militia, being necessary to the security of a free State, the right of the people to keep and bear Arms, shall not be infringed." Nevertheless, with regard to gun rights, these were mere words until *U.S. v. Cruikshank*.[40] As Justice Robert H. Jackson observed in a very different context: "The principle ... [lay] about like a loaded weapon, ready for the hand of any authority that can bring forward a plausible claim of an urgent need."[41] Unless and until a pertinent case arose, the Constitution's Second Amendment right to keep and bear arms was unrealized, existing merely as latent potential.

Three cases pertaining to the Constitution's Second Amendment arose between 1876 and 1939. Each of these decisions interpreted the text of the Constitution's Second Amendment. Each of these decisions addressed the meaning of the words "the right to keep and bear arms." All three decisions read the Constitution's Second Amendment "right to keep and bear arms" in "*collective*" terms. For instance, writing for a unanimous Court in *United States v. Miller*,[42] Justice James McReynolds linked "the right to keep and bear arms" to a "well regulated militia":

> The Constitution, as originally adopted, granted to the Congress power—'To provide for calling forth the Militia to execute the Laws of the Union, suppress Insurrections and repel Invasions...' With obvious purpose to assure the continuation and render possible the effectiveness of such forces, the declaration and guarantee of the Second Amendment were made. It must be interpreted and applied with that end in view.[43]

The Court abandoned its existing, collective, reading of the textual Second Amendment 69 years later. By a 5–4 vote, in *District of Columbia v. Heller*,[44] the justices interpreted the Constitution's Second Amendment as guaranteeing an *individual* right to keep and bear arms. Justice Scalia wrote:

> The two sides in this case have set out very different interpretations of the Amendment. Petitioners and today's dissenting Justices believe that it protects only the right to possess and carry a firearm in connection with militia service … Respondent argues that it protects an individual right to possess a firearm unconnected with service in a militia, and to use that arm for traditionally lawful purposes, such as self-defense within the home. … Putting all of [the] … textual elements together, we find that they guarantee the individual right to possess and carry weapons in case of confrontation…[45]

What occurred between 1939 and 2008, fueling such divergent readings of apparently identical words? In a word, constitutionalism.[46] For our purposes, constitutionalism should be understood as a verb, not a noun. As such, constitutionalism is an activity, a complex ongoing (re)configuring of competing factors, factions, and feelings. Constitutionalism entails tugging and pulling, pushing and shoving, thrusting and parrying. Constitutionalism is "structured in part by constitutional texts, in part by history, and in part by present politics."[47] If constitutionalism sounds familiar that is not surprising, because constitutionalism is politics. Politics is the social activity of choosing. Constitutionalism is a subset of that pursuit. One might say, with apologies to Carl von Clausewitz, that constitutionalism is the continuation of politics by law-full means.[48]

What occurred between 1939 and 2008 is that constitutionalism revised significantly the ℂonstitution (lower-case c—cultural) in ways that (1) legitimized an individual interpretation of the Constitution's Second Amendment; (2) undercut the collective interpretation of the Constitution's Second Amendment; and (3) profoundly polarized interpretation of and debate over the meaning of the Constitution's Second Amendment. The story of how and why the U.S. Supreme Court in *Heller* "caught up" with 21st century constitutional gun culture is fascinating and instructive. Its consequences are now daily news items. That story cannot be told here.[49] Suffice to say, that over time constitutionalism shaped ℂonstitutional values, attitudes, and beliefs, which eventuated in the High Court modifying the Constitution's Second Amendment.

Culture[50] is key. Americans' debates over guns underscore this situation. Referring to the Constitution's Second Amendment will never resolve disagreements over gun laws because, fundamentally, such discord is not about guns. Such discord is about us. Law professor Mark Tushnet concludes:

> As with many constitutional provisions, there's no definitive answer to what the Second Amendment means. And arguments over its meaning are affected, for the worse, by their ties to the culture wars. The arguments demonstrate the validity of what students of the Internet have called Godwin's Law (named after the Internet guru who first described it): As discussion proceeds, the probability that one's adversaries will be likened to Nazis and that Hitler will be invoked approaches one very quickly. Proponents of the right to own guns for personal use are 'gun nuts' and 'insurrectionists' to their opponents; proponents of gun control are fascists or socialists to theirs.... Like all battles in culture wars, then, fights over the Second Amendment are really about something else—not about what the Second Amendment means, or about how to reduce violence but ... about how we understand ourselves as Americans.[51]

The Constitution is a malleable governing "container," so to speak, into which we pour our deeply felt Constitutional assumptions, which mold—and are molded by—constitutionalism.

When theorizing free speech and the First Amendment in the context of contemporary social media and the Internet, a Hobbesian Constitutional culture of tribalism pervades. As tribalism in American society has infected our Constitution, anger, hostility, and annihilation prevail. The First Amendment has been weaponized. Here are three telling contemporary examples.

First, writing a guest column in the influential *Sabato's Crystal Ball*, political scientist Steven Webster analyzes how anger has diminished trust in government (and vice versa):

> **All politics is anger**
> Trust in government has declined precipitously over the past 60 years. [H]igh levels of trust in the national government were typical in the latter years of the Eisenhower Administration. However, by 2016, only 20% of Americans said they trusted the government 'always' or 'most of the time.' Because trust in government is essential for facilitating democratic representation and legitimacy, understanding the causes of this cratering trust in government is of paramount importance. My research ... suggests that the growth in anger within the electorate and Americans' declining trust in the national government are not separate phenomena. In fact, my work has shown that higher levels of anger within the electorate are actually one of the primary reasons citizens have lost trust in the national government.[52]

Webster parses the Constitutional interaction between political anger and distrust of government. His findings document the cancerous cycle whereby distrust-fuels-anger-anger-breeds-distrust ... and on and on. His data imply strongly that, with anger come factions and siloed identities. Webster provides one window into the miasma of tribalism presently afflicting American politics. Another window comes from the late Dave Frohnmayer, former Oregon Attorney General and University of Oregon President. Frohnmayer writes compellingly of what he termed "The New Tribalism." What is "The New Tribalism?":

> It is the growth of a politics based upon narrow concerns, rooted in the exploitation of divisions of class, cash, gender, region, religion, ethnicity, morality and ideology[;] a give-no-quarter and take-no-prisoners activism that demands satisfaction and accepts no compromise ... The result of this vituperation and negativity can be disastrous for our political system ... Terms like 'fascist' and 'wimp,' 'extremist' and 'FemiNazi' have become commonplace not only on radio and TV talk shows, but increasingly in our legislative halls. One United States Senator, leaving the chamber after a recent budget debate, was reported to declare, 'I'd like to take an Uzi in there and spray the place.'... This [is the] erosion of civility in public discourse...[53]

Frohnmayer pulls no punches in describing the contemporary state of nature that is American politics. Frohnmayer's New Tribalism is reminiscent of old Hobbes' war of each against all. Frohnmayer's analysis of poisonous contemporary American constitutionalism complements Webster's. Together they portray a society consumed by the "pursuit of loneliness,"[54] desperate to connect but clueless as to how to proceed. Increasingly, we yearn for a time (probably illusionary) when we were all in this together, while also engaging in the precise behaviors, and embracing the self-same attitudes, that pit us against one another.

Pew Center Findings as the Contemporary Leviathan

The Webster and Frohnmayer frontline reports are sobering. Still, they pale in comparison with findings reported in a Pew Research Center March 2017 publication entitled, "The Future of Free Speech, Trolls, Anonymity and Fake News Online." The report reads like *Leviathan* updated for the Internet age.

Between July 1 and August 12, 2016, the Center, collaborating with Elon University, surveyed almost 8,000 experts, scholars, practitioners, and leaders, of whom 1,537 replied.[55] Respondents were asked: "In the next decade, will public discourse online become more or less shaped by bad actors, harassment, trolls, and an overall tone of griping, distrust, and disgust?"[56] Forty-two percent replied that they expected no major change in the online social climate in the upcoming decade. Thirty-nine percent expected that climate to be more shaped by negative activities. Nineteen percent anticipated that the online social climate will be less shaped by harassment. The study's authors—Lee Rainie, Janna Anderson, and Jonathan Albright—distilled and synthesized their results into four themes about the future of the online social climate:

Theme 1: Things will stay bad, Part 1

While some respondents saw issues with uncivil behavior online on somewhat of a plateau at the time of this canvassing in the summer of 2016 and a few expect solutions will cut hate speech, misinformation and manipulation, the vast majority shared at least some concerns that things could get worse, thus two of the four overarching themes of this report start with the phrase, 'Things will stay bad.'

Theme 2: Things will stay bad, Part II

Many respondents said power dynamics push trolling along. The business model of social media platforms is driven by advertising revenues generated by engaged platform users. The more raucous and incendiary the material, at times, the more income a site generates. The more contentious a political conflict is, the more likely it is to be an attention getter. Online forums lend themselves to ever-more hostile arguments.

Theme 3: Things will get better

Most respondents said it is likely that the coming decade will see a widespread move to more-secure services, applications, and platforms and more robust user-identification policies. Some said people born into the social media age will adapt. Some predict that more online systems will require clear identification of participants. This means that the online social forums could splinter into various formats, some of which are highly protected and monitored and others which could retain the free-for-all character of today's platforms.

Theme 4: Oversight and community moderation come with a cost.

A share of respondents said greater regulation of speech and technological solutions to curb harassment and trolling will result in more surveillance, censorship and cloistered communities. They worry this will change people's sharing behaviors online, limit exposure to diverse ideas and challenge freedom.[57]

The Pew Research Center report paints a sobering picture.[58] Like Hobbes, the "vast majority" of the Pew respondents see skirmishes in the online war of each against all getting worse, not better. Echoing Hobbes, many respondents ground such conflict in the nature of human beings. It is notable that even those holding more sanguine opinions about the future of online combat temper their optimism with the recognition that efforts to mitigate contentiousness involve trade-offs and costs; "cures" potentially worse than the maladies themselves. Just as, from the standpoint of representative democracy, Hobbes' social compact that elevates an absolute monarch to the throne is unacceptable by being authoritarian, regulating the internet may well defeat its *raison d'être*—open communication.

Free Speech Theory in Our Hobbesian Era

We have arrived at a crucial juncture. Other chapters in this book analyze theories of free speech within various contexts. Fundamentally, though, all the chapters in this book describe and analyze free speech controversies in our Internet age—the "stormy present." The remainder of this chapter scrutinizes free speech theory amidst the Hobbesian constitutionalism that defines our time. Shifting from analyzing our stormy present, to thinking and acting anew, our focal point is engaging in imaginative constitutionalism, undertaking a new First Amendment narrative in order to fashion new social contracts (and vice versa). Our primary concerns here are (1) to change our political conversation, that is, reckon with if not necessarily transcend tribalism, and (2) ask concomitantly: must free speech always be freewheeling?

It is not difficult to make the case that the Internet is Hobbesian. Addressing the following question is much harder: what are we to make of this situation from the vantage point of free speech theory? In other words, What Is to Be Done (**Что делать**)?[59]

With regard to theorizing free speech in our Hobbesian Age—contemplating Where Do We Go from Here?[60] Hannah Arendt points in a fertile direction. Arendt's essay "The Crisis in Culture: Its Social and Its Political Significance"[61] provides a thought-provoking perspective and offers a stimulating point of departure. First, some necessary preparatory clearing away is required; demolition work, if you will. As Abraham Lincoln put it: "We must disenthrall ourselves…"

Lincoln understood "disenthrall ourselves" to entail liberating—unburdening—our minds from knee-jerk assumptions (i.e., "dogmas of the quiet past…") that were fueling civil war and threatening to destroy "our country."[62] In the context of this chapter's concerns, "disenthralling ourselves" entails disenchanting free speech. Paradoxically, those Fourteen Little Words[63] in the First Amendment simultaneously enjoy the status of being a (the?!) bedrock article of faith animating our secular constitutional religion, while suffering from being intellectually incoherent and under inclusive. One does not have to embrace Stanley Fish's iconoclastic "there is no such thing as free speech"[64] to realize that contemporary free speech theory and practice are troubled and problematic. Articulating this point in terms of our three key concepts: judges often interpret the Constitution's First Amendment in muddled and inconsistent ways because our Ȼonstitution is riven with divisions over free speech, which deeply fragment constitutional politics. Think of the anger and absolutism characterizing debates over professional athletes taking a knee during the national anthem. Think about the widely divergent responses to flag burning, to religious speech, and to hate speech. Reflect, as well, on the commentaries regarding free speech theory articulated in the other chapters in this book. Free speech theory is central to American constitutional law. It also is all over the map.

Disenthralling Ourselves (or Disenchanting the First Amendment)

There is a voluminous body of scholarship addressing the deficiencies and limitations of contemporary free speech theories that can facilitate disenthralling free speech. Two works, plus a third "posture," stand out among the huge library of works treating free speech. These three disenthralling works range from debunking free expression as a right, to a synthetic critique of free speech from an interdisciplinary perspective, to Hannah Arendt's admonition "to think what we are doing."[65]

Larry Alexander: Freedom of Expression is Not a Human Right

First, law professor Larry Alexander offers an abstract theoretical case for the proposition that freedom of expression is not a human right. His argument consists of three parts. Alexander defines a human right as "a moral right that can be validly invoked by any person at any time or place. ... Human rights as moral rights entail obligations on others. ... A right to freedom of expression is normally thought at its core to entail the negative obligation that *government* not penalize the exercise of a certain liberty or set of liberties."[66] Second, Alexander defines freedom of expression as entailing, at a minimum, "a requirement that government, at least in its capacity as regulator, maintain a stance of evaluative neutrality vis-à-vis messages."[67] In other words, "at its core [evaluative neutrality] requires regulators to abstain from acting on the basis of their own assessments of a message's truth or value."[68] Third, having rejected existing salient "general justifying theories of expression"[69] as not "tenable,"[70] Alexander concludes that evaluative neutrality is impossible in practice. The culprit is "liberalism," or rather liberal government's inherent contradiction:

> [O]perationalizing the idea that liberalism cannot take its own side in an argument is an impossibility. Liberal government cannot help but be partisan, which means that liberalism as governmental nonpartisanship (neutrality) toward religions, associations, and expression is an impossibility. ... Liberalism in any of its versions [must be 'partisan']. If liberalism is the correct political morality, all positions inconsistent with its tenets are incorrect. There is no neutral ground in these matters.[71]

For Alexander, free speech requires a governmental stance of "evaluative neutrality." Since liberal government is unavoidably partisan, free speech cannot exist. In other words, liberalism is inherently illiberal. Ergo, no right of free speech.

Alexander sets up an apparent straw man. By making freedom of expression contingent upon chimerical liberal "evaluative neutrality," his conclusion that no right of free speech exists is unavoidable: neutrality is necessary—and inconceivable. However one ultimately assesses Alexander's radical argument, for our disenthralling purpose his skeptical stance toward rights usefully erodes First Amendment dogmatism. Free speech rights neither exist in nature, nor inhere in humanity. One might say that rights are human-fabricated, rule-oriented "fences"; artificial barriers we erect, based on "hunches," so as to insulate specific valued activities from particular government interference (many of the Founding generation saw the constitutional republic they had created as a precarious experiment—noble, to be sure, but based on risky hunches nevertheless). Thus, although the right of free expression might not exist *per se*, in practice, such a right is a functional figment of our shared imagination.[72] The best we can do is "muddle through."[73]

Matthew D. Bunker: Critiquing "Classical First Amendment Theory"

Journalism Professor Matthew D. Bunker offers an interdisciplinary critique of First Amendment theory that expands one's imagination. He advances our disenthralling project by expanding our horizons. Bunker spells out his take on the state of free speech theory right at the outset. He writes:

> Mainstream First Amendment theory is under assault. Free speech should be protected, liberal theorists have proposed, for a number of important reasons, including democratic self-governance, self-realization, respect for individual autonomy, the search for truth, and a variety of other reasons. While these classical free speech justifications still have significant influence, free speech theory is nonetheless in a state of great ferment. The notion that government should extend to individuals the greatest possible right of free expression (long a truism among scholars in law, communication, and related disciplines) has become subject to significant challenges.[74]

"Under assault," "great ferment," "significant challenges"... Bunker chronicles and criticizes several late 20th century intellectual movements[75] within and across a variety of disciplines, challenging the "old consensus."[76] Broadly, that consensus consists of two loosely-related assumptions. First, law is an autonomous and self-contained discipline consisting (ideally) of "neutral principles."[77] Second, with regard to First Amendment protection of free speech, this right is an unalloyed good, defending individual actors from government discrimination. Bunker dubs the old consensus "Classical First Amendment Theory," and analyzes it critically as the "baseline ... to encapsulate, in brief, the tradition against which the interdisciplinarians are reacting..."[78]

For himself, Bunker settles upon what might be termed Classical Theory Lite (!) Having journeyed conscientiously through six chapters in which he closely interrogates prominent "interdisciplinarians," ferreting out salient flaws internal to their theories, as well as miscues in how they apply their critiques to First Amendment theory, Bunker returns to square one—sort of. One might say that, in the end, Bunker is a reconstructed adherent to semi-classical First Amendment Theory. As the title of his final chapter, Bunker poses this question: "Shall We Commit First Amendment Theory?" His reply is "yes"—qualified by a specific method. Working within a context of richly diverse options, Bunker urges a theoretical approach that avoids the *Scylla* (rock) of reductionism which diminishes the relative autonomy of law by assimilating law into, say, gender, and the *Charybdis* (hard place) of formalism which walls law off from social circumstances that clearly shape rules.[79] His approach "... does not advocate a quiet acceptance of the status quo. Instead, it critically examines the entire edifice of our constitutional tradition and forces us to reconsider those judgments that cannot be squared with wider clusters of knowledge."[80] The goal of the approach he advocates—"wide reflective equilibrium"[81]—is to fashion compelling, and impermanent, understandings, which reconcile a variety of materials and events. In short, "committing" First Amendment theory entails exercising judgment. As Lincoln would have it, thinking "anew."

Hannah Arendt: *"Thinking without Banisters"*

Next, Hannah Arendt adds her unique vantage point on how to approach thinking about matters such as free speech. Arendt survived the Holocaust, fortuitously escaping the murderous Nazi "Final Solution" that slaughtered millions during what British historian Niall Ferguson called "the single hundred-year 'War of the World.'"[82] For a time, she was a stateless Jew, eventually gaining refuge as an American citizen. Having found shelter from the firestorm engulfing the world, Arendt spent the remainder of her life reflecting on the causes and consequences of this catastrophe. She had a front row seat, as it were, on the cataclysmic collapse of the intellectual, religious, philosophical, and institutional foundations of Western Civilization that led to German fascism and Soviet Communism.[83] "[R]esponses to the most dramatic events of her time lie at the very centre of Arendt's thought."[84] She gleaned two basic lessons. First, she held that thinking—that is, people's capacity for thought—is essential to the human condition.[85] Second, in terms resembling Abraham Lincoln's, she argued that traditional thinking has proven utterly inadequate to surviving the dire straits amidst which we currently find ourselves (epitomized, for her, by totalitarianism). Loosening the grip of, and reconsidering, cherished bromides.[86] We require a genuinely *novus, ordo seclorum* (a *new* order of the ages).

Arendt held that the ability to think is intimately related to the human capacity to begin. "Men," she wrote (she meant humankind), "though they must die, are not born in order to die but in order to begin."[87] Essential to being perpetual beginners is "natality"—thinking creatively. Arendt dubbed such thinking "*Denken ohne Geländer*": "Thinking without Banisters." Richard J. Bernstein elaborates:

> 'Thinking without banisters' (*Denken ohne Geländer*) was one of the favorite expressions of Hannah Arendt—and it has a special meaning for her. Arendt was convinced that the eruption of twentieth-century totalitarianism meant a radical break with tradition. No longer could we rely on traditional political and moral categories to help us comprehend our times. If we are to engage in the activity of thinking after the break in tradition, then we can't rely on banisters or fixed points; we are compelled to forge new ways of thinking and new concepts. Thinking, which Arendt sharply distinguished from knowing, is primarily concerned with meaning—making sense of the world in which we find ourselves.[88]

Having surveyed our tribal Constitutional landscape, cleared some intellectual ground, and, per Arendt (resembling Lincoln) thought anew, we turn ultimately to the challenging task of beginning to reimagine free speech. While neither making it up as we go along, nor sailing off into *Terra Incognita*, the undertaking requires humility as well as resolve.

Arendt Again: Creating an "enlarged mentality"

The key to theorizing free speech in this, the Hobbesian tribal era during which we are living, is decidedly un-Hobbesian. Ironically, civil speech potentially can check uncivil speech: one path out of our current Hobbesian state of war (or, minimally, facilitating détente) is understanding free speech as the ongoing means of fashioning new social contracts. Instead of our chaotic, no neutrality state of war giving rise to an authoritarian Leviathan, civil speech can cultivate a humanized society. In our age of abusive speech, republican speech can act as a solvent. The indispensable insight underlying a republican theory of free speech is that republican speech is "cultivated" speech. The image/metaphor of one influential free speech theory is the marketplace where, per Justice Oliver Wendell Holmes, Jr., constructive ideas compete successfully with destructive ideas.[89] By contrast, the approach proposed here perhaps is best represented by gardeners[90]—certainly by Homer's Penelope.[91] In order to illustrate this approach, we turn again to Hannah Arendt.

Arendt offers a communications take on free speech.[92] For her, the First Amendment guarantee of free speech is all about nurturing discourse. Protecting speech promotes ongoing conversing by keeping multiple conversations going. Her understanding of speech is tied to her unique understanding of the key characteristic of political life—judgment, and communicating one's judgments. For Arendt, politics is the *sine qua non* of the human condition.[93] Without speech, politics is inconceivable. Speech requires "space." Political speech requires public spaces; spaces having physical, institutional, and psychological dimensions. From Arendt's point of view, the First Amendment fosters and shields debate; arguments which beat at the heart of politics and which, again, entail fashioning and conveying judgments about the world:

> Like Arendt, Aristotle connected politics, speech and judgment: The reason why man is a being meant for political association, in a higher degree than bees or other gregarious animals can ever associate, is evident. Nature, according to our theory, makes nothing in vain, and man alone of the animals is furnished with the faculty of language. ... [L]anguage serves to declare what is advantageous and what is the reverse, and it therefore serves to declare what is just and what is unjust. It is the peculiarity of man, in comparison with the rest of the animal world, that he alone possesses a perception of good and evil, of the just and the unjust, and of similar qualities.[94]

In other words, because we are speaking animals, humans are political animals, that is, judging animals. This association between talking, discerning, and choosing, brings us to one of Arendt's most powerful concepts: "Taste." In typical fashion, Arendt stands taste on its head, offering an analysis both instructive and audacious.

She starts by quoting the cliché: *gustibus non disputandum est* (in matters of taste, there can be no disputes). On the contrary, Arendt protests. Although arbitrary "private idiosyncrasies"[95] undeniably exist, "the activity of taste"[96] is neither ineluctably private, nor merely subjective.[97] Taste has a "public quality."[98] Taste is "open to discussion."[99] Unavoidably, taste entails chancy interpersonal communication. Arendt is interpreting Kant's *Critique of Judgment* here.[100] Arendt understands Kant as "disturbed by"[101] the clichéd definition that taste is exclusively one's own because such subjectivity "offended his political ... sense." Kant was concerned because "he insisted, in opposition to the commonplace adage, that taste judgments are open to discussion because 'we hope that the same pleasure is shared by others,' that taste can be subject to dispute, because it 'expects agreement from everyone else.' Therefore taste, insofar as it, like other judgments, appeals to common sense, is the very opposite of private feelings..."[102]

Taste, in short, is a debatable social construct. Arendt realizes that her speech-centered conception likely will occasion skepticism (or worse): "To classify taste, the chief cultural activity, among man's political abilities sounds so strange..."[103] Arendt explains by invoking two uniquely Kantian concepts—"wooing" and "enlarged mentality." With them, we arrive at the heart of the matter regarding her thinking and free speech theory.

Arendt explains what she terms "judgments of taste." Arendt's point of departure is Kant's definition of what taste judgments are, and what they entail:

> Taste judgments ... share with political opinions that they are persuasive; the judging person—as Kant says quite beautifully—can only 'woo the consent of everyone else' in the hope of coming to an agreement with him eventually. This 'wooing' or persuading corresponds closely to what the Greeks called ... the convincing and persuading speech which they regarded as the typically political form of people talking with one another ... Culture and politics, then, belong together because it is not knowledge or truth which is at stake, but rather judgment and decision, the judicious exchange of opinion about the sphere of public life and the common world and the decision what manner of action is to be taken in it, as well as how it is to look henceforth, what kind of things are to appear in it.[104]

Recapitulating two related points made earlier in this chapter, Arendt's Kantian notion of "wooing" illustrates, while elaborating on, (1) politics as the social activity of choosing; and (2) the quintessential political question, What Is To Be Done? Wooing—pressing one's suit with others—defines the character of politics. Wooing—pursuing and proposing—addresses the unavoidable political question. Ultimately, wooing is conducive to the frame of mind underpinning our Republic.[105] Novelist Barbara Kingsolver captures that republican frame of mind when she distinguishes between people talking *to* each other versus people talking *about* one another.[106] People talking to each other are connecting by conversing civilly. People talking about one another often are at odds, complaining and carping.

Hannah Arendt captures the essence of the republican ethos, again offering a singular reading of Kant:

> In the *Critique of Judgment* ... Kant insisted upon a different way of thinking ... which consisted of being able to 'think in the place of everybody else' and which he therefore called an "enlarged mentality" (*eine erweiterte Denkungsart*). The power of judgment rests on a potential agreement with others, and the thinking process which is active in judging something is not, like the thought process of pure reasoning, a dialogue between me and myself, but finds itself always and primarily, even if I am quite alone in making up my mind, in an anticipated

communication with others with whom I know I must finally come to some agreement. ... And this enlarged way of thinking, which as judgment knows how to transcend its own individual limitations ... cannot function in strict isolation or solitude; it needs the presence of others 'in whose place' it must think, whose perspectives it must take into consideration, and without whom it never has the opportunity to operate at all.[107]

For Arendt, speech is the connecting tissue of a republican body politic. By talking ceaselessly we constitute and reconstitute—as in ordaining and establishing—our Republic. By thinking out loud in the company of our fellow citizens our communication creates community. Wooing and enlarging: these twin activities are the knitting and purling by means of which We the People of the United States stitch together our fragile and resilient Union.

Slouching Our Way Toward a More Perfect Union

At the beginning of this book the reader was reminded that First Amendment theories do not exist in a vacuum. Every chapter in this book contextualizes controversies over First Amendment theory in the process of analyzing them. Each chapter unfolds its particular inquiry against the backdrop that we live in an age of Hobbesian tribalism. In our time, this clannish situation defines what Abraham Lincoln, more than a century and a half ago, called our "stormy present." Our imperfect Union is infected with discord. What is to be done?

Our journey toward addressing that ultimate political question has taken us through several dimensions of Hobbesian constitutionalism. The four vignettes provide windows into the social and individual consequences of weaponizing internet speech. Each scenario illustrates how tribalism warps civic discourse, vitiating civic virtue. Each scenario is grounded in a cultural Constitution rife with distrust, fear, and animosity. The three examples, which follow the four glimpses into ways Hobbesian tribalism corrupts our constitutionalism, complement those four vignettes. Steven Webster, David Frohnmayer, and the Pew Research Center situate the four vignettes within broader Hobbesian cultural trends playing out within our contemporary state of nature. Then, Alexander, Bunker, and Arendt serve to "disenthrall" us by disabusing us of cherished assumptions, namely that free speech is a human right (Alexander), that current "Classical" First Amendment theories accurately capture the social realities of free speech (Bunker), and that traditional Western principles provide sufficient guideposts (Arendt).

This preparatory work readies us to embark on a journey toward a more perfect union, addressing that overriding question: what is to be done?

Engaging that question, let alone answering it, seems daunting. The very pervasiveness and tenacity of Hobbesian constitutionalism appears likely to doom any and all efforts to undercut its grip on our imaginations and our actions. Perhaps, in the face of intractability, the only feasible response is chutzpah. Audacity meets single-mindedness. Emulating Hannah Arendt's role model, we might challenge Hobbesian constitutionalism with *Selbsdenken*: thinking for ourselves—without banisters. What might *Selbsdenken* entail in the face of Hobbesian constitutionalism?

Consider Arendt's appropriation of Kant's insight about "taste," and the implication of her adoption for overcoming Hobbesian tribalism. Recall the almost universal assumption that matters of taste are private matters—beyond public dispute. Similarly, the many modes of tribalism are usually assumed to be ubiquitous and existential—beyond doubt. But what if tribalism also were debatable, like taste, which is "open to discussion"? Taste is disputable because humans want others to share what gives them pleasure. People woo others in order to cultivate shared pleasures. Likewise, tribalism is disputable because humans want to join with others in sharing identities. Because we are other-oriented we woo others in order to cultivate shared attributes. Extending Kant's understanding of taste, then, to tribalism, tribalism is both a matter of opinion and open to discussion. As a beginning, cultivating conversation about tribalism might be an antidote to Hobbesian constitutionalism.

Benjamin Franklin: The Last Word?

There is a pertinent anecdote from the 1787 Philadelphia Convention. On the closing day of the Constitutional Convention a woman approached Benjamin Franklin as he departed the Pennsylvania State House (now Independence Hall). "Well Doctor," she queried Franklin, "what have we got, a Republic or a Monarchy?" With a wink, Franklin challenged his inquisitor: "A Republic, madam, if you can keep it." Fast forward almost two-and-a-half centuries. In the context of free speech theory in our Hobbesian Age, Franklin might just reply: "A Republic, fellow citizens, **if** you can keep the conversation going."[108]

Notes

1. Thomas Hobbes, *De Cive (The Citizen): Philosophical Rudiments Concerning Government and Society* (1642), ed. Sterling P. Lamprecht (New York: Appleton-Century-Crofts, 1949), 1–2.
2. Greg Sargent, "A GOP Senator's Remarkable Admission About Trump and Mueller," *Washington Post*, March 21, 2018, accessed May 26, 2019, https://www.washingtonpost.com/blogs/plum-line/wp/2018/03/21/a-gop-senators-remarkable-admission-about-

trump-and-mueller/?utm_term=.8a2958839ce5. Ben Sasse (R-NE), Bob Corker's senatorial colleague, analyzes the causes and consequences of contemporary tribalism in Ben Sasse, *Them: Why We Hate Each Other—and How to Heal* (New York: St. Martin's Press, 2018).
3. Sargent, "A GOP Senator's Remarkable Admission."
4. Thomas Hobbes, *Leviathan: Or The Matter, Forme and Power of a Commonwealth Ecclesiasticall and Civil* (1651), ed. Michael Oakeshott (New York: Collier Books, 1962), 100. Varieties of American tribalism are primordial, long antedating the formation of the United States. Essential reading on tribalism is Amy Chua, *Political Tribes: Group Instinct and the Fate of Nations* (New York: Penguin Press, 2018). Also see Colin Woodard, *American Nations: A History of the Eleven Rival Regional Cultures of North America* (New York: Viking, 2011). Also see Michael Shermer, "Evolution Explains Why Politics Is So Tribal," *Scientific American*, June 1, 2012, https://www.scientificamerican.com/article/evolution-explains-why-politics-tribal/; David Brooks, "The Retreat to Tribalism," *New York Times,* January 1, 2018, accessed May 26, 2019, https://www.nytimes.com/2018/01/01/opinion/the-retreat-to-tribalism.html; Kwame Anthony Appia, "People Don't Vote For What They Want. They Vote For Who They Are," *Washington Post*, August 30, 2018, accessed May 26, 2019, https://www.washingtonpost.com/outlook/people-dont-vote-for-want-they-want-they-vote-for-who-they-are/2018/08/30/fb5b7e44-abd7-11e8-8a0c-70b618c98d3c_story.html?utm_term=.555d18544d29; Jonathan Haidt, *The Righteous Mind: Why Good People Are Divided By Politics and Religion* (New York: Pantheon, 2012); and McKay Coppins, "The Man Who Broke Politics," *The Atlantic*, November 2018, https://www.theatlantic.com/magazine/archive/2018/11/newt-gingrich-says-youre-welcome/570832/. Compare this Lawcourt-l post from political scientist Lief Carter: "My misgivings about [our colleague,] Cornell [Clayton]'s thesis is his putting tribalism at the core of our current political problems. I think this is the equivalent of saying sex is the cause of our #metoo problems ... Alas, tribalism is woven into human nature at least as strongly as is the impulse to procreate. We are a social species of animal, and our huge brains contribute to making us an especially fearful one. We rely on our tribes—churches, business places, extended families, sports teams, neighborhoods, social clubs—to feel that we have allies when a fight breaks out, which in turn quells our fears and lets our big brains sleep at night. The Republicans figured this out long ago and play to it smartly, e.g., via the psychologically brilliant MAGA slogan. I just hope the Dems are seeing the light and building their own tribal solidarity around a different and less insidiously destructive set of flags and symbols and slogans. Women are surely the key to this effort, and for my money the only good news is that rise of women in opposing Trumpism, a rise which I hope the [Brent] Kavanaiugh [sic] [confirmation hearings] affair will only accelerate. . . ." Lief Carter, email to Law and Courts Discussion List—"LAWCOURT-L," October 5, 2018.
5. Caitlin Dewey, "The Only Guide to Gamergate You Will Ever Need to Read," *Washington Post*, October 14, 2014, accessed May 26, 2019, https://www.washingtonpost.com/news/the-intersect/wp/2014/10/14/the-only-guide-to-gamergate-you-will-ever-need-to-read/?utm_term=.a2a6342575d7.
6. Ibid.
7. Ibid.
8. Ibid.
9. Emily Chang, *Brotopia: Breaking Up the Boy's Club of Silicon Valley* (New York: Portfolio, 2018), 184.

10. Ibid.
11. Ibid., 41.
12. Ibid., 48, 49.
13. Ibid., 51.
14. Ibid., 53.
15. Ibid., 59.
16. Kate Conger, "Here's the Full 10-Page Anti-Diversity Screed Circulating Internally at Google," *Gizmodo*, August 5, 2017, https://gizmodo.com/exclusive-heres-the-full-10-page-anti-diversity-screed-1797564320. See Mike Rogoway, "Harassment, Stereotyping Remain Common in Oregon Tech, Survey Finds," *Oregonian* (Portland, OR), August 14, 2018, https://www.oregonlive.com/silicon-forest/index.ssf/2018/08/harassment_stereotyping_remain_1.html.
17. Dave Cullen, *Parkland: Birth of A Movement* (New York: Harper, 2019).
18. After much conversation and consultation, we have decided not to name the shooter, denying that person any notoriety that would come with identification. See No Notoriety website, accessed May 28, 2019, http://nonotoriety.com/.
19. Cleve R. Wootson, Jr., "NRA Taunts Parkland Teens: 'No One Would Know Your Names' If Classmates Were Still Alive," March 24, 2018, accessed May 26, 2019, https://www.washingtonpost.com/news/post-nation/wp/2018/03/24/nra-host-taunts-parkland-teens-no-one-would-know-your-names-if-classmates-were-still-alive/?utm_term=.139172f16963.
20. See Antonio Gramsci, *Selections From the Prison Notebooks*, ed. Quintin Hoare, trans. Geoffrey Nowell Smith (New York: International Publishers, 1971), chap. I.
21. Mari Uyehara, "The Sliming of David Hogg and Emma Gonzalez," *GQ*, March 30, 2018, accessed May 28, 2019, https://www.gq.com/story/the-sliming-of-david-hogg-and-emma-gonzalez.
22. Steve Collins, "Maine Candidate Calls Teen Who Survived Florida School Shooting 'a Skinhead Lesbian,'" *Press Herald* (Portland, ME), March 12, 2018, accessed May 28, 2019, https://www.pressherald.com/2018/03/12/maine-house-candidate-from-sabattus-calls-activist-teens-from-florida-a-skinhead-lesbian-and-another-a-bald-faced-liar/.
23. Kirby Wilson, "GOP Candidate in Maine Calls Parkland Student 'Skinhead Lesbian,'" *Tampa Bay Times* (Tampa Bay, FL), March 12, 2018, accessed May 26, 2019, https://www.tampabay.com/florida-politics/buzz/2018/03/12/gop-candidate-in-maine-calls-parkland-student-skinhead-lesbian/.
24. Collins, "Maine Candidate."
25. Tatyana Bellamy-Walker, "Conservatives Still Can't Stop Attacking Parkland Shooting Survivor David Hogg," *Daily Beast*, April 11, 2018, accessed May 28, 2019, https://www.thedailybeast.com/conservative-still-cant-stop-attacking-parkland-shooting-survivor-david-hogg.
26. Morgan Gstalter, "Infowars, Breitbart Compare Parkland's David Hogg to Adolf Hitler," *The Hill*, March 27, 2018, accessed May 29, 2019, https://thehill.com/blogs/blog-briefing-room/news/380546-right-wing-comparing-parklands-david-hogg-to-adolf-hitler.
27. Lisa Gutierrez, "Missouri Host Who Tweeted He'd 'Ram a Hot Poker Up' Parkland Survivor Resigns TV Gig," *Kansas City Star* (Kansas City, MO), April 9, 2018, accessed May 27, 2019, https://www.kansascity.com/news/state/missouri/article208351974.html.

28. Amanda Markotte, "Conservatives Can't Stop Themselves From Bashing Parkland Students: But Why?" *Salon*, March 29, 2018, accessed May 29, 2019, https://www.salon.com/amp/conservatives-cant-stop-themselves-from-bashing-parkland-students-but-why.
29. "Network Neutrality," accessed May 29, 2019, https://www.ocf.berkeley.edu/~raylin/whatisnetneutrality.htm.
30. Tim Wu, "Network Neutrality FAQ," accessed May 29, 2019, http://www.timwu.org/network_neutrality.html.
31. Brian Fung, "The FCC Just Voted to Repeal Its New Neutrality Rules, in A Sweeping Act of Deregulation," *Washington Post*, December 14, 2017, accessed May 26, 2019, https://www.washingtonpost.com/news/the-switch/wp/2017/12/14/the-fcc-is-expected-to-repeal-its-net-neutrality-rules-today-in-a-sweeping-act-of-deregulation/?utm_term=.0524da7fc600.
32. David Shepardson, "New FCC Chair Vows 'Light Touch' Approach to Regulation," *Reuters*, February 28, 2017, accessed May 29, 2019, https://www.reuters.com/article/us-usa-fcc/new-fcc-chair-vows-light-touch-approach-to-regulation-idUSKBN16720Z.
33. Edward C. Baig and Elizabeth Weise, "Millions of Net Neutrality Comments Were Faked. Turns Out Mine Was One," *USA Today*, December 6, 2017, accessed May 26, 2019, https://www.usatoday.com/story/tech/2017/12/06/fake-names-and-c-used-fcc-internet-regulation-debate-public-comments-includes-usa-today-tech-column/923576001/.
34. Brian Fung, "The FCC Just Voted." Compare "Marc Martin Quoted in *The Washington Post*—The FCC is Expected to Repeal its Net Neutrality Rules Today, in a Sweeping Act of Deregulation," General News, Perkins Coie, December 14, 2017, accessed May 29, 2019, https://www.perkinscoie.com/en/news-insights/marc-martin-quoted-in-the-washington-post-the-fcc-is-expected-to.html. Ironically, nearly every authentic FCC public comment supported net neutrality. See Jennings Brown, "Nearly Every Real FCC Public Comment Supported Net Neutrality, Stanford Study Says," *Gizmodo*, October 16, 2018, accessed May 29, 2019, https://gizmodo.com/nearly-every-real-fcc-public-comment-supported-net-neut-1829782244.
35. Jack Karsten and Darrell M. West, "Net Neutrality Debate Exposes Weaknesses of Public Comment System, *Brookings*, January 18, 2018, accessed May 29, 2019, https://www.brookings.edu/blog/techtank/2018/01/18/net-neutrality-debate-exposes-weaknesses-of-public-comment-system/.
36. David Z. Morris, "More Than 1 Million FCC Comments Opposing Net Neutrality Were Probably Fake," November 25, 2017, accessed May 29, 2019, http://fortune.com/2017/11/25/1-million-fake-fcc-comments-net-neutrality-were-probably-fake/.
37. One of the editors of this book observes: "...[W]e all know the rule book exists but what those rules actually are is a constant matter of tribal debate."
38. To one of the editors of this book this sentence is reminiscent of the World War Two slogan: "Loose lips sink ships." Rendering this slogan more directly pertinent to Hobbesian constitutionalism, one might suggest: sloppy conceptualization scuttles understanding.
39. Enclosing the "Second Amendment" within quotation marks is meant to suggest the essential contestability of the Amendment.

40. 92 U.S. 542 (1876).
41. *Korematsu v. United States*, 323 U.S. 214, 246 (1944) (Jackson, J. dissenting).
42. 307 U.S. 174 (1939).
43. Ibid., at 178.
44. 554 U.S. 570 (2008).
45. Ibid., at 577, 592.
46. See, for instance, Jacqui Shine, "How Civil Must Americans Be?" *New York Times*, August 12, 2018, accessed May 26, 2019, https://www.nytimes.com/2018/08/11/style/the-civility-paradox.html?hp&action=click&pgtype=Homepage&clickSource=story-heading&module=second-column-region&region=top-news&WT.nav=top-news.
47. Mark A. Graber, *A New Introduction to American Constitutionalism* (New York: Oxford University Press, 2013), 13.
48. Carl von Clausewitz, *On War*, trans. and ed. Michael Howard and Peter Paret (Princeton, NJ: Princeton University Press, 1976).
49. For a useful telling of this story see Adam Winkler, *Gun Fight: The Battle Over The Right to Bear Arms in America* (New York: W.W. Norton, 2011).
50. "I like to think of culture as the symbols that we share to understand each other." Composer John Adams quoted in Alex Ross, *The Rest Is Noise: Listening to The Twentieth Century* (New York: Picador, 2007), 535. The problem is that, in our tribal Hobbesian world, shared symbols are scarce; misunderstanding is rampant. To wit: Aaron Copeland once observed, "… that an artist who is forced to live in an atmosphere of 'suspicion, ill-will and dread' will end up creating nothing." Ibid., 383.
51. Mark V. Tushnet, *Out of Range: Why the Constitution Can't End the Battle Over Guns* (New York: Oxford University Press, 2007), xv-xvi; xix.
52. Steven Webster, "Mad as Hell: How Anger Diminishes Trust in Government," Sabato's Crystal Ball, University of Virginia Center for Politics, May 17, 2018, accessed May 29, 2019, http://www.centerforpolitics.org/crystalball/articles/mad-as-hell-how-anger-diminishes-trust-in-government/. Harvard History Professor and *New Yorker* staff writer, Jill Lepore, analyzed the distrust underlying the Victims' Rights Movement. Her conclusions are pertinent here: "[According to Raphael Ginsberg, University of North Carolina historian, the Victims' Rights Movement is] part of a larger conservative attack on expertise and on the notion of a public good. It's as if it came down to this: Don't trust the mainstream media, don't trust intellectuals, don't trust judges: protect yourself and your family and your freedoms; buy a gun; speak your truth … They are asking for an end to a set of arrangements under which what was once civil society has become a state of war." Jill Lepore, "Sirens in The Night: How the Victims' Rights Revolution Has Remade American Justice," *New Yorker*, May 21, 2018, accessed May 29, 2019, https://www.newyorker.com/magazine/2018/05/21/the-rise-of-the-victims-rights-movement
53. Dave Frohnmayer, "Speeches and Writings: 'The New Tribalism,'" The Office of the President Emeritus, University of Oregon, accessed May 29, 2019, https://frohnmayer.uoregon.edu/speeches/newtribalism/
54. Philip Slater, *The Pursuit of Loneliness: American Culture at the Breaking Point* (Boston: Beacon, 1970). Compare Robert D. Putnam, *Bowling Alone: The Collapse and Revival of American Community* (New York: Simon and Schuster, 2000).

55. See Lee Rainie, Janna Anderson, and Jonathan Albright, "About This Canvassing of Experts," Pew Research Center: Internet and Technology, March 29, 2017, accessed May 29, 2019, http://www.pewinternet.org/2017/03/29/social-climate-about-this-canvassing-of-experts/. Compare Maeve Duggan, "Online Harassment 2017," Pew Research Center: Internet and Technology, July 11, 2017, accessed May 29, 2019, http://www.pewinternet.org/2017/07/11/online-harassment-2017/; Michelle Goldberg, "Feminist Writers Are So Besieged By Online Abuse That Some Have Begun to Retire," *Washington Post*, February 19, 2015, accessed May 27, 2019, https://www.washingtonpost.com/opinions/online-feminists-increasingly-ask-are-the-psychic-costs-too-much-to-bear/2015/02/19/3dc4ca6c-b7dd-11e4-a200-c008a01a6692_story.html?utm_term=.ad56a8ab7528; and Ellen Pao, "Former Reddit CEO Ellen Pao: The Trolls Are Winning the Battle for the Internet," *Washington Post*, July 16, 2015, accessed May 27, 2019, https://www.washingtonpost.com/opinions/we-cannot-let-the-internet-trolls-win/2015/07/16/91b1a2d2-2b17-11e5-bd33-395c05608059_story.html?utm_term=.cf7ad97c3bd5.
56. Lee Rainie, Janna Anderson, and Jonathan Albright, "The Future of Free Speech, Trolls, Anonymity and Fake News Online," Pew Research Center: Internet and Technology, March 29, 2017, accessed May 29, 2019, http://www.pewinternet.org/2017/03/29/the-future-of-free-speech-trolls-anonymity-and-fake-news-online/. Compare Jennifer Kavanagh and Michael D. Rich, *Truth Decay: An Initial Exploration of the Diminishing Role of Facts and Analysis in American Public Life* (Santa Monica, CA: Rand Corporation, 2018).
57. Rainie, Anderson, and Albright, "The Future of Free Speech."
58. See Brian X. Chen, "The Internet Trolls Have Won. Sorry, There's Not Much You Can Do," *New York Times*, August 9, 2018, accessed May 26, 2019, https://www.nytimes.com/2018/08/08/technology/personaltech/internet-trolls-comments.html.
59. *What Is to Be Done* is the title of a utopian revolutionary novel by nineteenth-century Russian author Nikolai Chernyshevsky (1828–1889). His title—Что делатъ in Russian—poses the unavoidable, fundamental political question. Chernyshevsky's work inspired Vladimir (N.) Lenin to write his influential 1902 political pamphlet titled: *What Is to Be Done: Burning Questions of Our Movement*. Theorizing free speech entails addressing the question Chernyshevsky poses.
60. Where Do We Go from Here? is a variation on What Is To be Done?
61. Hannah Arendt, "The Crisis in Culture: Its Social and Its Political Significance," in *Between Past and Future: Eight Exercises in Political Thought*, rev. ed. (1961; repr., New York: Penguin, 2006).
62. Michael Pollan writes of our contemporary situation: "*Homo Sapiens* might have arrived at one of those periods of crisis that calls for some mental and behavioral depatterning." Michael Pollan, *How to Change Your Mind: What the New Science of Psychedelics Teaches Us About Consciousness, Dying, Addiction, Depression, and Transcendence* (New York: Penguin Press, 2018), 124.
63. "Congress shall make no law. . . abridging the freedom of speech, or of the press. . ."
64. Stanley Fish, *There Is No Such Thing as Free Speech: And It's a Good Thing, Too* (New York: Oxford University Press, 1994). See Matthew D. Bunker, *Critiquing Free Speech: First Amendment Theory and the Challenge of Interdisciplinarity* (Mahwah, NJ: Lawrence Erlbaum, 2001), chap 3. Compare Larry Alexander, *Is There a Right of Freedom of Expression?* (New York: Cambridge University Press, 2005), 178–80.

65. Hannah Arendt, *The Human Condition: A Study of the Central Dilemmas Facing Modern Man* (Chicago: University of Chicago Press, 1959), 5.
66. Alexander, *Is There a Right of Freedom of Expression?*, 3, 4.
67. Ibid., 11.
68. Ibid.
69. Alexander identifies these justifying theories as: "Consequentialist" (The Promotion of Truth, The Promotion of Autonomous Decisionmaking, The Promotion of Virtue); "Deontological"; and "As Concomitant to Democratic Decisionmaking" (The General Theory, Public Discourse Theory). Ibid., chap. 7.
70. Ibid., 146.
71. Ibid., 147, 149.
72. Jonathan Haidt's term is "consensual hallucination." See Brian Greene and Crawford Hunt, "The Other Side Isn't Your Enemy: Jonathan Haidt Speaks at TEDNYC," TEDBlog, November 3, 2016, accessed May 29, 2019, https://blog.ted.com/the-other-side-isnt-your-enemy-jonathan-haidt-speaks-at-tednyc/.
73. Alexander, *Is There a Right of Freedom of Expression?*, epilogue.
74. Bunker, *Critiquing Free Speech*, xi. See, e.g., Justice Jackson's statement, below, in *West Virginia State Board of Education v. Barnette*.
75. Specifically, feminist legal scholars, critical legal theorists, communitarian theorists, critical race theorists, and literary theorists practicing in Political Science, Communication, Philosophy, Economics, History, Psychology, Sociology, Literary Studies, and Critical and Cultural Studies. Among the diverse scholars whose work Bunker engages are: Susan H. Williams, Judge Richard A. Posner, Philip Bobbitt, Stanley Fish, John Rawls, Michael Sandel, Alasdair McIntyre, Mark V. Tushnet, Louis Michael Seidman, Cass Sunstein, Ronald Dworkin, Laurence H. Tribe, and Michael C. Dorf.
76. Bunker, *Critiquing Free Speech*, xi.
77. "The Legal Process School: Core Criticisms of the Approach," accessed May 29, 2019, https://cyber.harvard.edu/bridge/LegalProcess/essay3.txt.htm.
78. Bunker, *Critiquing Free Speech*, 2.
79. Ibid., 186.
80. Ibid., 188.
81. Ibid., 186–94.
82. Niall Ferguson, "The Next War of the World," *Foreign Affairs*, September/October 2006, accessed May 29, 2019, https://www.foreignaffairs.com/articles/middle-east/2006-09-01/next-war-world.
83. See Richard J. Bernstein, "Hannah Arendt on Violence and Power," in *Violence: Thinking Without Banisters* (Malden, MA: Polity, 2013); Margaret Canovan, *Hannah Arendt: A Reinterpretation of Her Political Thought* (New York: Cambridge University Press, 1992); and Elisabeth Young-Bruehl, *Hannah Arendt: For Love of the World* (New Haven, CT: Yale University Press, 1982). Also see Richard J. Bernstein, *The Abuse of Evil: The Corruption of Politics and Religion Since 9/11* (Malden, MA: Polity, 2005), 71–81.
84. Canovan, *Hannah Arendt*, 7.
85. Arendt, *The Human Condition*. Also see Hannah Arendt, "Thinking and Moral Considerations," *Social Research* 38, no. 3 (Autumn 1971).
86. For instance: "If there is any fixed star in our constitutional constellation, it is that no official, high or petty, can prescribe what shall be orthodox in politics, nationalism,

religion, or other matters of opinion or force citizens to confess by word or act their faith therein." Jackson, Robert, J., in *West Virginia State Board of Education v. Barnette*, 319 U.S. 624, 642 (1943).

87. Arendt, *The Human Condition*, 222. Referring to Calvin's metaphor of each human as an actor on a stage, author Marilynne Robinson has the Reverend John Ames, the narrator in her novel, *Gilead*, observe: "That metaphor has always interested me, because it makes us *artists of our behavior*, and the reaction of God to us might be thought of as aesthetic rather than morally judgmental in the ordinary sense." Later on, referring to humans' inclination to worry over/think about insoluble conundrums (such as predestination), Reverend Ames's friend Robert Boughton remarks: "To conclude is not in the nature of [that] enterprise." Marilynne Robinson, *Gilead* (New York: Picador, 2004), 124 (italics added), 152.

88. Bernstein, *Violence*, vi. Also see Hannah Arendt, *Thinking Without A Banister: Essays in Understanding, 1953–1973*, ed. Jerome Kohn (New York: Schocket Books, 2018); and Tracy B. Strong, *Politics Without Vision: Thinking Without a Banister in the Twentieth Century* (Chicago: University of Chicago Press, 2012).

89. See Bunker, *Critiquing Free Speech*, 2–8.

90. Gardeners cultivate nature, bringing forth the fruits of their labor. One might contemplate the significance of the verbs "to cultivate" and "to culture" in the context of free speech theory.

91. Homer's clever Penelope fended off the many admirers pursuing her during her husband Odysseus' twenty-year absence to fight the Trojan War, with the ruse that she would chose to marry one suitor only when she had completed weaving a burial shroud for Odysseus' elderly father. Never intending to complete her work, every night Penelope undid the weaving she had made the previous day. In the context of free speech theory, one might contemplate Penelope's twin acts of creating something new, only to undo that which she had just brought into being. See Hannah Arendt, *The Life of The Mind: Thinking* (New York: Harcourt Brace Jovanovich, 1977), 88. Arendt's conception of free speech as ceaseless conversing, abjuring conclusive absolutes, aligns her with a key aspect of pragmatist thought, specifically fallibilism that embraces practice over certainty.

92. Compare Jürgen Habermas and Thomas McCarthy, "Hannah Arendt's Communications Concept of Power," *Social Research* 44, no. 1 (Spring 1977).

93. In making this argument, Arendt is following Aristotle: "... man is by nature a social and political being." Aristotle, *Nicomachean Ethics*, trans. Martin Ostwald (Indianapolis: Bobbs-Merrill, 1962), 15; and "... man is by nature an animal intended to live in a polis. He who is without a polis ... is either a poor sort of being, or a being higher than man . . ." Aristotle, *The Politics of Aristotle*, trans. Ernest Barker (New York: Oxford University Press, 1958), 5.

94. Aristotle, *The Politics of Aristotle*, 5–6.

95. Arendt, "The Crisis in the Culture," 222.

96. Ibid.

97. Compare Linda Greenhouse: "[T]he opposite of objectivity isn't partisanship, or needn't be. Rather, it is judgment, the hard work of sorting out the false claims from the true and discarding or at least labeling the false." Linda Greenhouse, *Just a Journalist: On the Press, Life, and the Spaces Between* (Cambridge, MA: Harvard University Press, 2017), 62–63.

98. Arendt, "The Crisis in the Culture," 222.
99. Ibid.
100. Arendt's reading is not uncontroversial. See, for instance, Richard J. Bernstein's essay, "Judging—The Actor and the Spectator," in *Philosophical Profiles: Essays in A Pragmatic Mode* (Philadelphia: University of Pennsylvania Press, 1986).
101. Arendt, "The Crisis in Culture," 222.
102. Ibid.
103. Ibid., 223.
104. Ibid., 222–23.
105. See Hannah Arendt, *On Revolution* (New York: Viking Press, 1963). Preeminent Arendt scholar, Margaret Canovan, observes: "Arendt's version of republicanism is significantly different from any of the models she inherited: she was, for example much less interested than most of her predecessors both in military prowess and in the details of institutions, and *much more interested in free discussion*." Canovan, *Hannah Arendt*, 202–3 (italics added) (also see chapter 6 generally). Compare Jennifer Ring, *The Political Consequences of Thinking: Gender and Judaism in the Work of Hannah Arendt* (Albany: State University of New York Press, 1997), chap. 9.
106. Discussing her latest novel, *Unsheltered*, on NPR's Weekend Edition Sunday. "Author Interviews: 'Unsheltered' Tackles the Unhealed Divisions in America," NPR, October 14, 2018, accessed May 29, 2019, https://www.npr.org/2018/10/14/657238918/unsheltered-tackles-the-unhealed-divisions-in-america.
107. Arendt, "The Crisis in Culture," 220–21.
108. See Danna Bell, "'A Republic, If You Can Keep It," Library of Congress, September 8, 2016, accessed May 29, 2019, https://blogs.loc.gov/teachers/2016/09/a-republic-if-you-can-keep-it/. Jonathan Haidt suggests that an antidote to tribalism (one way to defuse disgust) is to "reach out to someone and say you want to talk." See Greene and Hunt, "The Other Side Isn't Your Enemy."

Bibliography

Alexander, Larry. *Is There a Right of Freedom of Expression?* New York: Cambridge University Press, 2005.

Arendt, Hannah. "The Crisis in Culture: Its Social and Its Political Significance." In *Between Past and Future: Eight Exercises in Political Thought*, 194–222. 1961. Reprint, New York: Penguin, 2006.

———. *The Human Condition: A Study of the Central Dilemmas Facing Modern Man.* Chicago: University of Chicago Press, 1959.

———. *The Life of the Mind: Thinking.* New York: Harcourt Brace Jovanovich, 1977.

———. *On Revolution.* New York: Viking Press, 1963.

———. "Thinking and Moral Considerations." *Social Research* 38, no. 3 (Autumn 1971): 417–46.

———. *Thinking Without A Banister: Essays in Understanding, 1953–1973.* Edited by Jerome Kohn. New York: Schocket Books, 2018.

Aristotle. *Nicomachean Ethics*. Translated by Martin Ostwald. Indianapolis: Bobbs-Merrill, 1962.

———. *The Politics of Aristotle*. Translated by Ernest Barker. New York: Oxford University Press, 1958.

Bernstein, Richard J. *The Abuse of Evil: The Corruption of Politics and Religion Since 9/11*. Malden, MA: Polity, 2005.

———. "Hannah Arendt on Violence and Power." In *Violence: Thinking Without Banisters*, 78–104. Malden, MA: Polity, 2013.

———. "Judging—The Actor and the Spectator." In *Philosophical Profiles: Essays in A Pragmatic Mode*, 221–37. Philadelphia: University of Pennsylvania Press, 1986.

Bunker, Matthew D. *Critiquing Free Speech: First Amendment Theory and the Challenge of Interdisciplinarity*. Mahwah, NJ: Lawrence Erlbaum, 2001.

Canovan, Margaret. *Hannah Arendt: A Reinterpretation of Her Political Thought*. New York: Cambridge University Press, 1992.

Chang, Emily. *Brotopia: Breaking Up the Boy's Club of Silicon Valley*. New York: Portfolio, 2018.

Chua, Amy. *Political Tribes: Group Instinct and the Fate of Nations*. New York: Penguin Press, 2018.

Cullen, Dave. *Parkland: Birth of a Movement*. New York: Harper, 2019.

Fish, Stanley. *There Is No Such Thing as Free Speech: And It's a Good Thing, Too*. New York: Oxford University Press, 1994.

Graber, Mark A. *A New Introduction to American Constitutionalism*. New York: Oxford University Press, 2013.

Gramsci, Antonio. *Selections from the Prison Notebooks*. Edited by Quintin Hoare. Translated by Geoffrey Nowell Smith. New York: International Publishers, 1971.

Greenhouse, Linda. *Just a Journalist: On the Press, Life, and the Spaces Between*. Cambridge, MA: Harvard University Press, 2017.

Habermas, Jürgen, and Thomas McCarthy. "Hannah Arendt's Communications Concept of Power." *Social Research* 44, no. 1 (Spring 1977): 3–24.

Haidt, Jonathan. *The Righteous Mind: Why Good People Are Divided By Politics and Religion*. New York: Pantheon, 2012.

Hobbes, Thomas. *De Cive (The Citizen): Philosophical Rudiments Concerning Government and Society*. Edited by Sterling P. Lamprecht. New York: Appleton-Century-Crofts, 1949.

———. *Leviathan: Or the Matter, Forme and Power of a Commonwealth Ecclesiasticall and Civil*. Edited by Michael Oakeshott. New York: Collier Books, 1962.

Kavanagh, Jennifer, and Michael D. Rich. *Truth Decay: An Initial Exploration of the Diminishing Role of Facts and Analysis in American Public Life*. Santa Monica, CA: Rand Corporation, 2018.

Pollan, Michael. *How to Change Your Mind: What the New Science of Psychedelics Teaches Us About Consciousness, Dying, Addiction, Depression, and Transcendence*. New York: Penguin Press, 2018.

Putnam, Robert D. *Bowling Alone: The Collapse and Revival of American Community.* New York: Simon and Schuster, 2000.

Ring, Jennifer. *The Political Consequences of Thinking: Gender and Judaism in the Work of Hannah Arendt.* Albany: State University of New York Press, 1997.

Robinson, Marilynne. *Gilead.* New York: Picador, 2004.

Ross, Alex. *The Rest Is Noise: Listening to The twentieth Century.* New York: Picador, 2007.

Sasse, Ben. *Them: Why We Hate Each Other—and How to Heal.* New York: St. Martin's Press, 2018.

Slater, Philip. *The Pursuit of Loneliness: American Culture at the Breaking Point.* Boston: Beacon, 1970.

Strong, Tracy B. *Politics Without Vision: Thinking Without a Banister in the Twentieth Century.* Chicago: University of Chicago Press, 2012.

Tushnet, Mark V. *Out of Range: Why the Constitution Can't End the Battle Over Guns.* New York: Oxford University Press, 2007.

von Clausewitz, Carl. *On War.* Translated and edited by Michael Howard and Peter Paret. Princeton, NJ: Princeton University Press, 1976.

Winkler, Adam. *Gun Fight: The Battle Over the Right to Bear Arms in America.* New York: W.W. Norton, 2011.

Woodard, Colin. *American Nations: A History of the Eleven Rival Regional Cultures of North America.* New York: Viking, 2011.

Young-Bruehl, Elisabeth. *Hannah Arendt: For Love of the World.* New Haven, CT: Yale University Press, 1982.

2. Freedoms of Speech in the Multiversity

Mark A. Graber

Free speech fights are taking place at institutions of higher learning across the United States and the world.[1] Professors are disciplined for wearing blackface at parties.[2] Students are disciplined for making racist or sexist remarks. Oxford University students are filing a petition asking the university to prohibit Professor John Finnis, a well-known legal theorist, from teaching because of his views on homosexuality.[3] Controversial speakers are disinvited or chased from college campuses.[4] Prominent thinkers proclaim, "Universities that should stand as bastions of open dialogue and free speech have too often become sites of intolerance and intimidation."[5]

These incidents receive substantial journalistic, political, and scholarly attention. Prominent media cover free speech fights on campus. Major political figures weigh in. The President tweets. Leading scholars write important books and articles about the subject. Notable authors include the Chancellor of the University of California, Irvine and the dean of the law school at the University of California, Berkeley,[6] the dean of Yale Law School,[7] one of the most distinguished literary theorists at the turn of the twenty-first century,[8] and the Cromwell Professor of Politics at Princeton University.[9]

This chapter explores four different approaches to regulating speech on campus: uninhibited speech, disciplined speech, weak inclusive speech, and strong inclusive speech. Uninhibited and disciplined speech advocates begin from the premise that universities are committed to "the production and dissemination of ideas."[10] Proponents of uninhibited speech think that mission is best achieved by combining academic freedom in the classroom and library with encouraging all forms of expression (within the bounds of the First Amendment) throughout the rest of the campus. Proponents of disciplined speech think that mission is best achieved by combining academic freedom in the classroom and library with modified disciplinary standards throughout the rest of the campus. Proponents of uninhibited and disciplined speech recognize that universities are really "multiversities," institutions charged with many missions including but not limited to the production and dissemination of knowledge. They nevertheless believe that either these other missions do not require altering contemporary notions of free speech and academic freedom, or, if intractable conflicts exist, the knowledge mission of the multiversity predominates.

Weak and strong inclusive speech advocates insist that the multiversity mission to include historically disadvantaged groups as equal members of the campus community promotes the university mission to produce and disseminate knowledge only when contemporary notions of free speech or academic freedom are adjusted. Proponents of weak inclusive speech think the knowledge and inclusiveness missions of multiversities are best harmonized by combining contemporary understandings of academic freedom in the classroom and library with adjustments to contemporary understandings of free speech that permit institutions of higher learning to impose civility and quality controls on racist, sexist, and related invective in other campus settings. Proponents of strong inclusive speech think the knowledge and inclusiveness missions of the multiversity are best harmonized by combining adjustments to contemporary understandings of academic freedom in the classroom and library that limit how professors may research and teach race, gender, and related subjects with adjustments to contemporary understandings of free speech that permit institutions of higher learning to impose civility and quality controls on racist, sexist, and related invective in other campus settings.

The University

Speech policies on campus differ from speech policies in other settings because institutions of higher learning have different missions than other institutions. The university mission to "produce and disseminate knowledge" justifies campus decisions to regulate some speech that other institutions routinely tolerate and campus decisions to tolerate some speech that other institutions routinely regulate. This mission to produce and disseminate knowledge guides public universities that must respect constitutional free speech protections and private universities that are constitutionally free to implement whatever free speech policies they believe appropriate.[11] For example, both the University of Maryland, Baltimore, a public institution, and Johns Hopkins University, a private institution, share a common commitment to academic freedom that explains why both protect some speech in the classroom and library that is not protected by other non-academic public and private institutions, while regulating other speech in the classroom and library that if uttered in a public park would be protected by the First Amendment.

The university commitment to producing and disseminating knowledge provides foundations for two distinctive approaches to speech policies on campus. Some commentators maintain the university mission justifies "uninhibited speech" policies. Universities foster uninhibited speech by designating numerous public spaces on campus as open public fora where persons are free to make any constitutionally protected assertion, using campus funds to subsidize open public fora, and refraining from regulating the private speech of campus employees and students. Speech outside the classroom and library that would be protected in a public park is also protected on campus, even when that speech does not meet appropriate disciplinary standards. Other commentators maintain that the university mission justifies "disciplined speech" policies. Universities foster disciplined speech by extending in modified form the quality and civility controls that uncontroversially regulate free speech in the classroom and scholarship to all or most public spaces on campus, to all uses of campus funds and, perhaps, to the private speech of campus employees and students. Speech that meets relaxed quality and civility standards is protected. Speech that falls short of those standards may not be.

Neither uninhibited speech nor disciplinary speech is identical to free speech, at least the free speech mandated by the Constitution of the United States as interpreted by the contemporary Supreme Court of the United States. Proponents of uninhibited speech insist universities achieve their mission by permitting speech that other public and private institutions may constitutionally regulate. Many campus spaces outside the classroom and library are open public fora. Subsidized student organizations may bring even the most outrageous speakers to campus. None of these policies is mandated by the First Amendment. Proponents of disciplined speech insist that universities serve their mission by regulating speech that in other settings is protected by First Amendment principles. Faculty whose publications do not meet high quality standards do not receive tenure. Racist, sexist, and related invective that is permitted on the town green may be prohibited in the campus dormitory.

One size does not fit all at any university or in any discussion of free speech on campus. Proponents of disciplined speech and proponents of uninhibited speech agree that disciplinary standards govern the classroom and scholarship. Students who as part of a class assignment write editorials in the college newspaper that include negligent falsehoods about public officials fail Journalism 101, even though they may not be sued for libel.[12] No proponent of disciplined speech claims that speech in the dorm room must meet the standards for speech in the classroom. Assertions made in the early morning at campus parties need not exhibit the same quality and civility necessary to pass a PhD examination.

The main dispute between proponents of disciplined speech and proponents of uninhibited speech on campus is over whether the core First Amendment principle that government officials cannot normally be trusted to distinguish between good and bad ideas has any application in a university setting. All prominent parties to disputes over campus speech policies agree that disciplinary experts can distinguish between good and bad scholarship and good and bad classroom performance. Tenured chemistry professors can tell the difference between science and pseudo-science, as well as the difference between an excellent sophomore paper and a failing sophomore paper. For this reason, a consensus exists that disciplinary standards rather than free speech principles govern research and the classroom. Proponents of disciplined speech insist that faculty have the same capacity to distinguish between good and bad speech outside the classroom as they do inside the classroom. Students may in principle be forbidden from holding signs on the campus green declaring "Women Enjoy Rape" because that assertion does not meet even the most relaxed standard for truth and civility. Proponents of uninhibited speech limit expertise to the classroom and scholarship. Campus authorities should leave even the most offensive speech unregulated partly because, outside specific sites for disciplinary expertise, faculty and university administrators have no better capacity to distinguish between good and bad speech than any other government official.

Academic Freedom

Academic freedom provides the foundation for discussions on free speech at universities. The "1940 Statement of Principles on Academic Freedom and Tenure" issued by the American Association of University Professors (AAUP) declares: "Teachers are entitled to full freedom in research and in the publication of the results," and to "freedom in the classroom in discussing their subject."[13] This "full freedom" is freedom only within certain disciplinary standards. The AAUP's "1915 Statement of Principles on Academic Freedom and Tenure" restricts academic freedom to "those who carry on their work in the temper of the scientific inquirer." Academic freedom is limited to "conclusions gained by the scholar's method and held in a scholar's spirit, that is to say, they must be the fruits of competent and patient and sincere inquiry, and they should be set forth with dignity, courtesy, and temperateness of language."[14] Political scientists cannot be sanctioned when acting within the scope of their university duties for speaking and teaching in ways that meet the standards of the political science discipline. Chemists cannot be sanctioned when acting within the scope of their university duties for speaking and teaching in ways that meet the standards of the chemistry discipline.

Academic freedom simultaneously expands and narrows the free speech protections enjoyed by members of the campus community. The university can produce and disseminate knowledge only if professors and students are free to teach and research according to disciplinary rather than political standards and when they adhere to those disciplinary standards when teaching and researching. This commitment to disciplinary standards in some circumstances compels universities to grant faculty more freedom than other public employees. Assistant district attorneys ordered to write a legal brief defending the constitutionality of capital punishment must express those sentiments, regardless of their beliefs about the death penalty.[15] Law school deans may not require assistant professors to write pro-death penalty articles or even articles that discuss capital punishment. Disciplinary standards in other circumstances restrict the speech of campus citizens. Academic freedom does not protect anyone whose speech fails to meet the quality and civility standards mandated by the relevant discipline.[16] Biologists who wish to opine on monetary policy may enjoy First Amendment rights when speaking privately but may be required to speak only on biology when acting within the scope of their university duties. Students are routinely sanctioned for examination answers that demonstrate they have neither mastered nor likely done the assigned reading. Professors are free to curse the government in public parks, but not in class.

Institutions of higher learning committed to academic freedom routinely violate every fundamental principle of contemporary free speech law.

- "Under the First Amendment, there is no such thing as a false idea."[17] Universities engage in quality control. This is called grading and tenure.
- First Amendment speech is "uninhibited, robust, and wide-open, and that … may well include vehement, caustic, and sometimes unpleasantly sharp attacks."[18] Universities engage in civility control. Students who insult other students in History 101 are asked to leave the class.
- First Amendment speech that does not substantially promote the justifications of a system of free expression is often protected in order to increase speech that does promote the justifications of a system of free speech. Chilling effects exist throughout the university. Paper requirements discourage ambivalent students from taking advanced seminars. Tenure requirements are designed to ensure that only the most highly motivated scholars seek academic employment.

The principles underlying academic freedom violate the free speech adage that "government censorship and control of ideas has always led to disaster."[19] Universities distinguish good research and writing from bad when they hire professors, tenure professors, grade students, and give out academic honors. Faculty whose scholarship is not considered sufficiently rigorous by university authorities are not hired or promoted. Students who claim that Abraham Lincoln was the president of Columbia or insist that Congress can repeal the law of gravity do not graduate. The values that justify uninhibited speech in a public park have no cache in Philosophy 209. A university barred from distinguishing good speech from bad would not be a university, but some other institution.

The practice of academic freedom in scholarship and in the classroom is constrained by some version of the Marquess of Queensberry rules, rules originally designed to civilize boxing. Professional norms consist of manners as well as footnotes. Scholarly papers refrain from language that is "uninhibited, robust and wide-open." Students in classroom settings may not make "vehement, caustic, and sometimes unpleasantly sharp attacks" on each other. Professors are just as bound by civility norms. Professional standards no more permit a professor to call a student an "idiot" than they permit students to call each other "idiots." "Professors who bully, abuse, degrade, or demean their students risk being found professionally incompetent in achieving their university's mission of education," Robert Post states, even though government could not regulate such behaviors in a public park.[20]

Academic speech policies have chilling effects. Policies that result in less speech are justified when they produce better speech. Universities discourage uninhibited speech in the classroom and in research because disciplinary health is measured by quality rather than quantity. Students and faculty are evaluated by the value of their scholarship, commentary, and written work, not by how often they speak in class or publish in suspect journals. Blunt criticism that leads less talented graduate students to seek some less academic line of work is an academic good, even if that means fewer dissertations are written. First Amendment standards protect some negligent falsehoods in order to encourage speech by the risk adverse.[21] Academic standards sanction negligent falsehoods rigorously in order to discourage shoddy scholarship.

The disciplinary standards that disciplinary experts enforce are neither fixed nor uncontroversial. That homosexuality is a mental illness was once unquestioned wisdom among psychiatrists. That homosexuality is not a mental illness is now unquestioned wisdom in that discipline. Political scientists engage in intense disciplinary wars over the relative merits of qualitative and quantitative research, as well as over the reliability of particular methods for doing qualitative and qualitative research. The crucial point underlying academic freedom is that judgments about disciplinary standards must be made by disciplinary experts, even as who counts as a disciplinary expert is contested.[22] As Stanley Fish points out, "disciplinary reasons are the reasons that count when a disciplinary norm is being challenged."[23]

Whether the principles of academic freedom cover students as well as professors is controversial, although the weight of both the authorities and argument favors encompassing all campus personnel engaged in disciplinary activities. The AAUP's *Joint Statement of the Rights and Freedoms of Students* declares that professors must "encourage free discussion, inquiry, and expression, [and evaluate students] solely on an academic basis, not on opinions or conduct in matters unrelated to academic standards."[24] Members of a chemistry department may neither refuse to promote a faculty member nor flunk a student in Chemistry 101 because they belong to the Communist Party or a white supremacist group. Some scholars restrict academic freedom to professors. J. Peter Byrne writes: "The term 'academic freedom' should be reserved for those rights necessary for the preservation of the unique functions of the university, particularly the goals of disinterested scholarship and teaching." In his view, "no recognized student rights of free speech are properly part of constitutional academic freedom, because none of them has anything to do with scholarship or systematic learning."[25] This seems mistaken. Students have the same right to be judged by disciplinary standards as their professors, even if the standards for Sociology 302 are far less demanding than the standards for becoming a tenured professor of sociology.

Uninhibited Speech

Proponents of uninhibited speech on campus limit the principles and practices of academic freedom to the classroom and research. Erwin Chemerinsky and Howard Gillman maintain that institutions of higher learning must balance disciplined and more uninhibited speech policies. They "think of campuses as having two different zones of free expression: a *professional zone*, which protects the expression of ideas but imposes an obligation of responsible discourse and responsible conduct in formal educational and scholarly settings; and a larger *free speech zone*, which exists outside of scholarly and administrative settings."[26] Quality and civility controls structure the professional zone. The "only restrictions" in the larger free speech zone are "those of society at large."[27] Leading proponents of uninhibited speech on campus go beyond the First Amendment to promote expression. They would have the university create open spaces for speech where the First Amendment might permit restriction,[28] and permit subsidized student groups to use university funds to invite the speakers of their choice when the First Amendment might permit conditions on sponsorship.[29]

Proponents of these larger free speech zones insist that history, and history's leading proponents of free speech, teach that intellectual progress is best made when speech is unregulated. Chemerinsky and Gillman channel John Milton when asserting, "beliefs should be tested by free-thinking human beings, and those free-thinking people would decide for themselves what [is] true after engaging in debate and experimentation."[30] Keith Whittington channels Oliver Wendell Holmes Jr. and John Stuart Mill when maintaining, "the university is precisely the type of environment where a 'free trade of ideas' is encouraged and ideas are placed in 'open and free competition.'"[31] "If truth and knowledge are to be pursued," Sigal R. Ben-Porath agrees, "speech and other modes of expression must be protected to the broadest extent possible."[32]

Uninhibited speech outside the classroom and library promotes the knowledge mission of universities. Other public institutions may justify restricting speech on public property, speech with the use of government funds, and speech by government employees because they have different missions. The military is concerned with defending the country, a mission that requires limiting speech on military property and the speech of military personnel.[33] Universities have no such mission that conflicts with free speech. Whittington declares, "the value of free speech is closely associated with the core commitments of the university itself."[34] "[T]he truth-seeking mission of universities," in his view, "dovetails with the truth-seeking function of free speech."[35] Chemerinsky and Gillman urge "campuses to more clearly identify liberty of thought, unfettered exchange, and robust debate as foundational values within higher education."[36]

Quality controls on campuses committed to uninhibited speech are limited to the classroom and research. The "free speech zones" Chemerinsky and Gillman champion "explicitly reject ... professional educational standards in order to allow a more raucous space of expression, governed only by the principles of the First Amendment."[37] Universities, Whittington asserts, "must foster an environment in which no beliefs are sacred, no ideas are safe from scrutiny, no opinions are immune from criticism."[38] Students must learn how to "fac[e] up to and judiciously engag[e] difficult ideas."[39]

Manners outside the classroom are subject to exhortation rather than regulation. Everyone agrees that institutions of higher learning should "emphasize ... civility, respect, and acceptance for all members of the community."[40] Those who champion uninhibited speech nevertheless vigorously insist that universities should not have rules prohibiting racist, sexist or related invective that would enjoy constitutional protection off-campus. Whittington asserts, "[d]issenters need the freedom to grab the attention of the public, to dramatize their concerns, and to convey their message in a way that makes sense and is accessible to both themselves and their intended audience."[41] Ben-Porath states, "[t]o protect inclusive free speech, much more room should be made for messy, inappropriate, challenging, and sometimes uncivil expression."[42] She fears civility "requires too much in that it further marginalizes those whose anger, frustration, and other emotions are deemed uncivil and thus unacceptable."[43]

Universities committed to uninhibited speech treat many campus spaces outside the classroom and library as public fora, subsidize additional public fora, and reject disciplined speech regulations outside of the classroom and professional research settings. Persons on the green and in the dorm may speak freely as long as they do not actually threaten others.[44] Student groups may spend campus funds as they please, even on speakers who have contempt for disciplinary standards,[45] provided, perhaps, that the student group is open to all university members.[46] Faculty, students, and other campus members are not disciplined for off-campus speech that does not meet disciplined speech standards.[47]

Uninhibited speech is not unlimited speech. Chemerinsky, Gillman, Whittington, and Ben-Porath approve efforts to ban speech on campus that the First Amendment permits to be banned off-campus. The university setting does not immunize persons who threaten, blackmail, or harass their classmates.[48] Campus protestors may no more disrupt university activities than they may interfere with any other lawful actions. Proponents of uninhibited speech scorn protests that silence speech. Whittington states, "If members of the audience can shout down a speaker, destroy a newspaper, or vandalize a sign, then the free exchange of ideas is at an end just as surely as it would be if government officials had arrested the speaker or confiscated the sign."[49] Universities may limit some public fora to members of the university community, provided they do not discriminate on viewpoints.[50] The Democratic Party may be banned from holding a rally in a university classroom, but not the Young Campus Republicans if the Young Campus Democrats have access to that site.

Disciplined Speech

Proponents of disciplined speech extend (in modified form) the principles of academic freedom to speech on campus, speech with university funds, and the speech of university employees. Campus spaces outside the classroom and library may be subject to civility and quality controls. Student groups may invite only outside speakers who meet certain disciplinary standards. University employees may be sanctioned for speech that does not meet disciplinary standards. The "may" in each sentence is important. Universities committed to disciplined speech have pragmatic reasons for not regulating speech that they believe does not contribute to the production and dissemination of ideas. Campus officials might decide that racist invective is best met by counter speech that demonstrates appropriate disciplinary standards rather than sanctions. They are just as free to prohibit racist invective because such language does not meet the quality and civility standards that proponents of disciplined speech deem appropriate for student speech outside the classroom.

The central principle underlying disciplined speech policies is that universities charged with distinguishing good speech from bad in the classroom should be trusted with distinguishing good speech from bad on the green and in the dorm room. Standards for assertions made in the classroom differ from appropriate standards for regulating assertions made on the green or in the dorm room, just as the standards for publishing in a peer review classics journal differ from the standards for passing Classics 106. Nevertheless, proponents of disciplined speech think the disciplinary experts who routinely calibrate their standards to account for differences between peer-reviewed journals and introductory courses are more than capable of calibrating their standards to account for differences between an introductory course and a political argument in the campus dining room.

Proponents of disciplined speech insist that, "universities are not Hyde Parks"[51] where the only limits on accuracy and rudeness are those of the Constitution. Post, the leading champion of disciplined speech, insists, "[w]hatever happens under the aegis of a university must be justified by reference to the university's twin missions of research and education."[52] These missions do not necessarily compel regulation. Allowing students to invite any speaker they wish to hear might "empower students to pursue research interests different from those offered by the faculty," "create a diverse and heterogeneous campus climate in which students can learn the democratic skills necessary to negotiate a public sphere filled with alien and cacophonous voices" or "educate students in practices of citizenship by encouraging a wide variety of student groups to invite outside speakers to recreate within the campus a marketplace of ideas."[53] Nevertheless, the university is as free to make the campus off-limits to speakers whose content fails to meet minimal disciplinary standards or who prefer insult to argument. Giving university sanction to the incompetent, the fraudulent, and the demagogue risks giving the false impression that these characters are engaged in the production and dissemination of knowledge.

Post limits disciplined speech to the campus. Speech on campus is regulated consistently with the university's "twin missions of education and research." Speech off campus by members of the campus community is subject only to the limits of the First Amendment. "Freedom of extramural expression protects an astronomer who wishes to write in public about NAFTA, or a computer scientist who wishes to speak about the war in Iraq," he writes. "When faculty engage in such speech," Post continues, "they attempt to influence public opinion so as to make it responsive to their views. They do not speak as experts conveying knowledge, but as citizens participating in public debate."[54]

Theory and Practice

General agreement exists that universities often fail to distinguish good speech from bad speech outside and sometimes inside the classroom.[55] Universities have sanctioned or threatened to sanction speech that clearly meets disciplinary standards. Too many cases exist in which rules ostensibly designed to prevent racist, sexist, and other invective are applied to shut down disciplinary conversations about race, sex, and other contested matters. John Finnis's publication history demonstrates that his work meets the disciplinary standards of philosophy, even if he concludes in his peer-reviewed works that homosexuality is unnatural. Whether children should be prohibited from wearing Halloween costumes that are "culturally unaware or insensitive," a claim that generated an intense free speech controversy at Yale, is the subject of legitimate debate among experts on early childhood.[56]

Disciplinary standards may function better in the classroom than on the green and in the dorm room partly because universities charge different persons with implementing disciplinary standards in different locations. Faculty implement disciplinary standards in the classroom and related settings. Professors have the expertise in their respective disciplines necessary to determine whether assertions about race, sex, and related subjects are within the realm of legitimate disciplinary conversation or mere invective. When making such decisions, faculty are likely to treat the production and dissemination of knowledge as the primary function of the university and make regulatory decisions on that basis. University staff and students often implement disciplinary standards outside the classroom. Both lack the expertise in the respective disciplines necessary to distinguish good, albeit controversial, disciplinary speech from bad invective. Both may be far more inclined than many, though hardly all, faculty members to make regulatory decisions that promote such values as inclusiveness, even when doing so is inconsistent with contemporary notions of free speech and academic freedom. Faculty, after all, are likely to perceive broad notions of free speech and academic freedom as promoting the knowledge mission of the university. The head of the campus diversity center may be more likely to perceive strong inclusiveness policies as better promoting that knowledge mission or as promoting an equally important institutional mission.

The line between uninhibited speech and disciplined speech at universities might better be drawn by determining who implements regulations rather than on where regulation occurs. Disciplined speech is appropriate when and only when disciplinary experts committed to the production and dissemination of knowledge are responsible for implementing regulations. Uninhibited speech is appropriate when the regulators have limited expertise in disciplinary standards, may not be as strongly committed to broad notions of free speech and academic freedom as faculty, or committed to missions other than the production or dissemination of knowledge. The resulting line is likely to be very similar to that proposed by most proponents of uninhibited speech, with disciplined speech being the rule in the classroom and uninhibited speech being the rule on the green and in the dorm room. Proponents of uninhibited speech think the green and dorm room are not appropriate sites for disciplined speech standards. Proponents of disciplined speech might justify the same policy on the ground that, given the decline of faculty governance in institutions of higher learning,[57] the persons the contemporary university charges with the daily responsibility for regulating the green and the dorm room are unlikely to implement disciplined free speech standards.

Institutions of higher learning might also consider an uninhibited/disciplined speech hybrid. On this model, universities may regulate speech outside the classroom or library as long as those regulations are not prohibitions. Administrators may issue non-binding guidelines detailing best practices for student speech on the campus green and the dorm. Student groups might be required to have faculty advisors, who must be consulted whenever those organizations invite outside speakers, even if the group is free to disregard the advice. Academic units on campus might provide additional funds in the form of co-sponsorship when student organizations invite speakers who meet that unit's quality and civility standards. Such policies are consistent with the claim that universities can distinguish good speech from bad outside the classroom and library. They are also consistent with claims that speech remain uninhibited as long as students remain free to decide for themselves whether to meet suggested quality and civility standards.

The Multiversity

Contemporary institutions of higher learning serve multiple functions. Clark Kerr, the former president of the University of California, Berkeley, who coined or popularized the term "multiversity," observes that

> The modern university [is] a 'pluralistic' institution—pluralistic in several senses: in having several purposes, not one; in having several centers of power, not one; in serving several clienteles, not one. It worship[s] no single God; it constitute[s] no single unified community; it ha[s] no discretely defined set of customers. It [is] marked by many visions of the Good, the True, and the Beautiful, and by many roads to achieve these visions; by power conflicts; by service to many markets and concern for many publics.[58]

Multiversities are often the cultural center, the leading employer and the largest landowner in a region. Students attend to learn the classics, to gain the skills necessary for employment, and for romantic opportunities. Campus properties range from classrooms and high-tech laboratories to food courts and softball fields. The only force that holds multiversities together, Kerr quipped, is "a common grievance over parking."[59]

Multiversities are charged with numerous missions that sometimes conflict. The softball field competes with the classroom for student attention because the multiversity must combine programs that educate young people with programs that entertain them. If *uni*versities are guided by a unifying purpose, *multi*versities struggle to harmonize, balance, and prioritize different imperatives. Kerr points out, "[t]he multiversity has many 'publics' with many interests; and by the very nature of the multiversity many of those interests are quite legitimate."[60] Multiversities develop extensive externship programs to make students more employable, even when faculty doubt whether those experiences enrich the learning environment.

The contemporary multiversity is different in degree rather than in kind from past institutions of higher learning. Universities have always been charged with multiple missions and employed specialized non-academic staff to carry out those missions. What distinguishes the contemporary multiversity is the diversity of institutional missions and a substantially increased number of non-academic staff with such specialized functions as job placement and swimming pool monitor. The number of career counselors has increased manifold at institutions of higher learning across the United States. Most have well-staffed diversity offices that did not exist 60 years ago.

The rise of non-academic staff and programs has consequences for the university knowledge mission. Many activities at most multiversities do not directly produce or disseminate knowledge. The varsity tennis team may increase alumni support in ways that facilitate the production and dissemination of knowledge, but the team trainer does not usually teach academic classes or write scholarly articles. Different members of the campus community are likely to have different beliefs about what promotes the knowledge mission of the multiversity and different beliefs about how to harmonize, balance, and prioritize that commitment in light of the other multiversity missions they carry out on a daily basis. Persons in the campus financial office are more likely to think large grants are particularly vital to the knowledge mission of the multiversity than assistant professors of English, who rarely obtain such largess. The football coach, hypothetically, might think team members should focus more on a winning record than on final examinations.

Controversies over free speech at a multiversity have a different structure than controversies over free speech at a university. Proponents of uninhibited and disciplined speech agree that the production and dissemination of knowledge is the exclusive or primary function of a university, while disputing the regulatory policies that best achieve that mission. Proponents of inclusive speech join the debate on multiversity campuses. They claim that institutions of higher learning must harmonize or balance the speech policies that best produce and disseminate knowledge with the speech policies that best treat all members of the campus community, members of historically disadvantaged groups in particular, with equal respect and dignity.

Inclusiveness

Multiversity commitments to inclusiveness present tougher challenges to free speech on campuses than the other missions the public charges contemporary institutions of higher learning with performing. Many faculty, if given the power, would do away with such accoutrements of the multiversity as fraternities, the football coach, and education specialists who believe that faculty time is far better spent providing the administration with detailed reports on learning outcomes than doing basic research.[61] Most faculty nevertheless support the work of the campus diversity center, even as many wish the staff had more sensitivity to free speech issues. Institutional commitments to inclusiveness must be harmonized or balanced rather than subordinated to institutional commitments to the production and dissemination of knowledge.

Contemporary institutions of higher learning are important sites for class mobility and overcoming past disadvantage. Multiversities provide opportunities for members of historically disadvantaged groups to improve their lot. Post-secondary education provides paths for the grandchildren of slaves and children of immigrants to rise to the middle class and beyond. "While maintaining its commitment to research and inquiry," Ben-Porath points out, "the university has grown from an institution that serves a small segment of the population deemed eligible to become religious, political, economic, and thought leaders to one that serves as an engine for social mobility and equal opportunity."[62] Substantial controversies exist over the relevant historically disadvantaged groups and the appropriate methods for improving their lot, but few doubt the importance of the commitment to inclusiveness.

The knowledge and inclusiveness missions of the multiversity may cohere without any need to adjust contemporary notions of free speech or academic freedom. A more diverse or more pluralistic campus is a campus on which a greater number of ideas are debated and a greater number of perspectives are brought to bear on the ideas being debated. Whittington speaks of "a false choice between inclusivity and free inquiry."[63] He and other proponents of uninhibited speech champion open public fora in which all members of the campus community are permitted to debate the points they feel ought to be debated in the way they believe appropriate for that debate.[64] Chemerinsky and Gillman discuss at length alternatives to quality and civility controls that they believe successfully promote inclusiveness without any threat to free speech principles.[65] University administrators may respond after controversial speakers attack members of historically disadvantaged groups or programs that benefit members of historically disadvantaged groups. Professors may correct rather than silence uninhibited speech in the classroom. Ben-Porath harmonizes free speech and inclusiveness when she declares, "[i]nclusive freedom demands that speech on campus be protected as broadly as possible while aiming to ensure that all members of the campus community are recognized—and know they are recognized—as members in good standing."[66] In her view, "[a] call for creating an inclusive environment in which all members are respected and where all voices can be heard should be framed and recognized as furthering rather than impeding the realization of a free and open campus."[67] Nevertheless, many proponents of inclusive and disciplinary speech insist on the priority of the knowledge mission of the multiversity should that mission clash with the inclusiveness mission. "Those who are welcomed to campus," Whittington writes, "must also understand what occurs there."[68]

Other proponents of inclusiveness question comfortable solutions to harmonizing the knowledge and inclusive missions of multiversities, as well as claims that contemporary notions of free speech and academic freedom should trump inclusiveness in cases of conflict. They would harmonize the knowledge and inclusiveness missions of the multiversity by adjusting either contemporary understandings of free speech or contemporary understandings of academic freedom. Critical race and feminist scholars challenge how Gillman, Chemerinsky, and others interpret the First Amendment. They claim that campus bans on racist, sexist, and related invective are consistent with maximum protection for free speech on campus because free speech principles do not justify protecting racist, sexist, and related invective inside the classroom, outside the classroom, and outside of institutions of higher learning. A largely underdeveloped line of thinking, though probably more important, calls on multiversities to modify principles of academic freedom when those principles trench too heavily on the inclusiveness mission of the contemporary multiversity. These claims rarely directly challenge the knowledge mission of the multiversity. Rather, proponents of weak and strong inclusive speech insist that universities will best produce and disseminate knowledge by abandoning inherited notions of constitutionally protected speech and implementing academic freedom in ways that ensure that all members of campus have an equal right and capacity to contribute to the academic project.

Inclusive Speech

Proponents of inclusive speech maintain that campuses may restrict speech that does not treat all members of the campus community as equals. President Michael Roth of Wesleyan University declares:

> The appeal to the free exchange of ideas, no matter what the cost to historically vulnerable groups, doesn't convince most of today's college students because many of them recognize that not all ideas make it to the marketplace and that, when all kinds of discourse are tolerated, certain groups tend to get hurt again and again—creating discriminatory hurdles for their members. Markets, including the ones for ideas, often work very well, but when they are unregulated, real pollution, real harm, occurs, all too often wounding people who historically have been abused by those with power and privilege.[69]

Arianna Shahvisi celebrates students who call for certain speech regulations that they believe will achieve "healthy, inclusive equitable workplaces."[70] Weaker versions of these justifications for campus speech regulations can be assimilated, with some tensions, into the frames of reference developed by proponents of uninhibited speech and proponents of disciplined speech. Stronger versions challenge the commitment to academic freedom underlying both uninhibited and disciplined speech.

The critical race and feminist scholars responsible for the initial burst of campus speech regulations insist that racist, sexist, and related invective is not protected by the Constitution.[71] Government officials and multiversity administrators, in their view, are constitutionally free to pass or impose content restrictions on speech that denies the equal citizenship of some members of the American or campus community. Richard Delgado claims that the interest of "personality and equal citizenship" entails "the right of all citizens to lead their lives free from attacks on their dignity and psychological integrity."[72] Catharine MacKinnon asserts that the First Amendment cannot protect advocacy of certain doctrines "if real equality is ever to be achieved."[73] "When equality is recognized as a constitutional value and mandate," she declares, "social inferiority cannot be imposed through any means, including expressive ones."[74] So called "campus hate speech codes" do not violate any rights or interfere with any institutional function either because no one has a right to utter racist, sexist, and related insults or because such speech does not make any contribution to any legitimate multiversity mission.[75]

Official decisions not to regulate hate speech on or off campus reinforce existing status hierarchies. Racist, sexist, and related invective adversely influence how persons of color, women, non-heterosexuals, and others see themselves and are seen by others. "[R]acist speech," Delgado claims, "is the means by which society constructs a stigma-picture of disfavored groups."[76] When bigoted messages flood the marketplace of ideas, the general populace typically does not hear the voices of those historically disadvantaged persons who are not dissuaded from speaking. Not only do "minority children" who "constantly hear racist messages ... come to question their competence, intelligence, and worth,"[77] but the "system of ideas and images" promoted by hate speech "constructs certain people so that they have little credibility in the eyes of listeners."[78] These biases create a dysfunctional marketplace of ideas. Mary Ellen Gale asserts, "the playing field is not level, but tilted to favor the status quo—in this case, racism and sexism."[79] Bans on hate speech "remove the tilt and level the field..."[80] Bans prohibit words, but not speech or at least what counts as constitutional speech. "Racial insults," Charles Lawrence asserts, "are undeserving of first amendment protection because the perpetrator's intention is not to discover truth or initiate dialogue, but to injure the victim."[81]

Critical theorists claim that officials who refuse to ban hate speech force persons of color and other members of historically disadvantaged groups to pay more than their fair share of the social price for free speech. Mari Matsuda regards "[t]he application of absolutist free speech principles to hate speech ... [as] a choice to burden one group with a disproportionate share of the costs of speech promotion."[82] "Tolerance of hate speech," she adds, "is a psychic tax imposed on those least able to pay."[83] Official toleration of hate speech aggravates the initial harm caused by such invective. Delgado charges that the "failure of the legal system to redress the harms of racism and racial insults conveys to all the lesson that egalitarianism is not a fundamental principle."[84] Matsuda speaks of "the pain of knowing that the government provides no remedy and offers no recognition of the dehumanizing experience that victims of hate propaganda are subjected to."[85] Progressives who defend the local bigot confirm perceptions that victims of hate speech are second-class citizens. "Nonwhite students feel abandoned," Lawrence reminds civil libertarians, "when the ACLU enters the debate by challenging ... efforts to provide a safe harbor for ... Black, Latino and Asian students."[86]

The first generation of inclusive speech regulations focused on student speech outside the classroom and library. Although such measures as the "Free Expression and Discriminatory Harassment" policy at Stanford University were phrased in general terms, they were primarily designed to "prohibit face-to-face insults"[87] that are far more likely to occur on the campus green and in the dorm room than in Physics 405 or in a computer lab. The (in)famous "water buffalo" incident occurred when a University of Pennsylvania student yelled an insult from his dorm window at African American women attending a loud sorority party.[88] The classroom was largely immune to first-generation speech regulations because racist and related invective were already prohibited in that academic setting.

Inclusive speech justifications for first-generation regulations were relatively weak. They challenged only speech policy outside the classroom, accepting how proponents of academic freedom regulated classroom and scholarly speech. Indeed, weak inclusive speech may be an offshoot of either disciplined or uninhibited speech. If, as such proponents of uninhibited speech as Chemerinsky and Gillman maintain, institutions of higher learning may ban constitutionally unprotected speech wherever uttered and, as such critical race theorists as Lawrence insist, racist, sexist, and related invective is constitutionally unprotected,[89] then, putting aside implementation problems, campuses committed to uninhibited speech may ban racist, sexist, and related invective inside and outside of the classroom. If, as such proponents of disciplined speech as Post maintain, all campus policies must contribute to the production and dissemination of knowledge and, as such proponents of inclusive speech as Thomas Grey insist, insults do not contribute to the production and dissemination of knowledge,[90] then, putting aside implementation problems, campuses committed to disciplined speech may also ban racist, sexist, and related invective inside and outside of the classroom.

Second-generation inclusive speech controversies pose more difficult challenges to inherited understandings of campus speech. Contemporary controversies over speech at many multiversities often concern what professors do in the classroom, in their research, and in their private capacity. Law professors are being sanctioned for wearing blackface at a class party[91] or using the word "nigger" in a classroom.[92] Calls are made to dismiss professors for anti-Israel tweets made in their personal capacity,[93] for publishing professional scholarship justifying sexual relationships between professors and students,[94] and for claiming in print that homosexuality violates natural law.[95] A Harvard Law School professor was removed from his position as dean of an undergraduate house after agreeing to help represent Harvey Weinstein, who was subsequently convicted of criminal sexual assault.[96] Unlike the student speech that was the target of the first-generation inclusive speech regulation, second-generation inclusive speech regulation targets the pedagogical, scholarly, and personal activities of professors historically protected by academic freedom.

Inclusive speech justifications for second-generation regulations must be strong in order to overcome traditional academic freedom barriers. The incidents discussed in the last paragraph illustrate how multiversity commitments to the production and dissemination of knowledge and to inclusiveness do not harmonize easily, at least when traditional academic freedoms are thought central to the knowledge mission. Many African Americans feel emotionally assaulted in a classroom when a professor uses the word "nigger," even if that usage is a professionally accepted way of making a pedagogical point. Many women feel emotionally barred from an undergraduate house whose dean jumps to the defense of an accused (and later convicted) rapist, even if such a defense is a legitimate exercise of professional judgment. Many sexual minorities feel emotionally excluded from classes taught by persons who publish articles claiming they are immoral, even if those articles are published by peer-reviewed journals. Many Jews feel emotionally unsafe in the presence of a professor who calls for Zionist genocide in tweets, even if that is a legitimate exercise of private free speech rights.

Historically marginalized groups pay as disproportionate a share of the price for policies that respect disciplinary standards in the classroom as they do for policies that protect broad free speech rights outside the classroom. Disciplinary standards are far more likely to permit criticisms of group members who have just been admitted to campus than those group members whose battles for inclusion were won long ago. Few inter-faith couples on campus are even aware of the critical commentary on such relationships published in the years immediately after World War II. Persons in gay and lesbian relationships, by contrast, must regularly confront robust arguments that the Constitution does not protect the rights of same-sex couples. Transgendered persons on campus must put up with claims, not yet fully rejected by psychiatrists, that persons who fail to identify as either male or female are suffering from gender dysphoria. Commentary on past discriminations is far less threatening than commentary on present discriminations. A "No Irish Need Apply" sign on a professor's door is an amusing historic relic. A poster of the Klan in a professor's office may communicate insensitivity to racial violence, even when the professor thinks the display is purely academic.

Proponents of uninhibited and disciplined speech may nevertheless be correct when they assert that institutions of higher learning will remain institutions of higher learning only if they maintain contemporary understandings of free speech and academic freedom when pursuing their knowledge missions, and prioritize the production and dissemination of knowledge when that charge conflicts with inclusiveness. This claim is partly consequential. Two champions for uninhibited speech maintain that restrictions inside and outside classrooms prepare students "poorly for professional life, which often demands intellectual engagement with people and ideas one might find uncongenial or wrong." "A campus culture devoted to policing speech and punishing speakers," Greg Lukianoff and Jonathan Haidt write, "is likely to engender patterns of thought that are surprisingly similar to those long identified by cognitive behavioral therapists as causes of depression and anxiety."[97] This claim for the priority of academic freedom and distinctive free speech principles is more firmly rooted in the identity of a university. Whittington points out, "[i]f universities are to operate at the outer boundaries of our state of knowledge and to push those boundaries further outward, they must be places where new, unorthodox, controversial, and disturbing ideas can be raised and scrutinized."[98] He might have added "as well as places where older ideas that justify marginalizing many persons on campus can continue to be maintained in the classroom until an overwhelming consensus exists among experts that they do not advance the production and dissemination of knowledge."

The multiversity undermines faculty governance solutions to free speech controversies. Faculty governance solutions make sense in universities. Faculty have special expertise in the production and dissemination of knowledge and are likely to be the persons on campus most committed to the production and dissemination of knowledge. This combination of expertise and commitment explains why faculty should make and implement free speech policy at a university dedicated solely or primarily to the production and dissemination of knowledge understood as a mission that can be engaged in independently from commitments to inclusiveness. Faculty have no special expertise or distinctive commitments to other multiversity missions. The persons who staff the campus diversity center are likely to have at least as much expertise about and commitment to inclusiveness as members of the physics department.

While most faculty who write about campus free speech issues are confident that campus commitments to free speech, and traditional notions of academic freedom and inclusiveness can cohere, anecdotal evidence suggests the campus diversity officers suspect that policies maximizing uninhibited speech and commitments to traditional notions of academic freedom do not maximize inclusiveness. Indeed, to the extent inclusiveness is a precondition for maximizing the production and dissemination of knowledge, traditional notions of academic freedom may not serve the knowledge mission of multiversities. This relative lack of faculty expertise on matters other than the production and dissemination of knowledge, differences in how the knowledge mission of multiversities is best pursued, and institutional commitments to matters other than the production and dissemination of knowledge, suggests multiversities mobilize the entire campus when making free speech policies that harmonize, balance, or prioritize producing and disseminating knowledge, inclusiveness, and other multiversity missions.

Conclusion

Institutions of higher learning diverge in how they welcome faculty and students. When I walk into my multiversity office building, I am greeted by a sign declaring the "core values" of the institution to be "accountability," "civility," "collaboration," "diversity," "excellence," "knowledge," and "leadership." When the prominent scholars who write about free speech on campus walk into their university office building, I imagine they are greeted by a big banner with the word "knowledge" inscribed. If the banner includes other words, their placement clearly indicates that such values are secondary to the production and dissemination of knowledge or fully cohere with that institutional mission. These greetings matter. Free speech policy on campus depends on whether the institution of higher learning is a university dedicated to either a single value or a set of harmonious values or a multiversity committed to a diversity of values that do not fully cohere.

The freedoms of speech at a multiversity present more complex challenges than the freedom of speech at a university. All institutions of higher learning determine not only what can be said on campus, but also what can be said where, who can say what where, and who can say what where and with campus funds. Universities rest content with balancing uninhibited and disciplined speech on campus in light of an institutional mission to produce and disseminate knowledge. Multiversities must balance uninhibited and disciplined speech on campus while juggling missions to produce and disseminate knowledge, promote inclusiveness, and satisfy other charges the public gives to an institution that is often the largest property holder, cultural center and major employer in the community. In the optimistic world of much literature, these functions cohere. Relatively clear lines exist between matters governed by uninhibited speech and matters governed by disciplined speech. Wise administration officials develop policies that simultaneously promote the production and dissemination of knowledge, inclusiveness, and the other missions assigned to the contemporary multiversity. The more pessimistic, skeptical account sketched here worries that multiversity missions more often collide than cohere. The line between the classroom of disciplined speech and the dorm room of uninhibited speech is murky. Wise administration officials balance and prioritize different institutional missions when setting speech policies on campus.

One response to this pluralism is more pluralism. Much literature on campus free speech promotes policies that all institutions of higher learning should adopt. The better practice may be to accept that at the present time legitimate normative and empirical disagreements exist about the proper balance between disciplined, uninhibited, and inclusive speech on campus, as well as the policies that maximize the different missions of the multiversity. If persons with disciplinary expertise on free speech debate the merits of different free speech policies on campus, institutions of higher learning do not betray their mission as long as they adopt a speech policy that can be justified by some disciplinary experts on free speech and academic freedom. The comfortable version of this pluralism suggests that campuses should be free to choose one of the many campus speech policies that meet disciplinary standards for balancing uninhibited, disciplined, and inclusive speech, as well as disciplinary standards for balancing the different missions of the multiversity. The less comfortable version of this pluralism acknowledges that the balancing at most multiversities in practice will often be done by mid-level staffers whose perspective may make them more sensitive to inclusiveness and institutional missions other than the traditional university mission of producing and disseminating knowledge than to contemporary notions of free speech and academic freedom.

Notes

1. For some of the incidents discussed below, see Erwin Chemerinsky and Howard Gillman, *Free Speech on Campus* (New Haven, CT: Yale University Press, 2017), 3–9.
2. Stephanie Francis Ward, "Law Prof Who Wore Blackface Violated School's Anti-Discrimination Policies, Report Finds," *ABA Journal*, December 22, 2016, accessed June 29, 2019, http://www.abajournal.com/news/article/law_prof_who_wore_blackface_violated_schools_anti-discrimination_policies_r/

3. Harriet Sherwood, "Oxford Students Call For Professor's Removal Over Alleged Homophobia," *Guardian*, January 9, 2019, https://www.theguardian.com/education/2019/jan/09/oxford-students-call-for-professors-removal-over-alleged-homophobia
4. Keith E. Whittington, *Speak Freely: Why Universities Must Defend Free Speech* (Princeton, NJ: Princeton University Press, 2018), 118–21.
5. Ibid., x.
6. Chemerinsky and Gillman, *Free Speech on Campus*.
7. Robert C. Post, *Democracy, Expertise, and Academic Freedom: A First Amendment Jurisprudence For the Modern State* (New Haven, CT: Yale University Press, 2012); Robert C. Post, "The Classic First Amendment Tradition Under Stress: Freedom of Speech and the University," in *The Free Speech Century*, eds. Lee C. Bollinger and Geoffrey R. Stone (New York: Oxford University Press, 2019).
8. Stanley Fish, *Versions of Academic Freedom: From Professionalism to Revolution* (Chicago: University of Chicago Press, 2014).
9. Whittington, *Speak Freely*.
10. Ibid., 13. For minor variations on this theme, see Sigal R. Ben-Porath, *Free Speech on Campus* (Philadelphia: University of Pennsylvania Press, 2017), 21 ("an open-minded search for truth and an equally open-minded climate for teaching"), 31 ("Colleges and universities are places where knowledge is developed and disseminated"); Post, "The Classic First Amendment Tradition," 121 ("twin objectives of research and education"); Post, *Democracy, Expertise, and Academic Freedom*, 25 ("the production and dissemination of expert knowledge"), 63 ("the preservation, advancement, and dissemination of knowledge"); Fish, *Versions of Academic Freedom*, 132 ("the advancement of knowledge and the search for truth").
11. See Chemerinsky and Gillman, *Free Speech on Campus*, xi. Private universities may be subject to federal and state statutory restrictions on their speech policies.
12. *New York Times Co. v. Sullivan*, 376 U.S. 254 (1964).
13. "The 1940 Declaration of Principles on Academic Freedom and Tenure," accessed June 29, 2019, https://www.aaup.org/report/1940-statement-principles-academic-freedom-and-tenure
14. "1915 Declaration of Principles on Academic Freedom and Tenure," accessed June 29, 2019, https://www.aaup.org/NR/rdonlyres/A6520A9D-0A9A-47B3-B550-C006B5B224E7/0/1915Declaration.pdf
15. See *Garcetti v. Ceballos*, 547 U.S. 410 (2006).
16. See Fish, *Versions of Academic Freedom*, 51.
17. See Post, "The Classic First Amendment Tradition," 107–8; Post, *Democracy, Expertise, and Academic Freedom*, xi, 28; Fish, *Versions of Academic Freedom*, 141; Whittington, *Speak Freely*, 34.
18. 376 U.S. at 270.
19. See Whittington, *Speak Freely*, 30.
20. Post, "The Classic First Amendment Tradition," 113, 114.
21. 376 U.S. at 279.
22. Post, *Democracy, Expertise, and Academic Freedom*, 97. See also Fish, *Versions of Academic Freedom*, 57–59.
23. Fish, *Versions of Academic Freedom*, 65.

24. "Joint Statement on the Rights and Freedoms of Students," AAUP, accessed June 29, 2019, https://www.aaup.org/report/joint-statement-rights-and-freedoms-students
25. J. Peter Byrne, "Academic Freedom: A 'Special Concern of the First Amendment,'" *Yale Law Journal* 99, no. 2 (November 1989): 262.
26. Chemerinsky and Gillman, *Free Speech on Campus*, 77.
27. Ibid.
28. Ibid., 126–28.
29. Whittington, *Speak Freely*, 124–41.
30. Chemerinsky and Gillman, *Free Speech on Campus*, 53.
31. Whittington, *Speak Freely*, 46.
32. Ben-Porath, *Free Speech on Campus*, 74.
33. See *Greer v. Spock*, 424 U.S. 828 (1976).
34. Whittington, *Speak Freely*, 6.
35. Ibid., 49.
36. Chemerinsky and Gillman, *Free Speech on Campus*, 156.
37. Ibid., 113.
38. Whittington, *Speak Freely*, 46.
39. Ibid., 93.
40. Ibid., 71.
41. Ibid., 96.
42. Ben-Porath, *Free Speech on Campus*, 71.
43. Ibid., 70
44. Chemerinsky and Gillman, *Free Speech on Campus*, 128.
45. Whittington, *Speak Freely*, 124–41.
46. Chemerinsky and Gillman, *Free Speech on Campus*, 142–43.
47. See Ben-Porath, *Free Speech on Campus*, 35, 82–83; Ibid., 77.
48. Chemerinsky and Gillman, *Free Speech on Campus*, 113.
49. Whittington, *Speak Freely*, 115. See also Chemerinsky and Gillman, *Free Speech on Campus*, 124–25.
50. See Whittington, *Speak Freely*, 124.
51. Post, "The Classic First Amendment Tradition," 118.
52. Ibid.
53. Ibid., 119.
54. Post, *Democracy, Expertise, and Academic Freedom*, 84
55. See Chemerinsky and Gillman, *Free Speech on Campus*, 87–108.
56. Ibid., 506.
57. See Benjamin Ginsberg, *The Fall of the Faculty: The Rise of the All-Administrative University and Why It Matters* (New York: Oxford University Press, 2011).
58. Clark Kerr, *The Uses of the University*, 5th ed. (Cambridge, MA: Harvard University Press, 2001), 103.
59. Ibid., 15.
60. Ibid., 20.
61. See Whittington, *Speak Freely*, 11.
62. Ben-Porath, *Free Speech on Campus*, 34.
63. Whittington, *Speak Freely*, 75.
64. Ibid., 77.
65. Chemerinsky and Gillman, *Free Speech on Campus*, 145–58.

66. Ben-Porath, *Free Speech on Campus*, 56.
67. Ibid., 37.
68. Whittington, *Speak Freely*, 75.
69. Michael Roth, "How Free Should Free Speech Be on Campus?" *Washington Post*, September 22, 2017, https://www.washingtonpost.com/outlook/how-free-should-free-speech-be-on-campus/2017/09/22/248ae04e-7e10-11e7-9d08-b79f191668ed_story.html?utm_term=.e283199f2803
70. Arianne Shahvisi, "From Academic Freedom to Academic Responsibility: Privileges and Responsibilities Regarding Speech on Campus," in *The Value and Limits of Academic Speech: Philosophical, Political, and Legal Perspectives*, eds. Donald Alexander Downs and Chris W. Suprenant (New York: Routledge, 2018), 280.
71. This paragraph and the next two are a loosely edited version of Mark A. Graber, "Old Wine in New Bottles: The Constitutional Status of Unconstitutional Speech," *Vanderbilt Law Review* 48 (1995): 359–62.
72. Richard Delgado, "Words That Wound: A Tort Action for Racial Insults, Epithets, and Name Calling," in *Words That Wound: Critical Race Theory, Assaultive Speech, and the First Amendment*, eds. Mari J. Matsuda, Charles R. Lawrence III, Richard Delgado, and Kimberlè Williams Crenshaw (Boulder, CO: Westview Press, 1993), 110.
73. Catharine A. MacKinnon, *Only Words* (Cambridge, MA: Harvard University Press, 1993), 108.
74. Ibid., 106
75. See Charles R. Lawrence, III, "If He Hollers Let Him Go: Regulating Racist Speech on Campus," in *Words That Wound*, 68–71; Thomas C. Grey, "How to Write a Speech Code Without Really Trying: Reflections on the Stanford Experience," *University of California, Davis Law Review* 29, no. 3 (Spring 1996).
76. Richard Delgado, "Campus Antiracism Rules: Constitutional Narratives in Collision," *Northwestern University Law Review* 85, no. 2 (January 1991): 387.
77. Delgado, "Words That Wound," 95.
78. Richard Delgado, "First Amendment Formalism is Giving Way to First Amendment Legal Realism," *Harvard Civil Rights-Civil Liberties Law Review* 29, no. 1 (Winter 1994): 171.
79. Mary Ellen Gale, "Reimagining the First Amendment: Racist Speech and Equal Liberty," *St. Johns Law Review* 65, no. 1 (Winter 1991): 157.
80. Ibid., 158.
81. Lawrence, "If He Hollers," 68.
82. Mari J. Matsuda, "Public Response to Racist Speech: Considering the Victim's Story," in *Words That Wound*, 48.
83. Ibid., 18.
84. Delgado, "Words That Wound," 93.
85. Matsuda, "Public Response to Racist Speech," 49.
86. Lawrence, "If He Hollers," 86.
87. Ibid., 67. For the text of the Stanford policy, see ibid., 66–67.
88. See Associated Press, "'Water Buffalo' Incident Settled by Penn Graduate," *New York Times*, September 10, 1997, https://www.nytimes.com/1997/09/10/us/water-buffalo-lawsuit-settled-by-penn-graduate.html
89. Lawrence, "If He Hollers."
90. Grey, "How to Write a Speech Code."

91. Ward, "Law Prof."
92. Richard Chess, "Paul Zwier Agrees to Bias Training, Barred From Teaching Mandatory First-Year Courses," *The Emory Wheel*, September 18, 2018, https://emorywheel.com/paul-zwier-bias-training-barred
93. Jodi S. Cohen, "Salaita Files Lawsuit Against U. of I. Over Documents in Job Dispute," *Chicago Tribune*, November 17, 2014, https://www.chicagotribune.com/politics/ct-steven-salaita-lawsuit-met-20141117-story.html
94. Chemerinsky and Gillman, *Free Speech on Campus*, 2–3.
95. See Sherwood, "Oxford Students."
96. Kate Taylor, "Harvard's First Black Faculty Deans Let Go Amid Uproar Over Harvey Weinstein Defense," *New York Times*, May 11, 2019, https://www.nytimes.com/2019/05/11/us/ronald-sullivan-harvard.html
97. Greg Lukianoff and Jonathan Haidt, "The Coddling of the American Mind," *The Atlantic*, September 2015, accessed June 29, 2019, https://www.theatlantic.com/magazine/archive/2015/09/the-coddling-of-the-american-mind/399356/
98. Whittington, *Speak Freely*, 178.

References

Ben-Porath, Sigal R. *Free Speech on Campus*. Philadelphia: University of Pennsylvania Press, 2017.

Byrne, J. Peter. "Academic Freedom: A 'Special Concern of the First Amendment.'" Yale Law Journal 99, no. 2 (November 1989): 251–340.

Chemerinsky, Erwin, and Howard Gillman. *Free Speech on Campus*. New Haven, CT: Yale University Press, 2017.

Delgado, Richard. "Campus Antiracism Rules: Constitutional Narratives in Collision." *Northwestern University Law Review* 85, no. 2 (January 1991): 343–87.

———. "First Amendment Formalism Is Giving Way to First Amendment Legal Realism." *Harvard Civil Rights-Civil Liberties Law Review* 29, no. 1 (Winter 1994): 169.

———. "Words That Wound: A Tort Action for Racial Insults, Epithets, and Name Calling." In Matsuda, et al., *Words That Wound*, 89–110.

Fish, Stanley. *Versions of Academic Freedom: From Professionalism to Revolution*. Chicago: University of Chicago Press, 2014.

Gale, Mary Ellen. "Reimagining the First Amendment: Racist Speech and Equal Liberty." *St. Johns Law Review* 65, no. 1 (Winter 1991): 119–85.

Ginsberg, Benjamin. *The Fall of the Faculty: The Rise of the All-Administrative University and Why It Matters*. New York: Oxford University Press, 2011.

Graber, Mark A. "Old Wine in New Bottles: The Constitutional Status of Unconstitutional Speech." *Vanderbilt Law Review* 48 (1995): 348–89.

Grey, Thomas C. "How to Write a Speech Code Without Really Trying: Reflections on the Stanford Experience," *University of California, Davis Law Review* 29, no. 3 (Spring 1996): 891–956.

Kerr, Clark. *The Uses of the University*, 5th ed. Cambridge, MA: Harvard University Press, 2001.
Lawrence, Charles R., III. "If He Hollers Let Him Go: Regulating Racist Speech on Campus." In Matsuda et al., *Words That Wound*, 53–88.
MacKinnon, Catharine A. *Only Words*. Cambridge, MA: Harvard University Press, 1993.
Matsuda, Mari J. "Public Response to Racist Speech: Considering the Victim's Story." In Matsuda et al., *Words That Wound*, 17–52.
Matsuda, Mari J., Charles R. Lawrence III, Richard Delgado, and Kimberlè Williams Crenshaw, eds. *Words That Wound: Critical Race Theory, Assaultive Speech, and the First Amendment*. Boulder, CO: Westview Press, 1993.
Post, Robert C. *Democracy, Expertise, and Academic Freedom: A First Amendment Jurisprudence for the Modern State*. New Haven, CT: Yale University Press, 2012.
———. "The Classic First Amendment Tradition Under Stress: Freedom of Speech and the University." In *The Free Speech Century*, edited by Lee C. Bollinger and Geoffrey R. Stone. New York: Oxford University Press, 2019.
Shahvisi, Arianne. "From Academic Freedom to Academic Responsibility: Privileges and Responsibilities Regarding Speech on Campus." In *The Value and Limits of Academic Speech: Philosophical, Political, and Legal Perspectives*, edited by Donald Alexander Downs and Chris W. Suprenant, 260–84. New York: Routledge, 2018.
Whittington, Keith E. *Speak Freely: Why Universities Must Defend Free Speech*. Princeton, NJ: Princeton University Press, 2018.

3. Free Speech, Free Press, and Fake News: What if the Marketplace of Ideas Isn't About Identifying Truth?

KEITH J. BYBEE AND LAURA E. JENKINS

In the run-up to the 2016 presidential election, the world of American politics seemed to turn upside down. This was not because the prominent Democratic political consultant John Podesta actually orchestrated a ring of pedophiles, or because Hillary Clinton really arranged the sale of military-grade weapons to ISIS, or even because Pope Francis, in fact, endorsed Donald Trump. Politics appeared topsy-turvy because fake news about Podesta, Clinton, the Pope, and many other public figures inundated public discussion and often overwhelmed the real news.[1] The completely fabricated article proclaiming the Pope had endorsed Trump was the most widely shared story on Facebook during the last three months of the 2016 presidential election.[2] And the most popular fake news stories were more widely shared on Facebook than the most popular true news stories.[3] Like moths to a flame, cursors and eyeballs swiftly flew toward a blaze of lies, and democracy was singed.

Fake news stories are not, of course, anything new. From posthumous slanders against the Roman Emperor Justinian[4] to mid-nineteenth-century newspaper stories trumpeting the existence of giant blue-skinned man-bats on the Moon,[5] misinformation (i.e., false information deliberately intended to deceive[6]) has long plagued news reporting in all its forms.

For many people, however, the tsunami of misinformation flooding the media today represents an unprecedented problem. A diverse assortment of commentators, scholars, and journalists have argued that fake news profoundly misleads the citizenry,[7] denies the possibility of developing agreement and compromise,[8] and fatally undermines open debate in the marketplace of ideas.[9] If these pundits and experts are right, then American democracy is on the verge of collapse.

But are these pundits and experts right? In this chapter, we survey the recent history of fake news beginning with the 2016 presidential election and ending with the early days of the Trump administration. We discuss the widely shared belief that nefarious political objectives, coupled with the economic incentives to produce "clickbait," rapidly transformed fake news from a harmless internet oddity into an existential threat to self-government.[10] We then describe a range of solutions that have been proposed to counter the mortal threat fake news ostensibly poses.

To gain some perspective on this consensus assessment of fake news, we look back to the nineteenth century, a period when American newspapers were directly affiliated with political parties and virtually all news was reported from a partisan point of view. Editors and journalists at the time did not think that their primary job was to provide objective information about events. Readers did not subscribe to newspapers simply to gather facts and make rational judgments about which policies best served the public interest. We argue consumption of the nineteenth-century partisan press cannot be explained by the dominant explanation of how free speech and the free press operate that was advanced by John Stuart Mill. Mill claimed that the main function of free speech and the free press is to inform readers and aid them in seeking truth in the marketplace of ideas. Given how the Millian explanation of free speech fails to explain why nineteenth-century readers eagerly and knowingly consumed fake news, we turn to nineteenth-century observer Alexis De Tocqueville's explanation of free speech and the free press. Tocqueville, a French man, visited the United States in 1831. Based on his observations, he penned *Democracy in America*,[11] one of the most important assessments of American politics and society ever written. In stark contrast to Mill, Tocqueville argued that the main function of free speech and the free press in the nineteenth century was to help Americans imagine the community in which they belonged. Truth seeking was not part of the equation for Tocqueville.

We conclude the chapter by applying Tocqueville's understanding of fake news to today's fake news. We argue that it is important to evaluate fake news not only for the misinformation it contains, but also for the forms of communal identity it facilitates. Fake news can certainly mislead and harm those who consume it. But fake news, like all news, is also used by the public to articulate and confirm a sense of membership. Armed with a Millian understanding of free speech, current efforts to weed out fake news stories from social media platforms and from public discussion are aimed at improving the accuracy of information in circulation. While such efforts may marginally improve the accuracy of information, they will not alter the underlying dynamic of identity formation that leads ordinary people to employ the news as a means of developing feelings of belonging.

A Brief History of Fake News

The story of fake news in 2016 begins in the small town of Veles, Macedonia, where teenagers looking to buy designer clothes and luxury cars began placing made-up news stories on Facebook's advertising platforms in the hopes of making money.[12] These politically ambivalent teens found that pro-Trump content was the most profitable kind of fake news, attracting the most eyeballs and generating thousands of dollars per month (if not per day).[13] As pro-Trump content became the black gold of the Internet, the overall amount of fake news in circulation quickly became heavily biased in his campaign's direction.[14] In the 2016 election, researchers found that 115 pro-Trump fake news stories were shared 30 million times on Facebook, while only 41 pro-Clinton fake news stories were shared 7.6 million times on the social media platform.[15]

People have always been able to find fake news stories online. Yet, in the early years of the Internet, fake news was limited to a smattering of harmless satire.[16] Only a small number of websites posted and spread fake news because it was too time consuming to create content in the days of dial-up and too cumbersome to share links with large audiences.[17] With the rise of social media (and with the development of algorithms or "bots" that autonomously interact with humans), the costs of producing and disseminating fake news have significantly dropped.[18] Lower costs mean higher potential earnings,[19] and the lure of easy money has made fake news far more common and far more appealing to profit seekers of all stripes, including Macedonian teens.

Fake news might have become just one more element in the flotsam and jetsam of the vast American media ocean. But then extraordinary things began to happen. Duped by a fake news story, a heavily armed Edgar Welch showed up at the Comet Ping Pong Pizzeria in order to free the children held in a fictitious pedophile ring supposedly run by the Democratic Party.[20] Even more remarkably, the fake news-fueled Trump campaign won the presidential election. Given these unanticipated developments, fake news became impossible to ignore, and experts and commentators began to search for an explanation of how misinformation could have become so important.

Many were quick to point their fingers at the structure of social media.[21] On social media, users often interact within "echo chambers" where (by virtue of how companies have built their platforms) users are continuously presented with information that supports their own ideas, and they rarely encounter contrary or challenging viewpoints.[22] When politically congenial fake news begins to reverberate in a user's echo chamber, the false information is easily integrated into that user's worldview and becomes impervious to refutation by any objectively valid facts.[23] As a result of this dynamic, the critics argued, fake news worked its way into a force potentially strong enough to determine the outcome of the presidential election.[24]

The story of fake news took another twist after the election when then President-elect Trump enthusiastically appropriated the term "fake news" to describe negative (but factual) press coverage of himself.[25] Trump first used the term "fake news" in this way on Twitter in December, 2016 (and he subsequently claimed, erroneously, that he coined the term).[26] Outside of Twitter, Trump first used "fake news" as a pejorative description of critical media coverage on January 11, 2017 in an attack on CNN's Jim Acosta.[27] Trump would go on to use the term "fake news" to refer to unfavorable press coverage of himself over 150 times in 2017.[28] CNN and the "failing *New York Times*" bore the brunt of Trump's fake news accusations.[29] Other world leaders would later follow Trump's example and use "fake news" to describe negative press coverage of themselves (no world leader had used the phrase before 2017).[30] The adoption of Trump's tactics around the globe made the pathologies of fake news one of America's leading exports.

The Nature and Depth of the Problem

Virtually everyone, experts and ordinary people alike, seem to agree that fake news is a threat to democracy.[31] And many believe that the threat targets democracy's very foundation: an informed citizenry. Despite the ludicrous headlines fake news often sports, a significant number of individuals who read fake news believe it, and 87% of Americans believe fake news creates at least "some confusion" about current events.[32] Fake news breeds this confusion in two related ways. First, fake news stories in and of themselves spread falsehoods that punch "holes in what is true."[33] Second, as ammunition for politicians looking to attack media outlets and to bolster their own causes, repeated denunciations of "fake news" cast doubt on the media's truth-seeking functions and, in doing so, further discredit the notion that there are any facts independent of any given person's preferred opinions—a development that allows misinformation to spread ever more easily.[34] By eroding citizens' trust in the media,[35] fake news erodes the "factual foundations" of citizens' viewpoints and in doing so erodes the "factual foundations" of democracy.[36]

Without a shared sense of facts and truth, citizens lose the ability to engage in meaningful political discussion and reach consensus.[37] As Yochai Benkler argues, "'[i]f everyone is entitled to their own facts you can no longer have reasoned disagreements and productive compromise.'"[38] Instead, you are "left with raw power" where everyone is caught in a war over who gets the monopoly on truth.[39] No one listens to all perspectives in order to develop a better understanding of how a policy or program works.[40] Free discussion and no-holds-barred argumentation seem only to multiply divisions and lies.[41]

The truth no longer wins out because John Stuart Mill's solution to false speech—to counter speech with more speech—does not work. Today more speech is likely to be only more false speech.[42] This is particularly true on social media. As one commentator described it:

> In the early days of Twitter, people would call it a 'self-cleaning oven,' because yes there were falsehoods, but the community would quickly debunk them. But now we're at a scale where if you add in automation and bots, that oven is overwhelmed ... There are many more people now acting as fact-checking and trying to clean all the ovens, but it's at a scale now that we just can't keep up.[43]

Far from being a vast marketplace trading in every conceivable notion and finding its way to truth, social media has become more like a lemonade stand, selling one sour serving of false ideas after another.

Potential Solutions

Given the serious threat that fake news is understood to pose, experts have proposed a wide range of solutions from more education to better news journalism to improved search and ranking algorithms. The search for solutions got off to an inauspicious start with social media companies initially denying there was any problem to be solved. Three days after the 2016 election, Facebook's Mark Zuckerberg argued that Facebook's impact on the election was minimal.[44] According to Zuckerberg, fake news and the echo chambers that amplify its destructiveness were not serious problems because "most users have friends who have different political views to their own."[45] After facing more than a week of criticism, Facebook ultimately conceded that fake news spread via its platform may have played a role in the election, and it laid out a plan to combat fake news.[46] One month later Facebook announced more measures, including a system to allow users to report stories they believe are false so that these stories can be sent to the non-partisan International Fact-Checking Network for review and (if warranted) marked by Facebook as "disputed."[47]

Across social media companies the consensus has been that changing algorithms would provide a technical panacea for fake news. Google altered its algorithms on YouTube and used revised algorithms to demote the ranking of fake news in its search results.[48] These changes in algorithms were intended to expose people to better information and to help minimize the deleterious effects of echo chambers.[49] The Google algorithm changes were also meant to demonetize fake news providers[50] and disrupt "fake news economics," with the goal of eliminating the incentives to fabricate stories about papal endorsements of Trump and their ilk.[51] Facebook adopted similar measures in May 2017, and decided to lower the rankings of "low-quality" information in Facebook newsfeeds (even though ranking algorithms have difficulty determining what qualifies as "low-quality" information).[52]

In September, 2018, Zuckerberg detailed how Facebook had adopted a multi-pronged "defense in depth" strategy to combat fake news "because no one tactic is going to prevent all of the abuse."[53] In total, Facebook has used machine learning to target over one billion fake accounts responsible for spreading fake news since the 2016 presidential election.[54] Facebook also hired more than 10,000 digital security personnel in 2018 alone.[55] Finally, Facebook has sought to publicize its efforts by creating a "Transparency Report" where users can track the company's removal of fake accounts.[56]

Twitter is likewise involved in an evolutionary arms race with fake accounts. From immigration controversies to mass shootings, bots comprise a significant percentage of Twitter activity on political hot-button issues.[57] In the classic battle between man and machine, Twitter waged combat against bots and in July, 2018, removed millions of bots from its platform.[58] To defeat bots, researchers have also created programs (available at FactCheck.me) to allow journalists to detect whether or not an account is real.[59] Unfortunately, the machines are winning this round and instead of tweeting automated tweets that Twitter can easily delete, bots are now retweeting politically divisive tweets produced by human pawns.[60]

Experts have also proposed legal solutions to address the problem of fake news, including holding Facebook liable for the spread of fake news on its platform.[61] Others have proposed changes to existing laws to allow for easier regulation of social media platforms more broadly (even though the prospect of more regulations raises fears about the stifling of speech).[62]

Finally, solutions have been proposed to put the Millian marketplace of ideas back in working order. Since the free trade in ideas can only run smoothly when citizens can distinguish fake facts from real facts, new educational curricula are being developed to provide future citizens with critical thinking skills.[63] And since the marketplace of ideas requires a sound factual foundation on which to stand, experts also argue that more high-quality reporting by traditional media outlets needs to be injected into the market.[64] This optimistic solution argues that once individuals are consistently presented with high-quality journalism, fake news will be the clear loser in the competition over what to believe.

Fake News, Nineteenth-Century Style

If the proposed solutions are not sufficient to eradicate the scourge of fake news, then American democracy is in truly dire straits. Unless, of course, the underlying diagnosis of the kind of problem that fake news represents is incorrect. What if the consensus assessment of fake news is rooted in a misunderstanding of how free speech and the free press actually work? To gain some perspective on this question, we turn to the nineteenth century, a time when all news was "fake."

The Worst of Times

When the nineteenth century dawned, the United States was in rough political shape. The unity of the founding generation had fallen apart as hard-fought elections divided the electorate into warring factions of Federalists and Democratic-Republicans. With the ink barely dry on the Constitution, American government seemed as fragile as the parchment on which the Constitution was written—parchment that was at risk of combusting from the heat of vicious political conflict. The generation that had banded together to form the Constitution's "We the People" had to band together once again to save the framework of government that they had so recently constructed. But how would Americans band together? And under what banner could they march as one?

Enter the partisan press. For a critical time, beginning in the disputes of the Federalist/Democratic-Republican period and ending with the rise of the commercial press in the late nineteenth century, the partisan press became the "linchpin" of politics in the United States.[65] Using the partisan press, party leaders could mobilize voters,[66] communicate the party's policy stances, advertise the party's candidates,[67] and focus voters' attention on pressing political issues.[68] Most importantly, party leaders believed that the partisan press could inculcate the values and principles needed to preserve the Constitution.[69]

As we shall see, the partisan press sought to instill the principles of the Constitution not through the impartial reporting of the facts, but through the broadcasting of partial truths, spin, and even outright lies to advance the party's cause.[70] In other words, the partisan press transmitted "fake news" to save the Constitution and the republic. This was not because partisan press and party leaders were wholly averse to the truth; nor was it because the editors and journalists of the day were greedy nineteenth-century versions of Internet trolls. The partisan press twisted facts and published lies in service of a higher purpose.[71] That higher purpose was to persuade, not dupe, the public into forming a community that was truly devoted to saving the republic.[72]

Rise and Fall of the Partisan Press

To understand how the partisan press helped its readers construct a communal identity, it is helpful to understand a bit more about how the partisan press first arose, as well as a bit more about how it finally fell. The Constitution was designed to make sure that the government could rise above partisan factions and operate on the basis of common interest and public reason. Before the election of 1800, newspapers maintained a veneer of impartiality to avoid accusations that they were feeding the flames of factionalism the Constitution had been created to smother.[73] After the election of 1800, however, the veneer of impartiality was stripped away and the press was drawn into the fray.[74]

Early political parties needed to fulfill the basic functions of modern political parties, including the development of rank-and-file membership and the reliable delivery of votes. Yet the incipient political parties of the early nineteenth century were too disjointed to rally their voters to the party's cause.[75] To form a cohesive political bloc, partisans need to feel connected to each other and to the larger party despite the time between elections and conventions, and despite the distance between individual citizens and the party organization.[76]

As they battled for office, both Democratic-Republicans and Federalists recognized that the press could be useful in convincing the public to coalesce around the party's cause.[77] The partisan press could help connect voters with their party and their fellow party members by providing the basis for a new communal identity.[78] In election after election, as the press proved that it could effectively mobilize voters, party leaders pulled newspapers into the politics of assembly and activation.[79] By providing the scaffolding for a new sense of identity and belonging, the partisan press effectively "link[ed] parties, voters, and the government together," and thus became the "central institution" of American politics.[80]

The partisan press would remain the keystone of American politics until the late nineteenth century when commercialism (the very catalyst for the rise of fake news in the twenty-first century) spelled the end of the partisan press's hegemony.[81] The rise of the "penny press" (a named earned by the newspapers' low price) gradually shifted the balance in favor of impartial journalism.[82] By injecting commercialism into the newspaper industry the penny press made the buying public, not politicians, its patrons.[83] Thus the creation of a highly profitable newspaper with a broad general readership, not the persuasion of the public to march to the party's drum, eventually became the ultimate goal of editors and publishers.[84] By the end of the nineteenth century, increased advertising, a growing distaste for partisanship, better printing technology, and a more literate public all contributed to the growth of more impartial journalism.[85]

The Utility of Fake News

The partisan press was ubiquitous in the early nineteenth century because it could fulfill almost any need the party had. If the party needed to defend itself from the slings and arrows of the other side, the partisan press could do that.[86] If the party needed to lob its own slings and arrows at the other side, the partisan press could do that as well.[87] Finally, if the party needed to convince its voters that they should adopt the party line, the partisan press could do that too.[88] The partisan press was the one-stop electioneering shop of the early American republic.[89]

Party leaders were responsible for the establishment of partisan newspapers across the country.[90] Party leaders also bought and circulated their newspapers in excessive numbers in the hopes they would convince the public to join and remain faithful to the party's cause.[91] For example, Thomas Jefferson and James Madison worked to establish the *National Gazette* in Philadelphia in the hopes it would be an "antidote to … Monarchy and Aristocracy" that would "inculcate genuine principles of our constitution."[92] Likewise, Federalists created the *New York Evening Post* to be the personal propaganda outlet for Alexander Hamilton.[93] The *Post*, like the *National Gazette*, regularly launched political crusades and aimed to provide people with "correct information, to enable them to judge of themselves what is really best."[94]

The partisan press was fully integrated into the party organization. Partisan press editors worked directly with politicians and even served as leaders in the party organization.[95] Newspapers' solvency often depended on the patronage of political parties, and patronage, especially presidential patronage, would only increase over time.[96] Presidents Jefferson, Madison, and Monroe patronized the *National Intelligencer*, while John Quincy Adams helped finance the *National Journal*.[97] Jackson's presidential campaign in

1824 caused the rapid growth of the partisan press on a national level,[98] and presidential patronage of the press soared dramatically during the Jackson and Van Buren presidencies.[99]

Given the clear economic incentives of partisan press editors to keep on the party's good side, we might be tempted to condemn these editors as politically ambivalent schemers publishing whatever views would keep the party dollars flowing in their direction. However, partisan press editors were not Macedonian teenagers looking to buy designer clothes, nor were they opportunist hacks.[100] Their ultimate motives were not economic, but political.[101] Whatever support editors received from political parties, the editors continued to support the party's cause because they believed their party could unite the people under the banner of protecting the Constitution.[102] Protecting this sacred document was far more important than the party's mammon. The partisan editors sincerely believed the cause of "good government" was at stake, and since their party's paper was the only way to save "good government," it was worth making financial sacrifices as necessary.[103]

If preaching the party's gospel was the only way to save "good government," then to be impartial was to be a blasphemer. As a consequence, partisan editors openly and proudly acknowledged their role in disseminating the party's propaganda and decried the impartial heathens.[104] William Cobbett, the editor of *Porcupine's Gazette*, made no "professions of impartiality" because he was not "a poor passive fool," but rather "an editor" who was partial "for the cause of good government."[105] Likewise, the editor of *The Portfolio* declared that he would "not publish an impartial paper" because impartial men are not "trusted by any."[106] Of such unprincipled men, he had "the deepest abhorrence, and for the silly scheme of Impartiality, he cherishes the most ineffable contempt."[107]

James Cheetham of the New York *American Citizen* likewise saw impartiality as "ruinous to the best interests of mankind."[108] Similarly, a Republican editor of the Baltimore *American and Daily Advertiser* in 1799 argued there was "too much at stake, in the contest of liberty against slavery, virtue against vice, and truth against sophistry, to admit of more than a limited impartiality."[109] This Republican editor would openly support "the principles of Republicanism" because it "is as incongruous for a publication to be alternately breathing the spirit of Republicanism and Aristocracy as for a clergyman to preach to his audience Christianity in the morning, and Paganism in the evening."[110] If an editor dared to be impartial toward the party's doctrine, he was doing the unforgivable—blaspheming against the spirit of the Constitution.

Dire Times Call for Fake News

Why did partisan editors use such apocalyptic language when advocating for partiality to the party's cause? The answer is simple: these editors thought they lived in dire times.[111] They lived in "times [that] demand[ed] decision."[112] As one Federalist argued, impartiality was a threat to the United States because politics is not value neutral—there is "a right and a wrong."[113] Therefore, no printer "under the specious name of impartiality" should mix "both truth and falsehood into the same paper."[114] The Constitution's "virtuous government" was so fragile, a Democratic-Republican editor warned, that it could only survive crises when "its virtues are protected ... by the means of diffusing truth."[115] Ironically, the chief means of diffusing this "truth" was the partisan newspaper.

The partisan press reported the "facts" (and twisted facts at that) when they supported the party's mission,[116] and in doing so the partisan editors saw their papers as means of diffusing a higher truth—the party's truth. Under the party's banner, partisan editors could unite the faithful and focus their attention on saving the Constitution.[117] The public accepted that saving the Constitution might call for scurrilous attacks on political rivals and outlandish claims of the party's deeds and the other party's misdeeds.[118] And if the fake news spread by the partisan press facilitated the formation of a communal identity centered on salvaging the republic, then the public would ultimately benefit from the misinformation they so eagerly consumed.

Fake News, Then and Now. A Case for Less Mill, More Tocqueville

No matter the era, it seems impossible that fake news could benefit its consumers. However, one early nineteenth-century observer of the partisan press, Alexis De Tocqueville, made exactly that argument and even argued that the partisan press's fake news cured a greater evil than it caused.[119] Tocqueville argued that collective action is difficult in democracies because individuals feel isolated from their compatriots.[120] He argued that newspapers, even ones rife with misinformation, make collective action possible because they communicate the same ideas simultaneously to those who would never meet in person, and thus provide a banner for "wandering spirits, who have been looking for each other for a long time in the shadows, [to] finally meet and unite" under.[121] Once united under the same banner with the same ideas, collective action becomes possible.

While Tocqueville's argument seems strange to our modern ears, given the ubiquity of fake news in the early nineteenth and twenty-first centuries, perhaps we need to evaluate whether Tocqueville's insights from the fake news of the past can provide us with insights into fake news today. After all, if nineteenth-century fake news cured a greater evil than it caused, then perhaps twenty-first century fake news also accomplishes something other than the destruction of democracy.

John Stuart Mill's understanding of free expression seems like common sense to many people today. Mill insisted that progress toward the whole truth can be made only through the free competition of ideas, a competition that he called "the rough process of a struggle between combatants fighting under hostile banners."[122] The ardent advocates participating in the competition of ideas are themselves unlikely to gain a better or more accurate understanding of issues. If anything, advocates tend to become more sectarian, inflexible, and extreme during heated disputes with their opponents. It is the audience, "the calmer and more disinterested bystander," that benefits from no-holds-barred argument.[123] It is the audience that identifies error, learns new truths, and gains a more vital grasp of the truths it already knows to be sound. And it is the audience's truth-finding capacities that are fatally compromised when public debate is overwhelmed with fabricated facts and false stories.

Mill's insights into free expression are always the first to spring to mind on the questions of the free press and truth in print, and Tocqueville never enters the conversation. It seems intuitive that individuals read the news to gain the facts they need to function in public life and that therefore ubiquitous falsehoods in print would seriously threaten truth in public life. However, when we look at the example of the nineteenth-century partisan press, Mill's explanation of free expression seems less intuitive, for why would people knowingly consume a twisted, overtly partisan version of the "facts?"[124] Given the similarity between nineteenth-century fake news and twenty-first century fake news, Tocqueville's insights on the purpose of news consumption in the nineteenth century deserve reconsideration.

Alexis De Tocqueville toured the United States in the early nineteenth century, and he understood the needs and capacities of the audience quite differently than Mill did. Tocqueville found American newspapers to be filled with wild exaggeration and scurrilous insults. In general, he observed, "the hallmark of the American journalist is a direct and coarse attack, without any subtleties, on the passions of his readers."[125] Indeed, the first American newspaper Tocqueville encountered denounced President Andrew Jackson as a "heartless despot" who "governs by corruption" and is little more than "a gambler without shame or restraint."[126] Like Mill, Tocqueville thought that the inflammatory rhetoric of the newspapers served a higher purpose. Unlike Mill, however, Tocqueville did not think that the higher purpose was the discovery of truth.

In aristocratic nations like nineteenth-century France, Tocqueville argued, the leading citizens all know one another. They belong to related families and travel in the same social circles. By contrast, in a democratic nation like the nineteenth-century United States, the mass of people lacks an aristocracy's sense of identity and membership. Compared to titled nobility, democratic citizens are "all very small and lost in the crowd."[127] Each democratic citizen is "anchored in the place in which he lives by the modesty of his fortune and a crowd of small necessary cares."[128] Ordinary individuals "do not see one another and do not know where to find one another" in the sprawling vastness of democratic society, and they cannot easily form a sense of the larger community in which they belong.[129]

According to Tocqueville, it is the press that furnishes the means for democratic citizens to imagine a larger community. Newspapers create the context in which a collective identity becomes possible, providing a way "of talking every day without seeing one another and of acting together without meeting." Newspapers are not only necessary to permit citizens to spot one another in the faceless crowd, but also necessary to continue to hold citizens together. Every day, the newspaper "speaks to each of its readers in the name of all of the rest," creating and constantly reinforcing a feeling of belonging. Tocqueville saw firsthand how American political parties made use of the newspaper's generative power. "The press rallies interest around certain doctrines and gives shape to party slogans; through the press, the parties, without actually meeting, listen and argue with one another."[130] The information and arguments found in the partisan press were often untrue and might "lead citizens to do very ill-considered things."[131] But readers were not coming to the press for objectivity and truth. They were instead seeking to identify and associate.

A Community of Lies

Viewed from the vantage point of Tocqueville and the nineteenth-century partisan press, today's fake news takes on a new dimension. Like the fake news of the nineteenth-century partisan press, today's fake news helps atomized individuals, lost in the faceless morass of social media, to construct a collective identity. From Mill's perspective, the echo chambers of social media, where fake news circulates unchallenged by truth, are devastating for democracy.[132] The audience, "the calmer and more disinterested bystander[s],"[133] cannot identify truth and cannot engage in politics armed with this truth because the Millian marketplace is flooded with falsity.[134] From Tocqueville's perspective, however, echo chambers rife with fake news are part of the grist in the mill of democracy.

By consuming fake news, social media users can imagine that they belong to a larger community devoted, much like the readers of nineteenth-century fake news,[135] to saving the republic. When users read that the Pope endorsed Trump or that Hillary Clinton sold weapons to ISIS, social media users can imagine that they are acting together with fellow partisans, despite never meeting them face-to-face or even knowing their real names. On the Internet, it is easy to feel "very small and lost in the crowd," but through news—both fake and real—users can talk "every day without seeing one another" and can act "together without meeting."[136] In this way, users can form a sense of the larger community of partisans to which they belong.

If Mill's understanding of free speech is mistaken and the higher purpose of news media is not providing its audience with truth but about helping them construct a collective identity, then the problem of fake news has been fundamentally misunderstood. Fake news is commonly viewed as an existential threat to self-government because it allegedly undermines the foundations of self-government: an informed citizenry.[137] From this perspective, social media is not a Millian marketplace of ideas where falsity is countered and conquered by truth, but a petri dish of ever-multiplying falsehood and spin.[138] This failure of the Millian marketplace has even prompted commentators to question the utility of free speech.[139] However, before we toss free speech onto the trash heap of history, we should first ask what the higher purpose of news media and free speech actually is.

If people engage in free speech and consume news media not to procure truth from the Millian marketplace, but to identify and associate with a community of like-minded partisans, then American democracy may not be on the verge of collapse. Using Tocqueville's understanding of free speech, we see that news media does not furnish American democracy with an informed citizenry, so much as it ensures American democracy is operated by citizens cemented together in a communal identity. Free speech does not exist to counter and conquer falsity with truth, but exists to help citizens to recognize, listen to, and argue with one another without ever meeting. Free speech and news media serve as the scaffolding for a sense of belonging that helps citizens fight against the atomizing forces of democratic society and act collectively with like-minded compatriots they have never met.

Tocqueville's perspective on fake news does not mean everything is rosy in American democracy. After all, fake news "might lead citizens to do very ill-considered things"[140] (like attempting to free nonexistent children from a fictitious pedophile ring run by John Podesta[141]). Additionally, if we value truth in public life, then forming a communal identity around lies, and outrageous ones at that, is an issue of concern. Nonetheless, the fundamental problem fake news poses to American democracy is not that it robs American democracy of an informed citizenry. News media's higher purpose was never to provide American democracy with a knowledgeable citizenry instructed by the Millian marketplace of ideas, but to provide American democracy with communal identities that allow citizens to act collectively. The consensus on fake news is simply accusing fake news of robbing American democracy of something the news media never provided American democracy with in the first place.

Conclusion

Fake news is nothing new. From the presidency of George Washington[142] to the presidency of Donald Trump, fake news has often played a role in politics. While today's fake news takes the form of clickbait that sports alluring but ludicrous headlines, the function of fake news has not changed since the early nineteenth century. Like the partisan press of the nineteenth century and like real news today, fake news facilitates the construction of communal identities of like-minded partisans. Using Tocqueville's understanding of free speech, we see that fake news does not undermine the argument for free speech because free speech was never about allowing truth to counter and conquer falsity. Instead, free speech (and the news media through which it is disseminated) is about combating the atomizing forces of American democracy and allowing citizens who feel "very small and lost in the crowd" to construct a shared identity that allows them to act in concert with strangers.[143]

If we rely on Mill's understanding of free speech, then fake news is a pox on the nation that must be combated with algorithms and education. However, if we rely on Tocqueville's understanding of free speech, fake news takes on a different hue. Fake news is still a problem, but it is a problem of a different kind that may call for different solutions. If fake news were a malfunction of the Millian marketplace of ideas, then perhaps algorithms to weed out falsehoods would be the much-needed panacea. Yet, if fake news facilitates the formation of communities built around lies, then a solution that recognizes the role that news media plays in identity formation (and not an algorithm-based solution) is needed. Since fake news does not appear to be going away soon, to address its pathologies we need to first understand what fake news is actually doing. We need to lay aside the Pollyannaish belief that truth seeking is why social media users consume news media, and instead need to recognize how fake news underwrites and supports collective action. Perhaps then we can understand how fake news allowed citizens to act collectively to elect Donald Trump to the presidency.

Notes

1. Hannah Ritchie, "Read All About It: The Biggest Fake News Stories of 2016," *CNBC*, December 30, 2016, accessed February 1, 2019, https://www.cnbc.com/2016/12/30/read-all-about-it-the-biggest-fake-news-stories-of-2016.html
2. Mike Snider, "Can the Fake News Trend Be Ironed Out?" *USA Today*, January 15, 2017, accessed February 1, 2019, https://www.usatoday.com/story/money/2017/01/15/can-fake-news-trend-de-escalated/96537288/
3. Craig Silverman and Lawrence Alexander, "How Teens in the Balkans are Duping Trump Supporters With Fake News," *BuzzFeed.News*, November 3, 2016, accessed February 1, 2019, https://www.buzzfeednews.com/article/craigsilverman/how-macedonia-became-a-global-hub-for-pro-trump-misinfo
4. Joanna M. Burkhardt, "Can Technology Save Us?" *Library Technology Reports* 53, no. 8 (November/December 2017).
5. Tom Standage, "The True History of Fake News," *1843*, June/July 2017, accessed February 1, 2019, https://www.1843magazine.com/technology/rewind/the-true-history-of-fake-news
6. "Misinformation | Definition of Misinformation," *English Oxford Living Dictionaries*, accessed February 1, 2019, en.oxforddictionaries.com/definition/misinformation
7. Vian Bakir and Andrew McStay, "Fake News and the Economy of Emotions: Problems, Causes, Solutions," *Digital Journalism* 6, no. 2 (2018).
8. Ibid., 162.
9. Philip M. Napoli, "What if More Speech is No Longer the Solution?: First Amendment Theory Meets Fake News and the Filter Bubble," *Federal Communications Law Journal* 70, no. 1 (April 2018).
10. Silverman and Alexander, "How Teens in the Balkans are Duping Trump Supporters."
11. Alexis de Tocqueville, *Democracy in America*, ed. J. P. Mayer, trans. George Lawrence (Garden City, NY: Doubleday, 1969).
12. Samanth Subramanian, "Inside the Macedonian Fake-News Complex," *Wired*, February 15, 2017, accessed February 1, 2019, https://www.wired.com/2017/02/veles-macedonia-fake-news/
13. Silverman and Alexander, "How Teens in the Balkans are Duping Trump Supporters."
14. Hunt Allcott and Matthew Gentzkow, "Social Media and Fake News in the 2016 Election," *Journal of Economic Perspectives* 31, no. 2 (2017).
15. Ibid., 212.
16. Burkhardt, "Can Technology Save Us?" 14.
17. Ibid.
18. Emilio Ferrara, Onur Varol, Clayton Davis, Filippo Menczer, and Alessandro Flammini, "The Rise of Social Bots," *Communications of the ACM* 59, no. 7 (July 2016).
19. Subramanian, "Inside the Macedonian Fake-News Complex."

20. Sabrina Tavernise, "As Fake News Spreads Lies, More Readers Shrug at the Truth," *New York Times*, December 6, 2016, accessed February 1, 2019, https://www.nytimes.com/2016/12/06/us/fake-news-partisan-republican-democrat.html
21. Bakir and McStay, "Fake News and the Economy of Emotions," 160.
22. Allcott and Gentzkow, "Social Media and Fake News in the 2016 Election," 211.
23. Leonard M. Niehoff and Deeva Shah, "The Resilience of Noxious Doctrine: The 2016 Election, the Marketplace of Ideas, and the Obstinacy of Bias," *Michigan Journal of Race and Law* 22, no. 2 (Spring 2017).
24. Bakir and McStay, "Fake News and the Economy of Emotions," 160.
25. Meg Kelly, "President Trump Cries 'Fake News' and the World Follows," *Washington Post*, February 6, 2018, accessed February 1, 2019, https://www.washingtonpost.com/news/fact-checker/wp/2018/02/06/president-trump-cries-fake-news-and-the-world-follows/?noredirect=on&utm_term=.2dd5361b0f4b
26. Callum Borchers, "Trump Falsely Claims (Again) That He Coined the Term 'Fake News,'" *Washington Post*, October 26, 2017, accessed February 1, 2019, www.washingtonpost.com/news/the-fix/wp/2017/10/26/trump-falsely-claims-again-that-he-coined-the-term-fake-news/
27. Kelly, "President Trump Cries 'Fake News.'" The sparring match between President Trump and Jim Acosta would continue into 2018, culminating in the White House revoking Jim Acosta's press pass after a heated exchange between the President and Acosta about misleading campaign ads about the migrant caravan on November 7, 2018. Brian Stelter, "White House Pulls CNN Reporter Jim Acosta's Pass After Contentious News Conference," *CNN*, November 7, 2018, accessed February 1, 2019, https://www.cnn.com/2018/11/07/media/trump-cnn-press-conference/index.html. Acosta's press pass was later restored by the White House on November 19. Michael M. Grynbaum, "CNN's Jim Acosta Has Press Pass Restored By White House," *New York Times*, November 19, 2018, accessed February 1, 2019, https://www.nytimes.com/2018/11/19/business/media/jim-acosta-press-pass-cnn.html. This came after a federal judge restored Acosta's press pass a few days earlier as a result of CNN suing the Trump administration. Paul Farhi, "Judge Hands CNN a Victory in Its Bid to Restore Jim Acosta's White House Press Pass," *Washington Post*, November 16, 2018, accessed February 1, 2019, www.washingtonpost.com/lifestyle/style/judge-hands-cnn-victory-in-its-bid-to-restore-jim-acostas-white-house-press-pass/2018/11/16/8bedd08a-e920-11e8-a939-9469f1166f9d_story.html?noredirect=on&utm_term=.20d249aca583.
28. Kelly, "President Trump Cries 'Fake News.'"
29. Angie Drobnic Holan, "The Media's Definition of Fake News vs. Donald Trump's," *Politifact*, October 18, 2017, accessed February 1, 2019, https://www.politifact.com/truth-o-meter/article/2017/oct/18/deciding-whats-fake-medias-definition-fake-news-vs/
30. Kelly, "President Trump Cries 'Fake News.'"
31. Snider, "Can the Fake News Trend Be Ironed Out?"
32. Amy Mitchell, Michael Barthel, and Jesse Holcomb, "Many Americans Believe Fake News is Sowing Confusion," *Pew Research Center: Journalism and Media*, December 15, 2016, accessed February 1, 2019, http://www.journalism.org/2016/12/15/many-americans-believe-fake-news-is-sowing-confusion/
33. Tavernise, "As Fake News Spreads Lies."

34. Hossein Derakhshan and Claire Wardle, "Ban the Term 'Fake News,'" *CNN*, November 27, 2017, accessed February 1, 2019, https://www.cnn.com/2017/11/26/opinions/fake-news-and-disinformation-opinion-wardle-derakhshan/index.html
35. Standage, "The True History."
36. Bakir and McStay, "Fake News and the Economy of Emotions," 160.
37. M. Mitchell Waldrop, "The Genuine Problem of Fake News," *Proceedings of the National Academy of Sciences of the United States of America* 114, no. 48 (November 2017).
38. Ibid., 12632.
39. Ibid.
40. Bakir and McStay, "Fake News and the Economy of Emotions," 162.
41. Niehoff and Shah, "The Resilience of Noxious Doctrine."
42. Napoli, "What if More Speech is No Longer the Solution?" 66–68.
43. Mike Wendling, "The (Almost) Complete History of 'Fake News,'" *BBC News*, January 22, 2018, accessed February 1, 2019, www.bbc.com/news/blogs-trending-42724320
44. Bakir and McStay, "Fake News and the Economy of Emotions," 162.
45. Ibid.
46. Mark Zuckerberg, "A lot of you have asked what we're doing about misinformation, so I wanted to give an update," Facebook, November 18, 2016, https://www.facebook.com/zuck/posts/10103269806149061
47. Mark Zuckerberg, "Preparing for Elections," *Facebook*, September 13, 2018, accessed February 1, 2019, https://www.google.com/search?q=facebook+preparing+for+elections&ie=utf-8&oe=utf-8&client=firefox-b-1-ab; Zuckerberg, "A lot of you have asked"; Adam Mosseri, "Addressing Hoaxes and Fake News," *Facebook Newsroom*, December 15, 2016, accessed February 1, 2019, https://newsroom.fb.com/news/2016/12/news-feed-fyi-addressing-hoaxes-and-fake-news/
48. James Carson, "Fake News: What Exactly Is It—and How Can You Spot It?" *The Telegraph*, January 31, 2019, accessed February 1, 2019, www.telegraph.co.uk/technology/0/fake-news-exactly-has-really-had-influence/
49. Dominic DiFranzo and Kristine Gloria-Garcia, "Filter Bubbles and Fake News," *XRDS* 23, no. 3 (Spring 2017).
50. Dominic Spohr, "Fake News and Ideological Polarization: Filter Bubbles and Selective Exposure on Social Media," *Business Information Review* 34, no. 3 (September 2017).
51. Zuckerberg, "A lot of you have asked."
52. Waldrop, "The Genuine Problem of Fake News," 12633.
53. Zuckerberg, "Preparing for Elections."
54. Ibid.
55. Ibid.
56. Ibid.
57. Issie Lapowsky, "Here's How Much Bots Drive Conversation During News Events," *Wired*, October 30, 2018, accessed February 1, 2019, https://www.wired.com/story/new-tool-shows-how-bots-drive-conversation-for-news-events/?fbclid=IwAR2IljkuDmUWKVSoO9zOrVX9lrzkvQKJJyRiwe8x6aYlTVNMiMP7GpTk9dc
58. Ibid.
59. Ibid.
60. Ibid.

61. Emma M. Savino, "Fake News: No One is Liable, and That is a Problem," *Buffalo Law Review* 65, no. 5 (2017).
62. Sheldon Burshtein, "The True Story on Fake News," *Intellectual Property Journal* 29, no. 3 (August 2017); Konrad Niklewicz, "Weeding Out Fake News: An Approach to Social Media Regulation," *European View* 16, no. 2 (December 2017), 335.
63. Waldrop, "The Genuine Problem of Fake News," 12634.
64. Bakir and McStay, "Fake News and the Economy of Emotions," 164–65.
65. Wm. David Sloan, "The Early Party Press: The Newspaper Role in American Politics, 1788–1812," *Journalism History* 9 (Spring 1982), 19; Michael Schudson, *Discovering the News: A Social History of American Newspapers* (New York: Basic Books, 1978); Jeffrey L. Pasley, *The Tyranny of Printers: Newspaper Politics in the Early American Republic* (Charlottesville: University of Virginia Press, 2001).
66. John Nerone, "Representing Public Opinion: US Newspapers and the News System in the Long Nineteenth Century," *History Compass* 9, no. 9 (2011).
67. Jamie L. Carson and M. V. Hood, III, "Candidates, Competition, and the Partisan Press: Congressional Elections in the Early Antebellum Era," *American Politics Research* 42, no. 5 (September 2014).
68. Sloan, "The Early Party Press," 18.
69. James Lyon to Jefferson, October 5, 1802, quoted in ibid., 22
70. Jeff Rutenbeck, "The Triumph of News Over Ideas in American Journalism: The Trade Journal Debate, 1872–1915," *Journal of Communication Inquiry* 18, no. 1 (Winter 1994).
71. Wm. David Sloan, "'Purse and Pen': Party-Press Relationships, 1789–1816," *American Journalism* 6 (1989).
72. Wm. David Sloan, "Scurrility and the Party Press, 1789–1816," *American Journalism* 5, no. 2 (1988).
73. Sloan, "The Early Party Press," 19.
74. Ibid.
75. Carson and Hood, "Candidates, Competition, and the Partisan Press," 761.
76. Pasley, *The Tyranny of Printers*, 11
77. Sloan, "'Purse and Pen,'" 104.
78. Carson and Hood, "Candidates, Competition, and the Partisan Press," 766.
79. Pasley, *The Tyranny of Printers*, 3–4.
80. Ibid.
81. Dan Schiller, "An Historical Approach to Objectivity and Professionalism in American News Reporting," *Journal of Communication* 29, no. 4 (December 1979).
82. Schudson, *Discovering the News*.
83. Nerone, "Representing Public Opinion," 755; Jeff Rutenbeck, "Editorial Perception of Newspaper Independence and the Presidential Campaign of 1872: An Ideological Turning Point for American Journalism," *Journalism History* 17 (Spring/Summer 1990), 18.
84. Richard Kaplan, "The American Press and Political Community: Reporting in Detroit 1865–1920," *Media, Culture & Society* 19, no. 3 (July 1997); Rutenbeck, "Editorial Perception," 18.
85. Rutenbeck, "Editorial Perception."
86. Sloan, "The Early Party Press," 19.
87. Sloan, "Scurrility and the Party Press," 100.

88. Ibid., 98.
89. Sloan, "The Early Party Press," 19.
90. Culver H. Smith, *The Press, Politics, and Patronage: The American Government's Use of Newspapers, 1789–1875* (Athens: University of Georgia Press, 1977).
91. Sloan, "'Purse and Pen,'" 109.
92. "Jefferson to Washington," in *Works of Thomas Jefferson*, vol. V, ed. Paul L. Ford (New York: G. P. Putnam's Sons, 1904), 336–37; "Madison to Edmund Randolph, Philadelphia, 1792," in *Writings of James Madison*, vol. VI, ed. Gaillard Hunt (New York: G. P. Putnam's Sons, 1906), 117–18; "Jefferson to Anthony Haswell," September 11, 1801, quoted in Sloan, "Scurrility and the Party Press," 111.
93. Sloan, "The Early Party Press," 19.
94. Quoted in ibid., 22.
95. Sloan, "'Purse and Pen,'" 105.
96. Carson and Hood, "Candidates, Competition, and the Partisan Press," 766; William E. Ames, *A History of the "National Intelligencer"* (Chapel Hill: University of North Carolina Press, 1971); Gerald J. Baldasty, *The Press and Politics in the Age of Jackson* (Columbia, SC: Association for Education in Journalism and Mass Communication, 1984); Smith, *The Press, Politics, and Patronage*.
97. Baldasty, *The Press and Politics*, 3.
98. Ronald P. Formisano, "Deferential-Participant Politics: The Early Republic's Political Culture, 1789–1840," *American Political Science Review* 68, no. 2 (1974); Ronald P. Formisano, "The 'Party Period' Revisited," *Journal of American History* 86, no. 1 (June 1999); Richard P. McCormick, *The Second American Party System: Party Formation in the Jacksonian Era* (Chapel Hill: University of North Carolina Press, 1966).
99. Jeff Rutenbeck, "Partisan Press Coverage of Anti-Abolitionist Violence: A Study of Early Nineteenth-Century 'Viewsflow,'" *Journal of Communication Inquiry* 19, no. 1 (Spring 1995).
100. Sloan, "'Purse and Pen,'" 117.
101. Ibid., 105.
102. Ibid.
103. William Cobbett, *Porcupine's Gazette* (Philadelphia), May 5, 1797.
104. Ames, *A History of the "National Intelligencer"*; Baldasty, *The Press and Politics*; Smith, *The Press, Politics, and Patronage*.
105. Cobbett, *Porcupine's Gazette*.
106. Joseph Dennie, *Prospectus of a New Weekly Paper, Submitted to Men of Affluence, Men of Liberality, and Men of Letters* (Philadelphia: Joseph Dennie and Asbury Dickins, 1800).
107. Ibid.
108. Quoted in Sloan "The Early Party Press," 19.
109. Ibid.
110. Ibid.
111. Sloan, "The Early Party Press," 19.
112. Quoted in ibid.
113. Sloan, "The Early Party Press," 19.
114. Ibid.
115. Quoted in ibid., 23.

116. Rutenbeck, "The Triumph of News Over Ideas."
117. Sloan, "The Early Party Press," 18.
118. William E. Ames, "Joseph Gales's Recollections," in *A History of the "National Intelligencer"* (Chapel Hill: University of North Carolina Press, 1972), 155–57.
119. Tocqueville, *Democracy in America*, 518.
120. Ibid.
121. Ibid.
122. John Stuart Mill, "On Liberty," in *John Stuart Mill, On Liberty: Annotated Text, Sources, and Background Criticism*, ed. David Spitz (New York: W.W. Norton, 1975), 46.
123. Ibid., 50.
124. Ames, "Joseph Gales's Recollections."
125. Tocqueville, *Democracy in America*, 185.
126. Ibid.,182.
127. Ibid., 518.
128. Ibid.
129. Ibid.
130. Ibid., 186.
131. Ibid., 517.
132. Napoli, "What if More Speech is No Longer the Solution?"
133. Mill, "On Liberty," 50.
134. Niehoff and Shah, "The Resilience of Noxious Doctrine."
135. Sloan, "Scurrility and the Party Press."
136. Tocqueville, *Democracy in America*, 518, 186.
137. Snider, "Can the Fake News Trend Be Ironed Out?"
138. Napoli, "What if More Speech is No Longer the Solution?", 66–68.
139. Ibid.
140. Tocqueville, *Democracy in America*, 517.
141. Ritchie, "Read All About It."
142. Sloan, "The Early Party Press," 18.
143. Tocqueville, *Democracy in America*, 518.

Bibliography

Allcott, Hunt, and Matthew Gentzkow. "Social Media and Fake News in the 2016 Election." *Journal of Economic Perspectives* 31, no. 2 (2017): 211–36.

Ames, William E. *A History of the "National Intelligencer"*. Chapel Hill: University of North Carolina Press, 1971.

———. "Joseph Gales's Recollections." In *A History of the "National Intelligencer,"* 155–57.

Bakir, Vian, and Andrew McStay. "Fake News and the Economy of Emotions: Problems, Causes, Solutions." *Digital Journalism* 6, no. 2 (2018): 154–75.

Baldasty, Gerald J. *The Press and Politics in the Age of Jackson*. Columbia, SC: Association for Education in Journalism and Mass Communication, 1984.

Burkhardt, Joanna M. "Can Technology Save Us?" *Library Technology Reports* 53, no. 8 (November/December 2017): 14–21.

Burshtein, Sheldon. "The True Story on Fake News." *Intellectual Property Journal* 29, no. 3 (August 2017): 397–446.

Carson, Jamie L., and M.V. Hood, III. "Candidates, Competition, and the Partisan Press: Congressional Elections in the Early Antebellum Era." *American Politics Research* 42, no. 5 (September 2014): 760–83.

De Tocqueville, Alexis. *Democracy in America.* Edited by J.P. Mayer. Translated by George Lawrence. Garden City, NY: Doubleday, 1969.

Dennie, Joseph. *Prospectus of a New Weekly Paper, Submitted to Men of Affluence, Men of Liberality, and Men of Letters.* Philadelphia: Joseph Dennie and Asbury Dickins, 1800.

DiFranzo, Dominic, and Kristine Gloria-Garcia. "Filter Bubbles and Fake News." *XRDS* 23, no. 3 (2017): 32–35.

Ferrara, Emilio, Onur Varol, Clayton Davis, FilippoMenczer, and Alessandro Flammini. "The Rise of Social Bots." *Communications of the ACM* 59, no. 7 (July 2016): 96–104.

Ford, Paul L. *Works of Thomas Jefferson*, vol. V. New York: G. P. Putnam's Sons, 1904.

Formisano, Ronald P. "Deferential-Participant Politics: The Early Republic's Political Culture, 1789–1840." *American Political Science Review* 68, no. 2 (1974): 473–87.

———. "The 'Party Period' Revisited." *Journal of American History* 86, no. 1 (June 1999): 93–166.

Hunt, Gaillard. *Writings of James Madison*, vol. VI (New York: G.P. Putnam's Sons).

Kaplan, Richard. "The American Press and Political Community: Reporting in Detroit 1865–1920." *Media, Culture & Society* 19, no. 3 (1997): 331–55.

McCormick, Richard P. *The Second American Party System: Party Formation in the Jacksonian Era.* Chapel Hill: University of North Carolina Press, 1966.

Mill, John Stuart. "On Liberty." In *John Stuart Mill, on Liberty: Annotated Text, Sources, and Background Criticism*, edited by David Spitz, 1–106. New York: W.W. Norton, 1975.

Napoli, Philip M. "What If More Speech Is No Longer the Solution? First Amendment Theory Meets Fake News and the Filter Bubble." *Federal Communications Law Journal* 70, no. 1 (April 2018): 1–7.

Nerone, John. "Representing Public Opinion: US Newspapers and the News System in the Long Nineteenth Century." *History Compass* 9, no. 9 (2011): 743–59.

Niehoff, Leonard M., and Deeva Shah. "The Resilience of Noxious Doctrine: The 2016 Election, the Marketplace of Ideas, and the Obstinacy of Bias." *Michigan Journal of Race and Law* 22, no. 2 (2017): 243–71.

Niklewicz, Konrad. "Weeding Out Fake News: An Approach to Social Media Regulation." *European View* 16, no. 2 (December 2017): 335.

Pasley, Jeffrey L. *The Tyranny of Printers: Newspaper Politics in the Early American Republic.* Charlottesville: University Press of Virginia, 2001.

Rutenbeck, Jeff. "Editorial Perception of Newspaper Independence and the Presidential Campaign of 1872: An Ideological Turning Point for American Journalism." *Journalism History* 17 (Spring/Summer 1990): 13–22.

———. "Partisan Press Coverage of Anti-Abolitionist Violence: A Study of Early Nineteenth-Century 'Viewsflow.'" *Journal of Communication Inquiry* 19, no. 1 (Spring 1995): 126–41.

———. "The Triumph of News Over Ideas in American Journalism: The Trade Journal Debate, 1872–1915." *Journal of Communication Inquiry* 18, no. 1 (Winter 1994): 63–79.

Savino, Emma M. "Fake News: No One Is Liable, and That Is a Problem." *Buffalo Law Review* 65, no. 5 (2017): 1101–68.

Schiller, Dan. "An Historical Approach to Objectivity and Professionalism in American News Reporting." *Journal of Communication* 29, no. 4 (December 1979): 46–57.

Schudson, Michael. *Discovering the News: A Social History of American Newspapers.* New York: Basic Books, 1978.

Sloan, Wm. David. "The Early Party Press: The Newspaper Role in American Politics, 1788–1812." *Journalism History* 9, no. 1 (1982): 18–24.

———. "'Purse and Pen': Party-Press Relationships, 1789–1816." *American Journalism* 6, no. 2 (1989): 103–27.

———. "Scurrility and the Party Press, 1789–1816." *American Journalism* 5, no. 2 (1988): 97–112.

Smith, Culver H. *The Press, Politics, and Patronage: The American Government's Use of Newspapers, 1789–1875.* Athens: University of Georgia Press, 1977.

Spohr, Dominic. "Fake News and Ideological Polarization: Filter Bubbles and Selective Exposure on Social Media." *Business Information Review* 34, no. 3 (September 2017): 150–60.

Waldrop, Mitchell M. "The Genuine Problem of Fake News." *Proceedings of the National Academy of Sciences of the United States* 114, no. 48 (2017): 12631–34.

4. *Free Speech and Confederate Symbols*

LOGAN STROTHER AND NATHAN T. CARRINGTON

Perhaps the most obviously visible link between the Civil War and the present day is the Confederate battle flag.[1] To many Americans, the Confederate flag and other monuments and memorials to the Confederate States of America are unambiguous symbols of racial hatred and a reminder of America's legacy of slavery and ascriptive racial hierarchy. The Confederacy, after all, was explicitly dedicated to the perpetuation of race-based slavery. Many others claim, however, that these Confederate icons are merely symbols of Southern heritage and reminders of our shared history, for good or ill. Some people in this latter camp go further, affirmatively rejecting any connection between contemporary displays of Confederate iconography and racial bigotry: "Heritage, not Hate" is the common refrain.[2] What is undoubtedly true, however, is that Confederate symbols convey a message, regardless of the way in which those symbols are viewed. Symbols that convey a message, or meaning, are by definition speech—they say *something*, even if what they say is contestable.[3] In this chapter, we address the free speech dimension of current controversies surrounding Confederate symbols and monuments.

Because of their fraught history, and perhaps also because of the multiple and potentially conflicting messages they might convey, Confederate icons are a source of recurrent controversy in American politics.[4] One major round of controversy was ignited when Dylann Roof murdered nine African American churchgoers in Charleston, South Carolina, in 2015. Roof's murders were motivated by a desire to start a race war, and an online manifesto was published along with a picture of Roof holding a handgun in one hand and a Confederate flag in the other. In the context of Roof's actions and intentions, the meaning of the flag, for him at least, is clear.

Roof's racially targeted murders led to calls throughout the nation for Confederate icons to be purged from public spaces. South Carolina Governor

Nikki Haley quickly called for the Confederate battle flag to be removed from the statehouse grounds.[5] Since that time, local governments around the country have removed Confederate monuments, renamed schools and parks that had been named for rebel leaders, and the like. For example, in 2017, the cities of New Orleans (LA), St. Louis (MO), and Memphis (TN) each made national headlines by removing Confederate statues and memorials from their public grounds.[6]

Removal of these symbols has aroused controversy at every turn because many people think that Confederate monuments should remain in the public square. Even in the wake of Roof's mass murder, several South Carolina lawmakers, including House member Jonathon Hill and former House member Mike Ryhal, opposed the removal of the Confederate flag.[7] A poll conducted by Reuters in August of 2017 found that 54% of American adults thought that Confederate monuments should remain in all public spaces, while only 27% felt that such monuments should be removed.[8] Numerous other polls from this period reached similar conclusions, with support for removal of Confederate monuments never surpassing 33% among the general public.[9] As time has gone on though, public sentiment has shifted: in a national survey conducted in July of 2018, we found that 44.3% of Americans thought Confederate monuments should be removed from public spaces.[10] A majority (55.7%) opposed removal, but these margins still suggested an important shift.

There are a variety of arguments advanced by supporters of these icons; most often these defenses are appeals to the importance of history and to free speech. The history argument holds that Confederate symbols serve as important reminders of our nation's history, with the implication that slavery, the Civil War, or Jim Crow might be forgotten in the absence of these public reminders. In research conducted with Spencer Piston and Thomas Ogorzalek, one of us has found that there is good reason to cast some doubt on the defense grounded in public history. That research shows that knowledge of Southern Civil War history is *negatively* correlated with support for the Confederate battle flag, even after controlling for ideology, partisanship, and education.[11]

The argument that removing these symbols from the public square constitutes a violation of someone's (or some groups') freedom of speech is an interesting one. These symbols, which undoubtedly convey meaning, *are* speech, even if what meaning they convey is contested—or, perhaps more likely, even if they convey different meanings to different people. When these symbols are removed from public spaces, the projection of their meaning(s) is also removed. Does this violate the "free speech" of people who like or otherwise support Confederate icons? Kenneth Warren, professor of political

Free Speech and Confederate Symbols

science at Saint Louis University, argues that the statues, even if offensive, are protected speech and should be left in place.[12] While the U.S. Constitution is silent on symbolic speech, Warren argues that the U.S. Supreme Court's precedents in this area support the constitutionality of these Confederate monuments. Indeed, Warren draws parallels between the fight to keep these monuments in place and the battle by the American Civil Liberties Union (ACLU) in support of the right of Nazis to march in Skokie, Illinois. Thus, Warren suggests that removing Confederate monuments violates the freedom of speech.

Although Warren makes the argument that free speech rights are violated if Confederate monuments are removed, he is not your average member of the public. Indeed, as a political science professor he holds views which are likely to be quite different from those of the average member of the public. However, because others have made similar claims, we sought to uncover how common this view is among the general public. To do so, we first described a common scenario to our nationally representative sample of 332 voting-age Americans.[13] We told them that "A city government recently decided to remove a statue of Confederate General Robert E. Lee from a public park because, in the words of a city spokesman, it 'does not reflect the city's values.'" We then asked them, "Do you think that removing this statue from public property violates citizens' freedom of speech?" Only 14% of our participants said they believe that removing the Confederate statue is a violation of free speech rights.[14] As Figure 4.1 indicates, this view is slightly

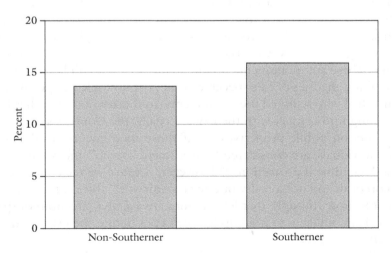

Figure 4.1: Does Removing the Confederate Statue Violate Free Speech Rights? Source: Logan Strother & Nathan T. Carrington

more common among people who identified as Southerners (15.9%) than those who considered themselves non-Southerners (13.2%), but it is still a decidedly minority position.

However, even if the belief that removing Confederate icons violates free speech rights is a minority position, it is still one that merits attention. This is especially true given the hallowed status of rights—especially freedom of speech—in the American civic religion.[15] In this chapter, we explore the free speech component of this heated national conversation.

The core of this chapter seeks to conceptualize the debate in terms of several prevailing theories of free speech. In what follows, we use some of the introduced theories to justify both removing and maintaining Confederate monuments on public property. As will become evident, some theories work better than others for their respective side of the issue. Similarly, it will be clear that strong theoretical justifications can be made for either of the positions. Consequently, we argue that the question of whether to remove or maintain Confederate monuments is a largely political question, and not one that can be solved by appealing to abstract justifications for free expression.

The Confederate Monument Controversy in Theories

It is worth emphasizing that the discussion in this chapter is concerned with Confederate monuments on public land. The analyses and arguments that follow do not apply to Confederate symbols on private property. This distinction is crucial when moving from a theoretical to legal discussion, as the U.S. Supreme Court has extended different levels of protection to public and private property. Moreover, it is important to highlight whose rights are being infringed—that is, who the "speaker" actually is. This is not an easy task, since these are monuments on public property. As will become evident, the prevailing theories of free speech can support multiple perspectives: from the individual who sculpted the monuments, to those whose speech is limited after coming into contact with the icons. Legally, the Court has decided that monuments on public property, even if those monuments are donated by private individuals, are considered "government speech" and are not subject to First Amendment protections.[16] However, because we are concerned with the theoretical, and not a real-world legal framework, this is of little concern. Suffice it to note, though, that legal arguments using a "freedom of speech" framework are unlikely to hold up in court considering the existing doctrine on government speech.

Finally, it is also worth emphasizing that the goal of this chapter is not to match theories up to popular claims made about Confederate monuments. Instead, it is to see how existing theories can be applied to the debate. Consequently, some theories may seem far-fetched and unrealistic. Nonetheless, they serve to demonstrate that the discussion surrounding Confederate icons can be grounded in respected theories of free speech.

The Millian Perspective: The Pursuit of Truth

As noted in the Introduction to this volume, one of the most ubiquitous and broad justifications for the freedom of speech originates from John Stuart Mill's *On Liberty*. There, Mill seeks to elaborate the nature of social liberty—that is, the extent to which power may be exercised by society over the individual. Concerned with the tyranny of the majority, Mill proceeds to outline the conditions under which the majority should not exert power over the individual. Of the several areas discussed in the essay, the one in which Mill spills the most ink is that which revolves around the "liberty of thought and discussion." As we outline below, Mill's work can be used to rationalize support for confederate monuments in terms of the pursuit of truth, but can also be used to justify removal in terms of tyranny of the majority.

For Mill, there are several reasons why society must not exert influence over the thoughts and discussions of individuals. However, among the most important for the present purposes is that the opinion that is silenced may, in fact, be true. If we acknowledge the fallibility of humankind, then it follows that neither an individual nor group of individuals can be absolutely certain the ideas they want to censor are untrue.

Even if the opinion were entirely false, however, Mill argues it would still be unwise to suppress it. As Mill so eloquently put it, "[i]f all mankind were of one opinion, and only one person were of the contrary opinion, mankind would be no more justified in silencing that one person, than he, if he had the power, would be justified in silencing mankind."[17] This is because those who hold the *true* opinion hold it more firmly because it is being challenged.

For Mill, even an entirely false opinion is nonetheless worth hearing, as it allows those who are against it to have a finer understanding of the truth. As Mill noted:

> The peculiar evil of silencing the expression of an opinion is, that it is robbing the human race; posterity as well as the existing generation; those who dissent from the opinion, still more than those who hold it. If the opinion is right, they are deprived of the opportunity of exchanging error for truth; if wrong, they lose, what is almost as great a benefit, the clearer perception and livelier impression of truth, produced by its collision with error.[18]

Mill goes on to argue that, "[h]e who knows only his own side of the case, knows little of that."[19] For example, Mill would argue that those who deny the Holocaust are valuable because they provide the rest of society a better understanding of the atrocities of the Holocaust and continuously require them to confront this truth.

Consequently, a Millian argument for keeping the Confederate monuments could go something like this: regardless of whether the monuments symbolize heritage or hate, they should remain in public spaces because they allow individuals the opportunity to exchange ideas and arrive closer to the truth.

This justification applies to a multitude of Confederate icons. For example, displaying the Confederate Battle Flag on vehicle license plates forces those who believe this symbolic expression is wrong to confront their own convictions and to offer a deeper, and more refined, understanding of their own beliefs. While the Supreme Court has ruled that states may resist calls to put the Confederate Battle Flag on license plates, these license plates nonetheless allow those who confront the icons on the roadway to reflect on their own beliefs, ultimately promoting the quest for truth. Similarly, efforts to rename roadways and schools after Confederate generals could serve the same purpose: those who enter the school or drive on the road will be offered the opportunity to sharpen their understanding of truth.[20]

While a pro-monuments argument rooted in a Millian foundation seems clear, there are additional questions that may cause problems. For example, monuments—perhaps more so even than ordinary speech—are imbued with different meanings by different individuals.[21] For some, a marble statue of Jefferson Davis on a horse may symbolize racial hatred, while others may see it as a commemoration to a man who died defending the Confederacy during "the War of Northern Aggression." And then there are those who may view the statue without ever having heard of Jefferson Davis. Likewise, those who enter a school or drive on a road named after a Confederate general may not have the slightest idea who the general was. A Millian framework justifying the existence of these monuments must also attempt to confront these questions. However, there is potentially a larger problem associated with the pro-monument Millian argument.

At the beginning of his seminal essay, Mill outlines the danger of the dreaded "tyranny of the majority," in which the majority uses the power of government to advance its mandates against a minority. As Mill notes, majority tyranny is "more formidable than many kinds of political oppression, since, though not usually upheld by such extreme penalties, it leaves fewer means of escape, penetrating much more deeply into the details of life, and enslaving the soul itself."[22] This applies to many realms of life. "Let us suppose," writes Mill,

> ... that the government is entirely at one with the people, and never thinks of exerting any power of coercion unless in agreement with what it conceives to be their voice. But I deny the right of the people to exercise such coercion, either by themselves or by their government. The power is illegitimate. The best government has no more title to it than the worst.[23]

In several municipalities in the South, a majority of the public (at least at one time) supported the Confederacy and, later, sought to commemorate that support by erecting monuments on public land. It is conceivable to argue—using a Millian framework—that this constitutes a tyranny of the majority against a minority viewpoint. Indeed, echoing Mill, an argument could be made (and, in fact, has been made) that this tyranny is especially heinous, since those who are descendants of those who were subjugated to the Confederacy must see the monuments daily as they travel around their town or state.[24] This constant reminder of the presumed inferiority of Black Americans undoubtedly "enslave[s] the soul forever."[25]

Of course, one concern with this theoretical anchoring is temporality: that is, as public opinion changes in favor of removing the monuments, which would make maintaining the monuments the minority viewpoint, does this justification for removal still apply? We believe that it does. While public opinion may shift in favor of removing the monuments, it does not necessarily follow that the Millian justification is reversed in favor of them being maintained with those favoring removal comprising a "tyranny of the majority." This comes, we believe, from the public versus private distinction outlined earlier, as well as Mill's discussion of the harm principle. Because these monuments are often government-funded and placed on public property, it is essentially the government using its authority to coerce a viewpoint against (what was at one point, and may still be) a minority viewpoint. Moreover, Mill does not preclude all censorship but, instead, simply government censorship. Indeed, Mill is accepting of public shaming. While you can speak—and, indeed, *should* speak—nobody is required to listen to you or to take whatever you say seriously. Moreover, Mill allows government coercion for the sole purpose of preventing harm to others. This "harm principle," as it is known today, allows a more solidified foundation for an anti-monument argument based on a Millian theoretical framework. While echoing critical theorists, it can be argued that the erection of the monuments sufficiently harms certain members of society and, consequently, coercion may be justified in their removal. Therefore, what began as a clear application of a Millian argument in favor of maintaining Confederate monuments has now been shown to apply to removing those very same monuments. In other words, Mill cannot resolve the free speech problem associated with Confederate displays.

Democratic Self-Governance

Since the Millian framework outlined above may not be the most convincing argument that can be levied in support of or opposition to Confederate monuments, let us turn our attention to another common theoretical justification for free speech: the importance of free expression to democratic self-government. As will become clear, the extent to which this theory can be used to support Confederate monuments is dependent on the extent to which they promote or hinder the democratic process.

While it was not until the 1927 case of *Whitney v. California*[26] that the Supreme Court recognized this justification in the context of the United States, it is certainly not new by any stretch of the imagination. Indeed, ancient Athenians recognized the connection between free and uninhibited expression and democracy over two millennia ago.[27] While this justification is as old as democracy itself, how well does it stand up in today's modern world and, specifically, when applied to debates surrounding Confederate monuments?

The contemporary scholar best known for arguing that there is a substantive and meaningful connection between democratic self-government and free speech is Alexander Meiklejohn. In his 1948 book, *Free Speech and Its Relation to Self-Government*, Meiklejohn makes the case against censorship of a member of the public on matters of *public* concern based on some authority's judgment.[28] As noted earlier in this volume, Meiklejohn makes some important caveats when discussing the First Amendment. First, the government is not entirely precluded from interfering with speech. For example, while the government may not limit speech on a public concern, it is allowed to encourage and promote that speech. Second, Meiklejohn is only concerned with speech that enhances the democratic process and he is entirely comfortable with the government limiting private speech. Indeed, as he argues, limiting some private speech is necessary for the success of public debate.[29] This speech includes that which is not relevant to promoting or enhancing the democratic process.

The question, then, becomes a conversation about which speech is related to the democratic process and which is merely private speech. For Meiklejohn, public speech protections apply "… only to speech which bears, directly or indirectly, upon issues with which voters have to deal—only, therefore, to the consideration of matters of public interest."[30] With this in mind, it becomes simple to make an argument for keeping Confederate monuments that is theoretically grounded within a democratic self-government framework.

It seems uncontroversial to claim that public Confederate monuments (especially contemporaneously) are matters of public concern. They could serve many functions (both direct and indirect) in society. First, they could commemorate a brutal Civil War that marked an important turning point in our society and our constitutional order. Indeed, immediately following that conflict, the U.S. Constitution was amended three times to prohibit slavery and grant citizenship and the right to vote to former enslaved persons. The ramifications of these amendments are still being felt today, especially as they relate to the Fourteenth Amendment's "due process" clause. Second, the monuments could spur public conversations about deeper controversies, particularly involving slavery and the historical and contemporary subjugation of Black Americans. Finally, and arguably most importantly for Meiklejohn, Confederate monuments can provide a useful heuristic for voters when evaluating public officials, and they may also serve as a gathering place for protesters.

For example, if a citizen wishes to vote for an elected official who upholds Southern traditions or values, however defined, attitudes of elected officials toward the Confederate monuments allow voters to make those connections when making electoral decisions. Likewise, a public official's statement denouncing Confederate monuments can also provide voters with useful information about that official's position on other important social issues.[31] All of this is to say that Confederate monuments can influence democratic self-government either directly or indirectly. Consequently, these monuments serve an important function in helping realize and maintain democratic self-government, and removing them would serve to impede the ability of citizens to engage in public discourse on important matters (that go deeper than just the monuments themselves) and to make educated electoral decisions.

However, as was the case with the Millian framework above, Meiklejohn's theory can also be used to justify removal of the monuments as long as one could make the case that the speech does not promote (or even actively hinder) the democratic process. For example, one could argue that the monuments represent private disputes—about, *inter alia*, the Civil War, slavery, and equality of the races—that just happen to be taking place on public property. If this is true, then the dispute is not relevant to the process of democratic self-government and could be limited without infringing on the freedom of speech.[32] Similarly, combining Meiklejohn with critical responses (addressed below in more detail) results in the same outcome, as the monuments actually serve to hinder, rather than promote, the democratic process. If, for example, monuments discourage individuals from voting on Election Day, then they could be removed without violating Meiklejohn's conception of free speech.

The discussion to this point also holds for non-monument Confederate icons, such as license plates and the renaming of roads and schools. To some, changing the name of roads and schools helps promote the democratic process by spurring mobilization and raising awareness. To others, these disputes are simply private in nature and do not relate to the democratic process. In summary, it seems again that this theory of free speech is not dispositive with regards to the controversy over Confederate symbols.

Individual Autonomy

Another theoretical justification for the freedom of speech is couched in terms of individual autonomy—that is, an individual's ability to develop and use their many faculties, including creativity and thinking. The individual autonomy justification for the freedom of speech is probably the least developed theory of free speech. Even so, as noted in the Introduction to this volume, this rationale for free speech was recognized by the U.S. Supreme Court in the 2002 case of *Ashcroft v. Free Speech Coalition*, and merits attention here.[33] As noted by the Court: "The right to think is the beginning of freedom, and speech must be protected from the government because speech is the beginning of thought."[34] We will argue that an individual autonomy argument can be made to maintain *or* take down the monuments depending on whether one believes that the monuments promote or hinder an individual's autonomy.

On its face, an argument for free speech that is rooted in individual autonomy seems unlikely to apply to Confederate monuments. One could make the argument that Confederate monuments should remain in place because taking them down would negatively affect the individual autonomy of the sculptor—just as the individual autonomy of owners of vehicles with Confederate license plates would be negatively affected if such plates were banned. However, this has a very limited scope and is not very convincing.

When it comes to Confederate statues, an argument could also be made that they serve to enhance the individual autonomy of not only the sculptor, but also those who encounter the monuments. For example, following a visit to Savannah where he saw numerous Confederate symbols, Marcus Amaker authored a poem directed at the country as a whole. The poem, entitled "Stagnation (a letter 2 America)" includes the following stanza:

> America,
> your fetish for warfare

> has erected stagnant symbols
> of oppression.
> Some of your people
> are just now awakening
> to the discomfort
> of the disenfranchised.
> Your body has been
> blemished by Southern battlegrounds,
> bound to a history of violence.[35]

Thus, not only do Confederate monuments support the individual autonomy of the sculptor, but also, they give those who encounter the monuments the chance to sculpt their own individual autonomy. Limiting the monuments serves but to limit "the beginning of thought." As a result, the "speakers" are not only the people who prefer the messages conveyed by the icons, but also those who confront the icons and develop their faculties as a result.

As should be evident by this point in the chapter, however, this is not the end of the story. An individual autonomy argument can also be made in favor of removing the monuments. Take the following example. In August of 2018, protesters toppled "Silent Sam"—a monument to the Confederacy showing a Confederate soldier—on the University of North Carolina (UNC), Chapel Hill campus. The rationale behind the monument was made clear when it was erected in 1913. Julian Carr, a former Confederate soldier himself, noted: "The present generation ... scarcely takes note of what the Confederate soldier meant to the welfare of the Anglo Saxon race during the four years immediately succeeding the war ... their courage and steadfastness saved the very life of the Anglo Saxon race in the South."[36] Carr went on to note that, "one hundred yards from where we stand ... I horse whipped a negro wench until her skirts hung in shreds because she had maligned and insulted a Southern lady."[37] Thus, the intent behind the statue is unambiguously about the inferiority of African Americans and the quest for their continued subjugation.

What does this have to do with individual autonomy? Consider the following statement made by Jerry Wilson (a graduate student at UNC Chapel Hill) following the toppling of Silent Sam. Reading from a letter that he wrote to Chancellor Carol Folt, Wilson noted that, "[w]hen you have to take the long way between classes in order to avoid the sight of a statue that denies your human dignity, the Southern Part of Heaven can feel an awful lot like hell."[38]

Thus, if we posit the development of human faculties and individual autonomy as a justification for the freedom of expression, then surely we must recognize that speech that impedes the individual autonomy of individuals is problematic. In this case, an argument could be made that the protesters were justified in removing the racist statue because it inhibited the individual autonomy of African Americans on the campus. Thus, as has been the case with all of our theories to this point, a theoretical foundation grounded in individual autonomy can be used to justify arguments for maintaining as well as removing Confederate icons.

Critical Perspectives: Are Confederate Symbols Hate Speech?

A chapter on Confederate monuments and free speech would be incomplete without a discussion of some of the critical responses to the monuments and the theories presented. Most of the responses that are critical of the Confederate icons and the theories used to justify their existence involve discussions about "hate speech" and the appropriate limits to freedom of expression. As will become clear, the answer to whether Confederate symbols are "hate speech" will determine whether the monuments should stay in place or come down. However, the answer to the question is likely to be motivated by an amalgam of factors, including racial attitudes, politics, and other non-theoretical factors.

Critical theorists recognize the importance and value of freedom of expression, but dispute the boundaries to appropriate expression. They recognize the need for robust and open debate in a quest for truth, but nonetheless acknowledge that certain speech is counterproductive. As a result, critical theorists argue that some speech is beyond the bounds of acceptable "free expression," since it only serves to devalue the person at whom the speech is directed, and to derail the conversation. In other words, communication that is aimed at limiting the speech of others (whether intentionally or in effect) is counterintuitive to the many justifications offered for free and robust debate and, consequently, should be prohibited.

Consider the following real-world example. In April, 2018, Larry Johnson, a former city commissioner, attempted to make a case for a "Confederate history month" by addressing the current commissioners in Griffin County, Georgia. During his remarks, Mr. Johnson repeatedly used a racial slur, saying that, "There were white folks. There were black folks when I was growing up. There was white trash—my family. There was n-----town. I lived next to n-----town."[39] When confronted by Rodney McCord, a city commissioner who is African American, asking, "You lived next to what town?" Johnson replied "N-----town, son!"[40]

For critical theorists, this scenario highlights the need for limits on the acceptable and legal limits of freedom of expression. While the conversation was taking place in a public forum, the racial slur used served no purpose but to limit the quality of the discussion and to derail the conversation. A debate that began as a good-faith effort to discuss the merits and demerits of having a "Confederate history month" abruptly shifted to a discussion about the humanity, dignity, and value of a group of citizens, even if implicitly.[41] The African American council member may feel devalued by society, personally attacked, and compelled to defend his mere existence. Therefore, some regulation of speech is necessary in order to help promote the core value of freedom of speech.[42]

It is easy, therefore, to make an argument against Confederate monuments using a critical theory approach. Monuments, as has been argued in court filings, have an effect on speech that disproportionately affects minorities.[43] This has the consequence of limiting debate and, therefore, is counterintuitive to the principal justifications for free speech.

However, we can also make an argument using a critical theory approach that justifies the existence of the Confederate monuments. While directly calling an individual a racial slur to their face is likely to result in the consequences that critical theorists seek to preclude, Confederate monuments are not necessarily comparable. Indeed, it could be argued that Confederate icons serve to embolden minorities into speaking out and engaging in the democratic process.

Consider the following example from West Virginia. In 1859, Heyward Shepherd, a Black man, died at Harpers Ferry during John Brown's raid for the abolition of slavery. A local Black college erected a monument in 1918, which caused the United Daughters of the Confederacy (UDC) to unveil their own memorial in 1931. As Caroline E. Janney explained in her *Washington Post* article:

> Although they discovered that Shepherd was a free man accidentally killed in the raid, they chose to celebrate him as a loyal and faithful slave who had refused to participate in Brown's abolitionist plot. With the rising prominence of civil rights groups like the NAACP speaking out against white supremacy, this narrative of Shepherd offered an alternative: a loyal black man who accepted his place in a segregated society.[44]

Janney goes on to note how some at the dedication refused to accept this narrative, and how the monuments fueled a countermovement led by several Black leaders and the Black press. As she notes:

> Condemning the memorial as the 'Uncle Tom Slave Monument,' black leaders and the black press … launched blistering attacks. But they did not settle for words alone. If whites insisted upon 'giving the Confederate point of view' in

memorializing a so-called faithful slave, African Americans would counter with their own. The following year, they dedicated another memorial to Brown—one that depicted him as a hero whose traits challenged acceptable black behavior in the Jim Crow South.[45]

In this scenario, at least, it seems that the monuments contributed to the democratic process and enhanced the marketplace of ideas by prompting more people to contribute. Similarly, following the toppling of "Silent Sam" mentioned above, first-year student Natalia Walker was quoted as saying, "I feel liberated—like I'm a part of something big. It's literally my fourth day here. This is the biggest thing I've ever been apart [sic] of in my life just activist wise. All of these people coming together for this one sole purpose and actually getting it done was the best part."[46] This direct form of participation is likely to continue into the future for many of those involved, not just regarding issues involving Confederate monuments. On balance, a critical theoretical perspective seems likely to tilt in favor of removing Confederate monuments, but even here a cogent pro-monument argument can still be made.

Conclusion

The purpose of this chapter has been to re-conceptualize the ongoing debate about Confederate icons in terms of theoretical justifications for free speech. Specifically, we have analyzed the controversy by tying it to the pursuit of truth, democratic self-governance, and individual autonomy. We acknowledged and discussed the critical responses that highlight the differing opinions on the range of acceptable speech. In doing so, we repeatedly stressed that sound justifications grounded in respected theory can be articulated on both sides of the debate. In other words, we are unable to solve the discussion around whether Confederate icons should remain by reference to theories of free speech alone. As has been shown, what might at first glance appear to be a clear application of Mill's "pursuit of truth" framework can be turned on its head and framed in terms of the dreaded "tyranny of the majority." Similarly, whether one recognizes the importance of the icons to the democratic process cannot be answered by referencing abstract theory. Finally, Confederate icons can both enhance and limit the individual autonomy of those whom encounter them. Thus, while theories can inform and guide the discussion, they cannot, on their own, provide the solution that some might seek.

Since theories of free speech cannot provide the answers to whether the icons should stay or go, what can? We contend that the problems presented by the continued presence of Confederate monuments in our public spaces are fundamentally political. Individuals' attitudes on questions relating to

Confederate imagery are powerfully influenced by racial attitudes, and to a lesser extent, identification as a "Southerner." Racial inequities have been a constant feature of American social and political institutions and public policies.[47] The Confederacy was defeated and slavery abolished, but the legacies of slavery and of the Civil War itself still persist.[48] Even today, attitudes toward and about racial and ethnic groups are crucially important to understanding an enormous range of political opinions and mass behaviors.[49] As a result, individual views about the best way to handle the controversial statues and the like are also driven in large part by racial attitudes. Shouting "Free Speech!" whether in defending Confederate monuments or advocating for their removal, is not going to get us very far.

Notes

1. The authors thank Valeria Sinclair-Chapman and Keith Bybee for helpful comments on previous drafts.
2. See, for example, Ben Jones, "The Confederate Flag Is a Matter of Pride and Heritage, Not Hatred," *New York Times*, December 22, 2015, accessed December 6, 2018, https://www.nytimes.com/roomfordebate/2015/06/19/does-the-confederate-flag-breed-racism/the-confederate-flag-is-a-matter-of-pride-and-heritage-not-hatred; Adam Smith, "'Heritage, Not Hate': Confederate Flag Supporters Emphasize Heritage, Love of Community," *News Courier* (Athens, AL), August 14, 2015, accessed December 6, 2018, http://www.enewscourier.com/news/heritage-not-hate-confederate-flag-supporters-emphasize-heritage-love-of/article_4f963ab0-4210-11e5-93ab-7beed50ba868.html.
3. Valeria Sinclair-Chapman, "(De)constructing Symbols: Charlottesville, the Confederate Flag, and a Case for Disrupting Symbolic Meaning," *Politics, Groups, and Identities* 6, no. 2 (2018).
4. See Logan Strother, Spencer Piston, and Thomas Ogorzalek, "Pride or Prejudice? Racial Prejudice, Southern Heritage, and Support for the Confederate Battle Flag," *Du Bois Review* 14, no. 1 (2017); Sinclair-Chapman, "(De)constructing Symbols"; John S. Reed, *Tears Spoiled My Aim and Other Reflections on Southern Culture* (New York: Harcourt Brace, 1993); John S. Reed, *Kicking Back: Further Dispatches From the South* (Columbia: University of Missouri Press, 1995); C. Vann Woodward, "The Search for Southern Identity," *Myth and Southern History* 2 (1958).
5. Frances Robles, Richard Fausset, and Michael Barbaro, "Nikki Haley, South Carolina Governor, Calls for Removal of Confederate Battle Flag," *New York Times*, June 23, 2015.
6. Tegan Wendland, "With Lee Statue's Removal, Another Battle of New Orleans Comes to a Close," *NPR*, May 20, 2017, accessed December 6, 2018, https://www.npr.org/2017/05/20/529232823/with-lee-statues-removal-another-battle-of-new-orleans-comes-to-a-close; Yasmeen Sherhan, "St. Louis to Remove Its Confederate Monument," *The Atlantic*, June 26, 2017, accessed December 6, 2018, https://www.theatlantic.com/news/archive/2017/06/st-louis-to-remove-its-confederate-monument/531720/; Ryan Poe, "Memphis to Remove Confederate

Statues Overnight Following Sale of Public Parks," *USA Today*, December 20, 2017, accessed December 6, 2018, https://www.usatoday.com/story/news/nation-now/2017/12/20/memphis-confederate-statues-removal/971882001/.
7. Rupali Srivastava, "Eight South Carolina Lawmakers Explain Why They Are Opposed to Removing the Confederate Flag," *ThinkProgress*, June 23, 2015, accessed December 6, 2018, https://thinkprogress.org/eight-south-carolina-lawmakers-explain-why-they-are-opposed-to-removing-the-confederate-flag-440c76925394/.
8. Ariel Edwards-Levy, "Polls Find Little Support for Confederate Statue Removal—But How You Ask Matters," *HuffPost*, August 23, 2017, accessed December 6, 2018, https://www.huffingtonpost.com/entry/confederate-statues-removal-polls_us_599de056e4b05710aa59841c.
9. Ibid.
10. This web-based survey was fielded by Survey Sampling International (SSI), in June of 2018; the sample was nationally representative of voting-age citizens, N=1,037.
11. Strother, Piston, and Ogorzalek, "Pride or Prejudice?"
12. Kenneth F. Warren, "Offensive Statues Should Be Protected Under First Amendment," *St. Louis Post-Dispatch*, August 24, 2017, December 6, 2018, https://www.stltoday.com/opinion/columnists/offensive-statues-should-be-protected-under-first-amendment/article_9acd6b76-cc9c-5be8-975c-85cc0d065165.html.
13. The survey was fielded by Survey Sampling International/ResearchNow (SSI) between May 9 and May 21, 2018. SSI maintains a large online (opt-in) panel of respondents from which it samples respondents to participate in surveys; each sample is balanced to be nationally representative.
14. Of course, this question wording does not permit us to ascertain exactly *whose* rights are perceived to be violated. Respondents could be thinking about their own right to freedom of speech, or the rights of other citizens or the sculptor of the statue, for example.
15. Mary Ann Glendon, *Rights Talk: The Impoverishment of Political Discourse* (New York: Free Press, 1991); Laura Beth Nielsen, *License to Harass: Law, Hierarchy, and Offensive Public Speech* (Princeton, NJ: Princeton University Press, 2009); Corey Brettschneider, "When the State Speaks, What Should It Say? The Dilemmas of Freedom of Expression and Democratic Persuasion," *Perspectives on Politics* 8, no. 4 (December 2010).
16. *Pleasant Grove City v. Summum*, 555 U.S. 460 (2009).
17. John Stuart Mill, *On Liberty* (Mineola, NY: Dover Publications, 2002; London: J.W. Parker, 1859), 14.
18. Ibid.
19. Ibid., 30.
20. See *Walker v. Texas Division, Sons of Confederate Veterans, Inc.*, 135 S.Ct. 2239 (2015)—rationalizing that government speech is the product of the democratic process, and also noting that people think of the state when they see licenses plates, the Court held that Texas prohibiting the Confederate flag on specialty license plates does not violate the First Amendment. In this regard, it is possible to argue that the Court is not protecting the freedom of speech in a Millian fashion, since it is precluding the quest for truth.
21. See, for example, *Pleasant Grove City v. Summum*, where the Supreme Court states: "The meaning conveyed by a monument is generally not a simple one like

"'Beef. It's What's for Dinner.'" Even when a monument features the written word, the monument may be intended to be interpreted, and may in fact be interpreted by different observers, in a variety of ways. . . . What, for example, is 'the message' of the Greco-Roman mosaic of the word 'Imagine' that was donated to New York City's Central Park in memory of John Lennon? Some observers may 'imagine' the musical contributions that John Lennon would have made if he had not been killed. Others may think of the lyrics of the Lennon song that obviously inspired the mosaic and may 'imagine' a world without religion, countries, possessions, greed, or hunger. Or, to take another example, what is 'the message' of the "large bronze statue displaying the word 'peace' in many world languages" that is displayed in Fayetteville, Arkansas? These text-based monuments are almost certain to evoke different thoughts and sentiments in the minds of different observers, and the effect of monuments that do not contain text is likely to be even more variable." 555 U.S. at 474–75 (internal citations omitted).

22. John Gray and G. W. Smith, eds., *J.S. Mill* On Liberty *In Focus* (London: Routledge, 1991), 26.
23. Ibid.
24. See, for example, *NAACP v. Hunt*, 891 F.2d. 1555, 1565 (1990) noting that: "The NAACP argues that the flying of the flag violates the Free Speech Clause in two ways. First, it argues that the presence of the flag chills free speech, as evidenced by the appellant Reed's testimony that he has difficulty saluting the American flag atop the capitol while the confederate flag flies." Also: "The NAACP's sole argument in support of the claim that the state has violated the Thirteenth Amendment is that the confederate flag, because of its inspirational power in the confederate army during the Civil War and its adoption by the Ku Klux Klan, is a 'badge and vestige of slavery.'" Ibid., at 1564. These efforts, however, have often failed to win support in courts, which often dismiss them as lacking any evidence of a deprived constitutional right.
25. "The Georgia state flag, through its incorporation of the Confederate battle flag, did not serve to bring Forman into the fold of public life. By conveying a message of intolerance, it acted instead to exclude him, to remind him of the subordinate role that Blacks have traditionally been forced into in the South. Instead of symbolizing a society in which he can be a member, it symbolizes a society in which he would have been a second-class citizen as a result of his race. Exclusion of this sort has no place in a nation that demands equality; Georgia's imposition of such exclusion on its Black citizens through its use of a discriminatory symbol denies them the equal protection of the law." Robert J. Bein, "Stained Flags: Public Symbols and Equal Protection," *Seton Hall Law Review* 28 (1998): 922.
26. 274 U.S. 357 (1927)
27. Jacob Mchangama, "Episode 1: Who Wishes to Speak?—Free Speech in Ancient Athens," *Clear and Present Danger: A History of Free Speech*, accessed December 6, 2018, http://www.freespeechhistory.com/2017/10/25/episode-1/. For additional information, see Arlene W. Saxonhouse, *Free Speech and Democracy in Ancient Athens* (Cambridge: Cambridge University Press, 2005).
28. Alexander Meiklejohn, *Free Speech and Its Relation to Self-Government* (New York: Harper, 1948).

29. For an example, see Meiklejohn's discussion of the city council meeting in which he acknowledges that private speech must be limited in order to enhance the public speech, which is the purpose of the meeting.
30. Meiklejohn, *Free Speech*, 94.
31. If doubts remain about the importance of confederate monuments to public discussion, attitudes, and policy, see: Cleve R. Wootson, Jr., "White Lawmaker Warns Black Attorney She May 'Go Missing' if Confederate Statues are Threatened," *Washington Post*, August 30, 2017, accessed December 6, 2018, https://www.washingtonpost.com/news/post-nation/wp/2017/08/30/white-lawmaker-warns-black-attorney-she-may-go-missing-if-confederate-statues-are-threatened/?noredirect=on&utm_term=.cfc1c3718894.
32. Parallels can be drawn between this and Meiklejohn's discussion of the city council meeting.
33. 535 U.S. 234 (2002).
34. Ibid., at 253.
35. Marcus Amaker, "Stagnation (a letter 2 America)," *MarcusAmaker*, August 17, 2017, accessed December 6, 2018, http://marcusamaker.com/stagnation/.
36. W. Fitzhugh Brundage, "I've Studied the History of Confederate Memorials. Here's What to Do About Them," *Vox*, August 18, 2017, accessed December 6, 2018, https://www.vox.com/platform/amp/the-big-idea/2017/8/18/16165160/confederate-monuments-history-charlottesville-white-supremacy.
37. Ibid.
38. Jane Stancill, "'Silent Sam' is Down: Protesters Topple Confederate Statue on UNC campus," *Fayetteville Observer*, September 6, 2018, accessed December 6, 2018, http://www.fayobserver.com/news/20180820/silent-sam-is-down-protesters-topple-confederate-statue-on-unc-campus.
39. John Bowden, "Former Georgia Official Uses N-Word While Advocating for a Confederate History Month," *The Hill*, April 7, 2018, accessed December 6, 2018, http://thehill.com/blogs/blog-briefing-room/news/382072-former-georgia-official-uses-n-word-while-advocating-for.
40. Ibid.
41. It is worth noting that a Meiklejohnian argument can be made against the speech here, too. The use of the racial slur derailed the conversation that was relevant to democratic self-governance. This is mere private speech and not relevant to the public consideration. Consequently, a democratic self-governing justification for free speech could be used to exclude this scenario from the boundaries of free expression.
42. This is similar to many of the European-style "hate speech" laws found today.
43. Merrit Kennedy, "Supreme Court Rejects Case Over Confederate Emblem on Mississippi Flag," *NPR: The Two-Way*, November 27, 2017, accessed December 6, 2018, https://www.npr.org/sections/thetwo-way/2017/11/27/566737228/supreme-court-rejects-case-over-confederate-emblem-on-mississippi-flag.
44. Caroline E. Janney, "Why We Need Confederate Monuments," *Washington Post*, July 27, 2017, accessed December 6, 2018, https://www.washingtonpost.com/news/made-by-history/wp/2017/07/27/why-we-need-confederate-monuments/?noredirect=on&utm_term=.25a02814fc7c.
45. Ibid.
46. Charlie McGee and Myah Ward, "Silent Sam Toppled in Protest the Night Before Classes Begin," *Daily Tar Heel*, August 20, 2018, accessed December 6, 2018, http://www.dailytarheel.com/article/2018/08/silent-sam-down.

47. See, for example, W.E.B. Du Bois, *The Souls of Black Folk* (Chicago: A.C. McClurg, 1903); Michael Dawson, *Behind the Mule: Race and Class in African-American Politics* (Princeton, NJ: Princeton University Press, 1994); Desmond S. King and Rogers M. Smith, "Racial Orders in American Political Development," *American Political Science Review* 99, no. 1 (February 2005); Katherine Cramer Walsh, *Talking About Race: Community Dialogues and the Politics of Differences* (Chicago: University of Chicago Press, 2007); Laura J. Hatcher, Logan Strother, Randolph Burnside, and Donald Hughes, "The USACE and Post-Katrina New Orleans: Demolitions and Disaster Clean-Up," *Journal of Applied Social Science* 6, no. 2 (September 2012); Paul Frymer, *Building an American Empire* (Princeton, NJ: Princeton University Press, 2017); Charles Menifield, Geiguen Shin, and Logan Strother, "Do White Law Enforcement Officers Target Minority Suspects?" *Public Administration Review* (June 19, 2018), https://doi.org/10.1111/puar.12956.
48. See Richard M. Valelly, *The Two Reconstructions: The Struggle for Black Enfranchisement* (Chicago: University of Chicago Press, 2004); Avidit Acharya, Matthew Blackwell, and Maya Sen, *Deep Roots: How Slavery Still Shapes Southern Politics* (Princeton, NJ: Princeton University Press, 2018); David A. Bateman, Ira Katznelson, and John S. Lapinski, *Southern Nation: Congress and White Supremacy After Reconstruction* (Princeton, NJ: Princeton University Press, 2018).
49. See, for example, Edward G. Carmines and James A. Stimson, *Issue Evolution: Race and Transformation of American Politics* (Princeton, NJ: Princeton University Press, 1989); Donald R. Kinder and Lynn M. Sanders, *Divided By Color: Racial Politics and Democratic Ideals* (Chicago: University of Chicago Press, 1996); Spencer Piston, "How Explicit Racial Prejudice Hurt Obama in the 2008 Election," *Political Behavior* 32, no. 4 (December 2010); Michael Tessler, *Post-Racial or Most-Racial? Race and Politics in the Obama Era* (Chicago: University of Chicago Press, 2016).

References

Acharya, Avidit, Matthew Blackwell, and Maya Sen. *Deep Roots: How Slavery Still Shapes Southern Politics*. Princeton, NJ: Princeton University Press, 2018.

Bateman, David A., Ira Katznelson, and John S. Lapinski. *Southern Nation: Congress and White Supremacy After Reconstruction*. Princeton, NJ: Princeton University Press, 2018.

Bein, Robert J. "Stained Flags: Public Symbols and Equal Protection." *Seton Hall Law Review* 28 (1998): 897–924.

Brettschneider, Corey. "When the State Speaks, What Should It Say? The Dilemmas of Freedom of Expression and Democratic Persuasion." *Perspectives on Politics* 8, no. 4 (December 2010): 1005–19.

Carmines, Edward G., and James A. Stimson. *Issue Evolution: Race and Transformation of American Politics*. Princeton, NJ: Princeton University Press, 1989.

Cramer Walsh, Katherine. *Talking About Race: Community Dialogues and the Politics of Differences*. Chicago: University of Chicago Press, 2007.

Du Bois, W.E.B. *The Souls of Black Folk*. Chicago: A.C. McClurg, 1903.

Dawson, Michael. *Behind the Mule: Race and Class in African-American Politics*. Princeton, NJ: Princeton University Press, 1994.

Frymer, Paul. *Building an American Empire*. Princeton, NJ: Princeton University Press, 2017.
Glendon, Mary Ann. *Rights Talk: The Impoverishment of Political Discourse*. New York: Free Press, 1991.
Gray, John, and G. W. Smith, eds. *J.S. Mill On Liberty In Focus*. London: Routledge, 1991.
Hatcher, Laura J., Logan Strother, Randolph Burnside, and Donald Hughes. "The USACE and Post-Katrina New Orleans: Demolitions and Disaster Clean-Up." *Journal of Applied Social Science* 6, no. 2 (September 2012): 176–90.
Kinder, Donald R., and Lynn M. Sanders. *Divided By Color: Racial Politics and Democratic Ideals*. Chicago: University of Chicago Press, 1996.
King, Desmond S., and Rogers M. Smith. "Racial Orders in American Political Development." *American Political Science Review* 99, no. 1 (February 2005): 75–92.
Meiklejohn, Alexander. *Free Speech and Its Relation to Self-Government*. New York: Harper, 1948.
Menifield, Charles, Geiguen Shin, and Logan Strother. "Do White Law Enforcement Officers Target Minority Suspects?" *Public Administration Review* (June 19, 2018). Accessed December 6, 2018. https://doi.org/10.1111/puar.12956.
Mill, John Stuart. *On Liberty*. Mineola, NY: Dover Publications, 2002. First published 1859 by J.W. Parker (London).
Nielsen, Laura Beth. *License to Harass: Law, Hierarchy, and Offensive Public Speech*. Princeton, NJ: Princeton University Press, 2009.
Piston, Spencer. "How Explicit Racial Prejudice Hurt Obama in the 2008 Election." *Political Behavior* 32, no. 4 (December 2010): 431–51.
Reed, John S. *Kicking Back: Further Dispatches From the South*. Columbia: University of Missouri Press, 1995.
———. *Tears Spoiled My Aim and Other Reflections on Southern Culture*. New York: Harcourt Brace, 1993.
Saxonhouse, Arlene W. *Free Speech and Democracy in Ancient Athens*. Cambridge: Cambridge University Press, 2005.
Sinclair-Chapman, Valeria. "(De)constructing Symbols: Charlottesville, the Confederate Flag, and a Case for Disrupting Symbolic Meaning." *Politics, Groups, and Identities* 6, no. 2 (2018): 316–23.
Strother, Logan, Spencer Piston, and Thomas Ogorzalek. "Pride or Prejudice? Racial Prejudice, Southern Heritage, and Support for the Confederate Battle Flag." *Du Bois Review* 14, no. 1 (2017): 295–323.
Tessler, Michael. *Post-Racial or Most-Racial?: Race and Politics in the Obama Era*. Chicago: University of Chicago Press, 2016.
Valelly, Richard M. *The Two Reconstructions: The Struggle for Black Enfranchisement*. Chicago: University of Chicago Press, 2004.
Woodward, C. Vann. "The Search for Southern Identity." *Myth and Southern History* 2 (1958): 119–32.

5. Speech and National Past Times: The NFL, the Flag, and Professional Athletes

AARON LORENZ

"Rosa Parks stood by sitting and changed the way people felt about lying down."[1]

"Sports and politics don't mix." When President Jimmy Carter announced that the United States would boycott the 1980 Summer Olympic Games to be held in the Soviet Union, this was the reaction of the Olympian Eric Heiden. After winning a record five individual gold medals at the Winter Olympics a few months earlier, Heiden unsuccessfully pursued a spot on the United States cycling team for the Summer games. Had he achieved that goal, he would have defied the President's decision. In saying that "sports and politics don't mix," Heiden demonstrated that quite the opposite is true.[2]

Indeed, countless examples show that sports and politics do, in fact, mix quite well. This is because athletes are often very aware that the platform their athletic skill affords them can be used to make profoundly important political statements. Tommie Smith and John Carlos at the Mexico City Olympics of 1968, raising their black-gloved fists in solidarity with the human rights movement, particularly the Black Power movement in the U.S.; Muhammad Ali refusing to serve in the military during the Vietnam War; LeBron James and other prominent NBA players wearing shirts that read "I Can't Breathe" to draw attention to the death of Eric Garner at the hands of New York City Police Officers; and, of course, Colin Kaepernick's decision to kneel during the national anthem at NFL games in order to bring attention to racial injustice in the United States—an action that cost him his job as a quarterback in that league.

State Action

To understand the relationship between free speech theories, sports, and political protests, the best place to start is with an issue briefly addressed in the Introduction to this volume. In 2014, then Seattle Seahawks running back Marshawn Lynch was fined $50,000 for failing to talk to the media after his team's game, a violation of the NFL Media Relations Policy. Some legal scholars have argued that the NFL Media Relations Policy is a due process violation of the First Amendment, positing that the NFL is a state actor. For Lynch, his issue hinged on the policy itself which stated, "players must be available to the media following every game and regularly during the practice week."[3] NFL rules mandate that players be available for interviews with the press after a reasonable waiting period following each game and during a normal practice week on Monday, Wednesday, Thursday, and Friday for a minimum of 45 minutes on each of those days. Failure to adhere to this policy would amount to a violation of league rules, unless one could argue that such a rule was a free speech violation. During the 2013 regular season, Lynch refused to talk to reporters and was subsequently fined $50,000. Lynch appealed the fine. As the season progressed, Lynch appeared at press conferences but gave only short responses and did not stay for the required 45 minutes. Legal scholar Sohil Shah argues that fining Lynch because of his refusal to follow the NFL's policy was a violation of his First Amendment right to freedom of speech.[4]

Lynch's First Amendment rights were violated by the NFL. The First Amendment states that "Congress shall make no law … abridging the freedom of speech…" The Fourteenth Amendment requires the First Amendment, and others in the Bill of Rights, to limit the actions of all levels of government—federal, state, and local. Specifically, the Fourteenth Amendment states that, "no State shall … deprive any person of life, liberty, or property, without due process of law." Fifteen years after the ratification of that addition to the Constitution, the Supreme Court, in the *Civil Rights Cases*, held that the Fourteenth Amendment only restricts state (government/public) actors; it does not speak to the *private* invasion of individual rights.[5] This has become known as the state-action doctrine, which, simply stated, means the constitutional amendments that protect individual rights only prohibit government action; they do not extend to private conduct that abridges or violates individual rights.[6]

How does this relate to the NFL and other such organizations? Shah posits that:

> … the state-action doctrine is not absolute and that private actors can be held liable under certain exceptions. When alleging a constitutional violation by a private

party, the issue is 'whether the state was sufficiently involved to treat that decisive conduct as state action.' The entanglement exception to the state-action doctrine states that the Constitution applies if the government 'affirmatively authorizes, encourages, or facilitates private conduct that violates the Constitution.' Government subsidies or financial support to a private entity can make the private entity a state actor and therefore liable under the state-action doctrine.[7]

The NFL is a State Actor. The NFL should be considered a state actor, whether it is the Lynch case or the Kaepernick case, because of its purpose. While the league is a private entity, its purpose is to promote, organize, and regulate professional football in the United States.[8] With significant government support, the NFL becomes a state actor. In free speech cases, the courts are typically tasked with balancing First Amendment rights of free expression against an individual's state-based right of publicity. Frank Ryan and Matt Ganas note that, in this context, First Amendment analysis generally turns on whether the defendant's publication qualifies as commercial or non-commercial speech.[9] While "commercial speech was initially viewed as being outside the ambit of the First Amendment altogether," precedent has held "that commercial speech is constitutionally protected but governmental burdens on this category of speech are scrutinized more leniently than burdens on fully protected noncommercial speech."[10] The clarity of the league as a state actor hinges on the NFL and its teams relying on public support (financial) which ultimately makes them public (enough) entities. The NFL receives government funding for its stadiums, a widely discussed issue among the taxpayers when a team begins to explore a new site. Take, for example, the new stadium for the Minnesota Vikings, built at a cost of nearly $1 billion, with state and local taxpayers footing nearly 70% of the bill (a percentage which is more the norm than the exception).[11]

The NFL enjoys the kind of status essentially reserved only for it. The United States provides federal and state assistance in the form of tax breaks not extended to other private corporations. However, the NFL is a tax-exempt, not-for-profit organization. The NFL has been classified as a nonprofit organization since 1942, and in 1966 Congress amended the tax code by adding "professional football leagues" to its definition of 501(c) not-for-profit organizations.[12] With this kind of protection, some legal scholars consider the NFL as a tax shelter for its teams and owners.[13] Of course, the league continues to make massive amounts of money selling licenses for things such as broadcasting contracts and apparel, and the individual teams then receive financial compensation. In turn, the teams pay dues to the NFL which are tax-deductible because of the NFL's status. This antitrust protection has allowed the NFL to function in such a manner for decades. In 1966, Congress enacted Public Law 89–800, which gave the NFL a monopoly regarding its broadcasting rights.[14] While the NFL maintains its nonprofit status, television rights are worth billions of dollars each year. Shah explains that the NFL also profits from its exclusive copyright license for games that are broadcast from its publicly funded stadiums,[15] and thus, the NFL's actions constitute its role as a state actor.

Scholar and theorist Alexander Meiklejohn helps provide a clear context for this discussion. He writes:

> But the 'consent' of free citizens is radically different in kind from this 'submission' of slaves. Free men talk about their government, not in terms of its 'favors' but in terms of their 'rights.' They do not bargain. They reason. Every one of them is, of course, subject to the laws that are made.[16]

Speech, for the athlete, is oftentimes simply an attempt to hold political institutions in check. Free speech, when exercised, is taking back dominance over the agencies that control society. For Meiklejohn, it was an opportunity, in chaotic and desperate situations, for the sake of a new order, to revolt and destroy.[17]

State Action and Free Speech Theory

The 1883 *Civil Rights Cases* were a group of cases that the Supreme Court considered to address racial discrimination by private businesses. The cases were consolidated and arose because of the recently passed Civil Rights Act of 1875 which provided people access to accommodations and public transportation regardless of race. Justice Bradley delivered the opinion of the Court and struck down the Civil Rights Act of 1875 arguing that the 13th Amendment only applied to slavery and the 14th Amendment did not provide Congress the power to forbid private discrimination. Essentially, Bradley posited that there was a clear differentiation between public and private acts. Private acts of racial discrimination were just that: private.

Justice John Marshall Harlan's dissent provided a somewhat progressive approach to racial discrimination, at least in terms of the year 1883. Harlan notes:

> What I affirm is that no State, nor the officers of any State, nor any corporation or individual wielding power under state authority for the public benefit or the public convenience, can, consistently either with the freedom established by the fundamental law, or with that equality of civil rights which now belongs to every citizen, discriminate against freemen or citizens, in their civil rights, because of their race, or because they once labored under disabilities imposed upon them as a race. *The rights which Congress, by the act of 1875, endeavored to secure and*

> *protect are legal, not social, rights.* The right, for instance, of a colored citizen to use the accommodations of a public highway upon the same terms as are permitted to white citizens is no more a social right than his right, under the law, to use the public streets of a city, or a town, or a turnpike road, or a public market, or a post-office, or his right to sit in a public building with others, of whatever race, for the purpose of hearing the political questions of the day discussed. Scarcely a day passes without our seeing in this court-room citizens of the white and black races sitting side by side watching the progress of our business. It would never occur to any one that the presence of a colored citizen in a court-house or courtroom was an invasion of the social rights of white persons who may frequent such places. And yet such a suggestion would be quite as sound in law—I say it with all respect—as is the suggestion that the claim of a colored citizen to use, upon the same terms as is permitted to white citizens, the accommodations of public highways, or public inns, or places of public amusement, established under the license of the law, is an invasion of the social rights of the white race.[18]

For Harlan, his dissent symbolized the rather blurred line between public and private. Private businesses were there for public consumption. Private railways were used by the public. Harlan was essentially arguing that nothing was unequivocally private and thus, it was public, even if only minimally. All of this was all in the interest of liberty.

Harlan's dissent hinges on the notion of public benefit or public convenience. Whether it is 1883 or the present, one need only ask: Does the benefit provided (or convenience to the user) belong to the public or private realm? Harlan's point is important because when one fails to see the overlap between public benefit or convenience and private rights or authority, it allows matters to be left in the hands of the powerful. In this case, the line between public and private is not as distinct as the NFL would have one believe.

Free Speech Jurisprudence: Connecting Theory to Content Neutrality

Speech restrictions that are enacted by the government are typically classified into two categories: content-neutral restrictions and content-based restrictions. Content-neutral restrictions are identified as limitations upon the time, place, or manner of speech.[19] To establish if a law is content-neutral, the law must be "justified without reference to the content of the regulated speech."[20] As the Supreme Court stated in *Ward v. Rock Against Racism*, "the principal inquiry in determining content neutrality … is whether the government has adopted a regulation of speech because of disagreement with the message it conveys."[21] The Supreme Court has historically considered the government's purpose in creating the law. In *City of Renton v. Playtime Theaters, Inc.*, the

Court concluded that a law is regarded as content-neutral if the government's ultimate purpose lies within the secondary effects of limiting speech, and not with the specific content of speech itself.[22] The Court held that a Washington state zoning ordinance prohibiting the presence of adult theaters was a content-neutral restriction. The rationale was that the ordinance was created to control external factors such as the city's crime rate, commerce, and property values. These external factors demonstrated the intent of the city, showing they were not concerned with suppressing the expression of unpopular views. Content-neutral restriction is appropriately narrowly tailored if the speech limitations directly align with the government's interest.[23]

Content-based restrictions limit speech because of the "message, its ideas, its subject matter, or its content."[24] Because of the consideration of substantive content, content-based restrictions are presumptively invalid. As Justice William J. Brennan, Jr. expressed in *Texas v. Johnson*, "if there is a bedrock principle underlying the First Amendment, it is that the government may not prohibit the expression of an idea simply because society finds the idea itself offensive or disagreeable."[25] This standard of judicial review, which legal scholars refer to as strict scrutiny, allows content-based restrictions to pass strict scrutiny if the limitation is "narrowly tailored to promote a compelling Government interest ... [and] if a less restrictive alternative would serve the government's purpose, the legislature must use that alternative."[26]

The Court heard a similar argument in *United States v. Playboy Entertainment Group, Inc.* and found "where the designed benefit of a content-based restriction is to shield the sensibilities of listeners, the general rule is that the right of expression prevails, even where no less restrictive alternative exists."[27] The Supreme Court held that a law requiring cable providers to block sexually explicit programs during the hours children were most likely to watch television was an unconstitutional content-based restriction upon speech. The Court noted, "even where speech is indecent and enters the home, the objective of shielding children does not suffice to support a blanket ban if the protection can be accomplished by a less restrictive alternative."[28] Of course, Colin Kaepernick's protest affected those in the stadium as well as those watching on television so *Playboy* might only loosely apply. The Court does explain that there are certain classifications of speech that the government may limit, even through content-based restrictions. For example, speech that exempts the government from the rigidity of content-based restrictions may be divided into six classifications: obscenity, defamatory language, incitement, fraud, speech integral to criminal conduct, and fighting words. That type of speech is regarded as "low value," and, in the eyes of the Supreme Court, does not warrant First Amendment protection. The public vs. private distinction remains consequential here because as noted earlier, the NFL is not completely disconnected from the U.S. government.

While content-based restrictions help contextualize the Kaepernick situation, prior restraint also needs to be addressed to better understand how the NFL is essentially violating Kaepernick's free speech. Prior restraint entails limiting or silencing speech before it occurs. If the speech is content-neutral or content-based, the government is generally not able to restrict the speech. When the government restricts speech in this manner, it is prior restraint. When a government entity, in this case the NFL, restrains speech before it is spoken, as opposed to punishing its effects afterwards, the action is also prior restraint. This kind of pre-emptive limitation on speech is highly frowned upon because it is an imposition on speech based "on predictions of dangers that would not actually materialize and thus would not be the basis for subsequent punishments."[29] In *New York Times v. United States*, the Supreme Court rejected the U.S. government's effort to preliminarily suppress the publication of select classified articles within the *New York Times*.[30] Justice Hugo Black explained in his concurrence that the government's justification of national security was far too overbroad and vague to constitute a compelling reason to override prior restraint. Kaepernick argues that the NFL owners colluded to keep him from re-signing with a team. Ultimately, if the government (or NFL in this case) would like to restrict speech, the restriction should be narrowly tailored to serve a governmental interest unrelated to the actual content of speech.

Social Activism and Sports

Columnist George F. Will sees efforts at separating sports and politics as decidedly peculiar, noting,

> Ancient Greek and Roman thinkers routinely discussed sports in the context of politics. Greek philosophers considered sport a religious and civic—in a word, moral—undertaking. Sport, they said, is morally serious because mankind's noblest aim is the loving contemplation of worthy things.[31]

This kind of political theatre was accepted then, and remains accepted today. We want our athletes in this country to blur the line between athlete and social critic. Yet, we also want to reserve the right to simultaneously critique them for their political views.

Social activism and sports have been connected for decades, with particular attention on the 1960s when student-athletes and the Civil Rights Movement/Black Power Movement overlapped. For much of the United

States, the San Francisco Bay Area became the focal point of civil disobedience campaigns and a good deal of it was linked to sports.[32] Many of the Black student athletes in the Bay Area protested their treatment, often feeling exploited. Black student athletes at San Jose State, called Good Brothers, sought to remedy some of the societal inequalities they saw present. About 35 Black student athletes worked together as a collective to use their status to effect social change.

The Good Brothers pressured their coaches to find them adequate housing similar to the support white student athletes were given. As Herbert Ruffin explains:

> In the 1950s and 60s, this home provided living space for Black students and African Americans new to the region. It was also one of the few places where people of racially different backgrounds freely intermingled in the South Bay Area before the 1960s. It received regular visits from liberal Whites that included legendary entertainer-activists the Smothers Brothers and NFL Hall of Fame coach Bill Walsh. In spite of this, most San Jose students and South Bay residents never really got to know the Good Brothers as people as much as they got to know their athletic excellence. Heading into the 1960s, this reality confronting the Good Brothers continued and steadily grew harsher as San Jose's color-line hardened in relation to the increase of Black student-athletes and the increase of civil rights activism sparked by the Greensboro Lunch Counter Sit-Ins in 1960.[33]

With sports and politics overlapping with race as well, Ruffin explains that while Black athletes participated in sports, much of it was heavily restricted. Black students could play sports, but not quarterback. Black students could play basketball, but there could not be too many on the court at one time. The result has been a history of blurred lines with sports, politics, and race.

The ways that politics and sports interface is across disciplinary subfields, time periods, locations, and topics, which essentially means that politics is everywhere in sports—in places both seen and unseen—and derives from the role of athletes, fans, teams, citizens, governments, markets, and institutions.[34] Sports may influence political alliances, governmental decision making, voting, interest group mobilization, and even social order and stability, ultimately shaping individuals, families, societies, countries, and international bodies. Both domestically and globally, sports implicate the biggest debates in political science.[35]

By 1967 in the Bay Area, San Jose State students continued to involve themselves in political issues and used sports as their platform. San Jose State only employed two Black professors at the time: a biologist and the famed sociologist, Harry Edwards. Meanwhile, the college maintained a quota of recruiting around 60 Black male athletes to play football as well as track and field.[36] While the college sought diversity, there was a limit to the diversity it envisioned. This resulted in the Revolt of September 1967. That Fall, of the 24,000 students, only 72 were Black and 60 of those 72 were Black athletes.[37] Student leaders planned to bring attention to the racial disparity, and they linked sports with their dispute. After meeting with President Clark at San Jose State, the students vowed to exercise their free expression. They informed President Clark that they intended to hold a rally at noon on the opening day of classes. They invited Clark to attend as well as all faculty and administrators. Over 700 people attended the rally and Professor Edwards was among the speakers. They delivered the charge of institutional racism and harped on the role that Black athletes were given at the college. With the upcoming game against Brigham Young, a religious institution whose central tenets professed black inferiority, the college was on edge:

> Within a week of the rally leading up to the game on September 23, an atmosphere of excitement and anxiety permeated the campus. While San Jose State officials sought to resolve the situation, controversies and tensions reverberated throughout the South Bay Area. A non-campus group from Oakland calling itself the 'Soul Brothers' contacted Edwards and proposed to take drastic measures at the game if needed.[38]

The sporting event on San Jose State's campus, a relatively small regional institution of higher learning, sparked a statewide—one could argue even a national—conversation on institutional racism. Politics and sports clearly overlapped. As Ruffin explains:

> White supremacist motorcycle group Hell's Angels publicly announced intentions to attend the football game to disrupt the proposed demonstration. Within two days of the rally, Black players at San Jose State and the University of Texas at El Paso systematically took themselves out of the game—some in support of the boycott and others fearing crowd violence. San Jose officials feared the boycott as the spark that could trigger urban unrest in a region that, until then, had settled racial problems through negotiation. According to President Clark, there were threats of arson aimed at fraternity and sorority houses, and burning torches were thrown on their lawns. Simultaneously, a critical mass of students reportedly left the campus several days after the rally, while athletic department officials such as Coach Winter were targeted by picketers with signs that read 'Stop exploitation of negro athletes now.' Finally, rumors that the college's football stadium would be burned to the ground by outside agitators forced President Clark to cancel the game on September 20, 1967 in the attempt to 'drain off the emotion.' This cancellation made San Jose State the first college in the United States to cancel a major athletic event under the threat of racial protest.[39]

Free speech leads to truth and individual self-fulfillment.[40] The efforts of the San Jose students help to clarify the justifications for speech outside the political process. In many ways, the case of Colin Kaepernick mirrors the San Jose

State story. For Kaepernick, exploitation by the NFL came in the form of being silenced once his protest impacted the pocketbooks of the league.

Colin Kaepernick. The genesis of the Colin Kaepernick story is well-chronicled. The crux of the story rests on Kaepernick's treatment by the league after he outlined his reasons for exercising his right to free speech. On August 26, 2016, Colin Kaepernick, a quarterback for the San Francisco 49ers, became the latest example in a long history of social activism in sports. Kaepernick's act provoked a national debate about the appropriateness of social protests in professional sports.[41] Despite the criticism, athletes are lawfully exercising their First Amendment freedom of expression rights.[42] In April of 2018, Kaepernick was recognized by Amnesty International for the Ambassador of Conscience Award. Kaepernick humbly accepted and said:

> It is only fitting that I have the honor of Eric Reid introducing me for this award. In many ways, my recognition would not be possible without our brotherhood. I truly consider him to be more than a friend. Eric, his wife, his children ... they are all a part of my family...
>
> People sometimes forget that love is at the root of our resistance ... And it is the people's unbroken love for themselves that motivates me, even when faced with the dehumanizing norms of a system that can lead to the loss of one's life over simply being Black ... History has proven that there has never been a period in the history of America where anti-Blackness has not been an ever-present terror. Racialized oppression and dehumanization is woven into the very fabric of our nation—the effects of which can be seen in the lawful lynching of Black and Brown people by the police, and the mass incarceration of Black and Brown lives in the prison industrial complex. While America bills itself as the land of the free, the receipts show that the United States has incarcerated approximately 2.2 million people, the largest prison population in the history of humankind.
>
> As police officers continue to terrorize Black and Brown communities, abusing their power and then hiding behind their blue wall of silence, and laws that allow for them to kill us with virtual impunity, I have realized that our love, that sometimes manifests as Black-rage, is a beautiful form of defiance against a system that seeks to suppress our humanity—A system that wants us to hate ourselves.
>
> I remind you that love is at the root of our resistance. It is our love for 12-year-old Tamir Rice, who was gunned down by the police in less than two seconds that will not allow us to bury our anger. It is our love for Philando Castille, who was executed in front of his partner and his daughter, that keeps the people fighting back. It is our love for Stephon Clark, who was lynched in his grandma's backyard that will not allow us to stop until we achieve liberation for our people.
>
> Our love is not an individualized love—it is a collective love, a collective love that is constantly combating collective forms of racialized hate. Chattel slavery, Jim Crow, New Jim Crow, massive plantations, mass incarcerations, slave patrols, police patrols: we as a collective, since the colonization of the Americas have been combating collective forms of systemic racialized hate and oppression.

> But I am hopeful. I am inspired. This is why we have to protest. This is why we are so passionate. We protest because we love ourselves, and our people ... When Malcolm X said, 'I'm for truth, no matter who tells it. I'm for justice, no matter who it is for or against. I'm a human being, first and foremost, and as such I'm for whoever and whatever benefits humanity as a whole.' I took that to heart.
>
> While taking a knee is a physical display that challenges the merits of who is excluded from the notion of freedom, liberty, and justice for all, the protest is also rooted in a convergence of my moralistic beliefs, and my love for the people.
>
> Seeking the truth, finding the truth, telling the truth and living the truth has been, and always will be what guides my actions. For as long as I have a beating heart, I will continue on this path, working on behalf of the people. Again ... love is at the root of our resistance ... To again quote Malcolm X, when he said that he, 'will join in with anyone—I don't care what color you are—as long as you want to change this miserable condition that exists on this earth,' I am here to join with you all in this battle against police violence.[43]

Critical race theorists help demonstrate the application of theory to a controversy to unearth the imbedded racial connections. Reginald Robinson writes,

> Critical Race Theory destabilizes the 'race' myth, on which a superior white identity depends. If race is really not there and if the social construction of superior whiteness depends on racialized myths, then Critical Race Theory reveals how fragile a White (or any racial) identity must be, and it shows us how white privilege perforce depends solely on force, violence, and oppression.[44]

Race, as a legal construct, enslaves Blacks and the Kaepernick example demonstrates this further.

Additionally, the importance of free speech hinges on protecting discourse for the sake of maintaining equality. When one is able to freely speak, they have greater self-fulfillment and a sense of truth and honesty. Free speech provides a greater possibility to express one's rights and facilitate public discourse, ultimately leading to the protection of all rights.[45] In order for one to have the opportunity to participate in public discourse as well as they will, free speech and its importance must be highlighted in society. This comes in the form of dialogue on free speech in school, in society, in public, in private, in government, and of course in the courts. Robust conversations on speech provide spaces for wide-open discourse. While not all speech leads to equality, advancing arguments on free speech leads to self-fulfillment and truth. Timothy Zick notes, "[v]isibility and voice are particularly important to oppressed minorities who challenge apartheid systems designed to displace or disappear them."[46]

The importance of speech can also be seen in social networking conversations, which begs the question: why is it protected in one space and not as vociferously in another? Davis Walsh writes: "Social networking, blogging and Internet speech may do very little original reporting, but Internet speech provides opportunities for people to play a role in public discourse, and these possibilities require the First Amendment protection. Through its conscious decision to guard against liability-causing regulations of the Internet, Congress appears to agree that Internet speech should be protected."[47]

The same principle should apply to speech by public figures (Kaepernick), employed by a government-subsidized "private" entity (the NFL), who exercise that right to highlight continued racial inequalities in society. Expression is not valuable exclusively for its own sake.

High School Football: The First Amendment Applies (Just as It Does With the NFL)

While fans have various sports to watch, football is one of the most popular, bringing in $14 billion in revenue in 2016 alone.[48] Kaepernick knew the platform he had could reach across color lines, across class, and across ages. He knew the connection to high school football programs, where the NFL uses the space as a training ground (also teaching the youth about the power of the NFL to dictate rules of speech) might result in the mimicking of his protest. Indeed, it did. High school players across the nation illuminated this issue when they began to mimic the act of kneeling during the national anthem in protest of police brutality against African American males.[49] Although this chapter argues that the First Amendment protects Kaepernick's symbolic act, in practice many high school players across the nation did not receive the same constitutional protection for mimicking his national anthem protest.[50] The students contended that the First Amendment protected their expressive conduct. They claimed that free expression protected their protests as long as such acts did not create a material disruption to the school learning environment.

Like Kaepernick, student-athletes have the constitutional right under the First Amendment to engage in protests during patriotic rituals, such as the national anthem. Any subsequent discipline is unconstitutional. The Supreme Court has stated that "[t]he vigilant protection of First Amendment freedoms is nowhere more vital than in our nation's public schools" because public schools serve as a training ground for our nation's future leaders and promote the preservation of our democracy.[51] The rationale for protecting the free speech rights of student-athletes in public schools is the same as the players in the NFL. It is equally vital to preserving democracy that public schools promote a marketplace of ideas by encouraging students to express their diverse perspectives openly. The Supreme Court has historically broadly interpreted the language of the First Amendment to include symbolic gestures as well as verbal speech. This is important, particularly at the K-12 level because it highlights the importance of speech for students, especially in their formative years. It is well established that students in K-12 hold First Amendment rights, reinforcing that adults like Kaepernick also need such protections.[52] First Amendment rights should supersede any limitations on those rights.

Social Protests and Consequences

As news of Colin Kaepernick's protest began to move across the country, many school administrators found themselves struggling to deal with how to best handle social protests during school sporting events. School authorities could either discipline students for engaging in a national anthem protest or support students' conduct as an exercise of their constitutional freedom of expression rights.[53] Both had consequences. Like the NFL, many schools failed to recognize this was an opportunity to demonstrate both the value of free speech and to properly define patriotism.

Some school administrators expressed public support for students while others issued sanctions or swiftly implemented policies prohibiting national anthem protests during school sporting events. For example, the Oakland School District in California retweeted news stories and supportive messages on the district's official Twitter page in acknowledgement of students' rights to engage in social activism during school-sponsored sporting events.[54] In Seattle, the entire high school football team at Garfield High School, including the coaches, kneeled during the national anthem in protest of social injustice.[55] Many of these acts were designed to display their solidarity with Colin Kaepernick and support his work to increase awareness about police brutality.

Of course, some schools disciplined their students. Mike Oppong, a football player at Doherty High School in Massachusetts, received a one-game suspension for kneeling during the national anthem in solidarity with Colin Kaepernick.[56] Similarly, another student, Bishop Gorman, was suspended from his Nevada high school and placed on a disciplinary contract for kneeling during the national anthem. Kaepernick was subjected to severe economic sanctions after his national anthem protest. Although Kaepernick was subjected to much harsher consequences than student protestors, he was afforded First Amendment protections and permitted to continue his national anthem protests.

In some circles, the kneeling was perceived as unpatriotic and an affront to the men and women who sacrificed their lives for their country. A principal at a high school in Honolulu responded to students kneeling during the national anthem by issuing the following statement in a letter to the faculty and staff:

> The behavior of that small group of students was disrespectful to our school and our country. It was particularly unfortunate that this occurred over Memorial Day weekend, knowing that thousands of KS Kapalama family members, faculty, staff and alumni have served our country's military to defend and uphold the freedoms we enjoy today.[57]

While one's feelings certainly cannot be critiqued, using a critical jurisprudential eye it is clear that Kaepernick's decision was one that attempted to use the podium to spotlight police brutality in the United States. The U.S. Supreme Court only limits freedom of speech under certain circumstances. "In light of the gross disparities in relation to whether students are disciplined for kneeling during the national anthem, it is of paramount importance to address the quandary surrounding the scope of students' freedom of expression rights outside the traditional school learning environment."[58]

Free Speech Jurisprudence: From Orthodoxy in Religion to Patriotism of Athletes

In *West Virginia State Board of Education v. Barnette*, the West Virginia Legislature amended a statute to require schools to offer courses in both history and civics for the purpose of "teaching, fostering, and perpetuating the ideals, principles and spirits of Americanism..."[59] The local Board of Education adopted a resolution making the flag salute part of the regular school program and activities. The flag salute mandate required students to give a salute while reciting the Pledge of Allegiance. Two students at Slip Hill Grade School in West Virginia, Marie and Gathie Barnette, refused to salute the flag because it conflicted with their religious beliefs as Jehovah's Witnesses. As a result, the Barnettes and several other children were expelled from school for their refusal to participate in the flag salute.

Barnette exemplifies the difficulty of balancing constitutionalism and patriotism. The Kaepernick story is no different. The *Barnette* Court explicitly acknowledged that socially-constructed notions of patriotism can create problems because they focus on the wrong issues. Kaepernick wasn't standing against the troops or the National Anthem or the police. He was using the First Amendment to bring light to an issue to which he thought Americans needed to pay more attention. His delivery, like that of Dr. King, should not have been critiqued because those critiques attempted to use the law to hide behind the substance of their argument: fear. Just like the Court noted in *Barnette*, the fear of not being able to indoctrinate was what opponents of Kaepernick's stance were afraid of. The NFL, or one might argue the State, was able to silence Kaepernick out of fear of losing corporate sponsors.

Although *Barnette* may be categorized as a free exercise of religion case, the Court emphasized that the students' right not to speak was part of their First Amendment freedoms under the Freedom of Speech Clause; therefore, the state did not have the constitutional right to compel students to profess any particular matter of opinion.[60] As Justice Robert H. Jackson eloquently stated: "If there is any fixed star in our constitutional constellation, it is that no official, high or petty, can prescribe what shall be orthodox in politics, nationalism, religion, or other matters of opinion or force citizens to confess by word or act their faith therein."[61]

Conclusion

The United States has an extensive history of sports, politics, and the law blurring lines. It is, therefore, surprising that more attention is not paid to the possible free speech implications of athletes making political statements. As this chapter has shown, those implications are numerous, and an analysis of the pertinent theories of expressive freedom serves to help us understand those implications. It is clear that free speech theories in society and free expression in sports often overlap. The very notion of sports hinges on the fanaticism of the group that follows the team. Rivalries are built on this fanaticism and the ensuing hatred that accompanies it. While the words and actions of fans, coaches, the media, and the players have all been dissected by both the courts and the court of public opinion, the question continues to be asked: When are the lines of free speech and expression in sports crossed? As we have seen, much of the answer lies in the money associated with sports, as that money pushes corporate responses that either encourage or limit speech and expression.

Colin Kaepernick's decision to use his platform as a professional athlete to draw attention to an issue he deemed important was certainly not novel. The response from the NFL/government was not novel either. There is only one way to view this story and that is the same way we must view virtually all First Amendment cases: through excess. With great freedoms come great excess. That means that we may not support the burning of the draft card, or Ali refusing to go to Vietnam, or Olympic athletes holding up their fists in a sign of solidarity but all of those moments make us "American." They help us better understand as members of a constitutional democracy that when we fail to support protest, we inch ever closer to authoritarian rule. The moment that we disallow an athlete to exercise their right to free speech, the closer we are to future rights being quashed as well. One may never know if those future rights are important to us and that is the very reason why we protect them now. But like Dr. King or Ali, Kaepernick stood up for what he believed in by kneeling and showed us how we mustn't ever allow the government to keep us from standing up for ourselves and others.

Notes

1. Unknown.
2. Thomas Gift and Andrew Miner, "Dropping the Ball: The Understudied Nexus of Sports and Politics," *World Affairs* 180, no. 1 (July 2017): 132.
3. Sohil Shah, "Free Speech, Football, and Freedom: Why the NFL Should Not Compel its Players to Speak to the Media," *Texas Review of Entertainment and Sports Law* 16, no. 1 (Fall 2014): 44.
4. Ibid., 43.
5. 109 U.S. 3 (1883).
6. Shah, "Free Speech, Football, and Freedom," 45.
7. Ibid.
8. Ibid., 46.
9. Frank Ryan and Matt Ganas, "Rights of Publicity in Sports-Media," *Syracuse Law Review* 67, no. 2 (2017): 422.
10. Ibid., 428.
11. Shah, "Free Speech, Football, and Freedom," 46.
12. Ibid.
13. Ibid.
14. Ibid., 47.
15. Ibid.
16. Alexander Meiklejohn, *Free Speech and Its Relation to Self-Government* (New York: Harper, 1948), 10.
17. Ibid., 12.
18. 109 U.S. at 59.
19. Tehrim Umar, "Total Eclipse of the Tweet: How Social Media Restrictions on Student and Professional Athletes Affect Free Speech," *Jeffrey S. Moorad Sports Law Journal* 22, no. 1 (2015): 317.
20. *Ward v. Rock Against Racism* 491 U.S. 781, 791 (1989).
21. Ibid.
22. Ibid., at 801.
23. Ibid., at 800.
24. *City of Renton v. Playtime Theatres*, 475 U.S. 41, 58 (1986).
25. 491 U.S. 397, 414 (1989).
26. *United States v. Playboy Entertainment Group*, 529 U.S. 803, 813 (2000).
27. Ibid.
28. Ibid., 814.

29. Umar, "Total Eclipse of the Tweet," 322.
30. 403 U.S. 713 (1971).
31. Gift and Miner, "Dropping the Ball," 132.
32. Herbert G. Ruffin, II, "'Doing the Right Thing For the Sake of Doing the Right Thing': The Revolt of the Black Athlete and the Modern Student-Athletic Movement, 1956–2014," *Western Journal of Black Studies* 38, no. 4 (Winter 2014).
33. Ibid., 265.
34. Gift and Miner, "Dropping the Ball," 131.
35. Ibid.
36. Ruffin, "Doing the Right Thing," 270.
37. Ibid.
38. Ibid., 272.
39. Ibid., 273.
40. John Stuart Mill, "On Liberty," in *John Stuart Mill, On Liberty: Annotated Text, Sources, and Background Criticism*, ed. David Spitz (New York: W.W. Norton, 1975).
41. Garry A. Gabison, "The Gray Problem: Should Athletes Be Punished for Their Social Media Posts?" *DePaul Journal of Sports Law* 13, no. 1 (2017): 41.
42. Ibid.
43. Amnesty International's Ambassador of Conscience Award, Transcript of Speech, Colin Kaepernick, accessed June 26, 2019, https://www.amnesty.nl/content/uploads/2018/04/Colin-Kaepernicks-Speech-Ambassador-of-Conscience-Final.pdf?x44402
44. Reginald Leamon Robinson, "Race, Myth and Narrative in the Social Construction of the Black Self," *Howard Law Journal* 40, no. 1 (1996): 38.
45. Timothy Zick, "The Dynamic Relationship Between Freedom of Speech and Equality," *Duke Journal of Constitutional Law and Public Policy* 12, no. 2 (2016): 25.
46. Ibid., 28.
47. Davis Walsh, "All a Twitter: Social Networking, College Athletes, and the First Amendment," *William and Mary Bill of Rights Journal* 20, no. 2 (2011): 629.
48. Laura Rene McNeal, "From Hoodies to Kneeling During the National Anthem: The Colin Kaepernick Effect and Its Implications for K-12 Sports," *Louisiana Law Review* 78, no. 1 (Fall 2017): 146.
49. Ibid., 146–47.
50. Ibid.
51. *Shelton v. Tucker*, 364 U.S. 479, 487 (1960); McNeal, "From Hoodies to Kneeling," 148.
52. McNeal, "From Hoodies to Kneeling," 150.
53. Ibid., 158.
54. Ibid.
55. Ibid., 159.
56. Ibid.
57. Ibid., 162.
58. Ibid., 163.
59. 319 U.S. 624, 625 (1943).
60. McNeal, "From Hoodies to Kneeling," 164.
61. 319 U.S. at 642.

References

Gabison, Garry A. "The Gray Problem: Should Athletes Be Punished for Their Social Media Posts?" *DePaul Journal of Sports Law* 13, no. 1 (Spring 2017): 31–60.

Gift, Thomas, and Andrew Miner. "Dropping the Ball: The Understudied Nexus of Sports and Politics." *World Affairs* 180, no. 1 (July 2017): 127–61.

McNeal, Laura Rene. "From Hoodies to Kneeling During the National Anthem: The Colin Kaepernick Effect and Its Implications for K-12 Sports." *Louisiana Law Review* 78, no. 1 (Fall 2017): 145–96.

Meiklejohn, Alexander. *Free Speech and Its Relation to Self-Government.* New York: Harper, 1948.

Mill, John Stuart. "On Liberty." In *John Stuart Mill, On Liberty: Annotated Text, Sources, and Background Criticism*, edited by David Spitz, 1–106. New York: W.W. Norton, 1975.

Robinson, Reginald Leamon. "Race, Myth and Narrative in the Social Construction of the Black Self." *Howard Law Journal* 40, no. 1 (1996): 1.

Ruffin, Herbert G., II. "'Doing the Right Thing For the Sake of Doing the Right Thing': The Revolt of the Black Athlete and the Modern Student-Athletic Movement, 1956–2014." *Western Journal of Black Studies* 38, no. 4 (Winter 2014): 260–78.

Ryan, Frank, and Matt Ganas. "Rights of Publicity in Sports-Media." *Syracuse Law Review* 67, no. 2 (2017): 421–48.

Shah, Sohil. "Free Speech, Football, and Freedom: Why the NFL Should Not Compel Its Players to Speak to the Media." *Texas Review of Entertainment and Sports Law* 16, no. 1 (Fall 2014): 43–50.

Umar, Tehrim. "Total Eclipse of the Tweet: How Social Media Restrictions on Student and Professional Athletes Affect Free Speech." *Jeffrey S. Moorad Sports Law Journal* 22, no. 1 (2015): 311–51.

Walsh, Davis. "All a Twitter: Social Networking, College Athletes, and the First Amendment." *William and Mary Bill of Rights Journal* 20, no. 2 (2011): 619–50.

Zick, Timothy. "The Dynamic Relationship Between Freedom of Speech and Equality." *Duke Journal of Constitutional Law and Public Policy* 12, no. 2 (2016): 13–75.

6. The Slants and Blurred Lines: The Conflict Between Free Speech and Intellectual Property Law

JASON ZENOR

In the United States, political debates often revolve around the idealistic rhetoric of our founding documents. We wax-poetic about a right to life, liberty, and happiness. We argue for our inalienable rights to free expression, freedom of thought, and a right to privacy. We cite the legal truism that we are all created equal, thus deserving of equal protection of the law. These pithy phrases often stoke the fires of patriotism and make us believe in the exceptionalism of our democracy. But a right that rarely ignites such rhetorical flare is one's right to private property. This is in part due to its terrible history, as people were once defined as property; but it is also because it reminds us of disputes over boundaries. And this right is inherently individualistic and combative—so, when building an aura of national pride, the other rights seem more conducive to one unified country.

However, property rights do appear in the founding documents. For example, in the Declaration of Independence, when the writers spoke of a "pursuit of happiness" they were thinking of a right to own land and the right to use that land as they wished. In many respects, it is as American as freedom of speech. Yet, there is a natural conflict between free speech principles and property law, especially when the property in question is creative (and lucrative) ideas. The First Amendment limits the government's ability to restrain speech without a showing of an immediate harm, but by contrast intellectual property (IP) law is government-created statutory law that provides a monopoly to an individual while restraining the speech of others (including allowing for imprisonment for those who willfully break such restraints).[1]

Within IP law, Congress created a property right in information. Property rights usually give the owners a right against the world as others cannot use the property without permission.[2] But intellectual property rights were meant to protect against any commercial competitor, not to be absolute rights against the world. Any intellectual property can be sold, borrowed, bequeathed, licensed (or rented), just like real property; but unlike real property, the public has a right to a fair use of intellectual property.

However, the relationship between the public's rights and the IP holder's rights has not always been balanced. For close to a century, intellectual property law has evolved to give greater protection to those who created the works than to the public who may want to build on them. In the digital era of remixing and sharing, free speech protections have started to pierce the once impenetrable IP protection as courts recognize the social and cultural importance of fair use. By contrast, other attempts to move IP law toward recognizing different values, such as diversity and equality, have floundered.

This chapter examines this conflict through the lens of free speech theory. The chapter first examines the constitutional underpinnings of IP law, specifically copyright and trademark. It then proceeds to discuss how free speech theory exists within the IP regulatory scheme. Finally, it analyzes two recent issues in IP law—disparaging trademarks and derivative works—and how free speech theory can guide our understanding of these two issues.

Intellectual Property Law

A prime consideration of IP law is that producers should be given an opportunity to profit from their creation. Like other public goods, which greatly benefit society—such as utilities and telecommunication—producers are given a monopoly over the product so that they will want to invest in it. Thus, the government created a legal regime that gives considerable protection to IP rights holders, especially in a commercial context. Though some scholars disagree,[3] it can be argued that IP law is a neutral regulation, in that the government does not focus on the content or message. So long as it is original and fixed to a medium, it will receive protection, no matter the message or subject.[4]

Content-neutral regulations only receive an intermediate level of judicial scrutiny, sometimes described as a balancing of interests.[5] However, when private parties enforce their IP rights this is often in the form of viewpoint discrimination. For example, Disney is notoriously aggressive in stopping any use of Mickey Mouse, especially when it is critical in nature.[6] Since most enforcement of IP rights is by private parties, this balancing of rights is often overlooked. The following sections examine the development of IP law and how it has heavily favored corporate IP rights holders.

Fundamentals of Copyright Law

Copyright infringement and protections date back to the beginning of mass production.[7] The origins of U.S. copyright law come from the U.S. Constitution. Article I, Section 8, Clause 8 grants Congress the power "to Promote the Progress of Science and useful Arts, by securing for limited Times to Authors and Inventors the exclusive Right to their respective Writings and Discoveries." Though the intended meaning of the words is not known, scholars have argued that "science and useful arts" did not specifically mean the product of scientists; rather, it was a reference to general knowledge. Others have argued that it was meant to be more instrumental, allowing authors to benefit from their works.[8]

The framers gave very little evidence that they contemplated the copyright clause.[9] Even when Congress passed the first Copyright Act in 1790, there was little deliberation as the act was a copy of England's copyright law—the Statute of Anne (1710). This act gave owners a 14-year copyright protection that could be renewed once for a total of 28 years. In 1919, Congress extended each term to 28 years, for a possible total of 56 years.

The last major overhaul to copyright came in 1976. This act protects any "works of authorship fixed in any tangible medium of expression, now known or later developed."[10] This includes the usual forms of media such as photography, literature, music, television, and movies, but it also includes other forms of expression such as dance, speeches, and architecture.[11] Some things are not protected, such as ideas, processes, methods, and scientific principles.[12] However, the compilation of facts or ideas may be protected if it is original (such as order choice, font, and cover-work).[13]

Today, copyrighted works often come with the warning that any use of the work without the express written consent of the right holder is forbidden. As copyright law moved from a social protection of ideas to an economic right, this disclaimer became a foregone conclusion for all published works. However, this statement is an exaggeration of the copyright holder's protection as the public is allowed a "fair use" of such products, including "criticism, comment, news reporting, teaching (including multiple copies for classroom use), scholarship, or research."[14] The four-part fair use test is codified in the Copyright Act of 1976, and is used to determine whether a use is an infringement:

(1) the purpose and character of the use, including whether such use is of a commercial nature or is for nonprofit educational purposes;
(2) the nature of the copyrighted work;

(3) the amount and substantiality of the portion used in relation to the copyrighted work as a whole; and
(4) the effect of the use upon the potential market for or value of the copyrighted work.[15]

In many ways, fair use is ambiguous and vague. Indeed, that may have been the design of Congress in passing the 1976 Act. The House of Representatives noted that it was "a rule of reason" that must be decided on a case-by-case basis.[16] Thus, courts have had difficulty in applying it and have often erred on the side of the copyright holder. Generally, if the original work is an older work of non-fiction and only a small unsubstantial portion of the original work is used, then it will be considered a fair use.

With the expansion of digital media and a share culture, copyrighted work has been used more and more by everyday people uploading parts of works onto social media or transforming published works altogether. The courts have been slow to catch up, but recently they have begun to recognize the need for a stronger fair use protection. For example, in *Lenz v. Universal* (2016),[17] the Ninth Circuit Court of Appeals held that before a copyright holder could send a cease and desist order, there must be a good-faith effort on the part of the copyright holder to discern whether or not fair use applies.

Fair use is sometimes described as a defense to a claim of copyright infringement, while on other occasions the argument is made that fair use is not a defense at all, because it can be conceptualized as a category of speech protected by the First Amendment.[18] It is akin to "actual malice" in libel law, which is a free speech protection that allows for "breathing space" in the discussion of public affairs.[19] Similarly, fair use doctrine recognizes that the original intention of IP law was to promote the dissemination of ideas in society.[20] Consequently, allowing the public to use copyrighted work in a limited way is in the public interest. However, the U.S. Supreme Court has never explicitly used the First Amendment as a constitutional defense for the use of a copyrighted work and, instead, has interpreted fair use as a statutory protection of free speech.[21]

Criticisms of copyrighted work are protected. In order to critique a work, the critic must reference it. But in order to fall within fair use, the critic cannot simply parrot the original work. Another type of critique that is protected is parody. In order to satirize a work, one has to use the original copyrighted work, but the parody has to be a commentary about it. In *Campbell v. Acuff-Rose* (1994), for example, a rap group used the lyrics and music from Roy Orbison's "Oh, Pretty Woman" for their sexually suggestive song "Pretty Woman."[22] The band altered the music and changed most of the lyrics, arguing that this was a fair use. The U.S. Supreme Court agreed and held that it was a transformative use because the band used the lyrics as a parody to comment on the naiveté of the original 1950s song.[23] "The heart of any parodist's claim to quote from existing material," wrote Justice David H. Souter, "is the use of some elements of a prior author's composition to create a new one that, at least in part, comments on that author's work."[24]

Oddly, critics are protected when making commentary, but fans who make derivative works (e.g., sequels, fan fiction, and merchandise) or give away parts of the work (e.g., a compendium of the work) are not protected,[25] even though they may be the biggest supporters of the artist. However, when a consumer purchases a copy of the work, they are able to give away that one copy, although they cannot make several copies to distribute.[26]

Though derivative work belongs to the original creator, if the new work is transformative or has artistic relevance then it will be protected.[27] For example, a parody may use much of the work while still being transformative. However, despite all of these defenses—parody, satire, transformative, artistic relevance—there is no clear definition as to when a use rises to this level.[28]

Fundamentals of Trademark Law

Trademark is considered intellectual property, but its origins are not in the Copyright Clause of the Constitution. Rather, the constitutional basis for federal protection of trademark law stems from the Commerce Clause, which gives Congress the power to "regulate Commerce with foreign Nations, and among the several States, and with the Indian Tribes."[29] Trademarks were protected in English common law, which, early on, was adopted by U.S. courts. The first statutory protections in the United States came in the 19th century at the state level; the first federal law came in 1870.[30] Today, the basis of U.S. trademark law is the Lanham Act passed in 1946.

Trademarks help customers and others identify a product as being from the trademark holder. Thus, customers can be confident that a trademarked product will have the same quality as any other products from the trademark holder. This allows the trademark holder to build goodwill with its customers. Trademark law allows companies to identify their goods through colors, slogans, packaging, and symbols. For example, the Coca-Cola Company has a trademark on the shade of red it uses, the font for the script, and the shape of its bottles. However, companies cannot have an absolute trademark on generic descriptions like "fast," "good," or "super." Although, when it is part of a name or slogan then a general description can be trademarked (e.g., Red Lobster, Boston Market, Speedy Lube).

Conversely, marks can become so popularly used that they lose trademark protection once they become generic terms. An example of this is Thermos, which is now a generic term for an insulated bottle.[31] Nonetheless, the Thermos company name is still trademarked and used for many other branded products. Ultimately, it is up to the company to police the use of its names to make sure they are not infringed upon by another product or used so ubiquitously that they become generic descriptors. The Copyright Dilution Act allows companies to do this by permitting them to sue anyone who uses these trademarks in a commercial context, even if it is a different industry, so long as the company can show that consumers may be confused.[32]

Unregistered trademarks may get limited protection under common law or state law. But companies would want to file for a federal registration of trademark with the U.S. Patent and Trademark office because that guarantees protection from any claim of infringement.[33] To be granted a registered trademark, the mark must be more than simply descriptive and cannot already be in use by another entity.[34]

The defenses to trademark infringement are very similar to the copyright defenses, such as news reports, creative works, criticism, and political speech. Generally, the defenses only apply in expressive arenas. News companies can discuss a story about a company such as Amazon without violating trademark law. Culture jammers who offer political commentary on corporate logos are protected, as is a comedy show like *Saturday Night Live* when it includes a character who works at Target. However, another restaurant could not call itself McDonalds and claim it was a parody.

...

In sum, intellectual property law is a restriction on free speech. IP law finds its roots in the U.S. Constitution and offers creators a temporally-limited protection over their works. Thus, copyright and trademark infringement have long been considered unprotected categories of speech. Nonetheless, IP protection is an individual right that has to be balanced with greater free speech principles such as "protecting political speech, promoting democracy or self-government, furthering the search for truth, or enhancing autonomy and enabling self-expression."[35] It is to this balancing act that this chapter now turns.

Free Speech Theory and IP Law

The following section examines the more prominent free speech theories and the scholars most associated with them. Generally, these theories have not been applied to IP law in the past, because IP is usually approached as an economic right rather than a free speech issue. Nevertheless, IP law protects expressions of creative ideas, so it is inherently related to free speech theory. An overview of each of the theories begins to reveal the principles that IP law is grounded in.

Free Marketplace of Ideas

Ultimately, the free marketplace of ideas is meant to support the search for truth. Or, as the U.S. Supreme Court said in *New York Times v. Sullivan* (1964), "debate on public issues should be uninhibited, robust, and wide-open."[36] The concept of a marketplace of ideas is taken from economics and the idea of a marketplace of goods. Intellectual property rights were meant to expand human knowledge, in other words, the marketplace of ideas.[37] As the U.S. Supreme Court has stated, copyright law is "the engine of free expression"[38] and without it, it is arguable that free speech would be chilled as creators would not fully benefit from their work. Regardless, many critics bemoan the commercial interests of cultural products, whether trademark or copyright, contending that they stifle the marketplace of ideas.[39]

Philosophers like John Milton, John Locke, and Immanuel Kant believed that every author had a "natural right" to own his or her work.[40] John Milton opposed the government's use of licensing and its requisite control of publishers. But Milton did admit that after an author dies the works continue to influence others.[41] Influential English jurist William Blackstone argued for perpetual copyright, just as one would have over any real property; but the House of Lords did not adopt this.[42]

In *The Federalist*, James Madison echoed these philosophers. "The utility of the power will scarcely be questioned," he wrote. "The public good fully coincides ... with the claims of individuals."[43] Throughout the history of American jurisprudence, the natural rights approach to IP has ebbed and flowed, but it has never been the dominant theory.[44] By contrast, in most European nations copyright laws do reflect the natural rights (or moral rights) model.[45]

The Anglo-American copyright tradition is based more on the "incentive" or utilitarian theory that it protects authors so that they will want to produce more works. This approach would not see intellectual property rights as natural rights, like free speech. Instead an individual's IP right is created to be an instrument of social growth.[46] Society offers a limited term for the author to profit, so as to encourage the creation of new ideas, which in turn benefits society. Without such a protection, it could be argued that there would be a limited number of authors.[47] But, when a use of a copyrighted work would expand the ideas available in the marketplace and the enforcement of the copyright would not, then the use is considered a "fair use" and is protected.

Trademarks are most often seen as having the utilitarian function of simply identifying the producer of the good in order to inform consumers. This has been the predominant approach in trademark law.[48] Yet, millions of dollars are poured into developing trademarks so that they transmit a message to potential consumers. Amazon's trademark smile moves from "A" to "Z" in the trademark to symbolize that it has everything from "A to Z." The rugged Marlboro cowboy has long been used in trademarks to symbolize the mythologized rough and tumble lands in the western United States. Therefore, the utility of the trademarks ends up moving beyond the commercial into the marketplace of cultural ideas.

Right to Information

Other theorists have argued that the right to free speech is really about the right to access information. Thomas Emerson argued that the First Amendment included a right "to hear the views of others and to listen to their version of the facts … the right to inquire … [and] to a degree, the right of access to information."[49] Such theorists argue that without it, the citizenry cannot be informed about the actions of its government, thus undermining democracy as voters cannot make informed decisions. However, the right to information has never received support from a majority of the justices at the U.S. Supreme Court.[50]

There is a "public interest" exception to IP law.[51] For example, informative works such as news, documentaries, and biographies are all protected works and the creators can protect the works so that audiences need to purchase them and others cannot use them without permission. However, the facts that are in the work (names, events, dates, etc.) will be part of the public domain open to public (and commercial) use, though the precise compilation of the facts, even if the whole work would serve the public interest, is not in the public domain. So, a rival news network could not air an entire interview. In fact, if the public is interested in the compilation itself, then the work may have more protection as it is worth more in the market and the commercial interest is one of the criteria in judging whether it was a fair use.[52] For example, in *Harper & Row Publishers, Inc. v. Nation Enterprise* (1985), a magazine was sued for publishing one page from President Gerald R. Ford's 500-page memoir, a page that include a quote from the President explaining why he pardoned Richard M. Nixon. The magazine argued that this was factual information in the public interest. However, the U.S. Supreme Court did not accept the magazine's argument, holding that the publisher's right in publication outweighed the public interest.[53]

Critics argue that, in a copyright regime dominated by corporate holders, the financial hurdles to accessing information may act as bars to self-government if people cannot access the information that they need in order to be civically engaged. The concern is not just for trivial entertainment content that must be purchased; copyright laws can also be used to block dissemination of biographies, news production, and misunderstood parody. For example, in the above case, the public would need to purchase the book in order to see the entire quote from President Ford.[54] Critics argued that without the precise details about events, the citizenry could not accurately judge its leaders.

Deliberation and Self-Governance

Scholars such as Alexander Meiklejohn[55] and Zechariah Chafee[56] were proponents of public deliberation as the goal of free speech. More recently, Robert Post[57] and Cass Sunstein[58] have also argued that self-governance is the main goal of free speech protections. This approach to free speech is more accepting of regulation of the marketplace of ideas, especially if it promotes discussion of public affairs.[59]

With the free marketplace of ideas metaphor, there would be an argument for almost no regulation of speech. But, in economic theory free markets cannot operate completely free of government regulation. Every so-called free economy in the world has some government regulations to promote competition, mainly antitrust law, to protect the capitalistic system. Without them basic laws of economics, such as the law of supply and demand, would not work.[60] Thus, with a deliberation approach to free speech, having more fair use exceptions may be beneficial to self-governance as they protect against a monopoly of ideas in the marketplace.

IP law does not often deal with issues of self-governance directly. As Alexander Meiklejohn argued, "the people do not need novels or dramas or paintings or poems, 'because they will be called upon to vote.'"[61] But, proponents of self-government often worry that copyright law protection could lessen political discourse as it stifles the amount of information available. Ultimately, defenses to IP infringement, such as fair use, educational use, comment and criticism, parody, and political speech, may be the protections for deliberative democracy and self-government.[62] These protections allow for the public to discuss public affairs without fear of being shut down by those with the economic incentive to do so. For example, Donald Trump may be able to obtain a trademark on "Make America Great Again" for purposes of selling merchandise. But, because of the commentary defense critics could use that phrase for political purposes and they should be protected from being sued (though the threat of being sued is often enough to chill speech).[63]

Though fair use can increase the amount of information available to the public, outright copyright infringement, such as piracy, will usually have little value to democratic debate. However, in nations such as China that regulate what media the public views, piracy may play a vital role in furthering self-governance as it might allow for access to content that would otherwise be blocked.[64] Although, the insistence of Western nations that China enforce international IP law has allowed for the government to "crack down on expression that it considers threatening, such as political dissent, religious information, and other so-called 'unhealthy' media" in conflict with international pressure to support free speech rights in the nation.[65]

Having exceptions to copyright, like information and political ideas, does serve the ideal of deliberation. But, when a copyrighted work fits within the category of information or political ideas, it may not be that easy to access. This is especially true in today's cultural landscape (as discussed in Chapter 1 by James Foster), where entertainment is more and more political and information has become infotainment. For example, would a Michael Moore documentary garner protection as a creative work or should it be in the public domain to increase public discourse?

Self-Fulfillment

Yet another free speech theory—the theory of speech as self-fulfillment—shifts the focus from the effect of the message on governance to individual autonomy to produce works. The theory moves beyond political speech by valuing aesthetics, meaning, and self-understanding, and is applicable to the moral rights approach to IP law because it protects the author's dominion over the work.

As economic goods, copyrighted material and trademarks are fixed to a medium. The author has an intended message and meaning for the work. IP law allows for authors to have self-fulfillment by expressing their ideas to the world. In turn, they are free to then profit from their creation. On the other hand, however, these are also ideas open to different meanings for the audience who consumes the work. Certainly, copyrighted works—from books, to films, and movies—are capable of multiple meanings. They may have a certain meaning and importance to a culture that is different from the author's intended meaning. Star Trek has a cultural meaning to Trekkies that goes beyond the intended message of Gene Roddenberry or Paramount Pictures for example. Trademarks may be more utilitarian, but trademarks often have a different meaning to a culture, appearing on clothing, tattoos, and other forms of individualistic expression. For example, Mercedes and Gucci are often mentioned in hip-hop,[66] and fans of punk rock often wore Doc Marten shoes.[67]

But this theory could also give protection to the use of copyrighted work and trademarks that are artistic or transformative, allowing the so-called infringer to express themselves. This use is not entirely selfish, because through this very act of expressing oneself a person may benefit society by creating transformative works and new ideas.[68] Fan fiction allows for a fan to create a community around a work where they often discuss larger political and cultural issues. Some fan fiction has become its own profitable venture, such as the *50 Shades of Grey* franchise which was a fan fiction derived from the *Twilight* series.[69]

Critical Race Theory

Critical race theory examines the ways in which law is not race-neutral. It has been used to engage in critical analysis of many areas of the law, including IP law. As international law, IP law has been criticized for perpetuating colonialism through cultural and economic forces. IP law heavily favors the global corporate conglomerates based in the Global North and West. As with past colonialism, the hegemonic powers exploit the labors of the Global South and East, often co-opting their culture and then criminalizing any attempts to co-opt the dominant cultures or attempts to take it back.

For example, in the United States modern pop music is rooted in jazz, which was rooted in the art of African slave culture. Yet, when modern hip-hop artists attempt to sample commercial music, they are cracked down upon by corporate record labels and are not recognized by courts as being transformative.[70] China has had a poor record of protecting international IP within its borders. The Western narrative was that the Chinese government did not care or was looking to hurt other countries. But what the narrative failed to recognize was that not all cultures fit into the Western ideal of private property. There is a long history of copying in Chinese culture and it can be seen as a form of honoring the past. The Chinese government eventually enforced Western IP law so that it could continue to be a player in the global market, even though it goes it against the cultural mores of the nation.[71] But as critical race theory argues, the hegemonic culture wins out, especially in a commercial context.

Balancing of Rights

Freedom of speech is a fundamental right; thus, it receives broad protection. However, it is not superior to other fundamental rights. For example, freedom of speech must be balanced with other fundamental rights such as privacy and right to a fair trial.[72] Yet, some scholars argue for a preferred position for free speech in this balancing of rights, making it more difficult for other rights to outweigh speech. Generally, the United States public strongly supports free speech.[73] However, this is often a preference for protection of their own speech, not necessarily that of others.[74]

Some theorists claim that intellectual property is a constitutional right given to an individual, thus it must be balanced against other rights such as free speech.[75] Moreover, it is a private right enforceable by individuals, thus not violative of free speech (which only applies to infringement by the government). Other scholars argue that IP law is just like any other property right. A person's right to expression does not allow them to trespass onto private property to protest; therefore, it similarly does not allow them to use other people's intellectual property in their own expression.[76]

In balancing these rights, intellectual property law allows for the restriction of speech by incorporating exceptions to when such restrictions cannot be allowed (such as fair use). In the alternative, free speech allows for some use of intellectual property by incorporating protections against unjust enrichment through thievery (such as piracy).[77] Ultimately, though, the question remains: is it a perfect balance or does one right get preferred positioning over the other? Some free speech advocates argue that as an amendment to the Constitution, the First Amendment changed the meaning of the Copyright Clause and the Commerce Clause.[78] But if one takes an originalist's viewpoint, both laws were passed by the First Congress and the legislators did not explicitly amend the Constitution to lessen copyright law. As the U.S. Supreme Court has stated, "[t]his proximity indicates that, in the Framers' view, copyright's limited monopolies are compatible with free speech principles."[79]

Current Issues in IP Law

The following section examines two recent cases in IP Law. The section begins by outlining the case of *Matal v. Tam* (2016) and the legal protection of disparaging trademarks. It then discusses the case brought by the Marvin Gaye estate against artists Robin Thicke and Pharrell for copyright infringement. The case expands the definition of infringement to include copying the essence and style of another artist. This section applies free speech theory to both of these cases to further understand their effect on the law.

Disparaging Marks and Free Speech

The Lanham Act of 1946 is a federal statute that regulates trademarks in the U.S. The original law did not allow for the registration of marks which "may disparage persons, institutions, beliefs, or national symbols, or bring them into contempt, or disrepute."[80] This changed in 2017 when the U.S. Supreme Court struck down the "disparagement clause." In *Matal v. Tam*,[81] an Asian-American punk-rock band named The Slants attempted to trademark its name, but was denied by the Patent and Trademark Office (PTO). The PTO cited Sec. 2(A) of the Lanham Act which barred any mark that may "disparage ... or bring ... into contemp[t] or disrepute" any "persons, living or dead."[82] The government argued that it wanted to protect under-represented groups from an onslaught of disparagement in commercial speech. However, the band members, who were all Asian-American, argued that the name was expressive and was an attempt to take back the power of the derogatory word just as African American hip-hop artists had done with the n-word.[83] The U.S. Supreme Court held that the clause was unconstitutional because it violated the First Amendment. The Court concluded that it was a content-based regulation and, as such, the disparagement clause was subjected to the strictest form of judicial scrutiny, meaning that the government would need to show that it had a compelling interest and that the law was narrowly tailored to serve that interest.

The Court stated that the trademark was more than simply commercial speech conveying the identity of the product, which would have received lesser scrutiny. Instead, the name chosen by the band concerned a social issue as the term "slants" is a derogatory statement regarding Asian Americans. Thus, the government could not block the trademark based on its message.[84] Though the Court agreed that the state had an interest in protecting groups from disparagement, the government could not censor one side of the debate. The Court held that free speech protects the speech we hate, and that the disparagement clause amounted to a "happy talk" clause.[85] Ultimately, the case not only allowed the band to proceed with its trademark, it also impacted a much more controversial use of derogatory trademarks—the Washington Redskins.

Uses of Native American Imagery in Trademarks

Native American imagery is seen throughout commercial speech, including Land O' Lakes, Spirit Cigarettes, and Calumet Baking. The imagery often associates the savage stereotype with sin products, such as cigarettes, alcohol, and strip clubs. Sports teams frequently use the imagery to associate with the warrior stereotype, including the Kansas City Chiefs, Chicago Blackhawks, and Atlanta Braves (whose fans do the Tomahawk chop).

The Slants decision impacted the long-standing challenge to the NFL's Washington Redskins trademark. The Redskins trademark was registered in 1933. The football team moved to Washington, D.C. from Boston in 1937, and a few years later came the first organized resistance from the Native American Congress of Indians.[86] By 2001, the U.S. Commission on Civil Rights called for the ceasing of American Indian imagery in sports. The NCAA followed suit and required its teams to either make an agreement with a tribe or stop use altogether.[87] For example, the North Dakota University Fighting Sioux changed its name to the Fighting Hawks in 2015. Florida State University was able to keep the Seminoles mascot after it came to an agreement with the Seminole Tribes in the state.[88]

In professional sports, however, no such requirement exists. Professional teams, which are individual companies, have to act on their own accord to remove such images. The Cleveland Indians MLB team has responded by removing its mascot, Chief Wahoo.[89] The Washington Redskins, however, has refused to change its name. The team's trademark was challenged in the U.S. Trademark Trial and Appeal Board (TTAB) twice. In 1999, the TTAB canceled the trademark as disparaging, but the case was overturned on appeal due to procedural issues. In 2014, TTAB once again canceled the mark, which was upheld by the Fourth Circuit (with the U.S. Supreme Court denying certiorari). However, the decision in the Slants case made any challenge of the Redskins' mark legally moot.[90]

Applying Free Speech Theory to the Disparaging Trademark Debate. On its own, the term "redskin" is offensive. It would be the equivalent of using "black skin" or "yellow skin," which would quickly be dismissed as offensive. Historically, "red skin" was a term for the scalps of Native Americans taken by U.S. soldiers in response to some tribes taking the scalps of Americans killed in wars between the two sides.[91] But today, on Sunday afternoons in the fall, the term "Redskins" means something else. It is a professional football team that has been in existence for almost 100 years. The meaning is so transformed that fans do not think about it as a racialized term.

In legal terms, the debate about disparaging marks is over. In the Slants case the Court supported a "free marketplace of ideas" value of free speech. The Court believed that the government could not decide which speech is acceptable and which is not (unless it is government speech). The Court believed that in the case of the Slants, there was an expressive element that added to the marketplace of ideas.[92]

Unlike copyright law, trademark law is not mentioned in the Constitution, so there does not necessarily need to be a balancing of rights. When the U.S. Patent and Trademark Office did not give federal protection to disparaging marks, it did not mean the trademark holder could not use the mark. It was not a prior restraint. Instead, it meant the government would not give it special statutory protection. But, in blocking disparaging marks the government was treating a mark differently based on the message of the mark. In doing so, the government was admitting that the trademark was more than just an identifier of a product—it had an expressive element; thus, it fell under free speech rights. So, the question with the Washington Redskins is: what is the expressive element? The team argues that it does not have the disparaging meaning of collected scalps. The team has made unsubstantiated claims that the name was in fact to honor a former coach who had Native American heritage;[93] but, how is a derogatory term an honoring?

Trademark law is most associated with the "right to information." It is meant to inform the public that a good is from whom the mark is associated with. But, if the Redskins were to change its mark, the fans of the team would still be able to recognize the product. Many teams in college and professional sports have changed their names and have not suffered a loss in a fan base.[94] In fact, in Washington D.C. the NBA team changed from the Washington Bullets to the Washington Wizards so the name would be less violent.[95] Of course, this was the team's own choice, not a requirement by the government.

As a self-fulfillment value, the question, then, is: who truly owns the mark? The Slants is entirely made up of Asian-Americans members who are artists, and by using the derogatory word they are making a social critique. This is obviously a form of self-fulfillment as they depict their own identity and how racial issues still permeate our nation. This can also be seen as self-fulfillment for its audience, which also deals with these issues, especially if the audience members also identify as Asian-American. But once again, for the Redskins mark there is a question as to the self-fulfillment value. The mark has been owned by a corporation long removed from anyone who played any part in naming the team, which was created through an economic incentive to connect to another trademark.

Admittedly, there is self-fulfillment for those who are fans of the teams and wear the paraphernalia. But, if the team changed its name the fans would still find fulfillment in being part of a community of fans, as much of it is tied to geography. For example, in the NFL the Baltimore Colts moved to Indianapolis in 1983 to become the Indianapolis Colts. Fifteen years later, the Cleveland Browns moved to Baltimore; however, the NFL required the trademark name to remain in Cleveland. So, the new Baltimore team became the Ravens (after native son Edgar Allen Poe's famous poem). The Cleveland Browns returned to the NFL in 1999 with a new team.[96] Though some fans certainly continued cheering for the logo and team colors, most fans stuck with the team that they associated with geographically (as seen through attendance).

With the Redskins, there is another issue with self-fulfillment and that is the effect it has on Native Americans. Tribal members on reservations are often culturally and physically removed from the rest of the U.S. So, for most Americans their contact with Native Americans comes through media, including the use of such imagery in sports and advertising. The negative stereotypes have an impact on young tribal members trying to figure out their place in the nation.[97] The depictions they see in the media do not reflect the modern indigenous life. Instead, the image connects to a myth from centuries ago.

The value of autonomy supports the Washington football club's right to continue to use the term Redskin. It has the liberty to use the name free of government restriction (with only the public pressure of the market to answer to). But the imbalance of power makes it difficult for Native Americans to have autonomy in this case. The use of derogatory names infringes on the dignity of indigenous persons; thus, they can never truly be culturally autonomous.[98] As critical race theorists have argued, this is an image that tribes can neither control nor stop because the power belongs to the moneyed interests in western IP law.

Ultimately, the Court in *Matal* stated that the government had an interest in protecting under-represented groups from disparaging speech.[99] But, in the end this attempt was not narrowly tailored and the government could not force "happy talk." In some ways, the Court was supporting deliberation and self-governance. Issues of race relations, hate groups, and equality are still prevalent. In allowing the derogatory trademarks to exist in the marketplace of ideas it allows for the political debate to continue. How do we want to use language? What is the power in these words? Do we want commercial markets to be a forum for such thoughts? If the goal of the First Amendment is for us to deliberate, then shutting down trademarks because of the message will stifle such debate.

Blurred Lines and Copyright Infringement

In 2013, Pharrell Williams, Robin Thicke, and T.I. had a billboard hit with the song *Blurred Lines*. They sold millions of copies and it was one of the most streamed songs in recent history. The artists were inspired by Marvin

Gaye's *Got to Give It Up*, and the artists admitted they were trying to mimic it. However, the Gaye estate found it to be too close of a copy and sued the artists for copyright infringement.

The artists argued that they did not maliciously copy the song. Instead, it was simply meant to capture the essence of the song and an era. The song did use similar instruments, but it had other key differences in its composition. However, at trial a jury disagreed and found the artists liable for copyright infringement. The court awarded $7.4 million to the Gaye estate (an amount which was eventually reduced to $5 million) and Marvin Gaye has since been given credit for the song.[100]

Derivatives and Inspiration

Many in the music industry found the case to be wrongly decided.[101] The song was simply a homage to an era and had a similar feeling to Gaye's song, and everything is derivative of previously released entertainment. To hold all artists liable in this manner would stifle creativity.[102] Many classic entertainment texts are derivatives of previous works. For example, most Walt Disney classics, such as Cinderella, Snow White, and Bambi are based on long-standing fairy tales. John Williams, who has produced the soundtracks for some of the most popular movie franchises, is heavily influenced by classical music. But, the difference with these two cases is that they are using works in the public domain.

At the end of the 20th century, the U.S. Congress extended copyright to 70 years after the death of the creator (95 years for corporate-owned copyrights).[103] This covers every entertainment work since 1923—essentially the beginning of Hollywood and modern pop culture (with the first copyrighted material entering the public domain in 2018). Moreover, even if a work is already in the public domain, if Congress decides to increase the term of copyright a work already in the public domain can go back into copyright protection.[104]

With the majority of recorded music, television, and film protected by copyright, what the Blurred Lines case does is extend protection beyond direct infringement or derivatives. The case also allows for the copyright owners to stop works that are inspired. So, does that mean Led Zeppelin can sue any musicians who have soaring guitars and vocals? Can Lucasfilm (Disney) sue any producers who create a movie about wars in space? Can Warner Bros. sue any television show that is about a group of *Friends*? If the artist admits that they were inspired, and the jury believes they are too close in facts, then maybe.

Applying Free Speech Theory to the Blurred Lines Debate

If we apply free speech values, certainly the Blurred Lines case does not promote the free marketplace of ideas. In many ways, it promotes the monopoly of the copyright owner—in this case, Marvin Gaye's estate. However, the case was not protecting against an outright theft. Instead it limited artists' ability to be inspired by previous works, going against the very spirit of the Copyright Clause of the Constitution. The chilling effects of this case could be far-reaching and long-lasting. In music, there are only so many notes, so many chords, and so many ways to put the music together. When entire genres of music are untouchable the marketplace of ideas suffers. Blurred Lines might not have been made if the artists (and more importantly the recording studio) had known it would be a possible infringement.

It is not only professional musicians who are impacted. Today there is a remix and sharing culture that flourishes through social media. Much of what people use in social media videos takes liberally from protected works. Unless it is parody or critique, then the use of these works is dubious. The large amount of the word that is used often makes a fair use defense unavailable. So, re-mixers then have to argue that the new work is transformative enough to have its own protection. The issue in music is that courts have been slow to recognize sampling as a separate form of art. Adding protection to entire genres will only chill more speech.

The autonomy value in copyright depends on whose autonomy controls. Certainly, future artists lose autonomy when previous works cannot inspire them. However, there is an argument for the autonomy or moral rights of the original artist who served as the inspiration, and how his or her works will be used. In the case of Blurred Lines, the original artist passed away decades ago, and it was the estate asserting its copyright, so the moral rights seem to be lessened. This issue becomes trickier with corporations that live in perpetuity. Their autonomy and moral rights would never cease; thus, they could always control how their works are used. This could become an issue of self-government when a corporation tries to block a parody or critique of its works by claiming it had moral rights over the original work.[105]

Moreover, several artists have blocked politicians from using their songs in political campaigns.[106] The artists argue that they have a moral right over how their song is used and if they do not support the candidate then they should be able to stop it. However, if the politicians believe the music best sums up their agenda and message then there is an argument that it is fair use that serves self-government by informing citizens.

The most important value applied to copyright is self-fulfillment. Certainly, for artists who create works they are often expressing themselves by analyzing the human condition. Copyright law gives them economic incentive to create the works (it is arguable that profiting off one's work is a form of self-fulfillment as well). However, with draconian copyright laws that bar others from creating derivatives, sampling or even being inspired by protected works, this restricts other people's ability to achieve self-fulfillment at least until a century or more passes and the work goes into the public domain.

Copyright protection is based in the U.S. Constitution and must be balanced with freedom of speech. Fair use is the free speech exception when it comes to copyright law and the problem for courts has always been defining what is a fair use. Courts have not recognized music sampling used in hip-hop music to be transformative enough to be a fair use. Thus, artists are required to clear rights with the rights holder of any song they wish to use. If the rights holder does not want the song to be used, then it cannot be used (unless it is parody or criticism).

With the Blurred Lines case, the scales tipped even further toward copyright protection. Allowing for estates to sue artists inspired by a song decades after it release does not seem to balance with free speech rights. Ultimately, in copyright the person who created the original work should get to profit from it. The question remains: what is truly original?

Conclusion

In terms of free speech, the two cases discussed were diametric in their outcome. In the Slants case, free speech won out over the intellectual property right. In the Blurred Lines case, the intellectual property right won out over the free speech rights. The cases show the shifting point where free speech meets IP protection. There will continue to be a conflict between the two, and legal battles will be fought among interested parties. But, as the focus of this book shows us, rarely will these issues be debated through the spectrum of free speech theory. Rarely will courts ask: what principles does IP law serve, and why?

Intellectual property is the nexus of the commercial and the cultural. Within a consumerist culture where large fandoms are built around franchises owned by international conglomerates, there is going to be a conflict between the respective ownership rights. Does Mickey Mouse belong to Disney or to the fans who have included the creation in much of their own self-fulfillment? Does the Apple logo belong to the company or to the legions of customers who identify as Apple product devotees?

For too long the law has erred on the side of the commercial owners. In some ways this is easier; if the works are the exclusive right of the owner there is not much for courts to consider. But, as we move further into a share culture with more works being created than ever before, then the utility of intellectual works moves beyond purely commercial. Thus, there needs to be a balance between the legal rights of the creators and the users.

Notes

1. 17 U.S. Code § 506.
2. *International News Serv. v. Associated Press*, 248 U.S. 215 (1918).
3. C. Edwin Baker, "First Amendment Limits on Copyright," *Vanderbilt Law Review* 55 (April 2002).
4. Neil Weinstock Netanel, "Locating Copyright Within the First Amendment Skein," *Stanford Law Review* 54, no. 1 (October 2001): 2.
5. *United States v. O'Brien*, 391 U.S. 367 (1968).
6. *Walt Disney Prods. v. Air Pirates*, 581 F.2d 751 (9th Cir. 1978).
7. Adrian Johns, *Piracy: The Intellectual Property Wars From Gutenberg to Gates* (Chicago: University of Chicago Press, 2010).
8. Malla Pollack, "The Right to Know?: Delimiting Database Protection at the Juncture of the Commerce Clause, the Intellectual Property Clause, and the First Amendment," *Cardozo Arts & Entertainment Law Journal* 17 (1999): 145.
9. Paul M. Schwartz and William Michael Treanor, "*Eldred* and *Lochner*: Copyright Term Extension and Intellectual Property as Constitutional Property," *Yale Law Journal* 112, no. 8 (June 2003): 2375.
10. 17 U.S.C. § 102(a)
11. Ibid.
12. Some of these fall into the public domain, while others—such as designs—are protected by another area of intellectual property: patent law. This chapter does not analyze patents because there is little argument that they have an expressive element.
13. *Feist Publications, Inc. v. Rural Tel. Serv. Co.*, 499 U.S. 340, 344 (1991).
14. 17 U.S.C. § 107 (2006).
15. Ibid.
16. H.R. Rep. No. 94-1476, at 65 (1976), reprinted in 1976 U.S. Code, Cong. & Admin. News. 5659, 5679.
17. 815 F.3d 1145, 1149 (9th Cir. 2016).
18. *Eldred v. Ashcroft*, 537 U.S. 186, 219-20 (2003).
19. *New York Times v. Sullivan*, 376 U.S. 254 (1964).
20. *Sony Corp. of America v. Universal City Studios, Inc.*, 464 U.S. 417, 477 (1984).
21. Russell K. Hasan, "Winning the Copyright War: Copyright's Merger Doctrine and Natural Rights Theory as Solutions to the Problem of Reconciling Copyright and Free Speech," *Engage* 14 (February 2013): 59.
22. The band 2 Live Crew sought permission to use the song, but was denied. *Campbell v. Acuff-Rose Music, Inc.*, 510 U.S. 569, 572 (1994).
23. Ibid., at 583.
24. Ibid., at 580.
25. *Warner Bros. Entertainment Inc. v. RDR Books*, 575 F. Supp. 2d 513 (S.D.N.Y. 2008). In this case, a Harry Potter Encyclopedia was considered an infringing derivative work.

26. This is called the first sale doctrine. See *Kirtsaeng v. John Wiley & Sons*, 568 U.S. 519 (2013).
27. 510 U.S. at 569.
28. David E. Shipley, "A Transformative Use Taxonomy: Making Sense of the Transformative Use Standard," *Wayne Law Review* 63 (2018): 336.
29. U.S. Const. Art. I, Sec. 8, Cl. 3. See also David W. Barnes, "A New Economics of Trademarks," *Northwestern Journal of Technology & Intellectual Property* 5, no. 1 (Fall 2006): 22–23. In the 19th Century, the U.S. Supreme Court held that trademarks are not created, but rather are a function of usage in the marketplace. *In re Trade-Mark Cases*, 100 U.S. 82, 93–94 (1879).
30. 100 U.S. at 92.
31. *King-Seeley Thermos Co. v. Aladdin Indus., Inc.*, 321 F.2d 577, 579 (2d Cir. 1963).
32. Trademark Dilution Revision Act of 2006 (PL 109–312).
33. *Matal v. Tam*, 137 S.Ct. 1744 (2017).
34. 15 U.S.C.§1052(d) - (e).
35. Rebecca Tushnet, "Copy This Essay: How Fair Use Doctrine Harms Free Speech and How Copying Serves It," *Yale Law Journal* 114, no. 3 (March 2004): 538.
36. 376 U.S. at 270.
37. Donald Diefenbach, "The Constitutional and Moral Justifications for Copyright," *Public Affairs Quarterly* 8, no. 3 (July 1994): 225.
38. *Harper & Row v. Nation Enterprises*, 471 U.S. 539, 558 (1985).
39. Lawrence Lessig, *Free Culture: The Nature and Future of Creativity* (New York: Penguin Books, 2004).
40. Mark Rose, "The Author as Proprietor: *Donaldson v. Becket* and the Genealogy of Modern Authorship," *Representations* 23, no. 23 (Summer 1988).
41. See, generally, William Poole, ed., *John Milton, Areopagitica and Other Writings* (New York: Penguin Classics, 2016).
42. Hannibal Travis, "Pirates of the Information Infrastructure: Blackstonian Copyright and the First Amendment," *Berkeley Technology Law Journal* 15, no. 2 (March 2000): 812–13.
43. James Madison, "Forty-Three," in *The Federalist Papers*, eds. George Carey and James McClellan (Indianapolis: Liberty Fund, 2016), 56. Conversely, Thomas Jefferson did not accept the natural rights theory of intellectual property, arguing that it was meant to create new knowledge. *Graham v. John Deere Co.*, 383 U.S. 1, 8–9 (1966).
44. The U.S. Supreme Court first rejected this theory in *Wheaton v. Peters*, 33 U.S. 591 (1834).
45. Cyrill P. Rigamonti, "Deconstructing Moral Rights," *Harvard International Law Journal* 47, no. 2 (Summer 2006): 362.
46. The U.S. Supreme Court has cited Thomas Jefferson's rejection of the natural rights theory of intellectual property. 338 U.S. at 8–9.
47. Lawrence Lessig, *Code: And Other Laws of Cyberspace* (New York: Basic Books, 1999), 133.
48. Robert Merges, et al., *Intellectual Property in the New Technological Age*, 6th ed. (New York: Wolter Kluwer, 2016), 11.
49. Thomas I. Emerson, *The System of Freedom of Expression* (New York: Random House, 1970), 3.
50. *Branzburg v. Hayes*, 408 U.S. 665, 684 (1972).
51. 471 U.S. at 560.

52. Eric B. Easton, "Who Owns 'The First Rough Draft of History?': Reconsidering Copyright in News," *Columbia Journal of Law & Arts* 27 (2004): 521–23.
53. 471 U.S. at 560.
54. Ibid.
55. Alexander Meiklejohn, *Free Speech and Its Relation to Self-Government* (New York: Harper, 1948).
56. Zechariah Chafee, *Free Speech in the United States* (Cambridge, MA: Harvard University Press, 1941).
57. Robert Post, "Meiklejohn's Mistake: Individual Autonomy and the Reform of Public Discourse," *University of Colorado Law Review* 64 (1993).
58. Cass Sunstein, *Designing Democracy: What Constitutions Do*, 2nd ed. (New York: Oxford University Press, 2001), 6–9, 96–101, 239–43.
59. Alexander Meiklejohn, *Political Freedom: The Constitutional Powers of the People* (New York: Oxford University Press, 1965).
60. "[T]he best free market systems should regulate themselves. Of course, no system is perfect, and regulation is necessary[.]" Christopher D. Luehr, "Red Banking: Chinese State-Owned Commercial Bank Reform and the Basel II Accord," *Minnesota Journal of International Law* 20 (2011): 196.
61. Alexander Meiklejohn, "The First Amendment is an Absolute," *Supreme Court Review* 1961 (1961), 263.
62. Robert Post, "Reconciling Theory and Doctrine in First Amendment Jurisprudence," *California Law Review* 88, no. 6 (December 2000): 2355.
63. Nina Golden, "SLAPP Down: The Use (and Abuse) of Anti-SLAPP Motions to Strike," *Rutgers Journal of Law & Public Policy* 12, no. 4 (Summer 2015): 428.
64. Lin Feng, "Online Video Sharing: An Alternative Channel for Film Distribution? Copyright Enforcement, Censorship and Chinese Independent Cinema," *Chinese Journal of Communication* 10, no. 3 (2017).
65. Stephen McIntyre, "The Yang Obeys, But the Yin Ignores: Copyright Law and Speech Suppression in the People's Republic of China," *Pacific Basin Law Journal* 29, no. 1 (2011): 79.
66. "Hip Hop's Favorite Brands," CNN.com, accessed June 28, 2019, https://money.cnn.com/infographic/luxury/rap-luxury-brands/index.html
67. Alex Tudela, "Doc Martens: From Punk to High Fashion," *New York Times*, November 30, 2015, https://www.nytimes.com/interactive/2015/11/30/fashion/mens-style/14MS-TRADINGUP.html.
68. David Tan, "The Lost Language of the First Amendment in Copyright Fair Use: A Semiotic Perspective of the 'Transformative Use' Doctrine Twenty-Five Years On," *Fordham Intellectual Property, Media & Entertainment Law Journal* 26, no. 2 (2016): 314–15.
69. "'Fifty Shades of Grey' Started Out as 'Twilight' Fan Fiction Before Becoming an International Phenomenon," *Business Insider*, February 17, 2015, accessed June 26, 2019, https://www.businessinsider.com/fifty-shades-of-grey-started-out-as-twilight-fan-fiction-2015-2
70. *Williams v. Gaye*, 885 F.3d 1150 (9th Cir. 2018).
71. Peter Yu, "Intellectual Property and Confucianism," in *Diversity in Intellectual Property: Identities, Interests, and Intersections*, eds. Irene Calboli and Srividhya Ragavan (Cambridge: Cambridge University Press, 2015).

72. *Chandler v. Florida*, 449 U.S. 560 (1981).
73. "State of the First Amendment: 2018 Report," Freedom Forum Institute, accessed June 26, 2019, https://www.freedomforuminstitute.org/first-amendment-center/state-of-the-first-amendment/
74. Nat Hentoff, *Free Speech For Me—But Not For Thee: How the American Left and Right Relentlessly Censor Each Other* (New York: Harper Collins, 1992).
75. Schwartz and Treanor, "*Eldred* and *Lochner*."
76. Adrian Liu, "Copyright as Quasi-Public Property: Reinterpreting the Conflict Between Copyright and the First Amendment," *Fordham Intellectual Property, Media and Entertainment Law Journal* 18, no. 2 (2008): 424.
77. Eugene Volokh, "Freedom of Speech and Intellectual Property: Some Thoughts After *Eldred*, *44 Liquormart*, and *Bartnicki*," *Houston Law Review* 40, no. 3 (2003): 725–28.
78. David McGowan, "Why the First Amendment Cannot Dictate Copyright Policy," *University of Pittsburgh Law Review* 65, no. 2 (2004): 281n1.
79. 537 U.S. at 219.
80. The "disparagement clause" read in full: "No trademark by which the goods of the applicant may be distinguished from the goods of others shall be refused registration on the principal register on account of its nature unless it (a) Consists of or comprises immoral, deceptive, or scandalous matter; or matter which may disparage or falsely suggest a connection with persons, living or dead, institutions, beliefs, or national symbols, or bring them into contempt, or disrepute...." 15 U.S.C. §1052(a) (2006).
81. 137 S.Ct. at 1744.
82. Ibid., at 1747.
83. Ibid.
84. Ibid., at 1763.
85. Ibid., at 1765.
86. "Mission & History," National Congress of American Indians, accessed June 26, 2019, http://www.ncai.org/about-ncai/mission-history
87. David Carl Wahlberg, "Strategies for Making Team Identity Change," in *The Native American Mascot Controversy: A Handbook*, ed. C. Richard King (Lanham, MD: Rowman & Littlefield, 2015), 122.
88. Chuck Culpepper, "Florida State's Unusual Bond With Seminole Tribe Puts Mascot Debate in a Different Light," *Washington Post*, December 29, 2014, https://www.washingtonpost.com/sports/colleges/florida-states-unusual-bond-with-seminole-tribe-puts-mascot-debate-in-a-different-light/2014/12/29/5386841a-8eea-11e4-ba53-a477d66580ed_story.html?noredirect=on&utm_term=.da4cf29db1e5
89. Camila Domonoske, "Cleveland Indians Will Remove 'Chief Wahoo' From Uniforms in 2019," National Public Radio, January 29, 2018, accessed June 26, 2019, https://www.npr.org/sections/thetwo-way/2018/01/29/581590453/cleveland-indians-will-remove-chief-wahoo-from-uniforms-in-2019
90. *Pro-Football, Inc. v. Blackhorse*, 112 F. Supp. 3d 439 (E.D. Va. 2015), vacated, 709 F. App'x 182 (4th Cir. 2018).
91. Baxter Holmes, "Update: Yes, a 'Redskin' Does, In Fact, Mean the Scalped Head of a Native American, Sold, Like a Pelt, for Cash," *Esquire*, June 18, 2014, accessed June 21, 2019, https://www.esquire.com/news-politics/news/a29318/redskin-name-update/

92. 137 S.Ct. at 1765.
93. Jesse A. Witten, "Taking the Stand: Time to Retire the 'R' Reference?" *Washington Lawyer*, June 2014, accessed June 26, 2019, https://www.dcbar.org/bar-resources/publications/washington-lawyer/articles/june-2014-taking-the-stand.cfm .
94. Neil Greenberg, "How Much Would it Cost to Change the Redskins Name?" *Washington Post*, June 18, 2014, https://www.washingtonpost.com/news/fancy-stats/wp/2014/06/18/how-much-it-would-cost-to-change-the-redskins-name/?utm_term=.97928f6340ab
95. Noah Frank, "Redskins Forever? A Lesson from the Bullets," *WTOP*, July 1, 2014, accessed June 26, 2019, https://wtop.com/news/2014/07/redskins-forever-a-lesson-from-the-bullets/
96. Kevin Chase, "Moving Franchises—Where Did Your NFL Team Come From?" *KBAT*, October 23, 2015, accessed June 26, 2019, http://kbat.com/moving-franchises-where-did-your-nfl-team-come-from/
97. American Psychology Association, "Summary of the APA Resolution Recommending Retirement of American Indian Mascots," accessed June 26, 2019, http://www.apa.org/pi/oema/resources/indian-mascots.aspx
98. Jason Zenor, "Tribal (De)termination: Commercial Speech, Native American Imagery, and Cultural Sovereignty," *Southwestern Law Review* 48 (2019): 96–99.
99. 137 S.Ct. at 1765.
100. Associated Press, "Pharrell Williams and Robin Thicke to Pay $7.4m to Marvin Gaye's Family Over Blurred Lines," *Guardian*, March 11, 2015, https://www.theguardian.com/music/2015/mar/10/blurred-lines-pharrell-robin-thicke-copied-marvin-gaye; 885 F.3d at 1150.
101. Randy Lewis, "Brian Wilson, Bonnie McKey and Others React to Blurred Lines Verdict," *Los Angeles Times*, March 14, 2015, https://www.latimes.com/entertainment/music/la-et-ms-blurred-lines-reaction-brian-wilson-bonnie-mckee-20150314-story.html#page=1
102. Randall Roberts, "How the Blurred Lines Case Could Have Chilling Effect on Creativity," *Los Angeles Times*, March 6, 2015, https://www.latimes.com/entertainment/music/la-et-ms-blurred-lines-notebook-pharrell-williams-robin-thicke-marvin-gaye-20150306-column.html
103. Sonny Bono Copyright Extension Act (CTEA) of 1998, 17 U.S.C. § 302 (1998).
104. *Golan v. Holder*, 565 U.S. 302 (2012).
105. 581 F.2d at 751.
106. Christian Holub, "Can Musicians Like Rihanna and Axl Rose Stop Politicians From Using Their Music?" *Entertainment Weekly*, November 5, 2018, https://ew.com/music/2018/11/05/can-musicians-stop-politicians-from-using-music/

References

Baker, C. Edwin. "First Amendment Limits on Copyright." *Vanderbilt Law Review* 55 (April 2002): 891–951.
Barnes, David W. "A New Economics of Trademarks." *Northwestern Journal of Technology & Intellectual Property* 5, no. 1 (Fall 2006): 22–67.

Chafee, Zechariah. *Free Speech in the United States*. Cambridge, MA: Harvard University Press, 1941.
Diefenbach, Donald. "The Constitutional and Moral Justifications for Copyright." *Public Affairs Quarterly* 8, no. 3 (July 1994): 225–35.
Easton, Eric B. "Who Owns 'The First Rough Draft of History?': Reconsidering Copyright in News." *Columbia Journal of Law & Arts* 27 (2004): 521–62.
Emerson, Thomas I. *The System of Freedom of Expression*. New York: Random House, 1970.
Feng, Lin. "Online Video Sharing: An Alternative Channel for Film Distribution? Copyright Enforcement, Censorship and Chinese Independent Cinema." *Chinese Journal of Communication* 10, no. 3 (2017): 279–94.
Golden, Nina. "SLAPP Down: The Use (and Abuse) of Anti-SLAPP Motions to Strike." *Rutgers Journal of Law & Public Policy* 12, no. 4 (Summer 2015): 1–37.
Hasan, Russell K. "Winning the Copyright War: Copyright's Merger Doctrine and Natural Rights Theory as Solutions to the Problem of Reconciling Copyright and Free Speech." *Engage* 14 (February 2013): 59–71.
Hentoff, Nat. *Free Speech For Me—But Not For Thee: How the American Left and Right Relentlessly Censor Each Other*. New York: Harper Collins, 1992.
Johns, Adrian. *Piracy: The Intellectual Property Wars From Gutenberg to Gates*. Chicago: University of Chicago Press, 2010.
Lessig, Lawrence. *Code: And Other Laws of Cyberspace*. New York: Basic Books, 1999.
———. *Free Culture: The Nature and Future of Creativity*. New York: Penguin Books, 2004.
Liu, Adrian. "Copyright as Quasi-Public Property: Reinterpreting the Conflict Between Copyright and the First Amendment." *Fordham Intellectual Property, Media and Entertainment Law Journal* 18, no. 2 (2008): 383–439.
Luehr, Christopher D. "Red Banking: Chinese State-Owned Commercial Bank Reform and the Basel II Accord." *Minnesota Journal of International Law* 20 (2011): 171–97.
Madison, James. "Forty-Three." In *The Federalist Papers*, edited by George Carey and James McClellan, 55–56. Indianapolis: Liberty Fund, 2001.
McGowan, David. "Why the First Amendment Cannot Dictate Copyright Policy." *University of Pittsburgh Law Review* 65, no. 2 (2004): 281–338.
McIntyre, Stephen. "The Yang Obeys, But the Yin Ignores: Copyright Law and Speech Suppression in the People's Republic of China." *Pacific Basin Law Journal* 29, no. 1 (2011): 75–134.
Meiklejohn, Alexander. "The First Amendment Is An Absolute." *Supreme Court Review* 1961 (1961): 245–66.
———. *Free Speech and Its Relation to Self-Government*. New York: Harper, 1948.
———. *Political Freedom: The Constitutional Powers of the People*. New York: Oxford University Press, 1965.
Merges, Robert, et al. *Intellectual Property in the New Technological Age*, 6th ed. New York: Wolter Kluwer, 2016.

Netanel, Neil Weinstock. "Locating Copyright Within the First Amendment Skein." *Stanford Law Review* 54, no. 1 (October 2001): 1–86.

Pollack, Malla. "The Right to Know?: Delimiting Database Protection at the Juncture of the Commerce Clause, the Intellectual Property Clause, and the First Amendment." *Cardozo Arts & Entertainment Law Journal* 17 (1999): 47–145.

Poole, William, ed. *John Milton, Areopagitica and Other Writings.* New York: Penguin Classics, 2016.

Post, Robert. "Meiklejohn's Mistake: Individual Autonomy and the Reform of Public Discourse." *University of Colorado Law Review* 64 (1993): 1109–37.

———. "Reconciling Theory and Doctrine in First Amendment Jurisprudence." *California Law Review* 88, no. 6 (December 2000): 2353–74.

Rigamonti, Cyrill P. "Deconstructing Moral Rights." *Harvard International Law Journal* 47, no. 2 (Summer 2006): 353–412.

Rose, Mark. "The Author as Proprietor: *Donaldson v. Becket* and the Genealogy of Modern Authorship." *Representations* 23, no. 23 (Summer 1988): 51–85.

Schwartz, Paul M., and William Michael Treanor. "*Eldred* and *Lochner*: Copyright Term Extension and Intellectual Property as Constitutional Property." *Yale Law Journal* 112, no. 8 (June 2003): 2331–414.

Shipley, David E. "A Transformative Use Taxonomy: Making Sense of the Transformative Use Standard." *Wayne Law Review* 63 (2018): 267–336.

Sunstein, Cass. *Designing Democracy: What Constitutions Do*, 2nd ed. New York: Oxford University Press, 2001.

Tan, David. "The Lost Language of the First Amendment in Copyright Fair Use: A Semiotic Perspective of the 'Transformative Use' Doctrine Twenty-Five Years On." *Fordham Intellectual Property, Media & Entertainment Law Journal* 26, no. 2 (2016): 311–79.

Travis, Hannibal. "Pirates of the Information Infrastructure: Blackstonian Copyright and the First Amendment." *Berkeley Technology Law Journal* 15, no. 2 (March 2000): 777–864.

Tushnet, Rebecca. "Copy This Essay: How Fair Use Doctrine Harms Free Speech and How Copying Serves It." *Yale Law Journal* 114, no. 3 (March 2004): 535–90.

Volokh, Eugene. "Freedom of Speech and Intellectual Property: Some Thoughts After *Eldred*, *44 Liquormart*, and *Bartnicki*." *Houston Law Review* 40, no. 3 (2003): 697–748.

Wahlberg, David Carl. "Strategies for Making Team Identity Change." In *The Native American Mascot Controversy: A Handbook*, edited by C. Richard King, 117–26. Lanham, MD: Rowman & Littlefield, 2015.

Yu, Peter. "Intellectual Property and Confucianism." In *Diversity in Intellectual Property: Identities, Interests, and Intersections*, edited by Irene Calboli and Srividhya Ragavan, 247–73. Cambridge: Cambridge University Press, 2015.

Zenor, Jason. "Tribal (De)termination: Commercial Speech, Native American Imagery and Cultural Sovereignty." *Southwestern Law Review* 48 (2019): 81–104.

7. Free Speech Debates in Australia: Contemporary Controversies

Katharine Gelber

Around the world freedom of speech is usually protected through explicit constitutional or statutory law. Australia is unusual for a Western liberal democracy, in that it does not possess any explicit federal constitutional or statutory protection for freedom of speech. Nevertheless, this does not mean the freedom is entirely unprotected; rather, that the mechanisms by which freedom of speech is protected are complex, multilayered, and weak.[1] The weak protection of freedom of speech in Australian constitutional and statutory law is in part reflective of the lack of a dominant theoretical approach to its defense throughout history. Free speech debates have taken place in the context of a broader political culture that historically has prioritized a utilitarian approach to governing over explicit rights protection.

Yet in contemporary political debate, freedom of speech is invoked rhetorically more frequently than has been the case before. Moreover, this invocation promotes a libertarian view of freedom of speech, which differs significantly from the approach to free speech that preceded these debates. This chapter investigates the ways in which current debates over free speech controversies reflect attempts to inject a libertarian view of free speech into Australian political culture. It also demonstrates the relative failure of this approach to build broad support for wider protections for a range of speech, including speech that harms.

In order to do this, first this chapter explains the unique set of circumstances surrounding Australia's lack of an explicit protection for freedom of speech in federal law. This includes consideration of the rationales underlying the decision of the Constitution's founders, and later legislatures, not to remedy this apparent lack. It then explains the *patchwork* framework in which freedom of speech is protected in Australian law, and the emergence of a democratic foundation. It then moves to examine two free speech controversies—racial hatred laws and the debate over marriage equality—to show how libertarian views are being injected into Australian political culture, and the relative inability of this theoretical approach to achieve broad traction and public support for wider protections for freedom of speech.

Australia's Unique Design

Australia's lack of an explicit constitutional or statutory protection for freedom of speech in federal law is due to two particular aspects of its unique design. The first is a merging of responsible government with federalism, and the second is a historical, strongly utilitarian political culture that prioritized practical measures over lofty idealism. This section explains how these aspects of Australia's constitutional framework resulted in its lack of explicit protection for freedom of speech when the Constitution was designed.

The task of those involved in drafting the Australian Constitution in the 1890s was to design a federal compact between previously freestanding colonies, which would retain their independence while simultaneously providing national government in areas of need. This involved merging principles of responsible, representative government derived from the United Kingdom and extant in the colonies, with federalism derived from the United States, which was designed to protect the colonies that were to become states by giving them equal representation in the Senate.[2] During the constitutional debates, there was an awareness of the United States Bill of Rights, and some attempts to include rights provisions in the founding document. One of the Constitution's founders, Andrew Inglis Clark, declared himself a firm "believer in the reality of the fundamental rights of man"[3] and attempted to insert a version of the United States 14th Amendment into the draft Constitution. His amendments would have secured citizenship rights, prevented the deprivation of life, liberty, or property without due process, and granted equal protection under the law. But they were unsuccessful, and only three explicit, "hedged and technical" rights provisions were adopted in the final document.[4]

The hostility expressed at Federation to the explicit inclusion of a bill of rights[5] in either constitutional or statutory law was heavily informed by utilitarian understandings of interests and practical utility.[6] Utilitarianism had been promoted since the late 18th century as a guide to government policy, with the aim being to achieve the greatest happiness for the greatest number.

Proponents of this philosophy included John Stuart Mill, who suggested that the correct way to choose between two alternatives is to select that which "all or almost all who have experience of both give a decided preference."[7] In Australia, the utilitarian view led to an emphasis on practicality and a valuing of the "majority will over minority rights," and was averse to abstract political ideas.[8] The combining of utilitarianism with principles of responsible government—in which the executive is drawn from the legislature and thereby held accountable through its activities to the people—and in which parliamentary sovereignty over decision making is the preferred mechanism for settling differences, explains the ongoing reluctance within the Australian polity to create a bill of rights that could result in a hard form of judicial review that might override parliamentary sovereignty.[9]

The fact that the Australian Constitution was developed with minimal attention to the explicit enunciation of rights has meant that a variety of other mechanisms has been used over time to effect the protection of freedom of speech.

Mechanisms for Protecting Freedom of Speech

The wide variety of mechanisms that is used to protect freedom of speech in Australia derives from what has been described as a "patchwork of human rights measures."[10] These include the common law, domestic statutory provisions at both federal and sub-national levels, the influence of international human rights law, and the role of an independent judiciary, including the development since 1992 of a doctrine of an implied constitutional protection for freedom of communication on political matters. As is to be expected from such a diverse range of measures, they lack a singular theoretical underpinning. This section explains the operation of these distinct mechanisms in protecting freedom of speech.

The common law tradition that Australia inherited from the United Kingdom has been described as the principle that, "everybody is free to do anything, subject only to the provisions of the law."[11] This has not always been used to protect freedom of speech in the way we understand it ought to today. In the early decades after European settlement in 1788, for example, government officials used the common law protection of freedom of speech to protect themselves from public censure.[12] However, over time the common law protection of freedom of speech came to be used in ways that are more recognizable to a 21st century audience. For example, in 1980, the Australian government sought to suppress publication of a book containing information about the invasion of East Timor by the Indonesian government.

The High Court declined to restrain publication, arguing that to do so would be inappropriate since, "[i]t is unacceptable in our democratic society that there should be a restraint on the publication of information relating to government when the only vice of that information is that it enables the public to discuss, review and criticize government action."[13] This reference to a democratic justification for freedom of speech—the need for citizens to be able to learn about and deliberate the actions of the government on their behalf—was to resurface later.

In 1987, the High Court declined to prevent the publication of former MI5 agent Peter Wright's book, *Spycatcher*, on similar grounds.[14] The following year, the common law protection of freedom of speech was relied upon when the High Court declared invalid the granting of exclusive commercial use to the Australian Bicentennial Authority of terms including, *bicentenary*, *200 years*, *Australia*, and *1788*. In making its judgment the Court declared that, "[i]n arming the Authority with this extraordinary power the Act provides for a regime of protection which is grossly disproportionate to the need to protect the commemoration" and that it was an "extraordinary intrusion into freedom of expression [that] is not reasonably and appropriately adapted to achieve the ends that lie within the limits of constitutional power."[15] Such cases, however, were relatively rare and the role of the common law in protecting human rights in Australia has been described as "limited."[16]

Second, from the 1970s onwards, the utilitarian, interests-based Australian political culture was challenged by internationalist human rights sentiments.[17] Australia adopted international obligations to combat racial hatred when it ratified the International Covenant on Civil and Political Rights (Article 20) in 1980, and the International Convention on the Elimination of All forms of Racial Discrimination (Article 4) in 1975. However, since international multilateral human rights treaties are not self-executing in Australia, ratification does not automatically translate into the domestic enforceability of their provisions,[18] although these provisions can help clarify interpretation where there is an ambiguity in domestic law.[19] Domestic implementation requires the passage of domestic law, and despite attempts to introduce specific human rights protections in the Constitution or federal statute in 1944, 1973, 1983, 1985, and 1988, these were unsuccessful in the face of the dominant utilitarian political culture.[20]

Third, and in partial domestic implementation of the human rights to which Australia is a signatory in international law, from the 1970s onwards new statutory provisions have been introduced that are rights-protecting. There are differences between the scope of the international legal protections and their more modest domestic counterparts, reflecting the founders' confidence in the role of the parliament.[21] Anti-discrimination provisions enacted federally include the *Racial Discrimination Act 1975* (Cth),[22] *Sex Discrimination Act 1984* (Cth), *Age Discrimination Act 2004* (Cth), and *Disability Discrimination Act 1992* (Cth). Similar provisions have been enacted at the sub-national level, such as the *Anti-Discrimination Act 1977* (NSW), *Anti-Discrimination Act 1991* (Qld), and *Discrimination Act 1991* (ACT). Federal privacy legislation has also been enacted (for example, the *Privacy Act 1988* (Cth)). This has resulted in the stronger protection of some human rights, but there has been no clear enunciation of the protection of free speech in federal statutory law. At the sub-national level, three jurisdictions have enacted statutory bills of rights that include an explicit provision protecting freedom of speech, all of which permit limitations to be placed on that right.[23] These bills of rights operate in a way that ensures parliamentary sovereignty, and they do not provide for a hard form of judicial review.

Fourth and finally, the operation of an independent judiciary has played an important but limited role in defending rights, including freedom of speech.[24] As early as 1977 High Court Justice Lionel Murphy[25] suggested that the proper operation of the Australian constitutional framework impliedly required the protection of freedom of speech and freedom of movement (among other things). He directly connected the need to protect freedom of speech to the proper operation of elections, the system of representative government, and "democratic principles." He said, "such freedoms are fundamental to a democratic society," and a "necessary correlation" to the Australian democratic system of government.[26] This articulation of a democratic justification for interpreting the Australian Constitution echoed the views of Alexander Meiklejohn, who described free speech as a "deduction" from democracy.[27] However, the view that the Constitution protected freedom of speech in an implied way remained in the minority for quite some time. It was not until 1992 that this view came to be accepted by a majority of the High Court justices, when they decided two landmark cases,[28] holding that freedom of communication on "political" matters was inherently protected in the representative and responsible system of government established by the Constitution. The freedom required that representatives be chosen by the people.[29] This implied a democratic theoretical underpinning for the freedom, since it was essential to the people being able to make informed decisions in elections. However, this theoretical underpinning was not explicitly elaborated in the judgments, as the freedom was interpreted as deriving from the text and structure of the Constitution. The freedom was clarified in a unanimous judgment in 1997,[30] which recognized it as an "indispensable incident" of the system of government.

The protection this "incident" offers is not robust. Where a law limits the implied freedom, it will not be held invalid as long as it is compatible with the maintenance of the constitutional system of government, and "reasonably appropriate and adapted" to serve a legitimate governmental purpose.[31] This so-called *Lange test*, named after the unanimous case of 1997, was updated slightly in 2004 in *Coleman v. Power*,[32] and significantly in 2015 in *McCloy*[33] to introduce a more structured type of proportionality test for assessing the validity of laws that are alleged to violate the implied freedom. Overall, although some critiqued the court in 1992 for over-extended reasoning and overstepping its judicial role,[34] the implied freedom has not led to significantly increased protection for freedom of speech. In fact, after the initial invalidation of two federal statutes in the 1992 cases, and in spite of numerous attempts to use the implied freedom as a basis for invalidating laws,[35] it was not until 2013 that another law was found constitutionally invalid under the terms of that freedom.[36]

The mechanisms used to protect freedom of speech in Australia have therefore been complex and varied. What is not apparent is a coherent theoretical underpinning to free speech protection. The development in the High Court of Australia of the implied doctrine of freedom of political communication suggested a democratic argument in favor of free speech, in so far as free speech was posited as inherent and vital to democratic deliberation in order for voters to exercise choice in electing their parliamentary representatives. However, perceptions of an underpinning of the Australian doctrine by a democratic argument are offset by the weakness of the implied doctrine, in the sense that proportionate laws which serve a legitimate government end can be interpreted as a valid exercise of governmental power even where they significantly restrain freedom of speech. This is arguably inconsistent with the premises of argument from democracy, which suggest a more protective approach to freedom of speech[37] that is not reflected in Australian practice.

...

Having established the mechanisms under which free speech has been protected historically in Australia, and the kinds of underpinnings that have emerged in that context, this chapter moves now to consider more recent controversies over freedom of speech. It will show that we have seen the emergence for the first time of a libertarian approach to free speech that has little historical antecedent in Australian political discourse. It will show how debates over racial hatred laws, and marriage equality, have evinced this approach and the relative lack of success of these attempts to shift the ground on free speech in Australian political culture.

Hate Speech Laws

Australia has a long history with anti-vilification laws (also known as hate speech laws), which have been introduced in states and federally since 1989. The introduction of these laws has always been resisted by some parliamentarians concerned about their impact on freedom of speech, but this concern has tended to result in the introduction of exemptions to the laws, rather than preventing their being enacted altogether. For example, New South Wales introduced a law prohibiting racial vilification in 1989 in response to reports of organized, right-wing racist activities, anti-Semitic attacks, and racist media commentary.[38] Similarly, federal anti-vilification laws were introduced in 1995 following the publication of the reports of the National Inquiry into Racist Violence in 1991, the Royal Commission into Aboriginal Deaths in Custody in 1991, and the Australian Law Reform Commission's report on Multiculturalism and the Law in 1992, all of which cited concerning levels of racial vilification in the community and said they warranted legislative remedy.[39] The international human rights sentiments generated by Australia's ratification of relevant multilateral human rights treaties also played a role in prompting legislatures to act.[40]

The free speech concerns articulated in response to proposals to introduce such legislation were generic and did not articulate specific theoretical arguments. Some described anti-vilification laws as "dangerous," an "attempt to stifle freedom of thought."[41] But the majority view was that such laws, when appropriately drafted, achieved the right balance between the competing rights of freedom of speech on the one hand, and the right to a life of dignity and a life free from discriminatory harms on the other. Parliamentarians achieved this balance by exempting fair reporting, and good-faith academic or scientific research or public debate, from the operation of the laws.[42]

Today almost all sub-national jurisdictions have adopted racial hatred laws and in many cases the laws have been extended to other grounds including sexuality, (trans)gender identity, HIV/AIDS status, disability, and religion.[43] Although criminal laws[44] exist, there have only been six successful prosecutions in nearly 30 years of their operation.[45] By design, and in order to protect free speech from excessive intrusion, the civil laws[46] are relied upon to manage the vast majority of complaints. Civil laws differ between jurisdictions, but they have in common that a person must make a complaint in writing with the relevant human rights authority, which investigates the complaint to see whether vilification has occurred and, if it has, seeks to conciliate a confidential settlement between the parties. Settlement can include an agreement to cease the behavior, an apology, a published retraction, or an agreement to conduct education in a workplace. A complainant may terminate a complaint and proceed to civil proceedings in a Tribunal (under State or Territory law) or the Federal Court (under federal law). Only 1.8% of complaints proceed to formal adjudication, with approximately half of those producing a finding that the impugned conduct was unlawful. The types of remedies that can be ordered are modest, and include an order to desist, an order to publish a retraction or apology, or a fine.[47] Responsibility for lodging a complaint rests on the person targeted, who must be of the requisite identity to have standing.[48]

There has never been a constitutional challenge in the High Court to the validity of Australia's anti-vilification laws, so the question of whether or not they would withstand constitutional scrutiny against the implied freedom of political communication remains open. Nevertheless, lower courts have suggested that the provisions would withstand such scrutiny. The Federal Court has stated this is because of the qualified nature of the implied freedom: "there are many examples of the High Court finding that laws which intrude upon free political discourse are nevertheless constitutionally valid because those laws reasonably serve a countervailing public purpose."[49] The Federal Court has recognized that hate speech laws are not limited to criminal laws targeting only the most egregious forms of racial hatred, but include civil laws designed to deter "public expressions of offensive racial prejudice which might lead to acts of racial hatred and discrimination." The Court has held that this renders them consistent with the provisions of international law that gave rise to them, and constitutionally valid exercises of power.[50] The Supreme Court of Victoria has similarly concluded that that state's hate speech law can be considered appropriate and adapted to serve the legitimate government end of preventing religious vilification.[51]

For many years, hate speech laws in Australia operated quietly and out of public view. The confidential nature of the civil complaints process assisted this. However, in 2011 controversy was raised after a finding in the Federal Court that a well-known journalist had engaged in unlawful vilification, by writing articles describing some Indigenous people of fair skin as not truly Indigenous and suggesting they had invalidly adopted Indigenous identities to take advantage of benefits only available to Indigenous people.[52] Even though the remedy ordered by the court was very mild—the offending articles remain accessible, but have appended to them a note that they were found to contravene Australia's federal racial hatred law—the journalist in question engaged in a campaign claiming to have been "silenced" as a result of the judgment.[53] The case enabled the media to engage in subsequent discourse questioning the legitimacy of racial vilification laws, and thereby to promote a more libertarian view of freedom of speech than had been previously typical in Australian political culture.[54] Commentary posited anti-vilification laws as inherently illegitimate restrictions on freedom of speech, and the journalist in question claimed erroneously that his views had been banned. Some politicians claimed the law was a "grotesque limitation on ordinary political discourse."[55]

This then led to attempts to amend the law in 2014 and 2016, both of which were designed to enact a more libertarian view on freedom of speech. In March, 2014, the federal Attorney General released an exposure draft bill[56] for public comment, which proposed narrowing the scope of the conduct captured, and expanding the exceptions to it very broadly. He famously defended the bill, declaring in the Senate that,

> People like Mr. Bolt should be free to express any opinion on a social or cultural or a political question that they wish to express. ... People do have a right to be bigots, you know. In a free country people do have rights to say things that other people find offensive or insulting or bigoted.[57]

In spite of his vigorous defense of the bill, it was dropped in the face of both staunch public criticism[58] and demonstrated ongoing public support for the restriction of hate speech in law. In parliament, the opposition Australian Labor Party criticized the 2014 amendments for seeking to override protections against discrimination. They said they would give, "a green light to racist hate speech in Australia," and were "an attack on fundamental values of tolerance and respect [that]... are at the heart of our diverse and multicultural society. ... This is not us. It's not the sort of country we are."[59] They spoke of the strong support from targeted community members for retention of the law.[60] Their defense of the law was premised on balancing the right to free speech against the right to live with dignity and free from discrimination and harm.

In 2016, another vilification complaint against university students received widespread media coverage,[61] and a report by the Australian Law Reform Commission on traditional rights and freedoms concluded that the terms used in the federal hate speech law may be an excessive intrusion into freedom of speech.[62] The federal government ordered a parliamentary inquiry into freedom of speech, but the report of that inquiry was unable to reach agreement on whether or not the wording of the federal law should be amended, and if so how.[63] The division amongst committee members demonstrated different views regarding the appropriate limits on freedom of speech, and the inability of those views to be reconciled. A subsequent attempt by the government to amend the wording of the legislation[64] failed to achieve sufficient support in the legislature. The parliamentary opposition also criticized the 2016 attempt to amend the law, noting that the exemptions in the law already protected freedom of speech where the speech was a matter of public interest: "If the speech [the Attorney General] wants permitted is a matter of public interest, it would be covered by [the exemptions]."[65] They proposed that, "racism, bigotry and discrimination are not an acceptable part of Australian life."[66] Additionally, opinion surveys consistently showed high levels of public support throughout Australia for retaining existing anti-vilification laws.[67]

This, then, is a good example of an attempt over time to enact and reinforce a libertarian view of freedom of speech, one in which content-based laws prohibiting racial hatred were posited as inappropriate, excessive and illegitimate incursions into freedom of speech. However, it had very limited success. Community and parliamentary opposition pushed back against the libertarian view being promoted, and the laws remained unchanged, reflecting an ambivalence in Australian political culture toward unfettered free speech.

The Marriage Equality Debate

A second example of a recent free speech controversy in Australia occurred during debate over the legality of same sex marriage. In 2004, and in response to same sex couples who married overseas announcing they would attempt to have their marriages legally recognized in Australia, the federal government amended the *Marriage Act 1961* (Cth) to specify that marriage could only legally take place between one man and one woman.[68] Thus began a national campaign to have same sex marriage legalized. The campaign was multifaceted and included attempts by states[69] and the Australian Capital Territory[70] to legalize same sex marriage in their jurisdictions. The latter failed when the High Court held that sub-national legislation could not operate concurrently with the federal *Marriage Act 1961* (Cth),[71] and that the federal legislation covered the field. Up to 2015, a total of 23 bills[72] to legislate for same sex marriage was introduced into the federal parliament, all of which were unsuccessful.

In 2015 the federal government, in the face of considerable and growing community pressure to legalize marriage equality, promised to hold a national plebiscite on the issue to ask the people their views. This promise was taken to the 2016 federal election, but the re-elected government was not able to pass legislation through the parliament to hold a compulsory plebiscite, due to concerns among non-government parliamentarians about the deleterious effects of such a vote on the LGBTQI community and the likelihood it would facilitate hate speech on the ground of sexuality.[73] The government subsequently chose to direct the Australian Bureau of Statistics to conduct a voluntary survey of all Australians on the electoral roll concerning whether or not they supported the right of same sex couples to marry.[74] This was unusual because the Australian Bureau of Statistics is normally responsible for collecting data on a five yearly basis for the census.[75] There was a failed legal challenge to the constitutional validity of the survey,[76] and it went ahead. It produced a very high participation rate of 79.5% of the eligible, voting-age population, with consistent participation among groups classified by age, gender, and geographical location. The result was a decisive 61.6% in favor of marriage equality rights, with 133 out of 150 electorates showing a majority of those surveyed in favor.[77] Following this result, in December 2017 the federal parliament legislated to enact marriage equality.[78]

Debate surrounding the conduct of the survey was of particular interest because opponents of same sex marriage pitched the issue of expressing one's view on same sex marriage as being primarily about freedom of speech. The Australian Christian Lobby, for example, claimed that marriage equality would "take away" people's right to free speech. They argued the very existence of same sex marriage was a "threat" to free speech because it would remove people's ability to speak publicly about their preferred definition of marriage.[79] Former Prime Minister Tony Abbott supported this, arguing that it was essential to vote "no" in the survey "if you're worried about religious freedom and freedom of speech."[80] He suggested that the enactment of marriage equality would have negative implications for freedom of speech, including in relation to how children are taught in schools, and suggested this had occurred in the UK and Canada. This is misleading because sex education content in Canada is voluntary and parents can exclude their children if they wish, and in the United Kingdom there is only a requirement that schools encourage respect for LGBTQI people, a requirement that was introduced before same sex marriage became legalized in that country.[81] Nevertheless, the issue of free speech was catalyzed by opponents of same sex marriage in an attempt to posit it as *the* key issue in the debate.

Although the *no* vote was a minority of voters, it is not possible to know how many of them believed they were voting in favor of free speech, and how many did not support same sex marriage. What can be seen in this case, however, is that the view that all social issues are about freedom of speech, and that freedom of speech should be conceptualized capaciously did not appear to win over a significant enough proportion of the public to put the survey result at risk.

Conclusion

Australia's unusual stance toward, and mechanisms for, the protection of freedom of speech have been heavily influenced by a strongly, but not uniformly, utilitarian political culture which reflected a distinctively white national identity coalescing with state-based and economic interests, and a myth of liberal egalitarianism that persists in spite of hard evidence of perpetual and ongoing inequalities.[82] The result has been a belief, promulgated as early as the Federation debates, that Australia did not need explicit protection of human rights in constitutional or federal statutory law. Since that time significant advances have been made both in relation to Australia's international obligations and domestically to secure the protection of human rights, and to protect vulnerable communities against discrimination. The protection of freedom of speech in this context has been unusual. There have been high watermarks throughout Australia's history when the preservation of freedom of speech has featured prominently both in jurisprudence and in parliamentary debates, and has been regarded as essential to its democratic system of governance. There is also evidence of ongoing broad support for, and acceptance of, the regulation of hate speech as a means of protecting the vulnerable against discrimination and harm.

In recent years there has been a surge in the popularity of the idea of freedom of speech in a vigorous public debate. Interestingly, this has been in the form of an injection of a libertarian understanding of freedom of speech into debate. This attempt to transform the theoretical underpinnings of popular understandings of this core freedom has not, however, resonated strongly enough to result in statutory amendments that significantly change the territory within which freedom of speech is regulated. Although the libertarian views being put forward would find themselves very much at home in any United States-informed debate on the topic, in the Australian context they have had little purchase. There is strong public support for retaining and extending legal protections, and resisting this emerging discourse. Pressures to adopt a more libertarian stance on freedom of speech have not, to date, found traction in Australian public sentiment, which still supports the retention of extant hate speech laws and recently introduced same sex marriage rights.

Australia's approach, therefore, has both strengths and weaknesses. Its strengths include an allowance for flexibility that can take account of harmful types of speech, legislate to remedy them, and engender strong, long-term public support for such laws that have thus far proven to be stable in the context of the whims of parliamentary majorities. Its weaknesses include potentially insufficient protection afforded free speech, especially in the face of legislatures that are determined to restrict speech, while paying rhetorical attention to its importance in public debate. On the whole, freedom of speech is relatively vulnerable in the Australian regulatory context, but there is also evidence that other political branches and civil society have succeeded in defending it at important moments. So, while it is usually recognized that the United States is an exception[83] in free speech terms, perhaps it can also be said that Australia is one too.

Notes

1. Michael Chesterman, *Freedom of Speech in Australian Law: A Delicate Plant* (Aldershot, UK: Ashgate, 2000); Katharine Gelber, "Pedestrian Malls, Local Government and Free Speech Policy in Australia," *Policy and Society* 22, no. 2 (2003).
2. James Warden, "Federalism and the Design of the Australian Constitution," *Australian Journal of Political Science* 27 (1992), 146–47; Hilary Charlesworth, *Writing in Rights: Australia and the Protection of Human Rights* (Sydney: University of New South Wales Press, 2001), 19.
3. Quoted in John M. Williams, "Race, Citizenship, and the Formation of the Australian Constitution: Andrew Inglis Clark and the '14th Amendment,'" *Australian Journal of Politics and History* 42, no. 1 (January 1996), 11; George Williams and David Hume, *Human Rights Under the Australian Constitution*, 2nd ed. (Melbourne: Oxford University Press, 2014), 25, 33.
4. Williams, "Race, Citizenship and the Formation of the Australian Constitution"; Charlesworth, *Writing in Rights*, 18, 20; Williams and Hume, *Human Rights Under the Australian Constitution*, 27.
5. There are competing explanations for this hostility, including a desire on the part of states to continue to discriminate against non-whites (Williams, "Race, Citizenship and the Formation of the Australian Constitution," 14–15, 18; Williams and Hume, *Human Rights Under the Australian Constitution*, 25–26); a concern that a bill of rights would imply the parliament intended to deprive citizens of their rights (Williams, "Race, Citizenship and the Formation of the Australian Constitution," 17–18; Andrew Byrnes, Hilary Charlesworth, and Gabrielle McKinnon, *Bills of Rights in Australia: History, Politics and Law* (Sydney: University of New South Wales Press, 2009), 25; Helen Irving, *To Constitute a Nation: A Cultural History of Australia's Constitution* (Cambridge: Cambridge University Press, 1997), 162); and a view that responsible government and the common law would be sufficient to protect rights (Williams, "Race, Citizenship and the Formation of the Australian Constitution," 19; Haig Patapan, "The Dead Hand of the Founders? Original Intent and the Constitutional Protection of Rights and Freedoms in Australia," *Federal Law Review* 25, no. 2 (1997), 219).
6. Paul Kildea, "The Bill of Rights Debate in Australian Political Culture," *Australian Journal of Human Rights* 9, no. 1 (2003), 84.
7. J.S. Mill, "Utilitarianism," in *John Stuart Mill and Jeremy Bentham: Utilitarianism and Other Essays*, ed. Alan Ryan (London: Penguin Books, 1987), 279.

8. Kildea, "The Bill of Rights Debate," 65, 69–72.
9. Brian Galligan, *A Federal Republic: Australia's Constitutional System of Government* (Cambridge: Cambridge University Press, 1995), 46–51.
10. Ibid., 135.
11. Gerard Brennan, foreword to *Freedom of Speech in Australia: A Delicate Plant*, by Michael Chesterman (Aldershot, UK: Ashgate, 2000), vii.
12. Nick O'Neill, Simon Rice, and Roger Douglas, *Retreat From Injustice: Human Rights Law in Australia*, 2nd revised ed. (Sydney: Federation Press, 2004), 369.
13. *Commonwealth v. John Fairfax and Sons Ltd.* (1980) 147 CLR 39, 52 cited in O'Neill, Rice, and Douglas, *Retreat From Injustice*, 372.
14. O'Neill, Rice, and Douglas, *Retreat From Injustice*, 373.
15. *Davis v. Commonwealth* (1988) 166 CLR 79, 100.
16. O'Neill, Rice, and Douglas, *Retreat From Injustice*, 28.
17. Kildea, "The Bill of Rights Debate," 75–76.
18. Anne Twomey, *Strange Bedfellows: The UN Human Rights Committee and the Tasmanian Parliament* (Canberra: Department of the Parliamentary Library, 1994).
19. Wendy Lacey, "In the Wake of *TEOH*: Finding an Appropriate Government Response," *Federal Law Review* 29, no. 2 (2001); Wendy Lacey, "The End for *Teoh*? *Re Minister for Immigration and Multicultural Affairs: Ex parte Lam*," (Gilbert + Tobin Centre of Public Law, 2004 Constitutional Law Conference and Dinner, February 20, 2004), accessed February 15, 2019, http://www.gtcentre.unsw.edu.au/events/2004-constitutional-law-conference-and-dinner.
20. Kildea, "The Bill of Rights Debate," 81; O'Neill, Rice, and Douglas, *Retreat From Injustice*, 27.
21. Louis Chappell, John Chesterman, and Lisa Hill, *The Politics of Human Rights in Australia* (Cambridge: Cambridge University Press, 2009), 27, 36–38.
22. "Cth" means a commonwealth, i.e. federal, law (as opposed to one of a state or self-governing territory).
23. Byrnes, Charlesworth, and McKinnon, *Bills of Rights in Australia*, 73–138; *Charter of Human Rights and Responsibilities Act 2006* (Vic), s 15; *Human Rights Act 2004* (ACT), ss 16, 28; *Human Rights Act 2019* (Qld), ss 13, 21.
24. Prime Minister Malcolm Fraser, 1979, cited in Kildea, "The Bill of Rights Debate," 77; Anika Gauja and Katharine Gelber, "High Court Review 2010: The Resurgence of Rights?" *Australian Journal of Political Science* 46, no. 4 (2011), 683–98.
25. Murphy was appointed to the High Court in 1975 after having previously served as a federal Senator (1962–1975) and Commonwealth Attorney-General (1972–1975).
26. George Williams, Sean Brennan, and Andrew Lynch, *Australian Constitutional Law and Theory*, 7th ed. (Sydney: Federation Press, 2018), 1329.
27. Alexander Meiklejohn, *Political Freedom: The Constitutional Powers of the People* (New York: Oxford University Press, 1965), 27.
28. *Nationwide News Pt Ltd v. Wills* (1992) 177 CLR 1; *Australian Capital Television v. The Commonwealth* (1992) 177 CLR 106. Political matters were not clearly defined, but in light of the cases being determined it was understood primarily to mean matters relating to government.
29. Adrienne Stone, "Freedom of Political Communication, the Constitution and the Common Law," *Federal Law Review* 26, no. 2 (1998), 219–57; Adrienne Stone, "Lange, Levy and the Direction of the Freedom of Political Communication Under

the Australian Constitution," *University of New South Wales Law Journal* 21, no. 1 (1998), 117–34; Adrienne Stone, "Rights, Personal Rights and Freedoms: The Nature of the Freedom of Political Communication," *Melbourne University Law Review* 25, no. 2 (August 2001), 374–417.

30. *Lange v. Australian Broadcasting Corporation* (1997) 189 CLR 520; Michael Chesterman, "When is a Communication 'Political'?" *Legislative Studies* 14, no. 2 (Autumn 2000), 8.
31. *Lange v. Australian Broadcasting Corporation*, 561–62; Gelber, "Pedestrian Malls"; H. P. Lee, "The 'Reasonably Appropriate and Adapted' Test and the Implied Freedom of Political Communication," in *Law and Government in Australia*, ed. Matthew Groves (Sydney: Federation Press, 2005), 81.
32. *Coleman v. Power* (2004) 220 CLR 1.
33. *McCloy v. New South Wales* (2015) 257 CLR 178; Williams, Brennan, and Lynch, *Australian Constitutional Law and Theory*, 1383–84.
34. Nicholas Aroney, "A Seductive Plausibility: Freedom of Speech in the Constitution," *University of Queensland Law Journal* 12, no. 2 (1995); Neil F. Douglas, "Freedom of Expression Under the Australian Constitution," *University of New South Wales Law Journal* 16, no. 2 (1993); Tom D. Campbell, "Democracy, Human Rights, and Positive Law," *Sydney Law Review* 16, no. 2 (1994), 195–212; Andrew Fraser, "False Hopes: Implied Rights and Popular Sovereignty in the Australian Constitution," *Sydney Law Review* 16, no. 2 (1994).
35. Williams, Brennan, and Lynch, *Australian Constitutional Law and Theory*, 1342–78.
36. *Unions NSW v. New South Wales* (2013) 252 CLR 530; Anne Twomey, "*Unions NSW v. New South Wales*: Political Donations and the Implied Freedom of Communication," *University of Notre Dame Australia Law Review* 16 (December 2014); Williams, Brennan, and Lynch, *Australian Constitutional Law and Theory*, 1378–1383.
37. See, for example, Eric Heinze, *Hate Speech and Democratic Citizenship* (Oxford: Oxford University Press, 2016).
38. Luke McNamara, *Regulating Racism: Racial Vilification Laws in Australia* (Sydney: Sydney Institute of Criminology, 2002), 121–22.
39. Ibid., 38.
40. Ibid., 36.
41. Ibid.
42. See, for example, *Anti-Discrimination Act 1977* (NSW), s 20C; *Racial Discrimination Act 1975* (Cth), s 18D; McNamara, *Regulating Racism*, 127–30.
43. Sexuality/homosexuality was added as a ground in 1993 in New South Wales, 1998 in Tasmania, 2002 in Queensland, and 2004 in the ACT. Transgender was added in New South Wales in 1996, gender identity in Queensland in 2002, and transsexuality in the ACT in 2004. HIV/AIDS status was included in New South Wales in 1994, and in the ACT in 2004. Disability was included in Tasmania in 1998. Religion was included in Tasmania in 1998, in Queensland in 2001, and in Victoria in 2001.
44. *Crimes Act 1900* (NSW), s 93Z; *Anti-Discrimination Act 1991* (Qld), s131A; *Racial Vilification Act 1996* (SA), s4; *Racial and Religious Tolerance Act 2001* (Vic), ss24, 25; *Discrimination Act 1991* (ACT), s67, *Criminal Code 1913* (WA), ss 76–80H.
45. There have been three prosecutions in Western Australia (Katharine Gelber and Luke McNamara, "The Effects of Civil Hate Speech Laws: Lessons from Australia," *Law and Society Review* 49, no. 3 (September 2015), 635); two prosecutions in

Queensland: one in 2015 involving racial abuse to which the accused pleaded guilty and received a suspended sentence (Anti-Discrimination Commission Queensland, "Submission to Religious Freedom Review," February 2, 2018, accessed February 15, 2019, https://www.pmc.gov.au/sites/default/files/religious-freedom-submissions/14531.docx; Australian Associated Press, "Teen's Racist Brisbane Train Rant Disgusting: Magistrate," *Brisbane Times*, September 14, 2015, accessed February 15, 2019, http://www.brisbanetimes.com.au/queensland/teens-racist-brisbane-train-rant-disgusting-magistrate-20150914-gjm2e7.html), and a second in which a transgender female was verbally threatened with physical harm (private correspondence to author from the Anti-Discrimination Commission, Queensland, April 19, 2018); and one in Victoria (James Oaten, "Far-Right Nationalists Found Guilty of Inciting Serious Contempt for Muslims After Mock Beheading Video," *ABC News*, September 5, 2017, accessed February 15, 2019, http://www.abc.net.au/news/2017-09-05/three-men-found-guilty-of-inciting-serious-contempt-for-muslims/8874804).

46. *Racial Discrimination Act 1975* (Cth), ss 18B-18F; *Anti-Discrimination Act 1977* (NSW), ss 20B-C, 38R-S, 49ZS-ZT, 49ZXA-ZXB; *Anti-Discrimination Act 1991* (Qld), ss124A; *Anti-Discrimination Act 1998* (Tas), ss19, 17(1); *Racial and Religious Tolerance Act 2001* (Vic); *Discrimination Act 1991* (ACT), ss 67A; *Civil Liability Act 1936* (SA), s73. See Katharine Gelber and Luke McNamara, "Anti-Vilification Laws and Public Racism in Australia: Mapping the Gaps Between the Harms Occasioned and the Remedies Provided," *University of New South Wales Law Journal* 39, no. 2 (2016), 490–99.
47. Typically, fines in anti-vilification matters are small, less than $10,000 (Gelber and McNamara, "The Effects of Civil Hate Speech Laws," 637).
48. Katharine Gelber and Luke McNamara, "Private Litigation to Address a Public Wrong: A Study of Australia's Regulatory Response to 'Hate Speech,'" *Civil Justice Quarterly* 33, no. 3 (2014), 307.
49. *Eatock v. Bolt* (2011) 197 FCR 261, 316–17.
50. *Toben v. Jones* (2003) 129 FCR 515, [19]-[21].
51. *Islamic Council of Victoria v. Catch the Fire Ministries Inc* [2006] VSCA 284, [113].
52. Katharine Gelber and Luke McNamara, "Freedom of Speech and Racial Vilification in Australia: The 'Bolt' Case in Public Discourse," *Australian Journal of Political Science* 48, no. 4 (2013).
53. Adrienne Stone, "The Ironic Aftermath of *Eatock v. Bolt*," *Melbourne University Law Review* 38, no. 3 (2015).
54. Katharine Gelber, *Speech Matters: Getting Free Speech Right* (St. Lucia, Australia: University of Queensland Press, 2011), 25–30.
55. Gelber and McNamara, "Freedom of Speech and Racial Vilification in Australia," 474–77.
56. Australian Government Attorney-General's Department, "Amendments to the *Racial Discrimination Act 1975*," April 30, 2014, accessed February 15, 2019, https://www.ag.gov.au/consultations/Pages/ConsultationsonamendmentstotheRacialDiscriminationAct1975.aspx.
57. The Hon. George Brandis, "Racial Discrimination Act," *Parliament of Australia: Questions Without Notice*, Senate Chamber, March 24, 2014, accessed February 15, 2019, https://www.aph.gov.au/Parliamentary_Business/Hansard/Hansard_Display?bid=chamber/hansards/6a5b8de8-212b-46a9-b00f-61b865fe92a2/&sid=0026

58. Stone, "The Ironic Aftermath of *Eatock v. Bolt*," 927.
59. Mark Dreyfus, "Brandis Gives Green Light to Racism," March, 25, 2014, "Portfolio Media," Mark Dreyfus QC MP, accessed February 15, 2019, http://markdreyfus.nationbuilder.com/government_gives_the_green_light_to_racism
60. Mark Dreyfus, Michelle Rowland, and Jason Clare, "Western Sydney Says No to Changes to 18C," April 24, 2014, "Portfolio Media," Mark Dreyfus QC MP, accessed February 15, 2019, https://markdreyfus.nationbuilder.com/western_sydney_says_no_to_changes_to_18c
61. Joshua Forrester, Augusto Zimmerman, and Lorraine Finlay, "QUT Discrimination Case Exposes Human Rights Commission Failings," *The Conversation*, November 6, 2016, accessed February 15, 2019, https://theconversation.com/qut-discrimination-case-exposes-human-rights-commission-failings-68235.
62. Australian Law Reform Commission, *Traditional Rights and Freedoms—Encroachments By Commonwealth Laws* (Sydney: ALRC, 2015), 113, 115–16, accessed February 15, 2019, https://www.alrc.gov.au/sites/default/files/pdfs/publications/alrc_129_final_report_.pdf
63. Commonwealth of Australia, Freedom of Speech in Australia: Inquiry into the Operation of Part IIA of the *Racial Discrimination Act 1975* (Cth) and Related Procedures Under the Australian Human Rights Commission Act 1986 (Cth) (Canberra: Parliament of Australia, 2017), February 28, 2017, accessed February 15, 2019, https://www.aph.gov.au/Parliamentary_Business/Committees/Joint/Human_Rights_inquiries/FreedomspeechAustralia/Report
64. Katharine Murphy, "Turnbull Pursues 18C Changes Despite Warning Over Marginal Seats," *Guardian* (London), March 21, 2017, accessed February 14, 2019, https://www.theguardian.com/australia-news/2017/mar/21/turnbull-pursue-18c-changes-despite-warning-marginal-seats
65. Tony Burke and Mark Dreyfus, "Another Backdoor Attempt to Weaken 18C," November 8, 2016, "Portfolio Media," Mark Dreyfus QC MP, accessed February 14, 2019, http://markdreyfus.nationbuilder.com/another_backdoor_attempt_to_weaken_18c
66. Tony Burke and Mark Dreyfus, "Abbott: Protections Against Race Hate Speech 'unAustralian,'" November 11, 2016, "Portfolio Media," Mark Dreyfus QC MP, accessed February 14, 2019, http://markdreyfus.nationbuilder.com/abbott_protections_against_race_hate_speech_unaustralian
67. Tim Soutphommasane, "In Bowing to Public Opinion, PM Shows Good Leadership," *Sydney Morning Herald*, August 7, 2014, accessed February 14, 2019, https://www.smh.com.au/opinion/in-bowing-to-public-opinion-pm-shows-good-leadership-20140806-100zqo.html; ABC News, "Racial Discrimination Act Changes Receive Little Support in New Nielsen Poll," *ABC News*, April 13, 2014, accessed February 14, 2019, http://www.abc.net.au/news/2014-04-14/race-law-changes-receive-little-support-in-new-poll/5387452; Andrew Jakubowicz, Kevin Dunn, Rosalie Atie, and Yin Paradies, "What Do Australian Internet Users Think About Racial Vilification?" *The Conversation*, March 16, 2014, accessed February 14, 2019, https://theconversation.com/what-do-australian-internet-users-think-about-racial-vilification-24280.
68. Marriage Amendment Act 2004 (Cth); Carol Johnson, "Fixing the Meaning of Marriage: Political Symbolism and Citizen Identity in the Same-Sex Marriage Debate," *Continuum: Journal of Media & Cultural Studies* 27, no. 2 (2013), 244.
69. George Williams, "Same Sex Marriage and the Australian States," *Alternative Law Journal* 40, no. 1 (2015), 4.

70. *Marriage Equality (Same Sex) Act 2013* (ACT).
71. *Commonwealth v. Australian Capital Territory* (2013) 250 CLR 441; Michael Kirby, "The ACT Marriage Equality Case: Losing the Battle But Winning the Constitutional War," *Southern Cross University Law Review* 18 (2016), 86–88.
72. Dierdre McKeown, "Chronology of Same-Sex Marriage Bills Introduced into the Federal Parliament: A Quick Guide," February 15, 2018, accessed February 15, 2019, https://www.aph.gov.au/About_Parliament/Parliamentary_Departments/Parliamentary_Library/pubs/rp/rp1718/Quick_Guides/SSMarriageBills
73. Odette Mazel, "The Politics of Difference: Posting My 'Vote' on Marriage Equality," *Alternative Law Journal* 43, no. 1 (2018), 5.
74. Australian Bureau of Statistics, "Report on the Conduct of the Australian Marriage Law Postal Survey 2017," 1, accessed February 15, 2019, http://www.abs.gov.au/ausstats/abs@.nsf/95553f4ed9b60a374a2568030012e707/7cbde85f96095fa-4ca25822400162fc2/$FILE/700652_ABS_AMLPS_A4_Report_Conduct_0118_FA4.002.pdf/700652_ABS_AMLPS_A4_Report_Conduct_0118_FA4.pdf
75. Paul Kildea, "Using the ABS to Conduct a Same-Sex Marriage Poll is Legally Shaky and Lacks Legitimacy," *The Conversation*, August 10, 2017, accessed February 15, 2019, https://theconversation.com/using-the-abs-to-conduct-a-same-sex-marriage-poll-is-legally-shaky-and-lacks-legitimacy-82245
76. Louise Yaxley, "SSM: High Court's Unanimous Decision Gives Government All Clear for Same-Sex Marriage Postal Survey," *ABC News*, September 7, 2017, accessed February 14, 2019, https://www.abc.net.au/news/2017-09-07/same-sex-marriage-postal-survey-greenlit-by-high-court/8881956.
77. Mazel, "The Politics of Difference," 8.
78. Australian Bureau of Statistics, "Report on the Conduct of the Australian Marriage Law Postal Survey 2017," iv; Marriage Amendment (Definition and Religious Freedoms) Act 2017 (Cth).
79. Lyle Shelton, "Why Gay Marriage Will Take Away Your Right to Free Speech," *Australian Christian Lobby*, August 17, 2016, accessed February 14, 2019, https://www.acl.org.au/why_gay_marriage_will_take_away_your_right_to_free_speech#splash-signup.
80. Fergus Hunter, "Marriage Plebiscite: Tony Abbott Urges a 'No' Vote to Reject Political Correctness and Protect Religious Freedom," *Sydney Morning Herald*, August 9, 2017, accessed February 14, 2019, https://www.smh.com.au/politics/federal/marriage-plebiscite-tony-abbott-urges-a-no-vote-to-reject-political-correctness-and-protect-religious-freedom-20170809-gxs6m6.html; Paul Karp, "Abbott Insists Marriage Equality a Threat to Religious Freedom After Brandis Calls it a 'Trick,'" *Guardian* (London), August 20, 2017, accessed February 14, 2019, https://www.theguardian.com/australia-news/2017/aug/21/abbott-insists-marriage-equality-threat-to-religious-freedom-after-brandis-calls-it-a-trick
81. "Fact Checking the 'No' Ad on Same-Sex Marriage," *ABC News*, August 30, 2017, accessed February 14, 2019, http://www.abc.net.au/triplej/programs/hack/fact-check-of-same-sex-marriage-survey-no-campaign-ad/8856496.
82. Rodney Smith, *Australian Political Culture* (Frenchs Forest, Australia: Pearson Education, 2001), 82, 96–97.
83. Frederick Schauer, "The Exceptional First Amendment," in *American Exceptionalism and Human Rights*, ed. Michael Ignatieff (Princeton: Princeton University Press, 2005).

References

Aroney, Nicholas. "A Seductive Plausibility: Freedom of Speech in the Constitution." *University of Queensland Law Journal* 12, no. 2 (1995): 249–74.

Brennan, Gerard. Foreword to *Freedom of Speech in Australia: A Delicate Plant*. By Michael Chesterman. Aldershot, UK: Ashgate, 2000.

Byrnes, Andrew, Hilary Charlesworth, and Gabrielle McKinnon. *Bills of Rights in Australia: History, Politics and Law*. Sydney: University of New South Wales Press, 2009.

Campbell, Tom D. "Democracy, Human Rights and Positive Law." *Sydney Law Review* 16, no. 2 (1994): 195–212.

Chappell, Louis, JohnChesterman, and Lisa Hill. *The Politics of Human Rights in Australia*. Cambridge: Cambridge University Press, 2009.

Charlesworth, Hilary. *Writing in Rights: Australia and the Protection of Human Rights*. Sydney: University of New South Wales Press, 2001.

Chesterman, Michael. *Freedom of Speech in Australia: A Delicate Plant*. Aldershot, UK: Ashgate, 2000.

———. "When Is a Communication 'Political'?" *Legislative Studies* 14, no. 2 (Autumn 2000): 5–23.

Douglas, Neil F. "Freedom of Expression Under the Australian Constitution." *University of New South Wales Law Journal* 16, no. 2 (1993): 315–50.

Fraser, Andrew. "False Hopes: Implied Rights and Popular Sovereignty in the Australian Constitution." *Sydney Law Review* 16, no. 2 (1994): 213–27.

Galligan, Brian. *A Federal Republic: Australia's Constitutional System of Government*. Cambridge: Cambridge University Press, 1995.

Gauja, Anika, and Katharine Gelber. "High Court Review 2010: The Resurgence of Rights?" *Australian Journal of Political Science* 46, no. 4 (2011): 683–98.

Gelber, Katharine. "Pedestrian Malls, Local Government and Free Speech Policy in Australia." *Policy and Society* 22, no. 2 (2003): 22–49.

———. *Speech Matters: Getting Free Speech Right*. St. Lucia, Australia: University of Queensland Press, 2011.

Gelber, Katharine, and Luke McNamara. "Anti-Vilification Laws and Public Racism in Australia: Mapping the Gaps Between the Harms Occasioned and the Remedies Provided." *University of New South Wales Law Journal* 39, no. 2 (2016): 488–511.

———. "The Effects of Civil Hate Speech Laws: Lessons from Australia." *Law and Society Review* 49, no. 3 (September 2015): 631–64.

———. "Freedom of Speech and Racial Vilification in Australia: The 'Bolt' Case in Public Discourse." *Australian Journal of Political Science* 48, no. 4 (2013): 470–84.

———. "Private Litigation to Address a Public Wrong: A Study of Australia's Regulatory Response to 'Hate Speech.'" *Civil Justice Quarterly* 33, no. 3 (2014): 307–34.

Heinze, Eric. *Hate Speech and Democratic Citizenship*. New York: Oxford University Press, 2016.

Irving, Helen. *To Constitute a Nation: A Cultural History of Australia's Constitution.* Cambridge: Cambridge University Press, 1997.
Johnson, Carol. "Fixing the Meaning of Marriage: Political Symbolism and Citizen Identity in the Same-Sex Marriage Debate." *Continuum: Journal of Media & Cultural Studies* 27, no. 2 (2013): 242–53.
Kildea, Paul. "The Bill of Rights Debate in Australian Political Culture." *Australian Journal of Human Rights* 9, no. 1 (2003): 65–117.
Kirby, Michael. "The ACT Marriage Equality Case: Losing the Battle But Winning the Constitutional War." *Southern Cross University Law Review* 18 (2016): 79–91.
Lacey, Wendy. "In the Wake of *TEOH*: Finding an Appropriate Government Response." *Federal Law Review* 29, no. 2 (2001): 219–40.
Lee, H.P. "The 'Reasonably Appropriate and Adapted' Test and the Implied Freedom of Political Communication." In *Law and Government in Australia*, edited by Matthew Groves, 59–81. Sydney: Federation Press, 2005.
Mazel, Odette. "The Politics of Difference: Posting My 'Vote' on Marriage Equality." *Alternative Law Journal* 43, no. 1 (2018): 4–9.
McNamara, Luke. *Regulating Racism: Racial Vilification Laws in Australia.* Sydney: Sydney Institute of Criminology, 2002.
Meiklejohn, Alexander, *Political Freedom: The Constitutional Powers of the People.* New York: Oxford University Press, 1965.
Mill, J.S. "Utilitarianism." In *John Stuart Mill and Jeremy Bentham: Utilitarianism and Other Essays*, edited by Alan Ryan, 272–338. London: Penguin Books, 1987.
O'Neill, Nick, Simon Rice, and Roger Douglas. *Retreat From Injustice: Human Rights Law in Australia*, 2nd revised ed. Sydney: Federation Press, 2004.
Patapan, Haig. "The Dead Hand of the Founders? Original Intent and the Constitutional Protection of Rights and Freedoms in Australia." *Federal Law Review* 25, no. 2 (1997): 211–35.
Schauer, Frederick. "The Exceptional First Amendment." In *American Exceptionalism and Human Rights*, edited by Michael Ignatieff, 29–56. Princeton: Princeton University Press, 2005.
Smith, Rodney. *Australian Political Culture.* Frenchs Forest, Australia: Pearson Education, 2001.
Stone, Adrienne. "Freedom of Political Communication, the Constitution and the Common Law." *Federal Law Review* 26, no. 2 (1998): 219–57.
———. "The Ironic Aftermath of *Eatock v Bolt*." *Melbourne University Law Review* 38, no. 3 (2015): 926–43.
———. "Lange, Levy and the Direction of the Freedom of Political Communication Under the Australian Constitution." *University of New South Wales Law Journal* 21, no. 1 (1998): 117–34.
———. "Rights, Personal Rights and Freedoms: The Nature of the Freedom of Political Communication." *Melbourne University Law Review* 25, no. 2 (August 2001): 374–417.

Twomey, Anne. *Strange Bedfellows: The UN Human Rights Committee and the Tasmanian Parliament.* Canberra: Department of the Parliamentary Library, 1994.

———. "*Unions NSW v New South Wales*: Political Donations and the Implied Freedom of Communication." *University of Notre Dame Australia Law Review* 16 (December 2014): 178–92.

Warden, James. "Federalism and the Design of the Australian Constitution." *Australian Journal of Political Science* 27 (1992): 143–58.

Williams, George. "Same-Sex Marriage and the Australian States." *Alternative Law Journal* 40, no. 1 (2015): 4–8.

Williams, George, Sean Brennan, and Andrew Lynch. *Australian Constitutional Law and Theory*, 7th ed. Sydney: Federation Press, 2018.

Williams, George, and David Hume. *Human Rights Under the Australian Constitution*, 2nd ed. Melbourne: Oxford University Press, 2014.

Williams, John M. "Race, Citizenship, and the Formation of the Australian Constitution: Andrew Inglis Clark and the '14th Amendment.'" *Australian Journal of Politics and History* 42, no. 1 (January 1996): 10–23.

8. Parliamentary and Judicial Treatments of Free Speech Interests in the UK

IAN CRAM

In the UK's system of parliamentary government, leading members of the Executive (such as the Prime Minister and all other members of the Cabinet) sit in the Legislature and are drawn from the ranks of the successful party at the most recent general election. Being supported by the majority of elected members to the House of Commons, the executive is thus able to dominate the legislative program in the legislature and can secure the passage into law of its policy programs. As for individual rights—such as the right to freedom of expression—these lack formal status in a document enjoying founding or constitutional status. The rule of recognition for the UK Constitution is that the law on any given topic is to be found in the latest Act of Parliament. Consequently, personal freedoms remain vulnerable as a matter of practice and obscure as to their fundamental nature: vulnerable because boundaries are subject to statutory incursion by legislators, which is often characterized by inattention to issues of principle;[1] and obscure, because disputes that reach the courts, and litigation involving questions about personal freedom, are more often than not settled by the application of canons of statutory interpretation or *stare decisis*, rather than a deeper level analysis of the autonomy/liberty interests that are implicated in the litigation.

At the outset, the preference that is shared by the legislature and judiciary alike for technical exercises as opposed to more principled reasoning should not however be surprising. In the instance of freedom of expression, the legislature for its part is motivated to regulate speech when convinced that existing laws insufficiently attend to a problematic form of expression. Online forms of hate speech, encouragement of terrorism, and revenge porn comprise three areas that have been the subject of recent legislative attention. When a new bill comes before Parliament, apart from isolated and initial discussion of points of principle, the focus of legislators tends in the main to settle upon practical aspects of definition, application, and enforcement. Few parliamentarians can be relied upon to raise principled concerns about speech limitations. As for the judicial branch, in the absence of entrenched constitutional precepts the courts lack a formal power of judicial review over an Act of Parliament. The latter constitutes the highest form of law known in the UK Constitution. The common law adjudication method favors judicial pragmatism and minimalism whereby rulings are confined to the terms of what is required to dispose of the case before the court and no more.[2] In this way the common law develops incrementally and the democratically elected legislature is left to effect more fundamental transformations. To be sure, judicial forbearance can also be found in jurisdictions where constitutional protections are entrenched. Consider *Borowski v. Canada (Attorney General)* where the Canadian Supreme Court took a decidedly minimalist approach in deference to the legislative sphere: "The Court must be sensitive to its role as the adjudicative branch in our political framework. Pronouncing judgments in the absence of a dispute affecting the rights of the parties may be viewed as intruding into the role of the legislative branch."[3] On the incrementalist view then, where constitutional questions do not *need* to be answered, it is prudent for a court to decide the case before it without having regard to questions of overarching constitutional principle,[4] even if this disregarding comes at the social cost of ongoing constitutional uncertainty.

The early part of this chapter argues that, until the formal incorporation of the European Convention on Human Rights into domestic law by the *Human Rights Act 1998* (HRA), the senior judiciary in the UK have been exemplars *par excellence* of pragmatic, under-theorized reasoning on free speech questions. Thus they failed to treat seriously and unbundle the range of concerns embedded in the idea of the "public interest" in expressive freedom. An account of the patchy shift toward a more theorized understanding of speech interests *post* HRA is then sketched. Parliamentary endorsement of the importance of (albeit qualified) rights such as freedom of expression might have been expected to conduce to a greater awareness of, and engagement with, principled concerns around the regulation of controversial speech forms across both the legislature and the judiciary. Accordingly, this section sheds light upon the receptiveness of each sphere toward the more abstract considerations implicated in any such legal treatment. If, as is maintained here, neither the UK legislature nor judiciary has since demonstrated a consistently principled approach, then the vulnerability of speech interests to apparently pressing counterclaims in national security and civility in public discourse online (and elsewhere) has been carried over into the HRA period. Ultimately, what is forsaken is a richer understanding of democratic pluralism. This is particularly regrettable in an era when digital communications make possible fuller engagement with politics by the *demos*. Instead, the impoverished state of elected representatives and judicial discourse lacks an account of citizens' participatory interests in self-government. Typically, elite-defined notions of civility in public speech remain without serious challenge or defense, setting the perimeters of permitted expression and excluding certain speakers and viewpoints on highly questionable grounds from the public domain.

Residual and Under-Theorized Protection for Individual/ Collective Rights Prior to the Human Rights Act

Eric Barendt, writing in 1985, noted the reluctance of UK judges to advance more theorized accounts of rights claims, remarking that, "[i]t is, however, very unusual for British judges to discuss the philosophical justifications for recognizing a free speech principle or interest."[5] This reluctance he traced to the absence of formal constitutional protection for human rights and the prevailing Diceyan orthodoxy that the English Constitution had developed a residual notion of personal freedom including liberty of expression. As A.V. Dicey himself put it:

> As every lawyer knows the phrases 'freedom of discussion' or 'liberty of the press' are rarely found in any part of the statute-book nor among the maxims of the common law ... The true state of things ... (is that) (a)ny man may, therefore, say whatever he likes, subject to the risk of, it may be, severe punishment if he punishes any statement ... which he is not legally entitled to make.[6]

For all the claims about "liberty of the press" in England, this in truth amounted to nothing more than an application of the general principle of the rule of law, namely that no one is punishable except for a distinct breach of the law. A person's freedom of speech was what was left after statutory and common law incursions into the freedom had been allowed for. As occurred in cases of seditious and blasphemous libel at the time, ordinary jurors determined whether a particular act of expression was protected or not.[7] Subsequently, the UK's major role in the drafting of the 1950 European Convention on Human Rights[8] with the latter's positive statement of rights of the individual is not to be read as a sudden loss of confidence in the common law and the residual method of rights protection. Indeed, as far as the

British were concerned, the Convention existed primarily to shield the citizens of *other* European countries from states' abuse of power. Domestically, the common law was thought to offer an effective mechanism for the protection of individual rights.[9] This confidence in the common law explains the United Kingdom's initial refusal to allow a right of individual petition to the European Court of Human Rights.[10]

The residual approach exposed minority and unorthodox expression to majoritarian forms of censorship whether expressed in parliamentary enactment or judicial pronouncements.[11] In the latter sphere, even where recognized as an important public interest, freedom of expression claims in the 1970s and 1980s almost always ceded precedence to an assortment of apparently weightier claims derived from an assortment of putative administration of justice, confidentiality, and national security interests in the more rarefied echelons of the House of Lords. Thus, in *AG v. Times Newspapers Ltd*[12] an injunction was upheld preventing publication of an article that was critical of the U.S. drug company Distillers in its handling of thalidomide claims from affected families. The article was thought to pose a "real risk" to the fairness of proceedings before a professional judge hearing the thalidomide claims.[13] The free speech interest that was deemed of lesser importance centered upon the public's interest in learning of Distillers' treatment of affected families. As such the injunction served to dampen pressures on members of the executive and/or legislature to intervene to secure a fairer funding settlement for affected persons now and in the future.

Further subordination of individual/societal interests in freedom of expression/information occurred in *BSC v. Granada Television*[14] where disclosure of a source's identity was ordered during a national strike of steel workers. The source had revealed confidential documents belonging to the state-owned *British Steel Corporation*, which revealed significant mismanagement. The House of Lords ruled that *Granada* had to disclose the identity of its source. The balance of competing interests lay "strongly" with the steel corporation. It had suffered a grievous wrong in which the broadcaster had become involved. Disclosure of the source's identity would enable appropriate disciplinary action to be taken against the disloyal employee.[15] The private law entitlements of the employer were not to be gainsaid by the public interest in uncovering mismanagement at the publicly owned corporation. That the accountability interests of taxpayers (electors) in not ordering disclosure were so lightly dismissed speaks to a poorly understood conception of the interests of the electorate as the owners and ultimate beneficiaries of a properly run national steel industry. A stronger commitment to the ideal informed level of participation by citizens and their political representatives in the oversight of governmental affairs would have led to the refusal of Granada's application for source disclosure.

Finally, the courts also saw fit to uphold a temporary injunction on the publication of the memoirs of a former MI5 spy Peter Wright in 1987 in *AG v. Guardian Newspaper Ltd*. Wright had alleged that the domestic security service had secretly bugged the offices of the then Labour Prime Minister Harold Wilson and sought to destabilize his government. Publication of these allegations, the majority held, would be a breach of the author's lifelong duty of confidentiality.[16] The notion that the accountability of security services entrusted with safeguarding the state and its institutions did not extend to informing the public about allegations of agents' misconduct is mystifying.

A bold dissenting judgment by Lord Bridge of Harwich did, however, lament the failure of the UK common law in the absence of a written constitution to safeguard

> fundamental freedoms essential to a free society such as freedom of expression ... I can see nothing whatever, either in law or on the merits, to be said for the maintenance of a total ban on discussion in the press of this country of matters of undoubted public interest and concern which the rest of the world now knows all about and can discuss freely.[17]

At their core, these cases reveal an apathy toward the idea of popular sovereignty, specifically the belief that the people must have access to ideas and information about the conduct of those in public power and powerful corporate interests. Only in this way can they participate in debates (not just limited to casting votes at election time) on matters of public interest and thus exercise meaningful sovereignty.

Key Features of the Human Rights Act 1998

The *Human Rights Act 1998* incorporates into domestic law a number of convention rights, mainly civil and political rights including the right to freedom of expression laid down in Article 10 of the convention that may be used to challenge the actions of public authorities.[18] The Act has a number of unique features that are discussed below. It requires inter alia a new methodology from the courts when assessing alleged infringements of a convention right under their expanded statutory interpretation role. The nature of this methodological innovation is outlined in the proceeding section of materials.

At the outset, it is crucial to note that the overarching doctrine of parliamentary sovereignty remains intact. Parliament remains free to legislate contrary to the convention since the latter is not (and cannot be) entrenched against future repeal. Unlike the U.S. Supreme Court, for example, where judicial striking down of the legislative enactments of Congress occurs, the UK Parliament remains, as noted above, the supreme lawmaker. Put simply, an Act of Parliament can never be unconstitutional. At the same time, three features of the 1998 Act mark it out as in an entirely different class of statute when compared alongside other Acts of Parliament. First, when introducing new legislation to Parliament, the Government must make a statement regarding the compatibility of the proposals with convention rights.[19] This feature alone might have been thought sufficient to prompt some consideration of matters of principle by members of the legislature. Regrettably, as will be detailed below, little such consideration has been forthcoming. This deficiency has extended even in cases where, as in the case of the Communications Bill of 2003, the government conceded that it was not able to make a statement of compatibility in regard to a clause that proposed to effect a total ban on political advertising in the broadcast media. This admission of non-compatibility in the regulation of political expression might have been expected to have been accompanied by a detailed explanation from the government but none was forthcoming.[20] The clause was subsequently successfully enacted into law along with the rest of the bill.[21] Second, the 1998 Act requires courts to read and give effect to primary and subordinate legislation (whether enacted before or after the commencement of the Human Rights Act) in a way which is consistent with the convention in "so far as it is possible to do so."[22] This is generally considered to allow a degree of linguistic straining of statutory terms in order to achieve compliance with the convention that exceeds the usual latitude afforded judges under established canons of statutory interpretation.[23] Finally, the Act's *sui generis* nature is evident from the wholly innovative "declaration of incompatibility" device created in section 4 (s. 4). This allows a court to issue a declaration to the effect that a domestic statute violates a litigant's Convention rights but in itself "does not affect the validity, continuing operation or enforcement of the provisions in respect of which it is given."[24] The choice then is for Parliament to decide whether to reform the offending provision or to leave it on the statute book. No court may force Parliament to amend the law.

The Impact of the Human Rights Act on Judicial Reasoning

Before addressing the matter of the extent to which the incorporation of convention rights has impacted parliamentary and judicial treatments of free speech claims, it is important to sketch in outline form how the HRA has generally altered judicial methodology in rights cases. The elements of this altered methodology are encapsulated in the twin principles of legality and proportionality. Both involve an increased role for the courts in rights adjudication and require brief discussion. According to the common law principle of legality, where Parliament intends to legislate contrary to fundamental principles of human rights, it must use express and unambiguous words. Where the statutory wording is overly general and/or imprecise, the courts will presume that Parliament intended the statute to be construed subject to the basic individual rights.[25] In identifying fundamental rights for the purposes of the legality principle, the claim to "fundamental" status would need to be explicated, an exercise that would be expected to connect the right to individual/societal interests and values. Some help is offered by the European Court of Human Rights' Article 10 jurisprudence which "must be taken into account" by domestic courts under the HRA (Article 10 is further discussed below).[26]

The search for deeper lying connections and purposes is also implicated by the concept of proportionality that features in cases involving qualified convention rights such as the core political freedoms of expression, assembly, and association. Proportionality interrogates the relationship between the end objective behind a rights-limitation and the measure chosen to advance that objective (including the rational connection between measure and objective). It allows the judges to inquire into the relative weights accorded by the political sphere to the assorted competing interests. More intense forms of judicial scrutiny are implicit in HRA-based judicial review of Executive/Legislative rule making than occurs in reviews where convention rights are not engaged.[27] As Lord Justice Laws, a senior Court of Appeal judge, put it:

> There is ... what may be called a sliding scale of review; the graver the impact of the decision in question upon the individual affected by it, the more substantial the justification that will be required. It is in the nature of the human condition that cases where, objectively, the individual is most gravely affected will be those where what we have come to call his fundamental rights are or are said to be put in jeopardy.[28]

The point to be taken from this statement is relatively straightforward. Any assessment of the gravity of a rights-reducing measure/decision requires first an account of why the freedom that is being restricted *matters* to that individual or any other.

Article 10 Freedom of Expression in the Courts

The language of the Freedom of Expression provision of Article 10 of the European Convention on Human Rights reads as follows:

1. Everyone has the right to freedom of expression. This right shall include freedom to hold opinions and to receive and impart information and ideas without interference by public authority and regardless of frontiers. This Article shall not prevent States from requiring the licensing of broadcasting, television or cinema enterprises.
2. The exercise of these freedoms, since it carries with it duties and responsibilities, may be subject to such formalities, conditions, restrictions or penalties as are prescribed by law and are necessary in a democratic society, in the interests of national security, territorial integrity or public safety, for the prevention of disorder or crime, for the protection of health or morals, for the protection of the reputation or rights of others, for preventing the disclosure of information received in confidence, or for maintaining the authority and impartiality of the judiciary.

In *Handyside v. UK* the European Court of Human Rights noted that freedom of expression was "one of the basic conditions for the progress of democratic societies and for the development of every man."[29] Shortly thereafter it stated in *Sunday Times v. UK* that "(F)reedom of expression constitutes one of the essential foundations of a democratic society."[30] Specific attention was paid in *Castells v. Spain* to the vital role played by media organizations in imparting political information and ideas to the public and hence the electorate.[31] Finally, the court has signaled that there is "little scope" under Article 10(2) for restrictions on political speech or matters of public interest.[32]

In the domestic jurisprudence of the higher courts, there has been a limited and unsatisfactory degree of engagement with ideas of principle. Technological advances have transformed patterns of communication of ideas and information. Previous rules developed from an era of "few speakers-many listeners/viewers" no longer reflect the empowerment of ordinary citizens *qua* speakers. More radical notions of viewpoint pluralism and citizen participation now exist in which the shaping of political agendas are less clearly the exclusive preserve of privileged mainstream political groupings and/or powerful corporate interests. An early (pre-Web 2.0) judicial foray in the HRA era is Lord Steyn's pronouncement in *R v. Secretary of State for the Home Department ex parte Simms*. The case concerned a challenge to a Home Office ban on prisoners being able to hold oral interviews with journalists to publicize alleged miscarriages of justice. Freedom of expression, Lord Steyn stated,

> ... serves a number of broad objectives. First, it promotes the self fulfillment of individuals in society. Secondly, in the famous words of Mr. Justice Holmes (echoing John Stuart Mill), 'the best test of truth is the power of the thought to get itself accepted in the competition of the market.': Abraham [*sic*] v. United States 250 U.S. 616, at 630 (1919), per Holmes J. (dissent). Thirdly, freedom of speech is the lifeblood of democracy. The free flow of information and ideas

informs political debate. It is a safety valve: people are more ready to accept decisions that go against them if they can in principle seek to influence them. It acts as a brake on the abuse of power by public officials. It facilitates the exposure of errors in the governance and administration of justice of the country...[33]

This welcome though rare declaration of underpinning values might have set UK free speech jurisprudence firmly on the path to greater conceptual clarity in the HRA era. Unfortunately, it disappoints. At the outset, Lord Steyn conflates the respective positions of Holmes and Mill on free speech. There is an inherent moral skepticism in Justice Holmes' position entirely absent from Mill's more earnest belief in rational decision making, namely that the better ideas win out over time. As Ten Cate has helpfully pointed out, Holmes does not claim that the better (i.e., more rational) ideas are the ones that *necessarily* gain acceptance in the marketplace of public opinion.[34] More centrally, however, to the facts in *Simms*, it is the "lifeblood of democracy" argument for freedom of expression that requires the closest attention. This undoubtedly is the most prominent justification for freedom of expression in domestic constitutional narratives. It features in judicial accounts[35] and is commonly invoked by politicians,[36] journalists,[37] and civic society groups[38] to defend particular instances of communication. Furthermore, a clear majority of members of the public believe that free speech on matters of public interest such as government policies on immigration, race, and other matters must include the right to cause offence.[39] According to evidence published in 2018, by a margin of 48%-35%, the British public feels that prevailing norms of civility in public speech in fact prevent people from saying what they really think and that debates are being shut down unnecessarily.[40] The idea that elite-defined notions of decorum have permeated into the legal framework in the UK and limited the political expression of non-elite sections of society is elaborated upon further below. Millian arguments from truth and more generalized claims to autonomy from paternalistic state interference feature much less visibly in public discourses in which free speech is defended.

In *Simms*, Steyn correctly identifies an array of interconnected democracy-supporting features of free expression, namely that the legitimacy of public bodies' decisions depends in part upon the opportunities afforded through freedom of expression to affected parties to influence those decisions; and the (i) scrutiny and (ii) exposure of error functions served by open discussion. This applies to prisoners who wish to publicize what they allege is their wrongful conviction in the courts. So far, so good; indeed, Simms went on to win his judicial review action against the Home Office on the basis that the ban represented an excessive interference with the prisoners' ability to challenge their convictions. The problem with this account of prisoners' freedom of expression emerges however when Steyn articulates the limitations upon such expression. No prisoner, he declares without further explanation, would be permitted to speak to journalists in order to publish pornographic materials, or join a debate on the economy or on political issues.[41] Why so? Plausible arguments can be made on self-fulfillment grounds (pornography) and rehabilitative democratic participation in societal debate to sustain a prisoner's right to speak and be heard on a range of matters beyond the justice of his/her own incarceration. There is a passing suggestion that Lord Steyn's limits are needed to maintain discipline and control, but it is never properly elaborated.

An alternative approach to regulating prisoners' freedom of expression might have recognized the vital role played by broad speech entitlements in conferring legitimacy upon rulemaking in society. Robert Post, for example, starts from a definition of democracy as active and mediated self-rule by the citizens. In this account, citizens can only experience government as their own government, if each possesses "the warranted conviction that they are engaged in the process of governing themselves."[42] For this conviction to be sustained, it is vital that the state is perceived to be responsive to the values of each citizen and that each might be able to influence the outcome of public discourse through our ideas and arguments. The opportunity to participate in public discourse promotes individual identification with the state and its decision-making processes even if the actual outcomes of public discourse are at odds (as they will of necessity be from time to time) with an individual's preferences. In the case of prisoners, a sanction for breach of the criminal law may be more easily justified when all have had the chance to participate in the making/re-making of the laws. Where the state excludes someone from participating in the speech by which public opinion (and subsequently public policy) is formed, that person will experience a loss of "democratic legitimacy" and become alienated from the process of self-government.

The senior judiciary's unwillingness to discard a pre-Web 2.0 account of communicative interaction (few speakers to many listeners/viewers) and thereby move beyond the model of the passive citizen who receives the speech of others persists to the present day. Giving her judgment in *R (Lord Carlile) v. Home Secretary* in 2015 Baroness Hale of Richmond (then deputy president of the UK Supreme Court) envisaged that the role played by citizens was confined to listening to the political speech of others, rather than one that entailed both listening *and* speaking.[43] The litigation centered upon a refusal by the Home Secretary to grant entry clearance to an Iranian dissident (Mrs. Rajavi) invited to London by a cross party group of parliamentarians. The refusal rested on the Home Secretary's assessment that Mrs. Rajavi's presence in the UK would not be conducive to the public good. For Baroness Hale, Article 10 of the convention covered

> the right of Mrs. Rajavi and of the parliamentarians both to receive and impart information and ideas without state interference ... Freedom of speech is the foundation of any democracy. Without it how can the electorate know whom to elect and how can the parliamentarians know how to make up their minds on the difficult issues they have to confront?[44]

That members of the public might also have been interested in learning what Mrs. Rajavi had to say in order to formulate their own views with a view to participating as speakers in their own right entirely escaped the deputy president. Instead, the more limited conception of the citizen held out here comprises a person who merely listens to the speech of elite opinion formers, namely parliamentarians and, indirectly, their guests.

Disciplining Uncivil and Offensive Speech

In the digital era, the UK courts' antiquated preference for a "few speakers–many audience" model of freedom of expression is complemented by the law's coercive demands for civility and inoffensive public expression when non-elite speakers do contribute to public discourse. For example, the lower courts' encounters with expression by ordinary citizens is framed to a significant, though not exclusive, extent by the contours of the criminal law and the disciplining demands of reasonableness and civility. The effects of this framing are clear, namely the privileging of communications from professional and highly educated persons, public officials and corporate entities, and the censoring of less refined speakers or those lacking a level of articulacy. The diminished pool of viewpoints generated by these constraints serves to limit the contours of public debate and deny an outlet to impassioned and angry speakers who are unable to modulate their tone and content to fit with prevailing standards of decency. The loss of legitimacy that results from these exclusionary practices means that certain sections of "the people" are not the authors of (or participants in the act of authoring) the laws by which they are governed. Consider, for example, the case of Azhar Ahmed who was convicted in October 2012 of "making a grossly offensive" communication under s.127 of the Communications Act 2003.[45] His crime consisted of posting the following comments on Facebook after learning of the DeathComs of six British soldiers in Afghanistan:

> People gassin about the deaths of Soldiers! What about the innocent families who have been brutally killed ... The women who have been raped ... The children

who have been sliced up..! Your enemy's were the Taliban not innocent harmful familys. All soldiers should die & go to Hell! The lowlife fokking scum! Gotta problem go cry at your soldiers grave & wish him hell because thats where he is going.

A police spokesperson was quoted as saying, "He didn't make his point very well and that is why he has landed himself in bother."[46] Ahmed was given a sentence of 240 hours of community service work and is thought to have avoided a jail sentence because he removed his post relatively quickly and made efforts to apologize for the distress caused to the families of murdered British soldiers.[47] Sentencing Ahmad, District Judge Jane Goodwin stated:

You posted the message in response to tributes and messages of sympathy. You knew at the time that this was an emotive and sensitive issue ... With freedom of speech comes responsibility and ... you failed to live up to that responsibility.

Imagine, however, if the defendant had written a more eloquent post in which he expressed his "profound disquiet at the hypocrisy of persons who grieve at the deaths of British soldiers but show little or no regard for the undoubtedly deep personal traumas and losses of innocent Afghani families caught up in conflicts that were not of their making." As the quoted remarks of the police spokesperson make clear, it is the tone of (and lack of sophistication in) Ahmed's words, in short, his incivility, that brings him to police attention in the first place. Had the speaker employed/been able to employ a more sophisticated choice of words, a prosecution might well have been avoided altogether. Ultimately, as signaled in *Ahmed*, dominant civility norms function to discipline unruly forms of political speech. As such they impoverish democratic pluralism.[48] Robust or crudely worded attacks on state policy are denied legal protection on account of their irresponsibility. This loss to popular participation in the scrutiny of official conduct passes largely unremarked in domestic commentaries.

Pre-emptive Strikes at the Enemies of the State (Government?)—Viewpoint Discrimination in UK Counterterrorism Laws.

History abundantly documents the tendency of Government—however benevolent and benign its motives—to view with suspicion those who most fervently dispute its policies ... The danger to political dissent is acute where the Government attempts to act under so vague a concept as 'domestic security.' Given the difficulty of defining the domestic security interest, the danger of abuse in acting to protect that interest becomes apparent.[49]

The compromised ability of ordinary speakers to participate in the shaping of the laws that govern them is arguably no better illustrated than recent legislation restricting expression in the arena of counter-terrorism. The full force of the criminal law is brought to bear preemptively on expressive conduct long before any evidence linking the expressive act to a subsequent harmful action is shown. Existing laws of incitement already penalized a speaker who incited another to act in a way that involved the commission of any criminal offence and intended or believed that the incited party would act with the requisite degree of fault needed for the offence so incited.[50] More recent restrictions introduced in counterterrorism legislation aim to disrupt speech that might be sympathetic to organizations proscribed under the Terrorism Acts 2000 & 2006, or that indirectly encourage acts of terrorism in the future. Section 12 of the 2000 Act for example makes it an offence to "invite support" for a proscribed organization. In 2016 the Court of Appeals ruled in *Choudhary* that the offence was made out when a speaker intentionally encouraged practical or moral support for an organization that had been proscribed.[51] It was not necessary for the prosecution to establish that the defendant speaker knew that the organization had been proscribed.[52] Nonetheless, the Court of Appeals did add a rider that "the (mere) expression of personal beliefs, or an invitation to someone else to share an opinion or belief did not fall within the s.12 offence."[53] Thus no offence may be committed under s.12 if all that a speaker does is express moral/intellectual agreement with a list of ideological objectives that corresponds closely (or even possibly exactly) with those of the proscribed organization or invites others to share those ideological positions.

Whatever its actual worth in protecting speakers who are critical of UK foreign policy, the residual degree of protection for freedom of political speech indicated by the Court of Appeals in *Choudhary* clearly troubled the government. It has since moved to close the gap identified there by proposing to make it a new criminal offence in clause 1 of the Counter-Terrorism and Border Security Bill 2018 to "express an opinion or belief that is supportive of a proscribed organisation" and to lower the *mens rea* requirement from an intentional invitation to support a proscribed organization in s.12 of the Terrorism Act 2000 to mere recklessness as to whether the listener will be encouraged to support a proscribed organization.[54]

This latest clumsy attempt to shut down dissenting opinion builds upon existing legal restrictions in section 1 of the Terrorism Act 2006 that prohibit "indirect encouragement" of terrorism. Before commenting upon the width of the offence of "indirect encouragement," it is important first to say something about the troublingly broad definition of "terrorism" preferred in UK law from previous counterterrorism legislation that serves as the platform for a panoply of counterterrorism powers and offences.[55] The latter is defined as the use or threat of action (serious violence against the person, serious damage to property, endangering a person's life, creating risk to the health or safety of the public or a section of it, seriously interfering with/disrupting an electronic system) designed to influence the government or an international governmental organization or to intimidate the public or a section of it for the purpose of advancing a political, religious, racial or ideological cause.

"Action" includes that done outside the UK.[56] The "person" need not be a UK national.[57] The "public" may be the public of another country.[58] The "property" may be outside the United Kingdom.[59] The "government" means any government in the world.[60]

Using that definitional platform, section 1 of the Terrorism Act 2006 makes it an offence for a person to publish a statement knowing, or having reasonable grounds to believe, that others are "likely to understand it as a direct or indirect encouragement or other inducement to the commission, preparation or instigation of acts of terrorism..." Within the category of statements that are likely to be understood as indirectly encouraging the commission or preparation of acts of terrorism under s.1(3) is a statement that

(a) glorifies the commission or preparation (whether in the past, in the future or generally) of such acts or offences; and (b) is a statement from which those members of the public could reasonably be expected to infer that what is being glorified is being glorified as conduct that should be emulated in existing circumstances.

The word "glorify" is defined to include any form of praise or celebration.[61] In assessing whether any statement falls under s.1, regard is to be had to both the contents of the statement as a whole and the circumstances and manner in which it is published.[62] The reach of the offence can be gauged by the facts that it need not be shown by the prosecution that the defendant's expression (i) actually encouraged anyone to commit a terrorist act or (ii) created any risk whatsoever of subsequent terrorist action, or (iii) that the speaker intended to encourage anyone to engage in acts of terrorism.[63] As Barendt notes, the maker of ineffective or idle threats and incitements is thus caught. The absence in the offence of a "dangerous effect" element directly contradicts the Council of Europe's Convention on the Prevention of Terrorism Article 5 which states that expression may only be punished where it causes a danger that one or more terrorist offences may be committed.[64] Heinze asks us to imagine the intended target of such laws—a bearded imam with raised fists quoting from Machiavelli's *The Prince* "It is much safer to be feared than to be loved"—in order to understand what is really prompting restriction in these cases, and concludes that the answer lies in the "ugliness" of the expression and its "disfiguring" effect on society rather than any demonstrably raised threat of terrorist action.[65] It can be conceded that a symbolic strike against minority groups who espouse anti-democratic viewpoints can serve to bind communities together through the muscular reinforcement of democratic values. Yet as Mill presciently noted, the disposition to censorship among governments and citizens alike is difficult to rein in, being as it was "energetically supported by some of the best and by some of the worst feelings incident to human nature..."[66] While doubtless reassuring at some level, symbolic strikes that deny the people access to the anti-democratic viewpoints of others betoken a form of paternalism that holds the sovereign demos unfit to discern what is anti-democratic about the expression at issue. It is not hard moreover to imagine how these vaguely drafted laws (and the proposed additional restrictions in the Counter-Terrorism and Border Security Bill) instill reticence on matters of politics, steering some citizens and some viewpoints away from active participation in the shaping of the laws and policies by which all are governed.

Enjoining Censorship by Non-State Actors. Supplementing direct state regulation of online expressive content, non-state actors such as social media corporations, search engines and Internet service providers are increasingly co-opted into the front line to sanction uncivil and dissenting opinion. Prime Minister May has led calls for social media platforms such as Twitter and Facebook to step up efforts to tackle "terrorist and extremist content."[67] Investors, she argued, could press digital intermediaries to "clean up their act." This echoes calls from the European Commission in Brussels, which called in March 2018 for Google, YouTube, Facebook, and Twitter to remove 'extremist' content more quickly or face legislative compulsion to do so. A commission spokesperson was quoted as stating that the digital intermediaries should be prepared to remove such content within an hour of being notified.[68] Digital Commissioner Andrus Ansip remarked that "while several platforms have been removing more illegal content than ever before ... we still need to react faster against terrorist propaganda and other illegal content which is a serious threat to our citizens' security, safety and fundamental rights."[69]

Outside of "terrorist" and "extremist" content, reforms to defamation law in 2013 have incentivized social media platforms to shut down expression on matters of public interest that are objected to by others on account of its allegedly defamatory nature. Intended to offer a defense to online platforms and digital intermediaries, s.5 of the Defamation Act 2013 and the accompanying regulations make clear that, where the platform is unable to contact the poster of the material, it is required to remove the material to retain immunity from a suit in defamation. Scott has described the current position as "placing a potentially heavy burden on website operators."[70] The "contracting-out" of speech regulation nonetheless throws up difficult questions about the (lack of) democratic accountability of for-profit privately run corporate bodies whose overriding loyalties are to shareholders and market share growth rather than assisting citizens to play their role in scrutinizing holders of public office.[71]

Conclusion

I have argued here that, notwithstanding the welcome move away from residual protection for freedom of expression in the domestic constitution brought about by the Human Rights Act 1998, the latter has not prefigured an era of principled determination of the boundaries of expressive freedom in the domestic constitution. Instead, contentious and minority forms of expression remain vulnerable to majoritarian pressures given voice by both the legislative and the judicial branches. At root, a limited though barely articulated conception of political pluralism explains the state of domestic regulation. Speculative notions of "harm" to national security sit alongside disciplining concepts such as the requirement to speak civilly to provide two linked bases for the banishment of non-mainstream speakers. Thus censored, audiences are denied opportunities first to evaluate and then to respond to a range of politically important claims. Such a limited account of the range and manner of expressive forms available to citizens strikes at the very core of self-government. Any effort to move toward a more principled treatment of the complex regulatory issues posed by digital communications would do well to start from a baseline that recognizes the vital interest all citizens have in being able actively to shape the laws by which they consent to be governed. Until this is acknowledged, elite-defined concepts of "appropriate speech" will continue to work in the UK in tandem with speculative risk assessments around expressive conduct to diminish political pluralism and the democratic legitimacy of law making. For the time being, the demos may look as if they are speaking but they do so on terms not of their making.

Notes

1. Of course, it does not follow for a moment that freedom of expression is more extensive by sole virtue of the fact that it enjoys constitutional status in a foundational document. The right is invariably set out in non-absolute terms that require senior judges to determine whether any interference by the state is constitutionally authorized. Broad readings of the state's power to curtail expressive freedom has been a feature at times of the U.S. and Canadian Supreme Courts' respective jurisprudence.

2. I don't wish, however, to be thought to make the different claim that judicial treatments of formal constitutional texts are always characterized by non-minimalist readings. Cass Sunstein's identification (and normative defense) of minimalist practices on the U.S. Supreme Court claims that minimalism is a recurrent feature of the Court's pronouncements: "... frequently judges decide very little. They leave things open. About both liberty and equality, they make deliberate decisions about what should be left unsaid. This is a pervasive practice: doing and saying as little as is necessary to justify an outcome." Cass R. Sunstein, *One Case at a Time: Judicial Minimalism on the Supreme Court* (Cambridge, MA: Harvard University Press, 2001), 3.
3. [1989] 1 SCR 342, 365.
4. See *Moysa v. Alberta Labour Relations Board*, [1989] 1 SCR 1572 where the Canadian Supreme Court was critical of the lower courts' engagement with questions of constitutional principle involving the protection of journalists' sources.
5. Eric Barendt, *Freedom of Speech* (Oxford: Clarendon Press, 1985), 30.
6. Albert Venn Dicey, *Introduction to the Study of the Law of the Constitution*, ed. Roger E. Michener (Indianapolis: Liberty Fund, 1982), 147, accessed June 28, 2019, https://oll.libertyfund.org/titles/dicey-introduction-to-the-study-of-the-law-of-the-constitution-lf-ed
7. Dicey drew on a 1799 case of seditious libel against a Holborn (a section of London) bookseller, *Rex v. Cuthell*, 27 St.Tr. 642, where it was held that freedom of speech was "neither more nor less than this: that a man may publish anything which twelve of his countrymen think is not blamable but that he ought to be punished if he publishes that which is blamable..."
8. Geoffrey Marston, "The United Kingdom's Part in the Preparation of the European Convention on Human Rights, 1950," *International and Comparative Law Quarterly* 42, no. 4 (October 1993); Ian Cram, "Judging Rights in the United Kingdom: The *Human Rights Act* and the New Relationship Between Parliament and the Courts," *Review of Constitutional Studies* 12, no. 1 (January 2007).
9. This attitude persisted into the 1990s among the senior judiciary. See the context of freedom of expression statements in *AG v. Guardian Newspapers* (No.2) [1990] 1 AC 109, 283–84 (Lord Goff of Chieveley) and *Derbyshire County Council v. Times Newspapers Ltd* [1993] AC 534, 550–51 (Lord Keith of Kinkel).
10. Lord Jowitt, the Labour Lord Chancellor, declared that the Convention was "'a half-baked scheme to be administered by some unknown court'" and would cause those with knowledge of the U.K. Constitution to "'recoil with a feeling of horror.'" Cram, "Judging Rights in the United Kingdom," 55n8.Labour figures worried that the party's nationalization program *inter alia* would be threatened by inclusion in Protocol 1 of a right to property.
11. Barendt, *Freedom of Speech*.
12. [1974] AC 273.
13. On appeal to the European Court of Human Rights in Strasbourg, a majority found that the injunction impermissibly interfered with the media's freedom to inform the public on matters of undisputed public interest, see *Sunday Times Ltd v. UK* (1979) 2 EHRR 245.
14. [1981] AC 1096.
15. For an invigorating sole dissent, see Lord Salmon who stated that a free press could not, outside of exceptional circumstances known to the common law, be made to

disclose the sources of their information. Failure to protect the press would lead to the drying up of media sources and the public would be denied information on matters of public interest. British Steel Corporation was a publicly owned company financed by the taxpayer and was in dispute with their employees in what was now a national strike. Ibid., at 1184 *et seq.*

16. *AG v. Guardian Newspaper Ltd* [1987] 3 All ER 316. Also see the excellent account in Keith D. Ewing and C. A. Gearty, *Freedom Under Thatcher: Civil Liberties in Modern Britain* (Oxford: Oxford University Press, 1990), 152–69.
17. Ibid. The Court did relent a year later, permitting publication when confronted with yet further evidence that the book was widely available in the UK. See *AG v. Guardian Newspaper Ltd.* (No. 2) [1988] 3 All ER 545.
18. For helpful background see John Wadham, Helen Mountfield, Elizabeth Prochaska, and Raj Desai, *Blackstone's Guide to the Human Rights Act 1998,* 7th ed. (Oxford: Oxford University Press, 2015).
19. S.19, HRA 1998.
20. For some limited discussion of issues of principle on the matter, see Joint Committee on Human Rights *Nineteenth Report of Session 2001–2002* Draft Communications Bill HL Paper 148, HC 1102, accessed June 26, 2019, https://publications.parliament.uk/pa/jt200102/jtselect/jtrights/149/149.pdf
21. As s.321(2) of the Communications Act 2003.
22. S.3(1), HRA 1998.
23. Thus not only could express language in an Act be 'read-down' to secure compliance (a pre-1998 Act technique for rendering statutes compliant with international treaties) but also courts might imply additional provisions *into* the legislation in question, see for a controversial use of this power *R v. A* (No. 2) [2001] UKHL 25. Of course, where Parliament is unhappy with the result of linguistic straining, it may amend the law to reverse the effect of the judges' interpretation.
24. S.4(6).
25. For a statement of the principle of legality, see Lord Hoffmann in *R v. Secretary of State for the Home Department ex parte Simms* [2000] 2 AC 115, 131–32 where it is acknowledged that this does entail some modification of the doctrine of parliamentary sovereignty.
26. S.2(1) HRA 1998.
27. *R (on the application of Daly) v. Secretary of State for the Home Department* [2001] UKHL 26 at para. 27. See, however, *Regina (Lord Carlile of Berriew and others) v. Secretary of State for the Home Department* [2014] UKSC 60 where the UK Supreme Court affirmed that the type of proportionality analysis would be conditioned by context-specific matters going to the relative competences of the political and judicial spheres as well as issues of democratic legitimacy. Thus in the context of a decision to refuse entry to a dissident Iraqi national on public good (national security) grounds, the Executive's greater institutional competence (derived in part from exclusive access to intelligence reports) coupled with the political accountability of the Home Secretary for predictions as to the likely future political/diplomatic consequences of that person's entry to the UK entitled the decision to refuse entry to considerable respect.
28. *Regina (Mahmood) v. Secretary of State for the Home Department* [2001] 1 WLR 840, 849.

29. (1979–80) 1 EHRR 737,
30. (1979) 2 EHRR 245, 280.
31. (1992) 14 EHRR 445.
32. *Wingrove v. United Kingdom* (1996) 24 EHRR 1, para 58; *Sürek and Özdemir v. Turkey* [1999] ECHR 50.
33. [2000] 2 AC 115, 126.
34. Irene M. Ten Cate, "Speech, Truth, and Freedom: An Examination of John Stuart Mill's and Justice Oliver Wendell Holmes's Free Speech Defenses," *Yale Journal of Law & the Humanities* 22, no. 1 (January 2010): 40, where she remarks that "Mill believes in the force of reason as a mechanism to identify the best ideas and ultimately uncover truth … while Holmes is more skeptical about the possibility, and desirability, of allowing reason to be the ultimate judge in the development of deeply held convictions by individuals."
35. Albeit sporadically in the pre- HRA case law as shown above.
36. For a recent selection from debates about the reform of UK libel and freedom of information laws see respectively Sadiq Khan MP (2012–13) HC Debs. Vol. 266 col. 274, accessed June 26, 2019, https://hansard.parliament.uk/Commons/2013-04-16/debates/13041655000001/DefamationBill?highlight=defamation%20bill%20public%20interest#contribution-13041655000075; and Nick Clegg's (then Deputy Prime Minister) speech on civil liberties (2011), accessed June 26, 2019, https://www.newstatesman.com/2011/01/government-british-information
37. See, among others, Will Gore "The Freedom of the Press in the UK has Declined Dramatically—Threatening the Basis of Our Democracy," *The Independent*, April 25, 2018, https://www.independent.co.uk/voices/press-freedom-uk-mainstream-media-democracy-phone-hacking-leveson-a8321216.html; Simon Jenkins, "Boris Johnson's Attitude to Free Speech Ought to Worry Us More," *Evening Standard*, March 26, 2013, https://www.standard.co.uk/comment/comment/simon-jenkins-boris-johnson-s-attitude-to-free-speech-ought-to-worry-us-more-8549824.html
38. For brief illustration of this point, see the following commentaries from Liberty (a campaigning NGO) "… freedom of expression is fundamental to our democracy," accessed June 26, 2019, https://www.libertyhumanrights.org.uk/human-rights/what-are-human-rights/human-rights-act/article-10-free-expression
39. Tom Clark, "Free Speech? New Polling Suggests Britain is 'less PC' Than Trump's America," *Prospect*, February 16, 2018, https://www.prospectmagazine.co.uk/magazine/free-speech-new-polling-suggests-britain-is-less-pc-than-trumps-america, revealing attitudes towards notions of "political correctness."
40. Ibid.
41. [2000] 2 AC 115, 127
42. Robert Post, "Democracy and Equality," *The Annals of the American Academy of Political and Social Science* 603 (January 2006): 24, 26.
43. [2015] AC 945, paras. 90–91.
44. Ibid.
45. More justifiably, s.127 catches threats of a "menacing character" made via a public electronic communications network. For a conviction in respect of a menacing message directed at female politicians campaigning for a woman (other than the Queen) to be represented on bank notes see *The Queen v. Nimmo & McSorley* (2014) January 24, accessed June 26, 2019, https://www.judiciary.uk/wp-content/uploads/JCO/

Documents/Judgments/r-v-nimmo-and-sorley.pdf. In their respective victim statements, the politicians gave evidence of how threats of rape had impacted adversely upon them.
46. Glenn Greenwald, "With Power of Social Media Growing, Police Now Monitoring and Criminalizing Online Speech," *The Intercept*, January 6, 2015, https://theintercept.com/2015/01/06/police-increasingly-monitoring-criminalizing-online-speech/
47. Jerome Taylor, "Azhar Ahmed, a Tasteless Facebook Update, and More Evidence of Britain's Terrifying New Censorship," *Independent*, October 9, 2012,http://www.independent.co.uk/voices/comment/azhar-ahmed-a-tasteless-facebook-update-and-more-evidence-of-britains-terrifying-new-censorship-8204212.html
48. See further Uta Kohl, "Islamophobia, 'gross offensiveness' and the internet," *Information & Communications Technology Law* 27, no. 1 (2018).
49. *United States v. United States District Court*, 407 U.S. 297, 314 (1972).
50. The incited party need not go on to commit that offence for the inciter to be liable. See David G. Barnum, "Indirect Incitement and Freedom of Speech in Anglo-American Law," *European Human Rights Law Review* 2006, no. 3 (January 2006): 263–67.
51. The offense was thus not confined to instances where the speaker invited listeners to provide practical help such as finance.
52. [2016] EWCA Crim 61, para. 48.
53. Ibid., para. 49.
54. For criticism from within Parliament, see the report of the Joint Committee on Human Rights *Legislative Scrutiny: Counter-Terrorism and Security Bill* (9th Report of Session 2017–19) HC 1208; HL Paper 167 (July 2018) para. 17. The Joint Committee feared that the new clause would limit entirely valid debates on the proscribed status of particular groups.
55. Terrorism Act 2000, s.1.
56. Ibid., s.1(4).
57. Ibid.
58. Ibid.
59. Ibid.
60. Ibid.
61. S.20(2)Terrorism Act 2006
62. S.1(4) Terrorism Act 2006.
63. Eric Barendt, "Incitement to, and Glorification of, Terrorism," in *Extreme Speech and Democracy*, eds. Ivan Hare and James Weinstein (Oxford: Oxford University Press, 2009), 447.
64. Council of Europe Convention on the Prevention of Terrorism, Details of Treaty No. 196, accessed June 26, 2019, https://www.coe.int/en/web/conventions/full-list/-/conventions/treaty/196
65. Eric Heinze, *Hate Speech and Democratic Citizenship* (Oxford: Oxford University Press, 2016), 173.
66. John Stuart Mill, *On Liberty and Other Essays* (Oxford: Oxford University Press, 1998), 18.
67. Heather Stewart and Jessica Elgot, "May Calls on Social Media Giants to Do More to Tackle Terrorism," *The Guardian*, January 24, 2018, https://www.theguardian.com/business/2018/jan/24/theresa-may-calls-on-social-media-giants-to-do-more-to-tackle-terrorism

68. Samuel Gibbs, "EU Gives Facebook and Google Three Months to Tackle Extremist Content," *The Guardian*, March 1, 2018, https://www.theguardian.com/technology/2018/mar/01/eu-facebook-google-youtube-twitter-extremist-content
69. Ibid.
70. Andrew Scott, "An Unwholesome Layer Cake: Intermediary Liability in English Defamation and Data Protection Law," in *The Legal Challenges of Social Media*, eds. David Mangan and Lorna E. Gillies (Cheltenham, UK: Edward Elgar Publishing, 2017), 232.
71. See Ian Cram, *Citizen Journalists: Newer Media, Republican Moments and the Constitution* (Gloucester, UK: Edward Elgar Publishing, 2015).

References

Barendt, Eric. *Freedom of Speech*. Oxford: Clarendon Press, 1985.

———. "Incitement to, and Glorification of, Terrorism." In *Extreme Speech and Democracy*, edited by Ivan Hare and James Weinstein, 445–62. Oxford: Oxford University Press, 2009.

Barnum, David G. "Indirect Incitement and Freedom of Speech in Anglo-American Law." *European Human Rights Law Review* 2006, no. 3 (January 2006): 258–80.

Cram, Ian. *Citizen Journalists: Newer Media, Republican Moments and the Constitution*. Gloucester, UK: Edward Elgar Publishing, 2015.

———. "Judging Rights in the United Kingdom: The *Human Rights Act* and the New Relationship Between Parliament and the Courts." *Review of Constitutional Studies* 12, no. 1 (January 2007): 53–82.

Ewing, Keith D., and C. A. Gearty. *Freedom Under Thatcher: Civil Liberties in Modern Britain*. Oxford: Oxford University Press, 1990.

Heinze, Eric. *Hate Speech and Democratic Citizenship*. Oxford: Oxford University Press, 2016.

Kohl, Uta. "Islamophobia, 'Gross Offensiveness' and the Internet." *Information & Communications Technology Law* 27, no. 1 (2018): 111–31.

Marston, Geoffrey. "The United Kingdom's Part in the Preparation of the European Convention on Human Rights, 1950." *International and Comparative Law Quarterly* 42, no. 4 (October 1993): 796–826.

Mill, John Stuart. *On Liberty and Other Essays*. Oxford: Oxford University Press, 1998.

Post, Robert. "Democracy and Equality." *The Annals of the American Academy of Political and Social Science* 603 (January 2006): 24–36.

Scott, Andrew. "An Unwholesome Layer Cake: Intermediary Liability in English Defamation and Data Protection Law." In *The Legal Challenges of Social Media*, edited by David Mangan and Lorna E. Gillies, 222–46. Cheltenham, UK: Edward Elgar Publishing, 2017.

Sunstein, Cass R. *One Case at a Time: Judicial Minimalism on the Supreme Court*. Cambridge, MA: Harvard University Press, 2001.

Ten Cate, Irene M. "Speech, Truth, and Freedom: An Examination of John Stuart Mill's and Justice Oliver Wendell Holmes's Free Speech Defenses." *Yale Journal of Law & the Humanities* 22, no. 1 (January 2010): 35–47.

Wadham, John, Helen Mountfield, Elizabeth Prochaska, and Raj Desai. *Blackstone's Guide to the Human Rights Act 1998,* 7th ed. Oxford: Oxford University Press, 2015.

Conclusion: It's Still Complicated

Helen J. Knowles and Brandon T. Metroka

Scenario #1—United States: *That* high school punk, the kid who lives just around the corner from you, the kid whose reputation precedes them, decides to fix a flag pole to the bed of their pickup truck, and fly a Confederate battle flag from it. The neighborhood consensus of opinion is that the kid has little (to no) understanding of the meaning of the flag, but knows it will "piss people off, so why not?"

Scenario #2—Great Britain: A highly regarded (by all that know her) writer, who frequently contributes to radio and television stories produced by the BBC, comments on one of her friend's Facebook posts. She defends the rights of the LGBTQ community, but makes the additional observation that "gender identity" is problematic because it is a fact that one's biological sex cannot be changed. The BBC fires her.

Scenario #3—Australia: A group of white students enters a facility on a university campus that is designated for the use of Indigenous students only. When asked if they are Indigenous, they reply no, and they are asked to leave, which they subsequently do. Afterwards, another student posts a comment on social media referring to the person in charge of the unit as a n****r.

These are real-world manifestations of expressive freedom, examples of the controversies this freedom generates around the globe. However, they have something else in common—none of them is easily addressed and/or resolved by applying free speech theories. This might seem like a strange statement with which to end a volume dedicated to using theories about freedom of speech to help understand contemporary controversies. However, note what we are *not* saying (and what our contributors have *not* said in their chapters): we are not claiming that free speech theories can be used to *resolve* confrontations and contestations. Rather, we share a far more modest (and realistic) belief that the theories delineated in this book can facilitate reasoned and rational discussion of the controversies that are generated when individuals and/or groups seek to make their myriad, divergent viewpoints heard.

"How can we answer the question of how things ought to be?" As we observed in the Introduction, there are numerous ways in which one might respond to this. We offered up Jonathan Wolff's answer:

> The uncomfortable fact is that there is no easy answer. But, despite this, very many philosophers have attempted to solve these normative political problems, and they have not been short of things to say ... philosophers reason about politics in just the way they do about other philosophical issues. They draw distinctions, they examine whether propositions are self-contradictory, or whether two or more propositions are logically consistent ... In short, they present arguments.[1]

It should now be clear that this response lies at the heart and soul of this volume. Freedom to express oneself is a subject about which a great many Americans, Australians, and Brits (to name the peoples of the three different countries discussed in this book) consider it important to freely express themselves. However, it is very *un*clear just where the bounds of that freedom lie (and/or where people think those bounds lie); what manifestations of that freedom are believed to be socially acceptable; and to what extent there are legally guaranteed and protected rights to engage in that expressive freedom. In short, there is nothing uncomplicated about crying "Free Speech!" The problem, as we observed from the outset, is that all too often the complexities of freedom of speech are divorced from consideration of the values which that freedom has been theorized to serve, and the result is an impoverished and bitter socio-political discourse. Stated differently, we value, defend, and even impugn free expression, in large part, for its *consequential* values and effects.[2] Even the classic defense of unfettered speech—its connection to finding "truth"—is not valuing speech for its own sake but instead for its ability to attain this subsequent value. Recognition of the right to expression is abundant; yet, thoughtful explanations of the values served and tensions created by free expression are in short supply. The contributors to this book have responded to the impoverished "Free Speech!" discourse by offering a course correction of sorts. They have steered interested readers away from the shoals of sloganeering and back to the vibrant seas of thoughtful, substantive discussion of underlying political values. They add *light* to the heat generated by political flashpoints.

That said, one of the greatest threats to this voyage might be the crew (aka humanity) itself, with its initial predisposition to dismiss, marginalize, or even shut (or shout) down "controversial" ideas inconsistent with deeply held worldviews. Even if the way in which one chooses to express oneself is legally permissible, that expression and/or its method of delivery is only likely to come to the attention of others if it is controversial—and since most things are deemed controversial by at least someone,[3] then virtually every expression should be considered "controversial." It therefore makes absolutely no sense simply to defend one's expression(s) by shamelessly hiding behind a "Free Speech!" shield. It is far more productive to take ownership of, and individual responsibility for one's speech, recognizing that those who disagree with you are just as entitled to express an opposing opinion. It is this second component to free expression that has the potential to generate "light" in addition to heat. In short, we believe that U.S. Supreme Court Justice Oliver Wendell Holmes, Jr. got it just right when he wrote the following in his dissenting opinion in *Gitlow v. New York* (1925):

> Every idea is an incitement. It offers itself for belief, and, if believed, it is acted on unless some other belief outweighs it or some failure of energy stifles the movement at its birth. *The only difference between the expression of an opinion and an incitement in the narrower sense is the speaker's enthusiasm for the result. Eloquence may set fire to reason* ... If, in the long run, the beliefs expressed in proletarian dictatorship are destined to be accepted by the dominant forces of the community, the only meaning of free speech is that they should be given their chance and have their way.[4]

Holmes is eminently quotable, and the fire metaphor he offers in his *Gitlow* dissent is, in part, an admonition to consider the consequences of expression. As James Foster explained in Chapter 1, although a great many people in contemporary American society would agree that indeed "every idea is an incitement," their interpretation of what that means generally looks a lot different from Holmes's interpretation. In a society dominated by "pervasive tribalism ... a potent combination of fear and hate, anger and distrust, combined with a zero-sum/in-group-out-group mentality,"[5] it is all too easy (and emotionally attractive) for people to view the *ideas* of "others" with suspicion. In this world, there is a tribalistic defense mechanism that *assumes* that others' (read different) ideas beget, or incite unwanted (read different, and dangerous) actions and/or responses.

But taking responsibility for expression requires more than simply recognizing another entity's right to convey a message. It also requires some introspection concerning the purpose of the expression, the values served by that expression, and a consideration of other social values we seek to realize. Doing so requires us to drop our tribalistic safeguards, which is easier said than done. As Mark Graber demonstrated in Chapter 2, one particularly potent location for the manifestation of such tribal instincts is the 21st century American college campus. All too often, we forget that the modern "multiversity" serves values that, while not always mutually exclusive, are often in tension with one another. Colleges are unique forums, at once more and less protective of speech dependent on the asserted purpose of the institution, forums within that institution (classrooms versus the campus "green"), and disciplinary contexts. While few (if any) would sincerely take issue with the statement that an institution of higher learning's core mission is to expand knowledge and pursue "truth," the "correct" or "preferred" means of achieving that mission are eminently debatable. If the "psychic tax" of unfettered expression is consistently imposed on those least able to pay for it, knowledge and the marketplace may contract rather than expand.

Despite these deeper concerns, prime for additional discussion and interrogation, modern debates rarely reach these themes. Instead, much hay has been made by the political right at the expense of the modern left, harvesting egregious examples of conservative speakers being shouted down by coddled, leftist students and complicit faculty in universities. President Donald Trump's executive order on campus speech, covered adoringly by right-leaning outlets on March 21, 2019, appeared to take great steps to assign blame wholly on the left wing of modern politics.[6] While there is no shortage of examples of speakers perceived as "conservative" being disinvited from college campuses, a 2014 report by the Foundation for Individual Rights in Education (FIRE) found that a significant (though fewer) number of disinvited speakers were perceived as "liberal."[7] Beyond college campuses, "hate speech" regulations, which are found in a number of western democracies (including the UK and Australia), are often questioned as "thought policing" of the right. These are hardly new flashpoints (and right-wing commentators' concerns are not without merit), but modern partisan warfare on the issue of free speech has often drifted between the Scylla of being shallowly derivative and the Charybdis of disingenuousness. Graber's chapter is a needed correction and an example of how faculty, students, administrators, and citizens may move beyond partisan bickering masquerading as some sort of deeper discussion of the values served by and values in tension with free expression.

It is of course all too easy to see the fault in someone else's stars and not our own. However, as Keith Bybee and Laura Jenkins showed us in Chapter 3, finding such fault by crying "fake news" is not the new phenomenon that so many people like to think it is. And, just like societal tribalism became that much easier to understand through the theoretical lens of Hannah Arendt; and the controversy of campus thought policing becomes far more nuanced when considering the rise of the multiversity and the competing conceptions of speech as "uninhibited," "disciplined," and "inclusive"; "fake news" takes on a whole new (and wholly educational) meaning when viewed from a Tocquevillian perspective. In a February 2019 interview with conservative Fox News entertainer Sean Hannity, former *CBS* reporter Lara Logan detailed a liberal echo chamber in the higher echelons of mainstream media, decrying the "bias" (a word that is used so ubiquitously and interchangeably in contemporary debate that it has been drained of meaning) against perspectives not conforming to those of far-left outlets like the *Huffington Post*.[8] The irony of such claims, delivered on one of the clearest platforms for right-wing consumers of information—was apparently lost on these two—and perhaps on all dyed-in-the-wool viewers of unapologetically partisan programming. We encourage such lost souls to spend quality time contrasting John Stuart Mill's search for truth with Tocqueville's communal values. If they do so, they will enhance not only their understanding of "fake news," but also, as Logan Strother and Nathan Carrington explained in Chapter 4, their knowledge of the cauldron of competing views that bubbles over any time a Confederate statue is removed, or a community contemplates taking such action. Clearly, there is more to these conflicts than the surface-level rhetoric lamenting *de facto* censorship.

Indeed, the Tocquevillian explanation of the value of free expression lingers in the background of many of the chapters in this volume. Serendipitously for interested readers (but perhaps ominously for those concerned with the health of our polity), scholarship by David Buttelman and Robert Bohm finds that the "us vs. them" impulse may be an innate feature of humanity, requiring little more than wearing different colored shirts to activate "in-group" biases among young children.[9] Believers in Mill's truth justification will likely be disheartened to know that when exposed to different viewpoints, people may dig their heels in further rather than compromise, trading searches for truth and enlightenment for the trenches and horrors of partisan and ideological war.

While cross-cutting deliberation is often offered as a remedy for group polarization, Cass Sunstein and Reid Hastie found that group attitudes may actually become more extreme in deliberative settings due to a combination of group members "self-silencing" out of deference because of "reputation effects"—social pressure dynamics that marginalize minority viewpoints, and cognitive biases like the "availability heuristic" (relying on anecdotal, personal examples as proxies for systematic probabilities).[10] Echo chambers abound in modern societies—perhaps as they always have—and (unfortunately) those who are the most knowledgeable and educated appear to be the most susceptible to the temptations of group-think. In a series of experiments examining citizen attitudes toward gun control and affirmative action, Charles Taber and Milton Lodge found that political sophisticates (those scored as more politically knowledgeable) are more likely to give greater weight to facts supporting their existing position, while it is the relatively *uninformed* who are more willing to engage in a conventional "pros and cons" analysis.[11] There is simply far more to these controversies than facile soliloquies valuing expression over all other considerations.

Newsworthy political events are (and always have been) a series of Rorschach tests,[12] allowing consumers of information to see what they want to see, albeit with the ever-present coaching and "leadership" of political elites.[13] Building a polity is a team activity, but team building can divide and destroy polities. If all values are subsumed by the team mentality, we are left with nothing but instrumental arguments. Indeed, there are many indicators that the values that free expression is designed to serve were cast overboard long ago:

- When Brett Kavanaugh and Dr. Christine Blasey Ford testified before the Senate Judiciary Committee in September of 2018, were you searching for truth or signaling your allegiance to a particular political community? Can you name one person who kept an open mind—or changed their mind—as more facts and testimony were made public?
- When Nick Sandmann and other students of Covington Catholic High School exercised their First Amendment right to assemble and express themselves at the 2019 March for Life and were later drawn into an altercation with Black separatists and a Native American elder exercising their own rights to speak and assemble freely—what did you see? Did your views change as new facts came to light, after the infamous "smirking" video went viral? Which values were being served by those intersecting efforts at expression? When Sandmann subsequently sued the *Washington Post* for $250 million (!) for defamation, did you take a step back and consider the values served by news reporting, and why we protect a free press? Or, were you a partisan cheerleader?
- When Colin Kaepernick took a knee—at the suggestion of a military veteran—just prior to nationally televised NFL games, did you see an individual using an efficient forum to express displeasure with our nation's sordid history (and present status) of race relations and policing? Did you give three cheers for political expression, or did you see an "other," an enemy combatant seeking to destroy that ever-instrumental, symbolic value of (and the last refuge of scoundrels) patriotism?

In recent free expression controversies, teams feature prominently in the athletic sense as well. In the case of Colin Kaepernick and politics in sports more

Conclusion: It's Still Complicated

generally, Aaron Lorenz in Chapter 5 illustrated how high-profile, expressive acts and statements by sports figures can and often do serve many consequential values that need not be viewed as mutually exclusive. Kaepernick—and those trailblazers who came before him—made use of his social status and image to offer a racial equality-based critique of the criminal justice system through an effective medium: NFL television broadcasts. Increasingly, as illustrated by stories posted on *Outsports* and other venues for members of historically silenced groups, athletes connect the marketplace and truth-values served by expression to fostering social inclusiveness and lowering the "psychic tax" imposed by speech that seems designed to injure, rather than empower, individuals.

If speech is worth protecting, in part, because of its meaningful impact on the thoughts and behavior of others and—if one supports this outcome—its ability to bring about a more socially egalitarian world, then intention, content, and effects ought to feature more prominently in free expression discussions. Consider a related example of speech in athletics concerning LGBTQ equality: former NHL prospect Brock McGillis,[14] through social media and intimate public forums, formally came out in 2016 to draw attention to the ways in which insular sports cultures denigrate non-masculine perspectives through language. If disinviting or deplatforming speakers can fairly be characterized as dangerous exercises in chilling speech, so too can insular cultures that adopt language that denigrates athletes who do not fit hypermasculine ideals. In these cases, unfettered expression actually crowds out dissenting ideas by creating anxiety and depression among minorities who might otherwise speak so as to attain self-fulfillment or expand the marketplaces of ideas and social equality. These are not merely theoretical abstractions: McGillis was apparently blacklisted by some in the hockey community upon discovering he was gay, confirming his fear of exclusion and highlighting again how expression may conflict with other values.[15] Clearly, the values of social equality and free expression can be complementary (as means or ends), but responses to these sorts of expression have often been vitriolic. The modern version of the pillory that followed Kaepernick's expression makes little sense through a Millian lens but is entirely consistent with a Tocquevillian view of free expression.

Other examples of commitments in tension with conventional justifications for expression are less obvious but no less significant, as Jason Zenor demonstrated in Chapter 6. Zenor dissected the problematic assumptions associated with constitutional and statutory copyright and trademark protections. The political and legal choice to protect copyrights is aimed toward motivating more, not fewer, valuable contributions to society in the form of ideas and products. Civil lawsuits concerning "song theft" illustrate the tension between generating more expressive material with a finite number of fundamental musical chords and a profit-driven motive to protect original works. If one accepts the underlying purposes of copyrights and trademarks as values worthy of protection (in this case, economic profit and protectionism), clearly free expression values, as conventionally understood, do not always triumph.

Due to some difficult editorial decisions, our volume could fairly be criticized as simultaneously overinclusive and underinclusive. Our vignettes and examples have been U.S.-centric, with the rationale that the idea of free expression has taken an outsized role in U.S. politics, law, and society, and therefore is deserving of a more circumspect evaluation than currently offered by self-serving ideologues, partisans, and punditry. We also recognize that nearly all sovereign nations carve out, at least formally, some degree of protection for expression, and that the United States is not the only game in town.[16] We view this volume as the beginning, not the end, of a discussion about the global status of expressive freedom. Fortunately, other scholars are shining much-needed light on free expression conflicts in the global South, finding that constitutional courts in these nations often grapple with difficult value trade-offs in the course of published opinions. The Global Free Speech Repository, a National Science Foundation-funded database in progress at Syracuse University, has already catalogued and qualitatively coded over 2,200 constitutional free expression decisions issued by constitutional courts worldwide, with a goal of better understanding who tends to benefit from free speech protections. Along the way, database collaborators have discovered divergent approaches to resolving these controversies that involve more than simply asserting the primacy of free expression.[17]

Our scope is more limited but no less interesting for its comparative value. In Chapters 7 and 8, Katherine Gelber and Ian Cram focused on two common law nations with free speech traditions notably different from that observed in the United States. These chapters are necessarily a bit more court-centric than other contributions to this volume due to the potential, relative unfamiliarity, on the part of our audience, with these legal systems. Of particular interest in the UK and Australian contexts is the explicit willingness of these courts (and polities) to weigh unfettered protection for expression against the values of democratic equality, dignity, and participation (particularly in the Australian case). Indeed, the U.S. approach to resolving legal free speech controversies may be somewhat at odds with other developed, western democracies. For example, the Supreme Court of Canada and the European Court of Human

Rights regularly engage in extended discussions of balancing restrictions on expression with laws protecting broader democratic commitments.[18]

It is, however, an unfortunate reality that our current polity lacks the measured leadership—from any and all persuasions—to guide us away from the dangerous tribal currents of human tendencies and toward extended, balanced discussions about expressive freedom. As with most political issues that might be addressed with actual solutions, cognitive biases loom large as obstacles. Shortsighted, selfish interests taking precedence over long-term, collective health is the *sine qua non* of collective action problems. The danger to our collective health, in the case of free expression, is forgetting *why* we protect certain values in the first place, and referencing rights without substance—often to the point of incoherence. Any individual who takes a moment to clear out the fog of ideological affinity and partisan bias can see that it makes little logical sense to argue that speech is important and should be protected, while simultaneously contending that it is so insignificant that we ought not take seriously or should simply ignore the potential effects of the words of prominent political leaders.

...

We hesitate to paint too grim a picture here: doomsayers come and go, and society has continued to muddle along. Indeed, there is evidence that "normal folks" (whatever that may mean) are not as bitterly divided and walled off from reasoned discussion as the chattering classes may think. For example, Seth Stephens-Davidowitz found that individuals who frequent the comment pages on major news sites often engage with opponents and air competing ideas (whether these discussions are of the second-order variety this volume advocates is another question, entirely).[19] Additionally, as we noted in the Introduction, the "survey says…" that most students can and do think about tensions between free speech, the values speech serve, and competing values far more, and far more frequently, than is often reported. However, the sad truth is, that enlightenment, cooperation, and agreement do not appear to make for good clickbait.

In 1994, physicist Stephen Hawking made the following observation:

> For millions of years, mankind lived just like the animals. Then something happened which unleashed the power of our imagination. We learned to talk and we learned to listen. Speech has allowed the communication of ideas, enabling human beings to work together to build the impossible. Mankind's greatest achievements have come about by talking, and its greatest failures by not talking. It doesn't have to be like this. Our greatest hopes could become reality in the future. With the technology at our disposal, the possibilities are unbounded. All we need to do is make sure we keep talking.[20]

Each in their own separate ways, the chapters in this book reflect the importance and profundity of Hawking's admonition, and its relationship to the ideal of taking individual responsibility for one's expressions. They all serve as powerful reminders that while free speech theories cannot *solve* expressive freedom controversies, they can surely help us to understand them.

Notes

1. Jonathan Wolff, *An Introduction to Political Philosophy* (New York: Oxford University Press, 2006), 3.
2. For a discussion and critique of consequentialism in U.S. First Amendment jurisprudence, see Erica Goldberg, "Free Speech Consequentialism," *Columbia Law Review* 116, no. 3 (April 2016).
3. Consider, for example, one law student's request that a teacher not use the "triggering" word "violate" when discussing the way in which an action might "violate the law." Jeannie Suk Gersen, "The Trouble With Teaching Rape Law," *The New Yorker*, December 15, 2014, https://www.newyorker.com/news/news-desk/trouble-teaching-rape-law.
4. *Gitlow v. New York*, 268 U.S. 652, 673 (1925) (Holmes, J., joined by Brandeis, J., dissenting) (italics added).
5. See Chapter 1, page 36.
6. See, for example, Alana Mastrangelo, "President Trump Signs Executive Order on Campus Free Speech," *Breitbart*, March 21, 2019, accessed June 19, 2019, https://www.breitbart.com/tech/2019/03/21/president-trump-signs-executive-order-on-campus-free-speech/.
7. FIRE, "Disinvitation Report 2014: A Disturbing 15-Year Trend," *FIRE*, May 28, 2014, accessed June 19, 2019, https://www.thefire.org/disinvitation-season-report-2014/.
8. Ian Schwartz, "Lara Logan: Any Journalist Not Beating the Drum Giving the Same Talking Points 'Pay the Price,'" *Real Clear Politics*, February 21, 2019, accessed June 19, 2019, https://www.realclearpolitics.com/video/2019/02/21/lara_logan_any_journalist_not_beating_the_drum_giving_the_same_talking_points_pay_the_price.html
9. David Buttelman and Robert Böhm, "The Ontogeny of the Motivation that Underlies In-Group Bias," *Psychological Science* 25, no. 4 (April 2014).
10. Cass R. Sunstein and Reid Hastie, "Four Failures of Deliberating Groups" (John M. Olin Program in Law and Economics Working Paper No. 401, 2008), accessed June 19, 2019, https://chicagounbound.uchicago.edu/cgi/viewcontent.cgi?article=1213&context=law_and_economics. For a broader review of scholarship concerning group polarization, see Cass Sunstein, *Going to Extremes: How Like Minds Unite and Divide* (New York: Oxford University Press, 2009). For an excellent treatment of human cognitive limitations, we recommend Daniel Kahneman, *Thinking Fast and Slow* (New York: Farrar, Straus, and Giroux, 2011).
11. Charles S. Taber and Milton Lodge, "Motivated Skepticism in the Evaluation of Political Beliefs," *American Journal of Political Science* 50, no. 3 (July 2006).
12. The Rorschach test reference appeared in some accounts of the Kavanaugh-Ford hearings. See, for example, Linda Chavez, "Kavanaugh Hearing Was Like a

Rorschach Test," *Chicago Sun Times,* September 28, 2018, https://chicago.suntimes.com/2018/9/28/18423411/kavanaugh-hearing-was-like-a-rorschach-test.
13. Geoffrey L. Cohen, "Party Over Policy: The Dominating Impact of Group Influence on Political Beliefs," *Journal of Personality and Social Psychology* 85, no. 5 (November 2003). A subsequent study of "contrast effects" found that some segments of the public may not adopt positions taken by political elites; see Lene Aaroe, "When Citizens Go Against Elite Directions: Partisan Cues and Contrast Effects on Citizens' Attitudes," *Party Politics* 18, no. 2 (March 2012). For a general account of the role political elites play in contributing to the perception of a polarized public by offering extreme choices, see Morris Fiorina, Samuel Abrams, and Jeremy Pope, *Culture War?: The Myth of a Polarized America* (New York: Longman Pearson, 2011).
14. Brock McGillis, "Brock McGillis: 'I Lived a Life of Denial, Because I am Gay,'" *Yahoo Sports,* November 3, 2016, accessed June 19, 2019, https://ca.sports.yahoo.com/news/brock-mcgillis-133805839.html.
15. McGillis's account, which includes an extended discussion of the relationship between anti-LGBTQ speech and mental illness, is available at John Matisz, "Homophobia, Diversity, Mental Health in Hockey With Brock McGillis, Rachel Doerrie," *Puck Pursuit Podcast,* January 24, 2019, accessed June 19, 2019, https://www.stitcher.com/podcast/thescore-inc/puck-pursuit/e/58365120.
16. See the Constitute Project, a database developed by contributors affiliated with the Comparative Constitutions Project at the University of Texas-Austin, accessed June 19, 2019, https://www.constituteproject.org/content/about?lang=en.
17. One of us has been a collaborator on this project. For additional details, see Scott Barrett, "Keck leads NSF-Funded Study of Global Free Speech," *Syracuse University News,* October 21, 2015, accessed June 19, 2019, https://news.syr.edu/blog/2015/10/21/keck-leads-nsf-funded-study-of-global-free-speech-40714/. For ongoing scholarship drawn from the database concerning the global South, see Sandra Botero, Rachel Ellett, Thomas M. Keck, and Stephan Stohler, "Free Expression and Judicial Power in the Global South," *SSRN,* June 6, 2019, accessed June 19, 2019, https://papers.ssrn.com/sol3/papers.cfm?abstract_id=3393063.
18. Section 1 of the Canadian Charter of Rights and Freedoms states: "The *Canadian Charter of Rights and Freedoms* guarantees the rights and freedoms set out in it subject only to such reasonable limits prescribed by law as can be demonstrably justified in a free and democratic society," while Article 10, Section 2 of the European Convention on Human Rights states: "The exercise of these freedoms, since it carries with it duties and responsibilities, may be subject to such formalities, conditions, restrictions or penalties as are prescribed by law and are necessary in a democratic society, in the interests of national security, territorial integrity or public safety, for the prevention of disorder or crime, for the protection of health or morals, for the protection of the reputation or rights of others, for preventing the disclosure of information received in confidence, or for maintaining the authority and impartiality of the judiciary."
19. Seth Stephens-Davidowitz, *Everybody Lies: Big Data, New Data, and What the Internet Can Tell Us About Who We Really Are* (New York: Harper Collins, 2017).
20. This passage comes from a 1994 British Telecom television advertisement featuring Hawking. It proved so inspirational to David Gilmour, one of the lead vocalists of Pink Floyd, that he subsequently included sections of Hawking reading this passage (and then the passage in its entirety) in two of the group's songs—"Keep Talking"

(1994) and "Talkin' Hawkin'" (2014). Jennifer Newton, "Professor of Rock: Stephen Hawking Puts in Cameo Vocal Performance on New Pink Floyd Album—On Song Titled 'Talkin Hawkin,'" *DailyMail.com*, Octoper 10, 2014, accessed June 19, 2019, https://www.dailymail.co.uk/news/article-2787639/Professor-rock-Stephen-Hawking-puts-cameo-vocal-performance-new-Pink-Floyd-album-song-titled-Talkin-Hawkin.html

References

Aaroe, Lene. "When Citizens Go Against Elite Directions: Partisan Cues and Contrast Effects on Citizens' Attitudes." *Party Politics* 18, no. 2 (March 2012): 215–33.

Buttelman, David, and Robert Böhm. "The Ontogeny of the Motivation That Underlies In-Group Bias." *Psychological Science* 25, no. 4 (April 2014): 921–27.

Cohen, Geoffrey L. "Party Over Policy: The Dominating Impact of Group Influence on Political Beliefs." *Journal of Personality and Social Psychology* 85, no. 5 (November 2003): 808–22.

Fiorina, Morris, Samuel Abrams, and Jeremy Pope. *Culture War?: The Myth of a Polarized America*. New York: Longman Pearson, 2011.

Goldberg, Erica. "Free Speech Consequentialism." *Columbia Law Review* 116, no. 3 (April 2016): 687–756.

Kahneman, Daniel. *Thinking Fast and Slow*. New York: Farrar, Straus, and Giroux, 2011.

Stephens-Davidowitz, Seth. *Everybody Lies: Big Data, New Data, and What the Internet Can Tell Us About Who We Really Are*. New York: Harper Collins, 2017.

Sunstein, Cass. *Going to Extremes: How Like Minds Unite and Divide*. New York: Oxford University Press, 2009.

Taber,Charles S., and Milton Lodge. "Motivated Skepticism in the Evaluation of Political Beliefs." *American Journal of Political Science* 50, no. 3 (July 2006): 755–69.

Wolff, Jonathan. *An Introduction to Political Philosophy*. New York: Oxford University Press, 2006.

Contributors

Keith J. Bybee is Vice Dean and Paul E. and the Hon. Joanne F. Alper '72 Judiciary Studies Professor at the Syracuse University College of Law. He is also Professor of Political Science in SU's Maxwell School of Citizenship and Public Affairs. His most recent book is *How Civility Works* (Stanford, 2016).

Nathan Carrington is a PhD student in the Department of Political Science at the Maxwell School of Citizenship and Public Affairs at Syracuse University, and a research associate with the Campbell Public Affairs Institute. His research interests include American law and courts, political psychology, and the freedom of speech.

Ian Cram is Professor of Comparative Constitutional Law, School of Law, Leeds University, in the United Kingdom. His research interests lie in the field of constitutional protection for free speech. He has published widely in this area. He currently serves on the Board of Editors of the *International and Comparative Law Quarterly*.

James C. Foster is Professor Emeritus of Political Science at Oregon State University (OSU)—Cascades. During thirty years of service at OSU (1985–2015), Foster held several administrative positions and presided over several professional organizations. Foster's dissertation, *The Ideology of Apolitical Politics: Elite Lawyers' Response to the Legitimation Crisis of Liberal-Capitalism, 1870–1920*, was published in 1990 as part of the Distinguished Studies in American Legal and Constitutional History Series. Foster also authored *BONG HiTS 4 JESUS: A Perfect Constitutional Storm in Alaska's*

Capital (2010) and, with Susan M. Leeson, former Oregon Supreme Court Justice, the two volume, *Constitutional Law: Cases in Context* (1992, 1998).

Katharine Gelber is Professor of Politics and Public Policy at the University of Queensland, and a Fellow of the Academy of Social Sciences Australia. She has jointly edited, with Susan Brison, *Free Speech in the Digital Age* (Oxford UP, New York, 2019) and recently published *Free Speech After 9/11* (Oxford UP, 2016).

Mark A. Graber is the Regents Professor at the University of Maryland Law School. He is an editor of the *American Constitutionalism* series as well as an editor of *Constitutional Democracy in Crisis?* He writes on constitutional law, constitutional theory, constitutional development, and pretty much anything in which "constitutional" may be used as an adjective.

Laura Jenkins is a Ph.D. candidate in political science at the Maxwell School of Citizenship and Public Affairs at Syracuse University. Her dissertation focuses on how the U.S. Supreme Court's decision in *National Federation of Independent Business v. Sebelius* (2012) stifled constitutional deliberation in Congress over the Affordable Care Act.

Helen J. Knowles is Associate Professor of Political Science at the State University of New York at Oswego. She authored *The Tie Goes to Freedom: Justice Anthony M. Kennedy on Liberty* and co-edited *Judging Free Speech: First Amendment Jurisprudence of US Supreme Court Justices*.

Aaron Lorenz is Dean of the School of Social Science and Human Services at Ramapo College in New Jersey. He earned a PhD in Political Science from the University of Massachusetts, Amherst, with a dissertation and book that focused on the constitutive nature of law in music. His current work addresses the relationship between comedy and law, with particular attention on issues of race and class.

Brandon T. Metroka is an Assistant Professor of Political Science and Pre-Law Advisor at the University of the Incarnate Word in San Antonio, Texas. He has authored and co-authored scholarly articles examining historical and contemporary trends in judicial behavior and free expression that have appeared in the *Justice System Journal, American University International Law Review*, and *Washington & Lee Law Review*.

Logan Strother is Assistant Professor of Political Science at Purdue University. His work has appeared in *Journal of Law and Courts*, *Public Administration Review*, *Political Communication*, and *Policy Studies Journal*, among others.

Jason Zenor is an Associate Professor in the School of Communication, Media and the Arts at SUNY Oswego. The courses that he teaches include Media Law, Media Economics, and Federal Indian Law & Policy. He has published a dozen articles on many legal topics, including government speech, appropriation, and disparaging trademarks.

Index

9/11
  terrorist attacks on 6, 21

Abbott, Tony 193
abolitionists
  suppression of the speech of 4
Abrams v. U.S. (1919) 14, 15, 18, 212–213
  See also Holmes, Oliver Wendell, Jr.; *Schenck v. U.S.* (1919)
absolutism 8
  See also Black, Hugo L.
academic freedom 2–3, 67, 68, 69, 70–73, 74, 75, 75–76, 77–78, 81, 82, 84–85, 86, 87, 88, 230
  See also multiversities; political correctness; trigger warnings; universities
Acosta, Jim 98, 111n27
actions as speech. *See* symbolic speech
Adams, John Quincy 103
Administrative Procedures Act (1946).
  See net neutrality
A Few Good Men (movie) 13
Age Discrimination Act 2004 (Cth) 187
AG v. Guardian Newspaper Ltd. (1987) 209

AG v. Times Newspapers Ltd (1974) 208
Ahmed, Azhar 215–216
  See also Communications Bill of 2003
Albright, Jonathan. *See* Pew Research Center
Alexander, Larry 48–49, 54
Ali, Muhammad 139, 154
  See also sports and free speech
Allman, Jamie 38
Amaker, Marcus 128–129
American and Daily Advertiser (newspaper). *See* partisan press
American Association of University Professors (AAUP) 70, 73
  See also academic freedom
American Booksellers Ass'n, Inc. v. Hudnut (1985) 30n72
  See also MacKinnon, Catherine
American Civil Liberties Union (ACLU) 5, 121
American Citizen (newspaper).
  See partisan press
Amnesty International Ambassador of Conscience Award.
  See Kaepernick, Colin
Anderson, Janna. *See* Pew Research Center
Ansip, Andrus 219
Anti-Discrimination Act 1977 (NSW) 187
Anti-Discrimination Act 1991 (Qld) 187

INDEX

Arendt, Hannah 47, 48, 50–54, 55, 230
Areopagitica. *See* Milton, John
Aristotle 52, 62n93
Ashcroft v. Free Speech Coalition
　(2002) 20–21, 22, 128
　See also Kennedy, Anthony M.;
　　pornography
Atlanta Braves (MLB team) 170
Atwood, Margaret 11
Australia
　Constitution of 184–185, 186, 187
　human rights protection in 186–187,
　　189, 190–191, 194
　marriage equality in 193
Australian Bureau of Statistics 192–193
Australian Christian Lobby. *See* Australia,
　marriage equality in
Australian Law Reform
　Commission 189, 191
　See also hate speech, in Australia
autonomy, argument from
argument from 20–21, 128–130, 132,
　147, 149, 166–167, 171, 174, 174–
　175, 214, 233

Baker, C.E. 20
　See also autonomy, argument from
balancing 87–88, 141, 152, 158, 162,
　168, 171, 191, 235
　See also intellectual property law
Baldwin, Adam 35
Baltimore Colts (NFL team) 171
Baltimore Ravens (NFL team) 171–172
Barendt, Eric 207, 218
Benkler, Yochai 99
Ben-Porath, Sigal 74, 75, 80–81
　See also academic freedom
Bernstein, Richard J. 51
　See also Arendt, Hannah
Bill of Rights to the U.S.
　Constitution 140, 184
Black, Hugo L. 30n63, 145
　"qualified absolutism" of 26n20
　See also absolutism; *New York Times
　　v. U.S.* (1971)

Blackstone, William 16, 17, 163
　See also prior restraint
Bland, Archie xi
"Blurred Lines" (song) 172–175
Bohm, Robert 231
　See also Buttelman, David
Borowski v. Canada (Attorney General)
　(1989) 206
bots 34, 97, 100
Bradley, Joseph P. 142
　See also Civil Rights Cases (1883)
Brandeis, Louis D. *See Whitney
　v. California* (1927)
Breitbart News 41
Brennan, William J., Jr. 2, 144
Bridge, Lord of Harwich. *See AG
　v. Guardian Newspaper Ltd.* (1987)
"brotopia." *See* Silicon Valley,
　"brotopia" in
Brown, John. *See* Harper's Ferry, WV,
　John Brown's raid on
BSC v. Granada Television (1981) 208
Bunker, Matthew D. 49–50, 54
Bush, George W.
　presidential administration of 40
Buttelman, David 231
　See also Bohm, Robert
Byrne, J. Peter 73
　See also academic freedom

Campbell v. Acuff-Rose (1994) 160–161
Canada
　free speech in 221n4, 237n18
Canovan, Margaret 63n105
　See also Arendt, Hannah
Carlos, John. *See* Olympic Games
　See also sports and free speech
Carr, Julian. *See* "Silent Sam" monument
　(University of North Carolina,
　Chapel Hill)
Carter, Jimmy 139
Castells v. Spain (1992) 212
Cato Institute 12
Chafee, Zechariah 165
　See also democracy, argument from

Index

Chang, Emily. *See* Silicon Valley, "brotopia" in
Charlottesville, VA 5
Cheetham, James 104
Chemerinsky, Erwin 73, 74, 75, 81, 82, 84
Chicago Blackhawks (NHL team) 169–170
Child Pornography Prevention Act (1996). *See Ashcroft v. Free Speech Coalition* (2002)
China
  intellectual property in 166, 167
  See also intellectual property law
Choudhary case. *See* Terrorism Act (2000)
Ciccariello-Maher, George 3, 7
  See also academic freedom
City of Renton v. Playtime Theaters, Inc. (1986) 143–144
  See also content-neutral restrictions; *Ward v. Rock Against Racism* (1989)
civic discourse 18
civil laws
  Australian 189–190, 190–191
Civil Rights Act of 1875 142
  See also Civil Rights Cases (1883); state action
Civil Rights Cases (1883) 140, 142–143
  See also state action
Civil Rights Movement 145–146
Civil War, U.S. 119, 120, 124, 127, 129, 133
Clark, Andrew Inglis 184
"clear and present danger" 12
Cleveland Indians (MLB team) 170
Clinton, Hillary 95, 97, 108
Cable News Network (CNN) 41, 98
Cobbett, William 104
Cohen, Paul Robert. *See Cohen v. California* (1971)
Cohen v. California (1971) 6, 26n22
  See also symbolic speech
Coleman v. Power (2004). *See Lange v. Australian Broadcasting Corporation* (1997)
college students
  attitudes toward free speech 7–8, 67, 82, 230
Commentaries on the Law of England. *See* Blackstone, William
commercial speech 141
common law
  in Australia 185–186
  in the United Kingdom 185, 206, 207, 208, 209, 211
Communications Bill of 2003 210, 215–216
communists
  efforts to suppress the speech of 4
conduct/speech distinction 5
  See also symbolic speech; *U.S. v. O'Brien* (1968)
Confederate flag 119, 120, 124, 135n25, 227, 231
"Confederate history month" 130–131
  See also Confederate flag; Confederate States of America, symbols of
Confederate States of America 119, 124, 125, 129, 133
  symbols of 119–133
consequentialism 6, 86, 228
  See also non-consequentialism
constitutionalism 41, 43, 44, 47, 54, 55, 152
Constitution, the 41, 43, 44, 47
Constitution, U.K. *See* United Kingdom, Constitution of
Constitution, U.S. *See* U.S. Constitution
content-based restrictions 143, 144, 145, 169, 192
  See also content-neutral restrictions; scrutiny, standards of judicial; *Texas v. Johnson* (1989); *U.S. v. Playboy Entertainment Group, Inc.* (2000)
content-neutral restrictions 143–144, 145, 158
  See also City of Renton v. Playtime Theaters, Inc. (1986); content-based restrictions; scrutiny, standards of judicial; *Ward v. Rock Against Racism* (1989); *U.S. v. O'Brien* (1968)

Copyright Act of 1790 159
　See also copyright law; intellectual property law
Copyright Act of 1976 159–160
　See also copyright law; intellectual property law
Copyright Dilution Act 162
　See also copyright law; intellectual property law
copyright law 158, 159–161, 162, 163, 164–165, 165, 166, 167, 168, 173, 175, 233–234
　See also intellectual property law
Corker, Bob 34
Council of Europe's Convention on the Prevention of Terrorism 218
Counter-Terrorism and Border Security Bill (2018) 217, 219, 224n54
　See also terrorism, speech related to
critical race theory 21, 22–23, 83, 84, 149, 167, 172
　See also critical theories of free speech
critical theories of free speech
　See also critical race theory; Delgado, Richard; feminist theory; Gale, Mary Ellen;
　　Lawrence, Charles; MacKinnon, Catherine; Matsuda, Mari; pornography
Critique of Judgment. See Kant, Immanuel
Cruise, Tom. See *A Few Good Men* (movie)
Cultural Cognition Project.
　See Kahan, Dan
cyber bullying 35, 36

Dallas Cowboys (NFL team) 10
Damore, James 10, 27n32, 37
　See also Google; Silicon Valley
Damore Memo. See Damore, James
Davis, Jefferson 124
De Cive: Philosophical Rudiments Concerning Government and Society.
　See Hobbes, Thomas

Declaration of Independence (1776) 157
Defamation Act (2013) 219
Delgado, Richard 83, 83–84
　See also critical theories of free speech
Democracy, argument from 17–19, 20, 126–128, 131, 132, 165–166, 185–186, 187–188, 194, 207, 212, 213, 214, 220
　See also Chaffee, Zechariah; Meiklejohn, Alexander; Post, Robert; Sunstein, Cass
Democracy in America 96
　See also De Tocqueville, Alexis
Democratic-Republicans 101, 102, 103, 104, 105
De Tocqueville, Alexis 96, 105–109, 230–231, 233
　See also *Democracy in America*
Dewey, Caitlin 35–36
　See also Gamergate
Dicey, A.V. 207, 221n7
dignity, individual 20, 80, 83, 129, 131, 172, 189, 191, 234
　See also autonomy, argument from
Disability Discrimination Act 1992 (Cth) 187
disciplined speech 67, 69–70, 75–77, 78, 80, 81, 82, 86, 87, 88, 230
　See also multiversities; Post, Robert; universities, free speech at
Discrimination Act 1991 (ACT) 187
Disney 158, 173, 175
District of Columbia v. Heller (2008) 43
　See also Second Amendment to the U.S. Constitution
doxing 35
Dworkin, Andrea. See *American Booksellers Ass'n, Inc. v. Hudnut* (1985)

Eason Monroe Courageous Advocate Award. See Kaepernick, Colin
Edwards, Harry 146, 147
egalitarianism 21, 83, 85
　See also critical theories of free speech

Index

Ellison, John 3
  See also academic freedom; trigger warnings
Emerson, Thomas 164
European Convention on Human Rights (ECHR) 206, 207–208, 211–212, 215, 237n18
European Court of Human Rights (ECtHR) 208, 211, 212, 234–235

Facebook 12, 37, 95, 97, 99, 100, 215, 219, 227
  See also social media; Zuckerberg, Mark
fair use 158, 159–160, 160–161, 163–164, 164, 165, 166, 168, 174, 175
  See also Copyright Act of 1976; intellectual property law
fake news 4, 13, 25n15, 25–26n16, 45, 95, 96, 97–98, 100, 101, 102, 102–103, 105, 106, 107, 108, 109, 110, 230–231
  See also Trump, Donald J., fake news and
Federal Communications Commission (FCC) 39, 40, 41
  See also net neutrality; Pai, Ajit
federalism
  in Australia 184, 187, 189, 192, 194
The Federalist 163
Federalists 101, 102, 103, 105
feminist theory 21–22, 82, 83, 84
  See also critical theories of free speech; MacKinnon, Catherine
Ferguson, Niall 50
Finnis, John 67, 77
"fire", "falsely shouting...in a crowded theater." *See Schenck v. U.S.* (1919)
First Amendment to the U.S. Constitution 8, 9–10, 19, 20, 33, 34, 41, 44, 47, 49–50, 52, 54, 69–70, 71–72, 73–74, 75, 83, 122, 140, 141, 144, 148, 150–151, 152, 153, 157, 160, 164, 168, 172, 232
  free press clause of 15

Fish, Stanley 47, 73
flag burning. *See Texas v. Johnson* (1989)
Flag of the United States 10, 47–48, 138, 152
  See also Kaepernick, Colin
flaming 34, 35
Ford, Christine Blasey 232
Ford, Gerald R. *See Harper & Row Publishers, Inc. v. Nation Enterprise* (1985)
Foundation for Individual Rights in Education (FIRE) 230
  See also academic freedom
Fourteenth Amendment to the U.S. Constitution 140, 142, 184
  due process clause of 127, 140
Franklin, Benjamin 55
"Freedom in the World Report" (Freedom House) 12
Free Speech and Its Relation to Self-Government. See Meiklejohn, Alexander
"free speech zones" on college campuses 8, 74
  See also academic freedom; universities, free speech at
Frohnmayer, Dave 44–45, 54
  See also tribalism
"fuck the draft." *See Cohen v. California* (1971)
Fung, Brian 40
  See also net neutrality

gag orders. *See* abolitionists, suppression of the speech of 4
Gale, Mary Ellen 83
  See also critical theories of free speech
Gamergate 35–36
Ganas, Matt 141
Garner, Eric 139
Gawker blog 37
Gaye, Marvin. *See* "Blurred Lines" (song)
gay rights and free speech. *See* LGBTQ+ community
Gillman, Howard 73, 74, 75, 81, 82, 84

Gilmour, David. *See* Pink Floyd.
Gitlow v. New York (1925) 229
Gjoni, Eron. *See* Gamergate
Global Free Speech Repository, Syracuse University 234
González, Emma 8, 38
   See also Parkland, FL, high school mass shooting
Good Brothers 146–147, 147–148
   See also Civil Rights Movement; sports and free speech
Goodwin, Jane 216
   See also Ahmed, Azhar
Google 10, 27n32, 37, 100
   See also Damore, James; social media
Gorman, Bishop 151
Got to Give It Up (song) 173, 180n100
government speech 74, 122, 125
Grey, Thomas 84

hacking 35
Haidt, Jonathan 86
Hale, Baroness (of Richmond).
   See R (Lord Carlile) v. Home Secretary (2015)
Haley, Nikki 119–120
Hamilton, Alexander 103
Handyside v. UK (1979–80) 212
Hannity, Sean 231
Harlan, John Marshall 142–143
harm principle 7, 125
   See also Mill, John Stuart
Harper & Row Publishers, Inc. v. Nation Enterprise (1985) 164–165
   See also right to information
Harper's Ferry, WV
   John Brown's raid on 131–132
Hastie, Reid 231
hate speech 8, 83, 84, 85, 86, 130–132, 230
   in Australia 189–192, 194
   in the United Kingdom 205–206
   See also academic freedom;
      LGBTQ+ community; racism, free speech and

Hawking, Stephen 235–236, 237–238n20
Hefner, Hugh 37
Heiden, Eric 139
   See also sports and free speech
Heyer, Heather 5, 7
Heyman, Stephen 20
   See also autonomy, argument from
Hill, Jonathon 120
Hobbes, Thomas 33, 34, 45, 46, 51
Hogg, David 8, 38
   See also Parkland, FL, high school mass shooting
Holmes, Oliver Wendell, Jr. 14–15, 17, 18, 51–52, 74, 212–213, 213, 223n34, 229
   See also Abrams v. U.S. (1919); marketplace of ideas; *Schenck v. U.S.* (1919); truth, the search for
Homer 52, 62n91
Huffington Post 231
Human Freedom Index (Cato Institute) 12
Human Rights Act 1998 (HRA) 206–207, 207–208, 209–211, 212–213, 220

"I Can't Breathe." *See* Garner, Eric
inclusive speech 67, 75, 78, 80–87, 88, 230
   See also multiversities; universities, free speech at
Indianapolis Colts (NFL team) 171
Ingraham, Laura 8
Instagram 12
intellectual property law 157–176
   See also China, intellectual property in; copyright; fair use; *Matal v. Tam* (2016); parody
International Convention on the Elimination of All Forms of Racial Discrimination (1975) 186
   See also Australia, human rights protection in; hate speech; racism, free speech and

Index

International Covenant on Civil and Political Rights (1980) 186
   See also Australia, human rights protection in
International Fact-Checking Network 99

Jackson, Andrew 103–104, 106
Jackson, Robert H. 42, 153
   See also West Virginia State Board of Education v. Barnette (1943)
James, LeBron 139
   See also Garner, Eric; sports and free speech
Janney, Caroline 131–132
Jefferson, Thomas 103, 177n43
Jehovah's Witnesses, persecution of 4, 152–153
   See also West Virginia State Board of Education v. Barnette (1943)
Jim Crow laws 120
   See also racism, free speech and
Johnson, Larry. *See* "Confederate history month"
Jones, Alex 38
Jones, Jerry. *See* Dallas Cowboys (NFL team)
Judging Free Speech 10–11
judicial review
   in the United Kingdom 209–210, 211
   in the United States 209–210
   See also scrutiny, standards of judicial

Kaepernick, Colin 5, 7, 139, 141, 144, 145, 147–148, 148–149, 150, 151, 152, 153, 154, 232–233, 233
   See also Flag of the United States; knee, taking a; sports and free speech; "The Star-Spangled Banner"
Kahan, Dan 38–39
Kansas City Chiefs (NFL team) 170
Kant, Immanuel 52, 53, 53–54, 55, 163

Kashuv, Kyle. *See* Parkland, FL, high school mass shooting
Kasky, Cameron. *See* Parkland, FL, high school mass shooting
Kavanaugh, Brett 232
Kennedy, Anthony M. 20–21, 22, 144
   See also Ashcroft v. Free Speech Coalition (2000); autonomy, argument from; dignity, individual; *U.S. v. Playboy Entertainment Group, Inc.* (2000)
Kerr, Clark 79
   See also academic freedom; multiversities
King, Martin Luther 152, 154
Kingsolver, Barbara 53
knee, taking a 5, 47–48, 139, 149, 150, 151, 151–152, 154, 232
   See also Kaepernick, Colin

Lange test. *See Lange v. Australian Broadcasting Corporation* (1997)
Lange v. Australian Broadcasting Corporation (1997) 188
Lanham Act of 1946 161, 169, 179n80
   See also Matal v. Tam (2016)
Lawrence, Charles 83, 84
Laws, Lord Justice 211
Led Zeppelin 173
Lenz v. Universal (2016) 160
Lepore, Jill. *See* Victims' Rights Movement
Leviathan. *See* Hobbes, Thomas
LGBTQ+ community 6, 227
   in Australia 192–193, 197n43
   sports and 233
   See also McGillis, Brock; marriage equality; *Masterpiece Cakeshop v. Colorado Civil Rights Commission* (2018)
libel 160, 207, 221n7
   See also New York Times v. Sullivan (1964)
libertarianism 16–17, 22, 183, 184, 188, 190–191, 192, 194
   See also Mill, John Stuart

Lincoln, Abraham 33, 34, 47, 51, 54, 72
Locke, John 163
Lodge, Milton 231–232
Logan, Lara 231
"Lost For Words" (song).
  See Pink Floyd
Lukianoff, Greg 86
Lynch, Marshawn 140, 141

McCloy v. New South Wales (2015). See
  *Lange v. Australian Broadcasting
  Corporation* (1997)
McGillis, Brock 233
  See also LGBTQ+ community; sports
  and free speech
McReynolds, James C. 42
Machiavelli, Niccolo 218–219
MacKinnon, Catherine 21–22, 83
  See also *American Booksellers Ass'n, Inc.
  v. Hudnut* (1985); critical theories
  of free speech; feminist theory
Madison, James 103, 163
Marjory Stoneman Douglas High School.
  See Parkland, FL high school mass
  shooting
marketplace of ideas 7, 13–17, 18–19,
  51–52, 74, 83, 95–96, 96, 99,
  100–101, 108, 109, 132, 150–151,
  163–164, 165, 170, 172, 174, 233
  See also *Abrams v. U.S.*
  (1919); Holmes, Oliver Wendell,
  Jr.; Milton, John; truth, the
  search for
Marriage Act 1961 (Cth) 192
marriage equality 192–193
  in Australia 188, 192–193
  See also LGBTQ+ community
*Masterpiece Cakeshop v. Colorado Civil
  Rights Commission* (2018) 6
  See also LGBTQ+ community
Matal v. Tam (2016) 168, 169, 170,
  171, 172, 175
  See also intellectual property law;
  Lanham Act of 1946
Matsuda, Mari 22–23, 83, 84

  See also critical theories of free speech
May, Theresa 219
Meiklejohn, Alexander 18–19, 21,
  29n58, 29–30n63, 126, 127, 128,
  136n29, 136n32, 136n41, 142,
  165–166, 187
  See also democracy, argument from
#MeToo movement 11, 22
Mill, John Stuart 16–17, 18, 21, 74,
  96, 98, 105, 106, 107, 108, 109,
  123–126, 127, 132, 134n20, 163,
  185, 212–213, 213, 219, 223n34,
  231, 233
  See also libertarianism; marketplace
  of ideas; utilitarianism; truth, the
  search for
Milton, John 15, 74, 163
  See also marketplace of ideas; truth, the
  search for
Minnesota Vikings (NFL team) 141
  See also sports and free speech
money and speech 29n48
Monroe, James 103
Moore, Michael 166
multiversities 68, 79–85, 86–88,
  229–230
  See also academic freedom; Kerr, Clark;
  universities, free speech at
Murphy, Lionel 187

NAACP v. Hunt (1990) 135n24
national anthem of the U.S. See "The
  Star-Spangled Banner"
National Basketball Association
  (NBA) 139, 171
  See also sports and free speech
National Football League (NFL) 5, 139,
  140, 141–142, 143, 144–145, 148,
  150, 153, 232
  See also Kaepernick, Colin; sports and
  free speech
National Gazette (newspaper).
  See partisan press
National Hockey League (NHL) 232
  See also sports and free speech

Index

National Inquiry into Racist Violence (1991) 189
National Intelligencer (newspaper). See partisan press
National Journal (newspaper). See partisan press
Native Americans 169–171, 172
See also trademarks
Nazis 44, 50, 121
See also hate speech
NCAA 170
net neutrality 34, 39, 40–41, 58n34
See also Federal Communications Commission (FCC); Pai, Ajit
New York Evening Post (newspaper). See partisan press
New York Times 4, 7, 8, 98
New York Times v. Sullivan (1964) 163
See also libel
New York Times v. U.S. (1971) 145
See also prior restraint
Nicholson, Jack. See *A Few Good Men* (movie)
Nike "Just Do It" campaign. See Kaepernick, Colin
Nixon, Richard M. See *Harper & Row Publishers, Inc. v. Nation Enterprise* (1985)
non-consequentialism 5–6
See also consequentialism

Obama, Barack
presidential administration of 40
O'Brien, David Paul. See *U.S. v. O'Brien* (1968)
Ogorzalek, Thomas 120
Olympic Games 139
See also sports and free speech
On Liberty. See Mill, John Stuart
Only Words. See MacKinnon, Catherine
Oppong, Mike 151
Orbison, Roy. See *Campbell v. Acuff-Rose* (1994)
Outsports. See LGBTQ+ community, sports and

Pai, Ajit 40
See also Federal Communications Commission; net neutrality
Parkland, FL high school mass shooting 8, 38
See also González, Emma; Hogg, David
Parks, Rosa 139
parliamentary government
in Australia 185, 187, 192–193, 194
in the United Kingdom 13, 205, 206, 208, 209–210, 220
parody 160–161, 165, 174
partisan political views about "free speech" 1–2, 6, 25n15, 48–49, 97–98, 108, 231, 232, 235
partisan press 96, 101–105, 106, 107, 108, 109
Patent and Trademark Office, U.S. 169, 171
patents 176n12
See also Patent and Trademark Office, U.S.
PayPal 37
See also Damore, James; Silicon Valley, "brotopia" in; Thiel, Peter
Pence, Mike 5
"penny press" 103
Peterson, Jordan B. 24n6
Pew Research Center 45–46, 54
Pink Floyd 1, 24, 27n25, 237–238n20
Piston, Spencer 120
Pizzagate (Comet Ping Pong Pizza conspiracy) 97
See also fake news
Pleasant Grove City v. Summum (2009) 124, 134–135n21
Podesta, John 95, 109
Poe, Edgar Allen 172
political correctness 2–3
Pope Francis 95, 108
Porcupine's Gazette (newspaper). See partisan press
pornography 20, 21–22, 21
revenge form of 205–206
See also *Ashcroft v. Free Speech Coalition* (2002); autonomy, argument from; critical theories of free speech

Portfolio (newspaper). *See* partisan press
Post, Robert 72, 76–77, 84, 165, 214
   See also democracy, argument from; disciplined speech
Powell, Michael 40
   See also Federal Communications Commission (FCC); net neutrality
Prager, Dennis 3
"preferred freedom" 7, 168
The Prince. See Machiavelli, Niccolo
prior restraint 15–16, 145, 171, 185–186
Privacy Act 1988 (Cth) 187
private property 122, 157–158, 167, 168
   See also intellectual property law
private speech (and the First Amendment) 10, 27n32
public fora 69, 72, 74, 75, 81, 232
   See also universities, free speech at
public opinion, court of 11–12

Quinn, Zoe. *See* Gamergate

Racial Discrimination Act 1975 (Cth) 187
racism, free speech and 119, 120, 127, 129–130, 130–131, 135n24, 188
   See also hate speech; International Convention on the Elimination of All Forms of Racial Discrimination
Rainie, Lee. *See* Pew Research Center
right to information 164–165
   See also Harper & Row Publishers, Inc. v. Nation Enterprise (1985)
R (Lord Carlile) v. Home Secretary (2015) 214–215
Roberts Court (and free speech cases) 27–28n35, 28n36
Robinson, Reginald 149
Roof, Dylann 119, 120

Roth, Michael 82
   See also inclusive speech
Royal Commission into Aboriginal Deaths in Custody (1991). *See* hate speech, in Australia
Rubin, Dave 24n6
Ruffin, Herbert 146, 147
R v. Secretary of State for the Home Department ex parte Simms (2000) 212–213, 213, 213–214
Ryan, Frank 141
Ryhal, Mike 120

Sabato's Crystal Ball 44
Sandmann, Nick 232
San Francisco 49ers (NFL team). *See* Kaepernick, Colin
Sasse, Ben 56n2
Scalia, Antonin 43
Schenck v. U.S. (1919) 12, 28n38
   See also Abrams v. U.S. (1919); Holmes, Oliver Wendell, Jr.
Scott, Andrew 219–220
scrutiny, standards of judicial
   in Australia 190
   in the United Kingdom 210–211
   in the United States 143–144, 158, 169
Seattle Seahawks (NFL team). *See* Lynch, Marshawn
Second Amendment to the U.S. Constitution 38, 42–43, 44, 58n39
   See also District of Columbia v. Heller (2008); *U.S. v. Cruikshank* (1876); *U.S. v. Miller*
Sedition Acts of 1798 4
self-fulfillment. *See* autonomy, argument from
self-government 18–19, 165–166, 172
   See also democracy, argument from; *Whitney v. California* (1927)
Sex Discrimination Act 1984 (Cth) 187
Shah, Sohil 140, 140–141, 142
Shahvisi, Arianna 82

Index

Shepherd, Heyward. *See* Harper's Ferry, WV, John Brown's raid on
"Silent Sam" monument (University of North Carolina, Chapel Hill) 129, 132
Silicon Valley 35
   "brotopia" in 36–37
   See also Damore, James; Thiel, Peter
The Slants. *See Matal v. Tam* (2016)
slavery 4, 119, 125, 127, 129, 131–132, 133, 135n24, 135n25, 142, 149
Smith, Tommie. *See* Olympic Games.
   See also sports and free speech
social media 12, 19, 34, 44, 97–98, 99, 100, 107, 110, 174, 219, 232
   See also Facebook; fake news; Google; Instagram; Twitter; YouTube
Souter, David H. 161
   See also Campbell v. Acuff-Rose (1994)
sports and free speech 47–48, 139, 140–154, 232–233
   See also Olympic Games
Spycatcher 186, 209
   See also AG v. Guardian Newspaper Ltd. (1987)
"Stagnation (a letter 2 America)".
   See Amaker, Marcus
"The Star-Spangled Banner" 5, 47–48, 138, 150, 151, 152
   See also Kaepernick, Colin
state action 10, 140–143, 144–145
Statute of Anne (1710). *See* Copyright Act (1790)
Stephens-Davidowitz, Seth 235
Steyn, Lord. *See R. v. Secretary of State for the Home Department ex parte Simms* (2000)
Sunday Times v. UK (1979) 212
Sunstein, Cass 165, 221n2, 231
   See also democracy, argument from
Supreme Court of Canada 234–235
Supreme Court of the U.S. 9–10, 124, 126, 128, 142, 143–144, 145, 150–151, 152, 160–161, 163, 164, 168, 169, 170, 209–210, 229
symbolic speech 5, 119, 120, 121, 124, 150, 151

Taber, Charles 231–232
Ten Cate, Irene M. 213, 223n34
Terrorism Act 2000 217
Terrorism Act 2006 217, 218
terrorism, speech related to 6, 21, 205–206, 216–218, 219, 219–220, 220
Tesla 37
Texas v. Johnson (1989) 2, 144
   See also content-based restrictions
Thatcher, Margaret 13
"theater" – "falsely shouting fire in a crowded ..." *See Schenck v. U.S.* (1919)
Thicke, Robin. *See* "Blurred Lines" (song)
Thiel, Peter 37
   See also Silicon Valley
Thirteenth Amendment to the U.S. Constitution 142
Thomas, Virginia 38
T.I. *See* "Blurred Lines" (song)
tolerance (of diverse viewpoints) 1–4, 21
trademarks 158, 161–162, 163, 164, 166, 167, 169, 169–170, 171, 177n29, 233–234
tribalism 33–37, 38, 39, 40–41, 42, 44, 45, 47, 51, 54, 55, 56n4, 229, 230
   See also Frohnmayer, Dave
trigger warnings 2–3, 236n3
   See also academic freedom
trolling 45, 46
Trump, Donald J. 4, 7, 34, 95, 108, 109, 110, 165–166, 230
   fake news and 4, 95, 96, 97, 98, 100, 109, 110
   presidential administration of 40, 41, 96
   press conferences of 4, 25n12
   Twitter usage by 4, 25n12, 98
   See also fake news
Trump, Lara 4
   See also fake news
trust in government 44
truth, the search for 13–17, 18, 20, 74, 96, 98, 99, 105, 106, 107–108, 109, 110, 123–124, 132, 134n20, 147, 163, 228, 231

See also Holmes, Oliver Wendell, Jr.; marketplace of ideas; Mill, John Stuart; Milton, John
Tushnet, Mark 43–44
Twitter 12, 35, 99, 100, 219
   See also social media

uninhibited speech 67, 69–70, 72, 73–75, 78, 80, 81, 82, 84, 86, 87, 88, 230
   See also multiversities; universities, free speech at
United Daughters of the Confederacy. *See* Harper's Ferry, WV, John Brown's raid on
"Unite the Right" protesters 5
United Kingdom
   Constitution of 205, 206, 207
   Supreme Court of 206, 214
universities, free speech at 68–69, 71, 72, 73–74, 77, 78, 80, 83, 86, 87, 88, 229–230
   See also academic freedom; multiversities
U.S. Civil War. *See* Civil War, U.S.
U.S. Commission on Civil Rights 170
U.S. Constitution 41, 42, 43, 44, 47, 101, 102, 104, 105, 127
   Commerce Clause of 161, 168
   Copyright Clause of 159, 161, 168, 174, 175
U.S. Patent and Trademark Office. *See* Patent and Trademark Office, U.S.
U.S. Trademark Trial and Appeals Board (TTAB) 170
U.S. v. Cruikshank (1876) 42
   See also Second Amendment to the U.S. Constitution
U.S. v. Miller (1939) 42–43
   See also Second Amendment to the U.S. Constitution
U.S. v. O'Brien (1968) 26n23
   See also content-neutral restrictions; *Ward v. Rock Against Racism* (1989)

U.S. v. Playboy Entertainment Group, Inc. (2000) 144
   See also content-based restrictions; Kennedy, Anthony M.; *Texas v. Johnson* (1989)
utilitarianism 184–185, 186, 194
   See also Mill, John Stuart
Uyehara, Mari 38
   See also critical theories of free speech

Van Buren, Martin 104
Victims' Rights Movement 59n52
Voltaire xi, 24n3

Walker, Natalia. *See* "Silent Sam" monument (University of North Carolina, Chapel Hill)
Walker v. Texas Division, Sons of Confederate Veterans, Inc. (2015) 124, 134n20
Walsh, Davis 150
Ward v. Rock Against Racism (1989) 143
   See also City of Renton v. Playtime Theaters, Inc. (1986); content-neutral restrictions; *U.S. v. O'Brien* (1968)
Warner Bros. 173
Warren, Kenneth 120–121
Washington Bullets (NBA team) 171
   See also sports and free speech
Washington, George 109
Washington Post 35, 38, 40, 131, 232
Washington Redskins (NFL team) 169, 170, 171, 172
   See also sports and free speech
Washington Wizards (NBA team) 171
   See also sports and free speech
Webster, Steven 44, 45, 54
Weinstein, Harvey 85
Welch, Edgar. *See* Pizzagate (Comet Ping Pong Pizza conspiracy)

Index

West Virginia State Board of Education v. Barnette (1943) 61–62n86, 152–153
  See also Jackson, Robert H.; Jehovah's Witnesses, persecution of
Wheeler, Tom 40
  See also Federal Communications Commission (FCC); net neutrality
Whitney v. California (1927) 17–18, 29n57, 126
  See also democracy, argument from
Whittington, Keith 74, 75, 81, 86
Will, George F. 145
Williams, John 173
Williams, Pharrell. *See* "Blurred Lines" (song)
Wilson, Jerry. *See* "Silent Sam" monument (University of North Carolina, Chapel Hill)
Wolff, Jonathan 2, 23–24, 228

Wootson, Cleve R., Jr. 38
Wright, Peter. *See Spycatcher*
Wu, Tim 39
  See also net neutrality

YouTube 100, 219
  See also social media

Zero to One: Notes on Startups, or How to Build the Future. *See* Thiel, Peter
Zick, Timothy 149
Zuckerberg, Mark 99, 100
  See also Facebook

STUDIES IN LAW AND POLITICS

The Studies in Law and Politics series is devoted to texts and monographs that explore the multidimensional and multidisciplinary areas of law and politics. Subject matters to be addressed in this series include, but will not be limited to: constitutional law; civil rights and liberties issues; law, race, gender, and gender orientation studies; law and ethics; women and the law; judicial behavior and decision-making; legal theory; sociology of law; comparative legal systems; criminal justice; courts and the political process; and other topics on the law and the political process that would be of interest to law and politics scholars. Submission of single-author and collaborative studies, as well as collections of essays are invited.

For additional information about this series or for the submission of manuscripts, please contact:

> Peter Lang Publishing, Inc.
> Acquisitions Department
> 29 Broadway, 18th floor
> NY, NY 10006

To order other books in this series, please contact our Customer Service Department:

> peterlang@presswarehouse.com (within the U.S.)
> order@peterlang.com (outside the U.S.)

Or browse online by series:

> www.peterlang.com